News and News Sources

News and News Sources

A Critical Introduction

Paul Manning

SAGE Publications
London • Thousand Oaks • New Delhi

First published 2001

SAGE Publications Ltd
6 Bonhill Street
London EC2A 4PU

SAGE Publications Inc
2455 Teller Road
Thousand Oaks, California 91320

SAGE Publications India Pvt Ltd
32, M-Block Market
Greater Kailash – 1
New Delhi 110 048

British Library Cataloguing in Publication data

A catalogue record for this book is available from the British Library

ISBN 0 7619 5796 0
ISBN 0 7619 5797 9 (pbk)

Library of Congress catalog card number is available

Typeset by M Rules
Printed in Great Britain by Biddles Ltd, Guildford, Surrey

Contents

For Winnie

Preface

The main aim of this book is as a contribution to the development of a framework for analysing the relationship between news sources and news media in contemporary liberal democratic, capitalist societies. A decade ago the question of news source activity was given scant attention by researchers. Now the literature is growing and we know more about the experiences of environmental activists, trade unions, penal reform groups, and other campaigning organisations in trying to develop news media strategies. There is a paradox in our experience of the news media: we suspect that the powerful have a very considerable ability to set agendas and control the supply of information to the public domain and yet, on a regular basis, we find news stories emerging which serve to highlight the inability of corporate organisations and governments to prevent information damaging to their interests from seeping out. As the range and variety of news media outlets expands in a multi-channel, 'media-saturated' world, there appears to be greater diversity and openness in news coverage, yet we as a public grow ever more suspicious of the ways in which news may be spun and controlled by the powerful.

This book suggests that we must look, in part, to the interaction between particular news sources and the organisations engaged in the various processes of news commodification, for an understanding of the nature of these paradoxes. In other words, both the model of a monolithic power structure controlling all news media from the centre, and the most naïve versions of pluralistic openness in news communication are wide of the mark. The institutional arrangements of corporate capitalism, government and the state allocate many of the best cards but not all the cards to the powerful, in the struggle around news agendas. The less powerful and the politically marginal do get a look in, but how and to what extent are empirical questions. This book tries to offer a framework for thinking through and exploring these issues. It is a framework which rests upon certain theoretical assumptions. Most important, it is assumed that interaction between news sources, journalists and news organisations involves a struggle to control information flows. Those involved may resort to coercion, implicit bargaining or even formal negotiation. Resources, both material and symbolic, are deployed in an effort to shape or control the information flows sustaining news production. Within the sociology of journalism, these sorts of themes have been traditionally approached through a variety of interactionist, ethnomethodological or organisational perspectives. However, if by political economy we mean the study of the ways in which material and symbolic resources promote or constrain action and are deployed to secure interests or advantage, then the study of the engagements between news sources, journalists and news organisations is an appropriate topic for a political economy. Such an approach is helpful, I think, because it reminds us that the battle to control information flows is a struggle around resources (material and symbolic) and, secondly, because it reminds us that all these micro-engagements occur in the context of the larger political–economic environment – market pressures, proprietorial interests, the formal and informal regulative capacities of government, and so on.

The first aim of this book, then, is to explore the nature of news source–news organisation interaction within a framework which could be described as political–economic. In doing this, the book reviews a wide range of evidence, including some important and well-known studies, but it tries to offer more than merely an introductory review. While some of the evidence is drawn from established work, other evidence is drawn from original research, or other original sources. The theoretical frameworks deployed, particularly in Chapters 6 and 7, draw upon several influences but try to offer a distinctive approach for theorising the activity of news sources.

A second aim of the book is to provide an accessible guide to the ways in which sources and news organisations interact to produce news, within the constraints imposed by markets, ownership structures and political institutions. Hopefully, students will find the book useful as a guide to the sociology of news sources, even if some of the material contained within strays from the familiar paths. I have tried to make the style and use of terminology as accessible as possible.

Chapter 1 serves as an introduction but does so by emphasising the importance of the question of news sources for the health of the public arenas that sustain the discussion and debate vital to democracy. Chapter 2 reviews the range of theoretical approaches available for analysing the relationship between news sources and news media. Chapters 3–5 deal with aspects of the political economic environment within which news is produced and news sources seek to operate. Chapter 3 explores the changing nature of news journalism and the organisation of the news room; Chapter 4 considers the constraints of markets, advertising, proprietorial power and the structures of capital, and Chapter 5 deals with the formal and informal controls over information flows at the disposal of governments and state. In each case, I have tried to draw examples and evidence from beyond the United Kingdom, though given the partisan nature of the English press and the preoccupation with spin which has characterised recent British governments, it is impossible not to dwell at some length upon the experience of the United Kingdom. Chapters 6 and 7 consider the position of news sources seeking to secure access to the news media. The central question concerns the extent to which politically marginal groups can find ways of countering the power and advantages associated with the material and symbolic resources at the disposal of corporations and state institutions, in the struggle to control or influence information flows. Chapter 8 returns to more familiar terrain by reviewing the available evidence concerning audiences for political communication. Does all the effort invested in news media work by the powerful or politically marginal signify among the public? Evidence from nearly five decades of audience research is hardly conclusive but it is now possible to describe the nature of public responses to political communication and news media work with some degree of confidence. There are signs that a sceptical public is growing ever more disillusioned with spin and political public relations. There is certainly evidence to suggest that political audiences are prepared to think critically and sceptically about the messages they receive providing they can draw upon alternative sources of evidence or information. It would be ironic if the political spin industry faced a terminal legitimation crisis produced by the very slickness of its own practices but such an outcome would not be a cause for regret among those who would welcome a politics prepared to acknowledge real social divisions and some awkward choices, rather than pay so much attention to presentation.

Acknowledgements

Many people have helped in various ways in the writing of this book. My colleagues in the Sociology Department at De Montfort University have provided encouragement in generous measure. Julia Hall at Sage has been equally patient and supportive. Although not in any way responsible for the ideas set out in this book, I should thank Professor Peter Golding for his invaluable guidance while I served my academic apprenticeship and for playing no small a part in securing the opportunity for this book to be written. De Montfort University granted study leave for one semester which allowed a start to be made. I am also grateful to the editors of Media Culture Society (Sage) and Ashgate Publications for permission to draw upon some evidence which has appeared in earlier publications. As always, my deepest thanks go to my family, Winnie, Michael, Peter and Dan, together with Barbara Manning, for their cheerful love and support.

Abbreviations

AFL-CIO	American Federation of Labor-Congress of Industrial Organisations
AFP	Agence France-Presse
AP	Associated Press
AEU	Amalgamated Engineering Union
AEEU	Amalgamated Engineering and Electrical Union
BBC	British Broadcasting Corporation
BECTU	Broadcasting, Entertainment, Cinematograph and Theatre Union
CGT	Confédération Générale du Travail
CNN	Cable Network News
COHSE	Confederation of Health Service Employees
EC	European Commission
GIS	Government Information Service
GMB	General and Municipal Workers Union
ITC	Independent Television Commission
NALGO	National Association of Local Government Officers
NASA	National Aeronautics and Space Administration
NHS	National Health Service (Britain)
NUPE	National Union of Public Employees
TGWU	Transport and General Workers Union
TUC	British Trade Union Congress
UPITN	United Press International Television News
WTN	Worldwide Television News
WWFN	World Wide Fund for Nature

1 Why Worry About the Sources of News?

This book is about news journalism but it is also about the importance of news sources. With the expansion of communication and media studies courses in recent years, there are now dozens of books available which describe the work of journalists and the processes involved in the making of news. Rather fewer studies give more than brief consideration to the question of where journalists get their information from, although there is now an emerging body of material on the activities of certain news sources, such as environmentalists, trade unionists, and those organisations campaigning in policy arenas such as criminal justice or health. Yet the study of news sources and their relationships with news organisations is absolutely central to the discussion of the 'big questions' that should be at the heart of any consideration of news journalism. Most accounts of 'democracy' assume that public choice between parties, individuals or policy options, is an important element. In the ideal model of the modern capitalist liberal democracy, 'free' and 'independent' news media are usually regarded as playing an important part in maintaining the flow of ideas and information upon which choices are made. However, this assumes first that those groups which have something important to contribute to these processes of information circulation can secure access to the news media and, secondly, that the representation of their arguments or perspectives will not be unreasonably constrained or misrepresented.

Can we make such assumptions about the accessibility of the news media and the transparency of the news communication process? Do all news sources enjoy the same degree of access and the same ability to communicate their perspectives, or encode their preferred agendas? The view that the powerful or wealthy in society may enjoy some advantages in these matters is not confined to academics or 'media experts'. The interests of wealthy media proprietors and the manipulative skills of 'spin doctors' working on behalf of political élites are images now familiar to the public. One of the important issues to consider, then, in thinking through the relationship between news media and democractic processes in liberal, capitalist societies, is whether or not the less powerful are significantly disadvantaged in the scramble to secure access to the news media. In turn, this will have an important bearing upon the question of just how diverse are the perspectives and interpretative frameworks that are presented through the news media.

Journalism and Democracy

What should the role of journalists be in a liberal democracy? Most commentators agree that at the simplest level, news journalists should have the task of gathering and communicating to the public, up-to-date information from home and abroad, in order to sustain political discussion and the democratic process. Yet beyond this, very little is agreed. For libertarians enamoured with the concept of the free market, news media in the business of selling information should acknowledge no obligation beyond that of yielding profits for proprietors or shareholders. The 'great' newspaper barons of the inter-war years, such as Beaverbrook or Northcliffe (see Chapter 4), insisted upon their right as owners to use their newspapers exactly as they pleased. For them, dictating the editorial line of their papers was simply one of the rights of ownership, and the task of their journalists was to follow the proprietorial line. As Beaverbrook, owner of the *Daily Express* famously and candidly admitted to the 1949 Royal Commission on the Press, 'I run the paper purely for the purpose of making propaganda, and with no other motive' (quoted in Driberg, 1956: 140).

There is, however, an inherent problem with the Beaverbrook doctrine. A sceptical public will submit what they read to even more severe critical scrutiny if particular newspapers reveal, in too blatant a fashion, the imprint of their proprietors' interests. In short, they may suffer a 'legitimation crisis'. It was Herbert Morrison, Peter Mandelson's grandfather, who warned Beaverbrook and Northcliffe that 'nobody in Great Britain is doing more to destroy the influence of the Press than you two specimens' (quoted in Driberg, 1956: 196). Anxieties about the public role of the news media, and particularly the power of newspaper barons, prompted some journalists and academics to propose an alternative vision or policy model for the press in the early post-war period. In the era of the Cold War, liberal academics and journalists searched for ways in which the legitimacy of the press in Western democracies could be distinguished from the party-controlled news media of state socialist societies. A picture of the press dominated by self-interested capitalists or newspaper barons was a little uncomfortable. Based upon an appreciation of news journalism's finer moments, the 'social responsibility' model placed the practice of journalism within a normative framework which required newspapers to acknowledge obligations beyond delivering profits or propaganda (Siebert et al., 1956). Journalists and their newspapers were encouraged to recognise the part they played in the circulation of political information as a necessary service for a healthy democracy; their role was to inform and educate citizens, and to provide electorates with the tools required to hold political élites to account. All this depended, of course, upon journalists maintaining a professional code which placed public before party or personal interest. While cynics might scoff, it is certainly the case that schools of journalism have traditionally encouraged the inculcation of these values in their graduates, and a number of news organisations, including, for example, the *Washington Post*, claim to operate according to formally identified codes of professional ethics.

A more recent variant of the same model places more emphasis upon the role of news organisations in mobilising an otherwise apathetic citizenry to participate in political processes. 'Mobilisation theory' (Protess et al., 1991) places more emphasis upon the capacity of the news media to *intervene* in the public interest by drawing public attention to issues of concern and encouraging public campaigning for reform. Campaigning stances have grown in popularity, cynics might suggest, as newspapers fight an ever fiercer battle with rivals for circulation. For supporters of the mobilisation model, however, journalists should sometimes aspire to trigger the agenda-building process (see Chapter 8), a collective process whereby interaction between citizens, journalists and members of political élites results in the placing of an issue of concern in the political and public domains. In this kind of account, journalists may be understood to operate on what Bardoel describes as the 'meso-level', a dimension above the micro-level of the ordinary citizen interacting and discussing with others, but below the macro-level of political élites and government decision-making (1996: 294). Bardoel suggests that journalists must be sensitive to the currents of opinion and interest circulating among the public at the micro-level but as the term 'meso-level' also implies, they are positioned hierarchically above the public as they exercise a greater capacity to control information flows and shape agendas.

Now, of course, there are several difficulties with this model and the 'social responsibility' approach. While newspapers are usually organised as private enterprises operating in the market-place, even those broadcasting institutions established as public service organisations are now frequently compelled to operate according to a commercial logic (see Chapter 4). Information that is generated for a public purpose by commercial organisations is likely to be, as Statham calls it, a 'cross-breed commodity' (1996: 543). In other words, while such information may serve the public purpose of sustaining political debate, it is also likely to bear the imprint of the commercial interests responsible for its production. The extent to which journalists working in an increasingly market-driven news environment can find ways of providing a comprehensive and truly diverse range of news perspectives is a key question in contemporary news journalism (see especially Chapter 3).

A further problem is identified by Protess. The picture of an actively engaged citizenry in dialogue with news media, which, in turn, interact with policy-makers and governments to build agendas and enact reforms, does not entirely fit with the evidence. Leaving aside the issue of how the news media represent political issues and in whose interests, a rather disturbing picture emerges of 'ordinary citizens', particularly in the United States. All the various indicators of political participation, from voting turn-out to party membership, suggest less engagement in recent decades. While it is not difficult to point to news media campaigns that have resulted in policy proposals or reforms, the evidence of extensive public participation in this process is more sketchy. For Protess, the 'golden age' in American investigative reporting, or 'muckracking', is to be found in the early decades of the twentieth century when newspaper circulations were expanding and readerships were radicalised by the experience of depression and unrestrained corporate power. In recent decades, according to Protess, investigative journalism has abandoned its responsibility to hold the corporate world to account and has, instead, tended to go for the soft target of 'government' and 'bureaucracy'. This has only reinforced a growing disenchantment among the public with politics and activism. News journalism has both reflected and encouraged a political apathy among citizens and a retreat from the public to the private domain (Protess et al., 1991).

The Public Sphere

The rather pessimistic conclusion drawn by Protess tends to underestimate the importance of new forms of politics and political engagement with environmentalism, the workplace, health, diet and sexuality, etc. However, it does underline the importance of tracing the relationship between journalists and groups campaigning around such issues (see Chapters 6 and 7). A healthy democracy in the contemporary late capitalist world must be one in which a variety of campaigning groups, if not all citizens, can circulate diverse and critical interpretations of issues and 'news events' through the news media. Once again, we return to the question of *access* to the news media.

In recent years a large number of media scholars have employed the concept of the public sphere as a framework for analysing this question. The term 'public sphere' comes from the German sociologist Habermas in his early study, first published in 1962, of the relationship between patterns of communication and social change (Habermas, 1989). Habermas argues that the emergence of capitalism from within European feudal societies in the seventeenth and eighteenth centuries, allowed a new sphere or space for the exchange of ideas through rational communication. In the feudal era, public communication was always bound by the power of the two most powerful feudal institutions. Through either patronage or the tools of repression, the feudal church and state exercised a very considerable degree of control over the circulation of ideas and information. In the Middle Ages, for example, 'the publicness of representation' (Habermas, 1989: 7) was entirely to do with the way in which the monarch or feudal lord represented his status and authority, rather than with the public exchange of ideas. As Peters puts it, 'representation was tied to persons not principles' (1993: 545). However, with the expansion of capitalist markets and production relations, a new space was opened up between church and state. Habermas says this space 'may be conceived as the sphere of private people come together as a public' (1989: 27) and he believes it was sustained by the emergence of a network of theatres, coffee shops, newspapers, journals, debating societies, circulating libraries, and learned associations, among other institutions, all of which were characterised by relatively low entry costs for those who wished to participate but which permitted rational debate. So for Habermas, in its early stages, the commodification of culture in Europe brought important benefits in terms of wider access and a democratisation of communication. In addition, the newly emerging patriarchal middle class family prepared individuals well for service within the public sphere through its emphasis upon rational argument and the extent to which it encouraged a demarcation between private subjective experience and outward public performance (1989: 50).Within this new public sphere, arguments could be weighed according to evidence and logic, the same universalistic criteria being applied to all communication, irrespective of the social position of those engaged in such exchanges. In other words, the philosophy and culture of the Enlightenment (the belief in the power of human reason as a force for progress) could find expression through the public sphere.

It was the energy of the newly emerging capitalist markets that stimulated the growth of the institutions and meeting places which made up the eighteenth-century public sphere, and for Habermas, it was precisely the same energies that by the nineteenth century were already weakening and contaminating it, through a process he terms re-fuedalisation. The re-feudalisation of the public sphere describes the process whereby communication and the exchange of ideas grow increasingly dependent upon a new group of sponsors and patrons, and upon new structures of authority which pose an increasing threat to the rationality of debate and the universalistic criteria by which arguments should be evaluated. In other words, capitalism replaces monarchs, church and feudal lords, with advertising, public relations and the commercial sponsorship of mass communication. Once again, the distinction between rational communication and the public representation of private interests grows blurred. As capitalism progressively re-feudalises the public sphere, the selection and representation of information placed in the public domain is undertaken according to commercial or political interests rather than 'pure' reason and rationality.

Of course, in the age of the 'spin doctor' and the global media corporation, Habermas's account has a particular resonance. This is the reason why the concept of the public sphere has received so much attention in academic writing on news media in recent years, and why media scholars continue to find the questions which Habermas's framework poses so central to media scholarship. Although first formulated in Habermas's earliest work, the concept of the public sphere is directly related to the more ambitious theoretical projects which preoccupy Habermas in more recent work. The public sphere is where the public experience of the *lifeworld* (i.e. interaction, social exchanges, the acting out of social customs, traditions, the dimension of individual meaning, etc.) is constituted, in contrast to the macro or *system* level, which comprises the structures of state, market and private corporation (Habermas, 1987). In other words, the interface between private experience and public power is structured through the public sphere. When somebody is made redundant by a private corporation, or told by a public official that their benefit has been reduced, the individual's responses in terms of subjective feelings and mode of analysis are conditioned by a number of factors, including conversation with family and friends but also by what they read in their newspapers or watch on television. Thus, public discourses and private subjectivities come together within the public sphere. This happens through the language and patterns of communication that individuals, social groups and, indeed, the mass media employ. This, in turn, provides a key to Habermas's later interest in the social conditions, or prerequisites, under which communicative action can occur.

Criticisms of the Concept of the Public Sphere

The concept of the public sphere has been subjected to considerable critical scrutiny. Indeed, Habermas himself agrees that in retrospect it could do with some revision (Habermas, 1994). Nevertheless, scholars both sympathetic and critical are reluctant to put the concept away because, both in its strengths and in its weaknesses, Habermas's account of the public sphere identifies what really are the vital issues and debates for the study of contemporary news media.

Central to questions both of theory and practical policy is the problem of rationality in communication. One feature of continuity in Habermas's work, as we have seen, is the assumption that communication and critical reasoning can be measured against an ideal type, or model, of perfect rationality, undistorted by interests or power structures. The extent to which a particular example of communication falls short of 'perfect rationality' then becomes an empirical problem to be described and then explained in terms of the particular social conditions in question. However, Habermas concedes that in practice communication, whether interpersonal or through mass media, can never entirely escape the effects of the conditions in which it is produced. The 'ideal speech act' can only ever be a theoretical possibility against which to measure empirical examples of communication. Critics, following Foucault, question the extent to which it makes sense to even contemplate 'rational communication', given that power relations permeate all human intercourse and all processes through which knowledge or communication is generated (Simon, 1995: 114).

Underpinning this is an epistemological question. In understanding all communication and all knowledge of the human sphere as a set of discourses, saturated by the interests of social groups and institutions, inseparable from the power networks underpinning their production, Foucault embraces a relativism which challenges the principles of the Enlightenment. The Enlightenment emerged in sixteenth- and seventeenth-century Europe as a cultural and philosophical movement founded upon the proposition that intellectual endeavour, in science or the arts, would achieve progress and reform, as knowledge of an objective world expanded. While Foucault's relativism encourages us to relate all such knowledge to the interests of particular social groups, and thus to abandon the pursuit of objective knowledge of the social world, Habermas is more ambivalent. Despite recognising the extent to which social interests may shape communication and the production of knowledge, he is reluctant to entirely relinquish the Enlightenment project (Habermas, 1983). The alternative seems to be to abandon the hope that political reason and the analytic tools of social science can be used to expose the 'truth' about inequalities, social injustice, oppression and exploitation. For Foucault (1979a), the forms of public communication which emerge through the Enlightenment are best understood as disciplinary tools, or mechanisms through which control and surveillance are achieved, while for Habermas, the Enlightenment concept of reasoned debate through public communication is still of central importance as a norm to guide communicative behaviour (Peters, 1993: 548).

This difference in epistemological understanding may seem rather remote from the day-to-day practice of journalism but is actually of vital importance. Politics in the age of the spin doctor can seem like a celebration of the irrational, with vested interests masquerading as impartial advice and sound bites being substituted for reasoned argument (Jamieson, 1992). Is it possible for current affairs journalists or studio interviewers to cut through the party propaganda to expose evidence of 'truths' below the surface? The Habermasian position implies that news journalism should still acknowledge this obligation, even if it is difficult, perhaps sometimes impossible, to achieve. Given that 'the politics of pleasure' has become rather a fashionable theme over the last decade, Habermas's vision of the public sphere is rather austere. Reason and argument based upon evidence rather than 'fun' or 'entertainment' appear to be the normative prescription in his public sphere and this has prompted some critics to suggest that Habermas has underestimated the extent to which ceremony, symbolism and ritual – the 'irrational' in Habermas's terms – continue to serve an important function in contemporary politics (Cottle, 1993: 110; Peters, 1993: 566). Political support is not secured through reasoned argument alone – perhaps hardly at all! Equally, in broadcasting and print journalism there must be entertainment value; news audiences are unlikely to warm to a format that has the feel of a sociology seminar, as several critics have pointed out (Bauman, 1992: 217; Collins, 1993: 251; Thompson, 1997: 41). And, in their day-to-day-'communicative activity', people exchange ideas and come to agreements in ways that may be 'reasonable', rather than 'purely rational' (Scannell, 1992: 341–-2). There are dangers in overemphasising the rationality in both media and audience discourses.

There are those who argue that a universal 'Enlightenment reason' may actually represent an oppressive force that refuses to become reconciled to fragmentary cultures and differences in outlook between cultures and groups. Drawing upon Foucault and recent postmodernist thought, critics argue that such a 'universal reason' contains an absolutism characteristic of bourgeois, patriarchal culture. In other words, the intellectual and cultural frameworks developed in other parts of the world, which represent alternatives to the Enlightenment tradition, are subordinated. There is, the critics suggest, a reluctance to tolerate 'difference' (Fraser, 1990; McLaughlin, 1993). In turn, this prompts questions about the way in which we should understand the public sphere in the contemporary world. First, just how diverse should be the discourses and perspectives articulated through a public sphere for late capitalist societies at the beginning of a new millenium? Must one 'Enlightenment standard' for reasoned argument and the presentation of evidence be maintained through all debates and communications within the public sphere? If one takes radio phone-ins which allow members of the public to 'join in', as an example of one news genre, the 'culturally grounded' nature of much public debate becomes obvious. Are we to dismiss such contributions if they fail to measure up to Enlightenment reason? Related to this is a second question concerning the epistemology, or status of knowledge, in journalism. Should journalists aim to produce 'objective' accounts of events to be presented in a public sphere as 'knowledge', or is objective journalism actually an unobtainable ideal? This question divides both journalists and academics and is considered more fully in Chapter 3.

A second area of criticism concerns Habermas's historical account of the public sphere. This has been subjected to intense criticism on two counts: that it rests upon an idealised account of its condition in the eighteenth century and on an over-pessimistic reading of its decline in the twentieth century (Garnham, 1986; Curran, 1991; Dahlgren, 1991). Habermas was well aware of the point that access to the European coffee houses, salons and libraries of the eighteenth century was far from universal; he intended the concept of the public sphere to be an ideal type against which real conditions could be assessed. Nevertheless, without discussion of the ways in which particular social groups were *excluded* from participation, there is clearly an important dimension missing from the original account. Only white bourgeois men enjoyed the authority and resources to participate freely; working class men, regional minorities, and almost all women other than a very small number of educated bourgeois wives, were all likely to experience very significant difficulties in securing participation and the right to communicate through the mainstream bourgeois public sphere. Indeed, in the preface to his original book, Habermas does acknowledge the 'submerged existence' of a 'plebian public sphere', represented by working class movements such as the Chartists (1989: xviii), but the point that subordinate groups were compelled to develop their own alternatives to the bourgeois public sphere is left unexplored. Critics argue that in his original formulation of the concept, Habermas failed to untangle and render visible the particular class and gender interests at play; that the public sphere represented a site of 'contested meanings' or even a mechanism through which the hegemonic dominance of particular class and gender interests could be secured, rather than a 'neutral space' in which discussion could occur (Fraser, 1990; Eley, 1992; Ryan, 1992; McLaughlin, 1993; Verstraeten, 1996). Thus, for example, the discourse of the nineteenth-century public sphere separated the public from the private, attaching importance to debates over how to achieve public reforms for the 'common good', and marginalising issues involving the personal, the private and the domestic sphere. In other words, the language and agendas of the nineteenth century were very much masculine in outlook.

If Habermas neglected issues of access and contestation in his original account of the early bourgeois public sphere, critics argue that he is overly pessimistic in his reading of developments in the twentieth century. A process of re-feudalisation has not been completed and to overestimate the influence of advertising, commercialism and public relations upon audiences and media workers is to misread a social science literature that points to the critical and discerning nature of media audiences or publics (see Chapter 8), and a sociology of journalism that finds many journalists (see Chapter 3) still actively engaged in critical commentary. Further to this, critics point to the emergence of a number of 'counter public spheres', including the radical working class press in the nineteenth century (Curran and Seaton, 1997), contemporary black and ethnic minority independent media (Gandy, 1998: 3) and the women's movement (Fraser, 1990). In line with recent developments in postmodernist thought, Fraser welcomes the pluralisation of counter public spheres in a de-centred, more fragmented social world. Following Foucault, some writers argue that the public sphere should be understood as a disciplinary mechanism and that its vitality is derived from the hegemonic struggles between subordinate and powerful groups over meaning and public interpretation (Verstraeten, 1996). Indeed, in a more recent reconsideration of his early work, Habermas agrees that the pluralisation of public spheres and the processes of contestation through which this occurs are important features of late capitalism (Habermas, 1992). Yet, as McLaughlin (1993) notes in the context of feminist strategies, campaigning groups may need to come to terms with the news media mainstream if they are to take their campaigns beyond the political micro-level (see Chapters 5–7).

There are weaknesses in terms of the way in which historical evidence is treated, and silences or omissions in the theoretical account, but Habermas's concept of the public sphere retains enormous value in guiding us towards what the really central issues are, both for media scholars and those policy-makers charged with media programming and regulation. In reading Habermas's original account, almost forty years old, we still find a contemporary agenda for research and debate. This is because Habermas, following Raymond Williams (1961), is interested in the central paradox of modern mass communication: contemporary political mass media offer the potential to involve and engage audiences in political debate at a deeper level than ever before, and yet this potential is rarely realised. Habermas believes that the explanation for this is bound up with the forces undermining the vitality and health of the public sphere.

Threats to the Public Sphere

Following the themes set out by Habermas, it is possible to identify four kinds of danger to the contemporary public sphere(s) in late capitalist societies: forces which may further undermine the rationality of political discourse and debate; a paradoxical process in which some new routes of access to the public sphere are opened up while others disappear; changes in the social fabric of society related, in turn, to aspects of globalisation; and finally, the progressive exposure of news media organisations to the pressures of market competition and the demands of news commodification.

The Nature of Political Discourse

In most parts of Europe and in the USA, politics has become slicker; politicians have grown more sophisticated in their use of image and language, while the political communications industry, consisting of spin doctors, advisors and image consultants, has grown from nothing to being huge in little more than two decades. The consequences of this for journalists and news sources are discussed in more detail in Chapters 5 and 6. Some critics believe that the rationality of political exchanges is undermined as politicians grow more adept at deploying sound bites and parrying questions, rather than engaging in genuine debate with opponents or interviewers (Jones, 1995). Some see the more frequent use of negative campaigning, personalised attacks and 'dirty politics' as part of the same pattern (Axford et al., 1992; Jamieson, 1992). More optimistic commentators argue that political public relations can bring benefits as well as dangers. Through a 'professionalisation' of political communication, politics can be made more accessible, political élites can communicate more effectively with voters, and democracy is thus strengthened (Shoemaker, 1989; Scammell, 1995).

There are some obvious dangers in constructing arguments around a vision of an earlier 'golden age' of politics in which opponents fought on policy and reasoned argument, each attempting to appeal to the rationality of the electorate. Political campaigning has always involved a fair degree of mendacity and image manipulation, while the partisan or even 'tribal' aspects of political support in earlier decades hardly square with the model of a rational electorate, guided by selfless reason. Nevertheless, undoubtedly television has changed the nature of political campaigning and with it political discourse. Even Ken Livingstone, a familiar personality on the political left in Britain, agrees that, 'It's a TV age . . . three minutes on the box . . . is worth hundreds of public meetings.'[1] If nothing else, politicians usually have very much less time in which to articulate their arguments in a television studio than they did in the pre-television era of hustings and meeting hall. If the nature of political communication has changed, this has important implications not only for political élites but for all campaigning groups and organisations. As we shall see with regard to the environment, for example, the more successful groups, such as Greenpeace, have developed media strategies which assume that in the contemporary media era, symbolism may be as important as the rigour of an intellectual argument. For some, there are dangers if the science involved in environmental debates is compromised (see Chapter 7) and this illustrates, very well, the dilemmas of a post-Enlightenment age. To what extent should we expect the debates around the environment to be conducted in terms of evidence, reason and Enlightenment rationality, or is it the case that the relations between campaigning groups, transnational corporations, governments and the news media, are constituted in such a way that the discourses of 'science' and 'environmentalism' are inherently shaped by the power relations and interests at play in this arena?

The Problem of Access

Access to the public sphere(s) of the contemporary age remains stratified and, indeed, with the arrival of digital broadcasting, Internet access, cable and other new communication technologies, the mounting costs of participation are further polarising the division between communication 'haves' and 'have nots' (Golding and Murdock, 1991). To the extent that senior figures in news organisations remain predominantly white and male, we can also say that the gatekeeping mechanisms regulating information flows to the news arenas of the public sphere remain stratified, too (see Chapter 3). However, while in these aspects, access to the public sphere(s) continues to be exclusive, in other important respects, developments in technology and format have made some news and current affairs arenas more inclusive and more participatory. Much speech radio, such as BBC Radio 5 Live or Talk Radio in the UK, bases a great deal of its programming around phone-ins and opportunities for engagement between presenters, studio guests and audience. Partly driven by market pressures to make current affairs programming more 'accessible', television now uses more studio audience discussion formats and other devices to engage more directly with viewers. Newspapers, particularly at the popular end, organise reader polls and invite comment on topical issues. Both broadcasting and print media employ e-mail and Internet resources to broaden channels of communication with news audiences, and it is possible to argue that broadcasting audiences are growing more confident and skilled in using these inquisitorial opportunities to challenge the public accounts provided by political élites on radio and television (Livingstone and Lunt, 1994). However, this is often an opening up of access for *individuals* rather than social groups or organisations. These kinds of programmes structure access in ways that invite individual members of news audiences to comment and, while it is sometimes possible for such individuals to formulate quite radical and incisive interventions, the 30-second phone-in contribution is not the best vehicle for an organisation to develop a complex analysis or contribute a detailed critique. As Simon Cottle (1995) has pointed out, the decline of the live studio interview format in favour of location reports by journalists has further restricted rather than opened up access.

Much depends upon how broad one's definition of 'current affairs' is. If daytime television chat shows are included, a rather more optimistic picture emerges than if all but 'heavy' flagship current affairs programmes, such as BBC 1's *Panorama*, are excluded (Connell, 1991). Nevertheless, while these developments may have opened some new routes to the public sphere(s), the counter-pressures should not be underestimated. The question remains, 'routes to what?' The ever growing pressures to deliver ratings, preserve circulation, trim costs and appease advertisers mean that, overall, the political and economic environment for news and current affairs journalism is less favourable now than in earlier decades (see Chapter 4). There are fewer 'serious' news and current affairs projects and this is likely to make life more difficult for the oppositional and campaigning groups that may be seeking to secure access to the public sphere in order to initiate or broaden debate (see Chapter 3).

Changes in Society

Habermas's original formulation of the concept of a public sphere assumes the existence of a consensual world in which there is a shared, mutual understanding of the conventions of debate and the criteria through which evidence should be evaluated. In other words, there is assumed to be a shared, consensually grounded rationality. There is also, by implication, a universally shared interest in the outcome of political or moral debates. Exchanges and controversies represented through the public sphere are thought to matter to people. In the immediate post-war period, radio and television really were collectively shared experiences and, in certain instances, broadcasting output could 'reach the nation'. Now, of course, things are very different. A common broadcasting experience, shared by the nation, is much rarer although they do still occur at certain times – major sporting events, the death of Princess Diana, and so on. However, routinely, the global, regional and local dimensions of cultural experience seem to resonate more strongly in people's lives than the national (Morely and Robins, 1995). Communities and identities are rather more fragmented in the contemporary world. Commentators suggest that this has precipitated a crisis for public service broadcasting which always depended for its rationale upon the concept of a *national* service (Hall, 1993; Mulgan, 1993). Given this fragmentation and that, as Habermas agrees, it is now more appropriate to think of a plurality of public spheres, the vision of a shared rationality and a consensually agreed set of criteria for debate, embraced by the national community, seems rather more problematic. With the pluralisation of broadcasting channels and specialist magazines, there is a danger that the public will retreat from arenas of national debate, preferring instead to inhabit local or specialist media communities, or even to withdraw entirely from national political processes. Politics, too, reflects this growing pluralisation or fragmentation. The rise of 'new social movements', new forms of protest and single issue politics, rooted more in identity, lifestyle or subculture than the creaking structures of the organised political parties, has prompted some commentators to question how long the stability of the familiar public sphere in which party politicians play out their set piece routines, will be preserved (Cottle, 1998: 22–3). A new counter-politics developed by those outside the political mainstream and sustained by the currents of the new social movements may be more symbolically exciting but, paradoxically, it may also be more vulnerable to media sensationalism and the charge that it contributes to a growing irrationality within, or even 're-feudalisation' of, the public sphere (see Chapters 6 and 7).

The Centrality of the Mass Media

In the eighteenth century, the circulating library, the coffee house and the newspaper each helped to sustain the public sphere. Now, at the beginning of the twenty-first century, the news media play a hugely dominant part in sustaining it. This, of course, may change as the Internet and more decentralised electronic communication systems grow in importance. There is a developing debate between those who envisage a new 'electronic commonwealth' of interneted cyber citizens, engaging in politics at the click of a mouse (for example, Negroponte, 1995), and those rather more sceptical critics who believe that the delivery of new electronic communications systems is likely to strongly bear the imprint of existing structures of power and dominance (for example, Golding, 1996, 1990; Barnett, 1997). However, at this point in time, the public spheres of the liberal democratic world are sustained primarily by the various news media, and there are good reasons for supposing that changes in the structure, ownership and organisation of the news media will drive them further and further from Habermas's ideal of universally accessible arenas through which rational dialogue can flow (see Chapters 4 and 5). One example will serve to illustrate the point. As our knowledge of health and medicine has grown, it has become feasible to make the public more knowledgeable regarding personal health issues than ever before. As Chapman and Lupton point out, 'The news media are therefore vital in mediating between specialised forums for the dissemination of medical and public health research and policy and the wider public' (1994: 25). In other words, it is through the news media that highly specialised knowledge located in exclusive professional domains can be made accessible to much wider audiences through the public sphere. However, the authors explain that too often this does not happen. Coverage of health and medical knowledge is frequently incomplete, oversimplified, partial, dependent upon a restricted number of powerful sources, or in certain circumstances, sensationalised in a way that is associated with 'health risk panics'. The reasons for these failures are complex but can be largely found through an examination of the organisation of news journalism and the intensification of commercial pressures within the newsroom (Lupton and Chapman, 1994: 25–35). In other words, it is largely to do with the commodification of news and the politics of news sources.

Many commentators, both academic and from within the industry, have argued that the intensification of commercial pressures is likely to lead to a drift away from 'hard' or 'serious' news formats, particularly within television (see Chapter 4). Some commentators have made explicit connections between the concept of the public sphere and the future of public service broadcasting (Garnham, 1986; Dahlgren, 1991; Keane, 1991; Scannell, 1992). While by no means embracing traditional public service models uncritically, such writers all identify public service institutions as a barrier against the progressive commodification of news media and all are deeply sceptical of the capacity of a fully deregulated market-driven media system to preserve the crucial features of a public sphere identified by Habermas. In a fully commercial system, it is audience ratings or direct subscriptions that drive scheduling and format decisions. Hence the diet of sensationalised reporting and studio audience spectacle. In public service broadcasting systems, there remains a degree of insulation from such pressures which allows a little more room not only for more 'serious' news and current affairs treatments but, as importantly, more diverse treatments, opening up access to a wider range of views and arguments. Yet, as numerous commentators have pointed out, the established definitions of public service broadcasting are increasingly questioned, not only by market liberals but those 'radicals' who associate public service broadcasting traditions with the 'totalising' tendencies of the Enlightenment.

The Debate Over Primary Definition

One of the important criticisms of the original Habermas formulation, as we have seen, is that he rather underplayed the issue of the relationship between power, structures of dominance and access to the public sphere. A second important debate within the sociology of the news media allows us to think this issue through in more depth. In a famous statement about the relationship between those seeking to gain access to the news media and the powerful, Stuart Hall and his colleagues argued that two aspects of news production – the pressures imposed upon journalists to meet deadlines, and the 'professional demands of impartiality and objectivity' – combine to bring about,

> a systematically structured over-accessing to the media of those in powerful and privileged institutional positions. The media, thus, tend faithfully and impartially, to reproduce symbolically the existing structure of power in society's institutional order. This is what Becker has called the 'hierarchy of credibility' – the likelihood that those in powerful or high status positions who offer opinions about controversial topics will have their definitions accepted, because such spokesmen are understood to have access to more accurate or specialised information on particular topics than the majority of the population. The result of this structured preference is that these 'spokesmen' become what we call the *primary definers* of topics. (Hall et al., 1978: 58)

The extent to which this observation, made over 20 years ago, remains true is one of the central questions of this book and lies at the heart of issues regarding the relationship between the news media and democracy and the vitality of the public spheres which sustain political contemporary discourse. Hall and his colleagues suggest that the powerful have a built-in advantage in the scramble to set news agendas or define news issues in particular ways, and that this is not necessarily a consequence of conscious or instrumental action taken by the powerful to deliberately manipulate, although it certainly does not preclude this; rather, the routine information gathering and news processing procedures operating in most news organisations make this likely to happen. By 'powerful', Hall and his colleagues have in mind the various departments of state, the leaders and senior figures within the main political parties, the institutions of law and security, but also the established interest groups close to government which in 1978 included both the Confederation of British Industry and the largest trade unions.

It is argued in *Policing the Crisis* (Hall et al., 1978) that such institutions will almost always succeed in shaping the news agendas and interpretative frameworks constructed by journalists because they are positioned at the top of a hierarchy of credibility. In other words, journalists would be very likely to take the frameworks for understanding events offered by such institutions as a starting point for their reports, for three reasons: first, precisely because such institutions *were* powerful and, therefore, newsworthy; secondly, because these institutions enjoyed a kind of legitimacy in the eyes of journalists by virtue of their status as representative either of 'the people' (governments, MPs, police, etc.) or of strategically important sections of society (trade unions, industry, the City, etc.); and thirdly, some sources enjoyed credibility not as representatives but as 'disinterested' or 'objective' experts, contributing expertise and authoritative knowledge (Hall et al., 1978: 58). It is not suggested in *Policing the Crisis* that other possible sources, including those who might contest the primary definitions of the powerful, will be barred from any access to news agendas but that their views or interpretations will be regarded as *secondary* definitions. Hall and his colleagues spent a considerable amount of time, both in *Policing the Crisis* and elsewhere, examining the textual devices in news reporting which in subtle, and less than subtle ways, signalled to audiences and readers the difference in legitimacy between primary and secondary sources (for example, Hall, 1971, 1973a, b, c; Morely, 1976).

Hall and his colleagues presented this conceptualisation as a way of thinking through in 'practical terms' how a sophisticated Gramscian Marxist theory (see Chapter 2) might avoid a 'crude conspiracy' model while still tracing the 'structured subordination' of the news media to the powerful primary definers in capitalist societies (Hall et al., 1978: 59). A decade later this conceptualisation was subjected to sustained empirical and theoretical criticism, led by Philip Schlesinger (1990), who, while wishing to retain 'a theory of dominance', still insisted that there were more opportunities for non-official news sources and politically marginal groups to intervene in the defining of news agendas than implied by the concept of primary definition. For Schlesinger, Hall's analysis seriously underestimated the 'potential openness' of distinct media sites (Schlesinger, 1990: 68) and suffered from a number of serious theoretical flaws.

First, the cohesiveness of primary defining institutions should not be overestimated. What happens if two such institutions offer contradictory or even competing definitions? This is not simply a theoretical possibility. Any political or lobby correspondent will cheerfully agree that some of their best stories come from individual ministers or departmental spokespersons briefing against their own side off the record. Sometimes departments of state feud with each other over fundamental policy differences or sometimes simply engage in turf wars, but these tensions frequently produce unofficial information flows which journalists happily convert into copy. Several studies have explored this process with regard to the war in Northern Ireland (Miller, 1993), tensions between the Treasury and other economic departments (Manning, 1998: 205–12), and food policy arenas (Miller and Reilly, 1994). Divisions within the Conservative Party played an important part in undermining the government's media strategy with regard to the notorious Community Charge or 'poll tax' in the United Kingdom (Deacon and Golding, 1994).

A second important criticism points to the difficulty in defining the precise boundaries that divide those with the power to primarily define the news from those with only a secondary status (Schlesinger, 1990: 66). In the British Parliamentary Labour Party, for example, ministers in government would presumably be regarded as primary definers while dissident left-wingers on the back-benches, it might be agreed, only enjoy an ability to offer secondary definitions. But what about those in-between, including aspiring back-benchers, 'senior' back-benchers, those occupying important positions on select committees and so on? Given that Hall includes organised interest groups in the definition of primary definers, how do we distinguish between those groups with a powerful capacity to set news agendas from the more politically marginal pressure groups.

At one time, the view that the British National Farmers' Union enjoyed a very real capacity to 'quietly' set news agendas through its co-operative relationship with the Ministry of Agriculture, Food and Fisheries would have prompted little dissent. Equally, the marginal status of even the more prominent environmental campaigning groups was fairly clear. Now, in the wake of numerous food, health and environmental scares, the capacity of government departments to primarily define news in these policy arenas is, arguably, significantly diminished and, according to some studies, the capacity of certain environmental groups such as Greenpeace to set news agendas in particular circumstances is much enhanced (Anderson, 1993, 1997). Similarly, while Hall may have included both trade union leaderships and the Confederation of British Industry in his account of primary definers in 1978, neither group appears to occupy a position in the hierarchy of credibility sufficient to ensure primary definition in the 1990s (Manning, 1998). In other words, there have been important historical shifts in the structures of dominance which Hall believes determine the capacity to primarily define the news. For Schlesinger, then, a third weakness in Hall's account is that it is atemporal, or fails to include a recognition of the possibilities for change in the distribution of capacities to primarily define (1990: 67).

Two further criticisms suggest that Hall oversimplified what are actually highly complex sets of interations and resistances involving political élites, media élites and the politically subordinate. Schlesinger and also Hansen (1991), for example, are critical of the assumption that the flow of influence travels in one direction only. It is frequently the case that political élites are influenced by the commentaries and agendas set in the news media. Critics of New Labour sometimes suggest that it is a government rather too eager to pander to tabloid headline writers in its policy deliberations. Beyond this point, Schlesinger argues, Hall's original definition underestimates the extent to which definitions are contested and negotiated. There is an emerging literature on the news media strategies employed by groups and organisations seeking to contest the way in which issues and events are defined through news media coverage in areas such as health, sexuality, environmentalism and labour relations (Anderson, 1997; Manning, 1998; Miller and Williams, 1998). The strategies employed by particular subordinate, or politically marginal, groups to gain access to the news agenda setting process have been charted and the relationships of exchange or negotiation between journalists and such groups described in detail. The evidence suggests, then, that it *is* possible in certain circumstances to contest or resist definitions offered by the powerful and to exert power in a counter direction.

Conclusion

Does this sustained critique mean that the concept of primary definition has little to offer media sociologists at the turn of a new century? On the contrary, the list of weaknesses or omissions rehearsed above, underlines just how fruitful Hall's original formulation was in marking out a research agenda for both empirical and theoretical work. Quite a lot of work has been undertaken since then in gathering empirical data about how the more or less powerful institutions contest the news arenas and attempt to offer competing definitions of events and issues. Inevitably, this has, in turn, demanded a theoretical effort in thinking through how we are to understand the power relationships between political élites, media élites and the politically marginal. Hall's original framework may have oversimplified complex relationships and underplayed the conceptual difficulties in getting to grips with processes of news definition and agenda setting but, as Cottle comments, it at least had the virtue of

> identifying the structural and institutional linkages between the mass media and other centres of power – linkages that can be examined and that promise to help explain the 'hierarchies of credibility' (Becker, 1967) and the differential opportunities of media access granted by the mass media to contesting . . . voices and interests. (Cottle, 1998: 18)

The view taken in this book is that if we want to assess the health of the public sphere(s) and its (their) capacity to serve the democratic good in contemporary capitalist societies, we must consider issues of access and the debate over the concept of primary definition provides, in this light, an excellent starting point. The questions and themes raised through the critique of Hall's early formulation are central to an understanding of news production and the part played by news sources, whether powerful or marginal, in this process. How do journalists assess the credibility of the sources they depend upon? How do potential sources earn such credibility and how do such 'hierarchies of credibility' change over time? How should we explain the dependence of journalists upon routine sources of information and how can this be placed in the context of the political–economic environment and the commodification of news information? What strategies can subordinate and politically marginal groups use to open up the news agenda setting process?

Chapters 3–7 deal with these questions but before addressing these, Chapter 2 will briefly consider the most useful theoretical frameworks available for analysing struggles around news definitions and information flows.

Notes

1. Quoted in *Labour Party News*, No. 1, 1987.

2 Theorising News Media and News Sources

This chapter is not intended to provide an overview of media theory, or even a comprehensive account of theoretical debates with regard to news media. There are plenty of alternative texts that can provide a fuller treatment for these purposes. Rather, what this short chapter will attempt is to provide some indication of the theoretical positions that have helped to sharpen the focus of this book. Accordingly, there will be little discussion in this chapter of the ways in which content, representation or reception can be theorised, although such issues will be touched upon in Chapter 8. The much less ambitious aim here will simply be to consider the insights that a limited range of theory has to offer with regard to the control and mobilisation of information through the relations between news sources and news media. A brief consideration of three important theoretical themes will help to locate the theoretical traditions discussed below.

First, throughout this book there is an interest in the ways in which information can be controlled and deployed. Powerful political élites may pull formal levers or apply informal pressures to promote or restrict the circulation of information through news media; politically marginalised groups may try, perhaps in vain, to use information as a bargaining chip in a complex series of exchanges with journalists; news beat correspondents will seek to sort the valuable 'contextual information' upon which they may lay claim to a specialist knowledge, from that which they regard as contaminated by political spin. In each of these examples, information is deployed through a variety of social practices and more or less consciously devised strategies. However, just as light travelling through space may be bent by the presence or gravitational pull of a gigantic object, so some would suggest information flows can be influenced not only by the conscious intentions of social actors but also by the existence of certain dominant social structures. As media progressively globalise, so the commercial significance of news grows also. The energies and processes of news commodification (the transformation of information into palatable packages to be sold) bring with them certain constraints and imperatives. The market position of any particular news organisation; the extent to which the news organisation may depend upon advertising revenues or, equally, upon finding a formula that successfully addresses key segments of the news audience; and the strategic importance of a newspaper's raison d'être in fostering an organic relationship with a particular political constituency or élite grouping, all represent examples of the kinds of structures that loom large in journalists' lives as 'givens' – parts of the social, political and economic environment that are less amenable to modification by human agency than others. In other words, to study the position of journalists within the news organisation or the attempts by news sources to gain access to the news encoding process, is also to consider one of the classic preoccupations in sociological theory – the problem of the interface between action and structure. One of the conundrums of the human condition is that in the social sphere, we make and modify but are also subject to the constraints of social structures. As Marx famously put it: 'Men make their own history but they do not make it just as they please; they do not make it under circumstances chosen by themselves, but under circumstances directly encountered, given and transmitted from the past' (Marx, 1968: 97). The theoretical approaches discussed below all offer some kind of judgement as to the extent to which those engaged in the struggles and processes of news encoding can make their own history and communicate it, or alternatively, are subject to the given circumstances of news production. In the attempts of various social groups to control and deploy information to their own advantage we can clearly see the interplay of structure, choice and action. Each of the theories below prompts questions and insights into this process.

A second theme which helps to locate each theoretical tradition concerns the very status of knowledge and the assumptions we make about the nature of social reality. At its modernist high point in the mid-twentieth century, much theorising in sociology and communication studies assumed that knowledge, both the kind produced by academics and that produced by journalists, could grasp the 'real' world in a more or less unproblematic way. Journalists described what happened 'out there' in the 'real world' just as sociologists could develop theory which captured, illuminated and even explained the 'reality' of social processes. However, few social scientists would now claim that either their empirical research or conceptual theorising grasped 'reality' in a direct and unproblematic way. Perhaps a slightly larger proportion of journalists might cling to such a naïve empiricism but even among journalists there is now a widespread understanding that facts about human beings rarely speak for themselves and that as we select aspects of this complex social world for discussion, and further select vocabularies, either those of the academy or those of journalism, with which to describe these aspects, we are in a certain sense constructing reality.

However, there are considerable differences among both academics and journalists as to what the implications of abandoning such a naïve empiricism actually are. For 'social realists', an external and objective social world remains out there and the task for both social scientists and journalists is to find a method and a conceptual vocabulary that allow us to provide the description and, perhaps, explanation which most closely approximates to this reality, even if the production of an account that entirely reproduces objective truth is never possible. Against this, a view which has become much more influential in recent social and cultural theory can be termed the 'strong' social constructionist position. The influence of phenomenological and pragmatist philosophy during the 1960s and 1970s promoted the argument in social theory that, in the social domain at least, we cannot untangle our understandings of reality from the value commitments and interpretative assumptions which guide us through our daily lives as we engage in social interaction with others. Social realities are 'constructed' as social actors interact with each other and exchange interpretative meanings.

A decade later, prompted by the writing of Foucault and Derrida, a new generation of social and cultural theorists arrived at a rather similar position. Social relationships, including the exercise of power, were sustained through the discourses which were generated socially but which also 'positioned' subjects or social actors. A 'strong' social constructionist position has profound implications for both journalism and media sociology. A 'strong' social constructionist position suggests that rather than reporting reality, journalists socially construct it. For Tuchman (1972), for example, the hugely complex social world outside the newsroom can never be grasped through the production of one definitive, objective account. Rather, journalists engage in 'strategic rituals', as they work with each other and sources to construct news reports. If one party's version of 'reality' is balanced by a competing account within the news text, then the 'objectivity' of the report can be defended. For media sociologists, the implications of a 'strong' social constructionist position are equally radical. In the past, communication scholars frequently attempted to measure the 'gap' between news media reporting of an issue or event, and another benchmark measure of 'reality' – sometimes official data, or, in certain instances, a set of eyewitness accounts. For some more recent media scholars, influenced by post-structuralist and postmodernist writing, such attempts are entirely misguided because there are no independent benchmark measures of reality. All is discourse. Stuart Allan (1995), for example, insists that the social world is constituted through the discourses which emerge to describe it. Eyewitness accounts and official statistics are merely alternative discourses, rather than benchmark measures of reality. The task must be to explore how news texts present themselves as 'truthful', rather than to test them against truth.

The implications of the 'strong social constructionist' position for the analysis of news sources, news media and information flows are important. In the sphere of party politics, for example, it is generally agreed that media work has become a more central part of political activity in recent years in the United States and most European democracies. As the spin doctors weave on behalf of political élites and even many politically marginal groups invest resources in developing 'media strategies', the temptation is to become wholly preoccupied with the processes of political symbolisation and spin – the ways in which political groupings seek to represent themselves through language and image – rather than attempting to hold political or media élites to account by assessing spin against alternative sources of evidence.

This prompts, in turn, a third theme, or rather an acknowledgement that the social and historical context is important for social and cultural theory, just as much as for an understanding of shifts in the practice of politics and journalism. Several theories that offer insights regarding news media, information flows and the role of news sources, strongly reflect the perspectives and concerns of the modern age. They are based upon a set of assumptions about the nature and functioning of political and economic structures which appeared more or less permanent from the vantage point of the mid-twentieth century. While there are many definitions, most agree that the emerging characteristics of modernism reached a full fruition by the mid-point of the twentieth century. It is by this point that Fordist social relations had come to typify the organisation of capitalist enterprises; commodity production was geared towards mass markets; an interventionist state was widely welcomed as an instrument to promote 'rational' policy not only in the economic but also the social sphere and, of course, much social science was integrated within what Wright-Mills called the 'administrative apparatus' (1970: 66), generating technical knowledge to achieve the state or corporate defined goals understood as 'progress'. In this era, it was possible for social scientists to regard large social aggregates – nation states, social classes, mass markets, welfare systems, etc. – as more or less unproblematic objective features constituting the subject matter of their disciplines. In contrast, more recent social and cultural theorising reflects recent and rapid processes of social change, particularly the growing centrality in society of processes of communication and symbolic representation, and the progressive globalisation of information flows. With this, there is a greater sensitivity to the dangers of reifying the social world, and of overestimating the capacity of social science to provide meta-explanations of its workings. It is something of an oversimplification to divide social and cultural theory according to its modern or late modern/postmodern orientation. Nevertheless, the social and historical context in which particular accounts of news media and information flows emerged is important for a proper understanding of the arguments which they offer. Structural functionalism, to which we turn first, is an excellent illustration of precisely this point.

Structural Functionalism and the Mobilisation of Information

Structural functionalism is unmistakably a product of the high modern age. With roots in the work of Durkheim, Spencer and, before them, the Enlightenment philosophers preoccupied with questions of social order, structural functionalism blossomed in the mid-twentieth century as sociology established itself in the American academy. Beyond its historical context, two central assumptions underpinning structural functionalism signalled its modernist outlook. First, while particular exponents of structural functionalism acknowledged the complexity and value-laden nature of the social world in contrast to the natural world, nevertheless functionalist writing employed the discourse of science to develop comparisons between society and the organic world. Societies, like organisms, could be analysed in terms of their component parts. Each part was understood to *function* in ways that contributed to the overall survival of the system, and the *structure* of the system, like that of an organism, was secured through the co-ordination of each functioning part. Secondly, while there is an ambivalence in functionalist writing which, as we shall see below, reflects the upheavals and traumas of a century of 'total war' and mass industrialisation, there is also an optimism characteristic of the modern era, a belief in the possibility of social progress and the promise of social science as a source of technical expertise upon which social policy and reform could be based.

Two well-known papers published by American social scientists in the mid-twentieth century provide a good starting point for considering the functionalist analysis of media and information flows. The shadow of war, the growing ideological crisis in relations between the West and Soviet Russia, and the alarming prospect of a technology that might as easily precipitate human kind's destruction as prove its saviour, loom large in their thinking. With public radio only two decades old and television still an emerging technology, Louis Wirth believed that in 'mass communication systems we have unlocked a new social force of yet incalculable magnitude' (1948: 12). Rather like nuclear fusion, mass communication systems appeared to offer simultaneously the hope of tremendous progress and huge potential danger. Turning first to the potential societal benefits, Lasswell identifies three societal functions in which the communication of information is central to the process: surveillance of the external environment, the correlation (or co-ordination) of internal parts, and 'the transmission of the social heritage from one generation to the next' (1960, first published 1948: 118). Lasswell argues that what both the single-cell organism and the complex human society share in common is the need 'to maintain an internal equilibrium and to respond to changes in the environment that maintains that equilibrium'. Thus, in the social domain, information flows carry intelligence or information about 'foreign affairs' back to the metropolitan, political centres of world, which can be understood as functioning like the cortical and subcortical centres in the organic nervous system. And, internally within particular societies, editors, journalists, political élites and communicators relay information in ways which assist in the 'correlation' or co-ordination of functions and parts, in a manner equivalent to the co-ordinated functioning of the living organism.

At the heart of structural functionalism there was an interest in the processes through which consensus could be secured in society. Stability and social equilibrium could only be ensured if there was more or less common adherence to a set of shared values, beliefs and normative patterns. This is, of course, a 'classic' modernist vision: the 'good society' secured through collective commitment to common goals. However, for Wirth and Lasswell things were not quite as simple as this. Common collective subscription to agreed values and normative patterns was likely to be problematic in societies 'where relatively abundant shares of power, wealth and other values' are concentrated in a few hands (Lasswell, 1960: 123). In other words, in societies characterised by wide inequalities in the distribution of wealth, political power and prestige, there would always exist the potential for what later critical theorists would describe as a legitimation crisis: the commitment of citizens to the existing normative order might weaken as they came to question the justice of existing social arrangements. Mass communication systems could play an important role here, according to both Lasswell and Wirth, in helping to mobilise consent:

> Modern society exhibits two major aspects. On the one hand, it consists of organised groups, ranging from informally constituted intimate groups to highly formalised organisations, such as the modern corporation, the union, the church and the state. On the other hand, there are the detached masses that are held together, if at all, by the mass media of communication. . . . On every level of social life calling for concerted action whether it be that of organised groups or the mass, we need a degree of consensus capable of mobilising the energies of members or at least of neutralising their opposition or apathy. (Wirth, 1948: 5)

In a manner which anticipates more recent theoretical debates, both Lasswell and Wirth distinguished two dimensions through which mass communication systems, particularly news media, might contribute to the engineering of social cohesion, but in making this distinction both writers betray an ambivalence in their picturing of news media audiences. On the one hand, both regarded the news media as first and foremost information carrying systems (hence the references to the organic nervous system). One of the most important problems for modern, industrialised societies was the very size of their component institutions which worked against the formation of close-knit or *gemeinschaft* social relations. One of the great challenges for social scientists, according to Wirth, and one upon which the future of democracy rested, was to explore ways in which mass communication systems could be used to promote 'effective contact between members and two-way communication between leaders and the membership of these giant structures' (Wirth, 1948: 4). Political communication here is understood as a *rational* process, through which leaders and citizens engage in dialogue. Lasswell called this process of mutual exchange and education, a process of 'equivalent enlightenment', adding that while political élites and full-time specialists might have 'more elaborate and refined . . . attention structures' with regard to particular policies, nevertheless, 'it is quite possible for the specialist and the layman to agree on the broad outlines of reality' (1960: 129). News media could play an important part in facilitating the exchange of ideas and information upon which such rational political dialogue needed to be based.

On the other hand, however, the use of the term 'masses' betrays a rather different understanding of the nature of political communication. This term has echoes of the nineteenth-century liberal preoccupation with the assumed 'irrationality' of the new urban masses, released from the stabilising influence of traditional rural social ties. In this context, there is a role for the symbolic and charismatic in political communication. Consent is secured not only

through rational dialogue but also through the mobilisation of a
symbolism which addresses political audiences along the emotive ra
rational dimension. Lasswell discusses the function of imagery,
ideology in securing political consent (1960: 123). Wirth points t
played by symbols such as the 'Stars and Stripes' or 'Hammer and Sickle', and the importance of stereotypes and slogans, 'which are the stock-in-trade of so much of our present day propaganda and public relations' (Wirth, 1948: 6).

> The instrumentalities of mass communication lend themselves particularly well to the dissemination of these symbols on a scale hitherto thought impossible. We happen to live in a world in which, despite the barriers of technology and politics, the whole human race becomes potentially exposed to the same symbols. They are weapons of offence and defence, and they are bonds of union or discord, depending upon the purposes which those who use them have in mind. (Wirth, 1948: 6)

Written at the mid-point of the twentieth century, these two papers seem remarkably prescient in their anticipation of the growing centrality of the mass media to the political process, and the dawning of the era of the spin doctor and sound bite. Indeed, at one point, Lasswell tries to distinguish between two groups of 'symbol specialists': those who are simply message 'handlers' and those who control or manipulate the content of messages. Of course, more recent theorising would question the distinction between message handling and message manipulation: all information or knowledge processing is likely to bear the imprint of particular power relations. There is a tension in these early functionalist accounts between the recognition that all information flows are sustained through mechanisms of control and the play of particular political interests, on the one hand, and a desire to present the question of mass communication as a 'technical problem', to be constituted as a suitable object for technical-scientific enquiry, on the other. Thus, various technical aspects of mass communication were explored through the organic analogy and the search for equivalents between communication in the social domain and the function of communication in the animal world but, at the same time, there was also a recognition that the extent to which *actual* mass communication systems functioned to fulfil 'technical specifications' depended greatly upon the ways in which certain political problems were resolved in practice. In particular, both Lasswell and Wirth acknowledged that so long as the control of print and news media was associated with large concentrations of wealth, there would also be a danger that the functional model of two-way neutral information exchange between 'parts' of society would be undermined by the play of powerful interests (Wirth, 1948: 11; Lasswell, 1960: 121).

In the reference to 'offence' and 'defence' in the passage above, Wirth seems also to anticipate the ideas explored by Gramscian theorists and those who have understood the news media as an arena in which particular political struggles are fought out. While structural functionalism has sometimes been criticised for overstating the tendency towards equilibrium and consensual stability in modern society, in the cases of Lasswell and Wirth at least, there is an understanding that consensual stability is never assured but, rather, depends at every stage upon the consensual function of particular social agencies, including the news media. In an analysis which could be Gramscian (see pp. 40–41) in everything but terminology, Wirth points to the 'spheres of human interaction', where struggles around political or industrial issues might undermine or even fatally weaken consensual social relations (1948: 12). Wirth acknowledged that such struggles might partly be fought out through the systems of mass communication in which case the news media might not function as mechanisms for the forging of consent but rather as sites of contestation.

While there has been a recent revival of interest in Durkheim's ideas in recent years, for much of the post-war period structural functionalism became unfashionable in sociology and is often ignored on communication and media studies courses, other than in discussions of how media 'function' to gratify audience needs. This seems a pity because, as we have just seen, some of the early functionalist writing represents a fascinating example of how communication theorists tried to think through the implications of new mass communication technologies as they were emerging and connecting with social and political structures at the high point of the modern era.

Nevertheless, functionalist concepts and arguments continue to be deployed both explicitly and implicitly within other theoretical frameworks.[1] Often theorists draw upon functionalist frameworks in considering the actual or potential role of the news media in relation to formal political processes and democratic government. Graber (1993), for example, has recently discussed the ways in which the performance of the news media in functioning to supply political information to political audiences can be improved by making broadcasting news formats more accessible. Kuhn (1995) organises his analysis of French media around a framework that identifies six media functions: the provision of information; communication between the various social strata in society; the performance of a watch-dog function through which political élites are held to account both by journalists and electorates via phone-ins and the like; a socialization and legitimation function to ensure social stability; an entertainment function; and finally, a 'nation building function' which some media may perform in consolidating a sense of shared national identity. A revival of interest in Durkheim's sociology has been partly prompted in recent years by anxieties about an apparent decline in social cohesion in late capitalist societies. In turn, the contribution which mass media might make to strengthening nation or communal ties once again became the focus for neo-functionalist approaches (Wylie, 1974; Alexander, 1981). Alexander's contribution is interesting because it returns to the question of the relationship between values, power and the nature of news information. As we have seen, a tension existed in early functionalist writing between a model of news communication as a value-neutral process of information dissemination and an acknowledgement that information flows are controlled and sustained through the exercise of power and political interests. Alexander agrees that news communication serves a cognitive function as an 'information conduit' (1981: 21) to news audiences but he is also quite emphatic in rejecting the proposition that news can be wholly objective or value neutral. Indeed, news communication is functional precisely because it is value laden: 'a major function of the news media is to produce "bias", to create through the framework of cognitive statements certain non-empirical evaluations . . . the production of moral bias is also a "good" and necessary social function' (1981: 19).

The news media partly function to disseminate appropriate values and reinforce moral boundaries but, according to Alexander, the news media are more flexible and can adjust to gradual normative shifts in public opinion in a way that is more responsive than other normative institutions such as law. However, the capacity of the news media to function normatively and maintain flexibility in this process depends upon the extent to which the news media have become structurally differentiated, so that they are free of 'economic, political, solidary and cultural entanglements' (1981: 33). In other words, just as Lasswell and Wirth acknowledged, where the influence of capital in owning and controlling news organisations is too transparent, or where the mechanisms of control operated by the state are too obvious, the credibility and legitimacy of the news media in the eyes of the public can be undermined.

Functionalism Assessed

The weaknesses of structural functionalist approaches have frequently been rehearsed. Most important, for the purposes of this discussion, are the questions which are now posed by the development of late capitalist societies in the second half of the twentieth century and the new millennium. First, as we shall see below, for some theorists, the influence of post-structuralist ideas encourages a sceptical view of any theoretical model which assumes that certain social structures are 'essential' or that social behaviour can be explained in terms of the determining influence of such 'essential' structures. There certainly is a tendency in functionalist writing on news communication to rather play down or simply ignore the degree to which news discourses are complex and contested. It is assumed that news journalists will produce copy in accordance with the functional imperatives specified by the structural role of news organisations. And yet, we know that news texts reflect a variety of currents, interests and political pressures which, in turn, reflect the complex social relationships through which news journalists produce news.

Secondly, the very idea that news media can contribute to consensus building processes now looks, at the beginning of a new millennium, a little dated; an idea rooted in the conditions of high modernity and rather less appropriate for the complex, highly differentiated and multicultural societies of late modernity. Can one shared normative order organise late modern societies and would it be desirable? On the other hand, news journalists do tend to organise their work on the basis of a consensual model, at least with regard to the formal political process, and perhaps with regard to moral and social issues too. Thus, as several commentators have pointed out in the past, mainstream broadcast news and much political print journalism too, reflect a set of normative boundaries which may be fuzzy around the edges but which, nevertheless, serve to set out the sphere of 'legitimate', 'moderate' liberal democratic politics and identify those groups and parties beyond the normative boundary as 'extremist' (Hall, 1971; Morley, 1976).

Pluralism: Élite Conflict and the Control of Information

The consensual role of news media provides one point of overlap between structural functionalism as a sociological perspective of the high modern era, and its contemporary in political theory, pluralism. Both became influential during the middle years of the twentieth century – the high point of the era of modernity – and both shared a preoccupation with problems of political stability and the relationship between the political centre and the 'ordinary citizen'. Both also looked forward to a period of political stability following the political turbulence and upheavals of the first half of the twentieth century. Pluralism as much as functionalism pictured legitimate politics as a process in which competition and political conflict could occur but within a normative framework of agreed rules and shared values. As Wirth put it:

> Consensus in mass democracies, therefore, is not so much agreement on all issues, or even on the most essential substantive issues, among all members of society, as it is the established habit of intercommunication, of discussion, debate, negotiation and compromise, and the toleration of heresies, or even of indifference, up to the point of 'clear and present danger' which threatens the life of society itself. (1948: 10)

Political contestation and conflict would not de-stabilise the polity providing it occurred within the normative limits defined by the consensually agreed boundaries of 'legitimate' politics. As Wirth implied, the stability of this model of liberal democracy depended upon the extent to which political ideas and information circulated freely. However, at this point, pluralists faced the same problematic issues as Wirth and Lasswell. To what extent did command over key material and symbolic resources, including capital, allow the powerful to exercise an unequal control over the flow or circulation of political information?

Pluralism represents, as Tony Bennett once put it, an 'emergency repair job on the liberal democratic tradition' (1982: 40), or an attempt to reconcile the ideals of liberalism with the 'practical realities' of politics in the post-war era. Traditional varieties of liberal theory appeared, in the context of the times, vulnerable to the radical and Marxist charge that while all in a liberal democracy might enjoy the right to vote and to formally hold governments to account, *real* power was rather less transparent and concentrated much more exclusively in the hands of those who owned or mobilised capital. Post-war American pluralism represented an attempt to address this central problem for liberal theory and it did so through the formulation of the principle of élite representation and counter-vailing power. Pluralists, such as Schumpeter (1976) and Dahl (1961, 1982), writing in the two decades after the Second World War, developed the argument that while power clearly was unequally distributed in liberal democracies, nevertheless, political power structures were characterised by a vital fluidity. There existed a *plurality* of élite groups, mobilising influence through pressure groups, political parties, corporate organisations and communal associations. Citizens, as individuals, might be relatively isolated and powerless, but most were indirectly enfranchised or represented by the activities of one or more organised interests, each competing within the normative framework of 'legitimate' politics. Through the activities and energies of these numerous organisations, the power of capital could be held in check. Marxist and élite theories underestimated the counter tendencies towards decentralisation and the dissemination of influence in modern liberal democracies: 'Views of domination like those found in Marxism and Italian élite theory are surely correct in emphasising the strength and universality of tendencies towards domination. Where these views go wrong is in underestimating the strength of tendencies toward political autonomy and mutual control' (Dahl, 1982: 33).

Pluralist writers generally conceded that certain organised interests, particularly those associated with business, would enjoy important material advantages in the struggle for political influence. Wealth, of course, could provide the staffing and means of political campaigning. Perhaps more importantly, given the strategic importance of wealth creation to national economies, governments would always be disposed to place the interests of capital high on their lists of priorities. In this light, even the early pluralists such as Trueman acknowledged that the state could not be understood as a neutral institution (Trueman, 1951: 322). Nevertheless, it was argued, business élites and associated organisations rarely enjoyed consistent and uninterrupted influence in government for several reasons. In the first place, business élites and associated organisations were often in competition with each other for influence, rather than acting as a unified class. Secondly, and most importantly for our purposes, material wealth represented just one kind of political resource. Other kinds of political resource could be equally important, and in some instances more so. For example, the communication or political skills which certain organisations might mobilise; the political standing, legitimacy or public image of campaigning organisations; the dynamism of their leaderships; or the extent to which they could mobilise activist support, might all make an important difference (Truman, 1951; Eckstein, 1960; Dahl, 1961). In other words, political and symbolic resources might compensate for disadvantages in terms of wealth and material resources

The implication here is important for the concerns of this book. If political and symbolic resources were to be mobilised, some of the most important arenas within which this could be achieved were likely to be offered by the news media. Implicit in the pluralist case was the suggestion that here, at least, the command of wealth counted for less, and that skilful use of symbolic resources, the arts of political presentation and even reasoned argument might count for more. As Finer put it, 'there is no perfect correlation between wealth and the amount of favourable publicity which one receives' (1966: 119). Rose put the argument even more baldly: 'money is of declining importance in politics in England', because pressure groups with little money could always rely upon 'publicity' (1974: 252). The news media, then, were understood to play an important role in liberal democracy because they appeared to represent a political terrain upon which the authority of capital was not sovereign and where other political currents could be enfranchised. A further important implication follows. In developing this kind of argument, pluralism directed attention towards the mechanics and strategies of power, as revealed at the empirical level; the ways in which both material and symbolic resources might be deployed in attempts to produce effective political communication, secure political influence, shape agendas or mobilise public opinion. While much of the orthodox pluralist case warrants more than a degree of scepticism, the suggestion that the mechanics of power, the strategies through which not only material but political, symbolic and communicative resources are mobilised, should be studied empirically is a useful one and one that informs the recent flourish of work on the sociology of news sources (for example, Miller, 1993; Schlesinger and Tumber, 1994; Deacon, 1996; Anderson, 1997; Manning, 1998; Davis, 2000; Miller and Dinan, 2000).

These approaches are, in the main, critical of the pluralist proposition that the power and authority associated with capital is partly nullified in the news arena. Indeed, Schlesinger, in the seminal article that was partly responsible for encouraging a new interest in news sources, insisted that questions about the strategies and mechanics of news media work should be posed 'from within a theory of dominance' (1990: 63). Nevertheless, a debt to pluralist traditions is reflected in three aspects of these studies. First, there is a commitment to the empirical observation of *how* particular groups mobilised available resources to develop media interventions or influence agendas. Secondly, attention is given to competition and conflict between groups located beyond government for access to public arenas. As we shall see, some, though by no means all, radical and Marxist approaches have rather downplayed the importance of such struggles between campaigning groups, preferring instead to concentrate upon the 'big picture' of class relations and the state. Lastly, there is an assumption that, at least at one level, the outcome of such strategies was uncertain, i.e. that the success or failure of such political or media interventions was a matter of empirical investigation and could not be predicted in advance. The problems in trying to reconcile a theoretical approach which assumes that the dominance associated with capital and the other major structures of power *does* shape and constrain news media processes, with an approach which acknowledges a degree of fluidity, openness or unpredictability in the contests and struggles around news agendas, are not easy to resolve (the complexity of the social reality in which news is produced is one of the attractions of the field!), but these are some of the most important issues which media sociologists have had to try to grasp and we will return to them in the course of this discussion and in the remaining chapters of the book.

Pluralism and News Production

The pluralism of the high modern era has given us, then, a model of political structures and processes which emphasises the fluidity of power, an empirical interest in the 'nuts and bolts' of the political and media strategies employed by groups and organisations struggling to shape agendas, and the suggestion that normative frameworks or political cultures play an important part in the regulation and stabilisation of political conflict. How have these broad themes been applied to the analysis of news production? One obvious difficulty with the pluralist argument described above was that even at the height of the modern era, most news media in most liberal democratic societies were privately owned, frequently by rich and powerful individuals or corporations hardly inclined to place the effective circulation of a variety of political perspectives at the top of their list of business priorities. The film *Citizen Kane*, the famous critique of wealthy press barons unaccountable to anyone other than their own interests, had appeared in 1938 and, as we have already seen, early functionalist theory had tried to grapple with precisely the same issue. Early post-war pluralism tried to address the problem in two ways: by an appeal to the market and by reference to the political norms and values which it was hoped might encourage a civic responsibility among news organisations. It was argued by some, and sometimes still is argued, that market processes and disciplines might mitigate against the dangers of the concentration of the ownership of news organisations in the hands of capital. For some pluralists, newspapers in competitive markets had to prioritise readers' interests rather than proprietors' prejudices, or risk commercial disaster; for others, ownership structures were likely to become increasingly fragmented as media companies raised new investment funds in the capital markets (Seiden, 1974; Whale, 1977).

However, as Chapter 4 discusses in more detail, expectations regarding the capacity of the market to dilute power or check the influence of proprietors have hardly been justified by recent newspaper or broadcasting history. A more subtle approach acknowledges the dangers that market pressures and economic power may produce but places more hope upon the robustness of the political culture and associated normative framework. This version of a pluralist approach is sometimes called social responsibility theory (Siebert et al., 1956). The mass media can be encouraged to fulfil society's expectations regarding their responsibilities providing the political culture and normative order is sufficiently vibrant. For example, in a society in which the mainstream political culture values the independence of the news media and the importance of the circulation of a diverse range of political perspectives, journalists will be encouraged to resist 'inappropriate' proprietorial pressures and the expectations of the public at large will act as a further safeguard. More recently, pluralist writers have been less sanguine regarding the capacity of the normative order alone to do the job. Some have noted with alarm the deregulatory tide that has weakened or washed away public service broadcasting systems in Europe and the growing difficulties, given the market-driven nature of globalised news, in trying to deliver the kind of comprehensive news and current affairs coverage which had in the past often been taken for granted as a prerequisite of a healthy democracy (Blumler, 1992). State as well as moral regulation to protect the 'valuable' in news broadcasting is now more frequently advocated.

What is important here is the view that relationships between news media and political élites are embedded in a political culture. Pluralist writers anticipate significant conflict between political and media élites. Indeed, such conflicts can be read as a sign that journalists are doing their job in holding politicians and governments to account and it is suggested that such conflicts can usually be managed without severe crisis or rupture in political–media relations providing the political culture defines appropriate role expectations for each side (Gurevitch and Blumler, 1977). A healthy modern political culture will include a commitment to the values and expectations of public service broadcasting. Party politics, pluralists conceded, could be a dirty business and political journalism could be equally sordid, but robust public service broadcasting values could ensure that at least some channels in political communication remained uncorrupted:

> We take our stand, then, not with 'the broadcasters' but with the values of public service broadcasting. These are precious and should not be cavalierly dismissed as mere myths and shams. Because they are often neglected or twisted does not mean that they lack beneficial impact. Indeed, in so far as they are applied, they confer fairness, reason and dignity on the struggle for votes through campaign communication. We are not blind to what is sordid or imperfect in the workings either of competitive democracy or of broadcasting. But that is exactly why public service standards are so vital – to serve as spurs to improvement and guides to correction. (Blumler and Gurevitch, 1979: 219)

Once again, while some of the important difficulties associated with this kind of analysis will be considered below, the attention to the empirical detail of power as it is expressed through interaction between political and media élites is valuable. Relationships between political and media élites are typically complex in modern liberal democratic societies, being characterised by a mutual dependency but equally by inherent tension. Pluralist writers have made a valuable contribution in charting the ways in which, for example, particular political parties develop 'organic' relations with particular newspapers or particular journalists (for example, Seymour-Ure, 1974, 1991) but equally valuable is the work which reminds us that politicians and journalists, political élites and media élites, frequently become locked in struggles around issues of control and access to information (for example, Tracey, 1978). In more subtle pluralist writing, the outcomes of these conflicts are not 'given' but remain a matter for empirical enquiry. The potential threats posed by the 'big power battalions' (Gurevitch and Blumler, 1990: 272) to the open circulation of information are acknowledged: official sources may use their position and influence to encourage a dangerous dependency on the part of journalists, and wealth can be mobilised to promote or suppress news. In this kind of pluralist account, such outcomes are considered possible but perhaps not likely providing the norms and values shaping political and journalistic behaviour are sufficiently robust to encourage 'a principled resistance to external forces attempting to subvert media autonomy' (Gurevitch and Blumler, 1990: 270).

As we shall see below, those media sociologists working from within a theory of dominance, to use Schlesinger's phrase, are inclined to be more sceptical regarding the capacity of a liberal political culture to withstand attempts on the part of the dominant and powerful in society to exert control over the information flows to the public sphere(s). Nevertheless, one of the contributions of pluralist writing in this area is to remind us that there is a degree of openness or fluidity permitted by the institutional arrangements and structures supporting political communication in most liberal democracies, and that this recognition has to be squared with the equally undeniable point that those dominant groups and institutions enjoy structured advantages in the struggle to control information flows supplying the public sphere(s). This is where the sociology and politics of news sources begins. In societies where the powerful enjoy very significant communicative advantages and yet subordinate groups do achieve some significant successes in accessing certain news agendas, we need to ask questions about news media strategies, the ways in which organisations mobilise material and symbolic resources, and the nature of the relationships that can be established between press or publicity staff within organisations and news journalists. Blumler appeared to recognise the value of moving in this direction more than two decades ago, outlining a research agenda in which political communication was understood as a 'three legged stool' involving not only journalists and audiences but also 'political and other interest groups' (1980: 373) but, with one or two exceptions,[2] an interest in the communicative strategies of subordinate, or even dominant, groups did not emerge within mainstream pluralism and it was left to media sociologists, such as Schlesinger, in the late 1980s to expand this research agenda.

Pluralism and the One-dimensional Approach to Power

The failure of pluralism to develop Blumler's 'three legged stool' can be explained partly in terms of the impact of a powerful radical critique which encouraged large numbers of social scientists in the 1970s and early 1980s to question not only the empirical propositions offered by pluralism but the very theoretical and epistemological assumptions underpinning the approach. The main thrust of this critique has been rehearsed on numerous occasions.[3]

In terms of theoretical considerations the important point is that in its commitment to the empirical investigation of power, pluralism has traditionally ignored dimensions of power and structure that are not amenable to conventional social scientific investigation. Pluralism focused upon the instrumental dimension of decision-making. Pluralist studies frequently assessed the distribution of power between competing interest groups by 'noting' political outcomes – how many decision-making successes were particular organisations able to secure in policy-making arenas. A simple extension of this to the news editorial room would clearly be inadequate. It is not enough simply to observe decision-making either in public policy-making arenas or news production: one has to be aware of two further dimensions, as Lukes (1974) has famously argued. The focus on decision-making misses the point that certain agendas may be shaped by 'back stage' activities: certain dominant interests may exert power to keep sensitive issues off the agenda and, perhaps by extension, also off the front page of the newspaper. This kind of influence is hard to observe empirically for obvious reasons – 'back-stage' zones are normally kept off limits for inquisitive social scientists. But beyond this, there is a 'structural' dimension which operates above and beyond the level of conscious decision-making. This might include the 'gravitational pull' of capital referred to in the introduction to this chapter. Just as a local paper might simply not even think of running with the issue of air quality in a small one-plant steel town (Crenson, 1971), so certain issues which might prompt more fundamental criticism of the political and economic status quo may rarely surface in news reporting, not because editors or senior journalists deliberately smother such stories but simply because the organisational culture and practices of the newsroom prompt journalists in other directions.

There are, then, dimensions of power that are neglected by traditional pluralism. The 'classic pluralists' of the mid-twentieth century were certainly aware of the 'deeper' ways in which structures might influence political outcomes – Dahl (1961) in a famous footnote acknowledges that the observation of decision-making only addresses one aspect of power – but the methodological thrust of mainstream social science during the heyday of pluralism was towards the empirical and observable. Structures or power relationships that could not be 'captured' using conventional, usually quantitative, methodologies, were regarded as beyond the limits of an empirical social science. The neglect of 'deeper structures' may partly explain the more optimistic pluralist accounts of the capacity of the normative order and culture within the polity to check or restrain the pressures undermining news media autonomy. Those approaches, characterised by Schlesinger as theories of dominance, which assume that we must start our investigations of political–news media relations with the assumption that power relations are characterised by significant structural inequalities, are likely to take a rather less optimistic view of the efficacy of mainstream political culture as a 'buffer' against predatory material interests.

The tensions, fractures and competition between powerful groups described in orthodox pluralist accounts is real enough. Indeed, such divisions among the powerful have been acknowledged in radical accounts too (for example, Hallin, 1986; Deacon and Golding, 1994). It is also undeniable that the dominant sometimes fail in their political or media strategies. However, at another level, a dimension not necessarily amenable to direct empirical observation, structures of dominance do shape news production and the struggles around the generation of information flows. Before thinking through the ways in which these two pictures of political communication can be reconciled, we need to turn to the theoretical traditions that describe and explain such structures.

Marx, Political Economy and Neo-Marxisms

Marx's writing is absolutely central to our theoretical understanding of news media and yet, perhaps, few media sociologists would now describe themselves baldly as 'Marxists'. This partly reflects a movement in recent years away from structural, 'essentialising' theories in media and cultural studies. However, Marx helpfully left only rather sketchy comments regarding journalism, ideology or the nature of control over 'ruling ideas', which has allowed scholars ample opportunity to work on a bewildering variety of interpretations, revisions and adaptations during the course of the 117 years since his death. It is now possible to identify several quite distinct theoretical traditions, each of which owes a huge debt to Marx but does not necessarily now claim the appellation 'Marxist'. To attempt an adequate review of all would require a volume in itself. However, in focusing upon the way in which struggles around the control of information flows may be understood, it will be helpful to start with Marx and Engel's famous statement:

> The class which has the means of material production at its disposal, has control at the same time over the means of mental production, so that thereby, generally speaking, the ideas of those who lack the means of mental production are subject to it. . . . The individuals composing the ruling class possess among other things consciousness, and therefore think. Insofar, therefore, as they rule as a class and determine the extent and compass of an epoch, it is self-evident that they do this in its whole range, hence among other things rule also as thinkers, as producers of ideas, and regulate the production and distribution of ideas of their age: thus their ideas are the ruling ideas of the epoch. (Marx and Engels, 1970: 64)

This is an important passage because it is one of the few places where Marx and Engels begin to sketch out how they believed the powerful in society exercised control over the circulation of ideas. There are sufficient ambiguities even here to support more than one interpretation. However, it is possible to discount certain approaches. For example, in the writing of some twentieth-century Marxists an account is presented in which the mass media 'function' to generate a kind of ideological fog which descends like a blanket upon the masses to cloud their thinking with 'ruling class ideas'. Marx and Engels certainly argue that in order to secure its legitimacy a ruling class must 'give its ideas the form of universality' (1970: 66); in other words, it must represent its interests as those of society as a whole. However, the passage quoted at length above makes it clear that they did not believe that nineteenth-century media consumers were simply overwhelmed by ideological fog. Rather, it was a matter of the *circulation* of ideas. It was the case that 'generally speaking', or usually but not always, ideas which challenged the political and economic status quo were not widely circulated because those advocating such ideas lacked 'the means of mental production'. Radical and subordinate groups experienced more difficulty in promoting critical perspectives because usually they did not enjoy editorial access to newspapers with mass circulations, or popular publishing houses. This argument in itself does not make any assumptions about the vulnerability of the public to media messages or propaganda. Rather, it simply makes the point that 'ruling class ideas' were very much more widely circulated given the institutional practices and economic relationships of nineteenth-century capitalism.

How was the exclusion of the subordinate from the main channels of communication or information flows to be explained? The passage implies that this has to be understood in terms of the distinct dimensions of power discussed above. On the one hand, in this passage Marx and Engels refer to the 'consciousness' of members of the ruling class and their capacity to 'regulate' the production and distribution of ideas. This is the dimension of instrumental action: power consciously exercised to promote or restrict the flow of information to the public domain. But by implication there is another dimension here. The capacity to circulate information through society is determined by access to the 'means of mental production'. In turn, the means of mental production are subject to the structures of the market and the imperatives of capital. Even in 1846, when *The German Ideology* was completed, the industrialisation of newspaper publishing was already beginning to develop; new, more sophisticated printing presses demanding huge amounts of capital investment were on the point of introduction, circulation wars and advertising markets would soon begin to drive editorial strategies, and the division of labour in journalism was already raising the cost of staffing (Curran and Seaton, 1997). Such structural features meant that already access to the means of mental production was unequal and that proximity to capital afforded significant advantages. If a ruling class enjoyed a dominant position with regard to the circulation of ideas, or information flows, this was both a product of instrumental action and a consequence of structure. This is why Marx and Engels argue that the class which has the means of material production at its disposal also has control over the means of mental production.

Although both instrumental and structural dimensions of power seem to be acknowledged in *The German Ideology*, Marxist scholars devoted much of the 1970s and 1980s to arguing the case for *either* an instrumental or a structural approach to the problem of power in capitalist societies. Marxist scholars focusing upon the instrumental dimension gathered data on the common backgrounds, shared beliefs and personal networks which bound members of financial, business, political and media élites together. Those with power within media institutions shared economic and political interests with other powerful élites and yet tended to represent these as a national rather than class interest. Miliband, for example, insists that 'there is no question' that the dominant classes in capitalist societies exercise control over the main means of communication (1994: 31). Yet he also recognises that in contrast to the former Communist regimes there is also an 'extraordinary diversity in the production and dissemination of ideas'. He reconciles these two propositions in the following way:

> It means that in some areas, in which ideology and politics are directly and obviously involved, views which jar sharply with those of the controllers of the means of communication, whether private or public – in other words views strongly at odds with conventional ones – will have some difficulty, to put it no higher, in getting a fair hearing. This, it should be emphasized, is not to say that all such views are suppressed. That is certainly not so; and there are, in any case, alternative 'minority' channels of expression for them. The point is rather that the views which the controllers of the main means of communication find obnoxious will have to run an obstacle course, which some survive, in a more or less battered condition, and others do not. (1994: 31)

How does the 'obstacle course' operate inside the organisations and agencies which circulate ideas and operate information flows? The role of the press as a critical voice, Miliband continues, should not be underestimated but neither should its limits be overlooked.

> One reason for its limits, of great importance, is that the people who actually produce and disseminate the products are themselves subject to one of the most effective forms of censorship – self-censorship. The people concerned generally *know* what is likely to produce problems with their bosses; and for the most part try to avoid these problems. (1994: 32)

This is true, Miliband insists, in both the private sector where 'major shareholders are not likely to pine for the representation of radical views' and the public sector in which senior managers and 'external pressures' encourage regimes of self-censorship.

This kind of analysis, with its emphasis upon chains of command within media organisations, mechanisms of self-censorship and perceived 'external pressures', is clearly instrumental in its emphasis upon action and understanding. For some 'structural' Marxists, the main problem with instrumental approaches is that they fail to break with the methodological and ontological assumptions underpinning pluralism. By focusing too much upon the background and actions of those in power, whether politicians, bankers or newspaper editors, there is a danger that the structural constraints which operate irrespective of personnel, would be overlooked (Poulantzas, 1969). Would the editorial line of a popular tabloid newspaper change very much if the editor changed: if a woman rather than a man took charge, or some one on the political left, rather than right? A structural analysis might suggest not, because the overriding imperative to commodify news using a particular format, to reach a target audience through specific market strategies and to acknowledge the interests of shareholders or proprietors, are structural 'givens' constraining the decision-making process, irrespective of whom is in charge. And yet, one of the merits of the instrumental approach, and one Miliband fiercely emphasised, is its insistence upon 'the absolute necessity of empirical enquiry' (1972: 256).

Miliband shared with pluralists a desire to show how power worked empirically. For structuralists such as Poulantzas, this was an error because the *essential* underlying reality of power was not amenable to empirical observation. Nevertheless, some of the pioneering news production studies have shown that valuable insights into the workings of power and control over information flows can be obtained by studying how mechanisms of control and self-censorship operate, using both ethnography and historical case studies (for example, Schlesinger, 1978; Tracey, 1978; Miller, 1994), even if it is acknowledged that these empirical studies, in themselves, are unlikely to reveal how power works at every level.

There is a danger, as Jessop (1990) has recently argued, in presenting the instrumental and structural as a false dichotomy: there is always a dialectic between the two, as structural constraints find expression through the negotiated strategies of thinking, reflecting actors. Indeed, in analysing the reasons for the restricted range of perspectives in the main news media, Miliband refers to structural features including corporate ownership patterns and advertising markets, as well as the intention of ruling classes to wage 'ideological class struggle from above' (Miliband, 1991: 145–7). Nevertheless, to systematically think these issues through is by no means a waste of time. It is partly necessary in order to trace the development of the distinct theoretical approaches which share a common root in Marx, and partly in order to separate out the more subtle from the cruder kinds of Marxian analysis. It would be surprising if a theoretical framework formulated 150 years ago, during the emergence of the modern industrial age, was not in need of some revision in the light of twentieth-century history. The things which Marx got wrong have been noted on numerous occasions, although it is surprising how applicable many of his ideas still are in an era of globalised capitalism (Hobsbawm, 1994, 1997; Miliband, 1994). If there is one main lesson which is as important now as it was in Marx's day, it is that capital continues to exert its 'gravitational pull' upon the social and economic life of society. The danger that critics of Marxism are quick to alert us to is that in acknowledging the continuing centrality of capital we treat it as an *essential* structure, to which we can turn in order to 'explain' all other social or political practices; in other words, economic reductionism.

Neo-Marxist Approaches: Hegemony or Political Economy?

Marx was highly critical of these kinds of analyses and when he turned his attention to matters beyond writing *Das Kapital*, showed a subtle understanding of the interplay between the economic, social and political.[4]

Nevertheless, assessments of Marxist and neo-Marxist writing in recent times have continued to wrestle with the problem of how to acknowledge the centrality of capital and yet avoid the oversimplifications of reductionist analyses. It cannot be denied that in approaching the role of the mass media in capitalist societies, some accounts have collapsed into forms of reductionism. This is not the time to provide a comprehensive account of twentieth-century Marxist scholarship. For the purposes of focusing upon news media and the control of information, three kinds of approach in neo-Marxist theorising are important.[5] These are first, what is sometimes called the propaganda model; second, the hegemonic model; and third, political economy.

To return to the passage from *The German Ideology*, contemporary political economy takes as its starting point the relationship between material production and mental production. One neo-Marxist approach develops a political economy of mass communication systems but does so in a way that stresses instrumental relationships. Herman and Chomsky (1988), for example, begin with themes central to a political–economic analysis – the consequences of corporate control over the main channels of mass communication, the impact of advertising, and the dependence of news organisations upon official government sources. However, in the development of what the authors describe as a 'propaganda model' to account for how US news media 'manufacture consent', most emphasis is placed upon the filtering process involved in editorial decision-making and the relationships between government, business, 'experts funded and approved by these primary sources and agents of power' and senior journalists or editors (Herman and Chomsky, 1988: 2). Chomsky dismisses the value of examining the politics of news sources; alternative more critical sources could always be found if journalists really wished to do so (1989: 77). American news media coverage of US foreign policy was equivalent to propaganda or 'thought control' because too often, 'the media simply refused to investigate the facts or report what they knew' (1989: 81).

There are several problems with this kind of analysis, as critics have pointed out (Schlesinger, 1989; Schudson, 1991). The model of the relationship between news media and audiences is simplistic – as Chapter 8 discusses in more detail, political audiences are receptive to media agendas in particular circumstances but are rarely directly 'controlled' in the way suggested here. More importantly, the emphasis upon instrumental connections between journalists and powerful government or business personnel can easily collapse into a conspiracy model. Conspiracies do occur – and Chomsky may be correct in suggesting that sections of the American media set out to demonise the Sandinistas in Nicaragua – but a conspiracy model simply cannot deal with all the available evidence. Conspiracy models cannot account for the times when the news media significantly undermine the authority of the powerful; when, as Schudson reminds us, American presidents are compelled to resign, or when a giant biotech corporation concedes that it has lost the public relations battle in Europe over genetically modified food. Production studies suggest that many, perhaps most, journalists and certainly those working for public sector broadcasting organisations do not experience the pressures of conspiracy in their everyday working lives. Rather, power and constraints operate in more subtle ways within the newsroom. The 'propaganda model' really is oversimplistic in reducing US foreign news coverage simply to the economic and political objectives of corporate capitalism and US imperialism. The tradition of empirical investigation within the sociology of journalism demonstrates that relationships between journalists and the powerful are more complex; that conspiracies may occur but that the interests of the powerful are expressed through a variety of complex relationships and that their dominance is rarely fully guaranteed.

The dangers of reductive analysis and economic determinism prompted a revival of interest in the writings of Gramsci during the 1960s and 1970s (see Gramsci, 1971). Althusser (1971) also appeared to offer a framework for developing a Marxist analysis that acknowledged the 'relative autonomy' of the political and ideological, from the economic. Gramsci's starting point can also be found within *The German Ideology*: Marx and Engels observe that every new ruling class strives to 'represent its interest as the common interest of all members of society . . . to give its ideas the form of universality' (1970: 66). According to Gramsci, hegemony is secured to the extent that the ideas and perspectives of a dominant class or class fraction come to be regarded as 'commonsense' – a universality widely embraced by social groups throughout society. However, the hegemony of the powerful is rarely permanent or secure: subordinate groups are always likely to contest dominant ideas and offer alternative perspectives. The Gramscian approach focuses attention upon the cultural and political arenas (schools, newspapers, theatres, etc.) in which societal tensions, and engagements between classes and fractions of classes, found expression in tussles over the meaning of ideas, political concepts, symbols, and even particular words.

The Gramscian and Althusserian influence stimulated what could be described as the *hegemonic model*, associated with recent neo-Marxism. This approach emerged during the 1960s and 1970s and was characterised by a new interest in the news media text as a site of struggle – an arena through which the powerful sought to secure hegemony but within which the subordinate might also resist and where oppositional readings, or elements of critical agendas, might surface. The desire to avoid 'reducing' news texts simply to the cultural expression of economic class interests, prompted the decision to start with the text itself, rather than the social relationships involved in the production of texts, as traditional Marxist and political economic perspectives usually did. This was justified on the grounds that the production of media texts could not be treated just like any other political economic process of commodity production. Rather, the production of media texts involved 'the articulation together of social and symbolic elements' and it was this 'symbolic practice' that was the distinctive feature of media and cultural production (Hall, 1982: 68). The task for numerous content-focused studies, then, was to trace the contested nature of news coverage (among other media forms); to chart the way in which the language and symbolism of the news text tended to displace critical, subordinate interpretations and privilege dominant ideological frameworks which articulated the perspectives of the powerful. Thus, through the work of the Centre for Contemporary Cultural Studies at Birmingham University, among many other subjects, the 'unwitting bias' of radio news in demarcating legitimate consensual politics from 'illegitimate' political protest (Hall, 1971, 1973a) was analysed; the ideological structure of news photographs deconstructed (Hall, 1973b); the marginalisation of militant trade unionists and in television current affairs described (Morley, 1976); and the prioritisation of conservative 'law and order' explanations in crime reporting demonstrated (Hall et al., 1978). At the same time, the Glasgow University Media Group documented the distortion of industrial coverage in mainstream television (1975), the privileged access to studios and interviews which the powerful enjoyed (1980), and the extent to which the state could 'manage' news coverage of military conflict (1985).

These kinds of studies represented an important step forward because they *did* avoid the dangers of economic reductionism and offered radical or Marxist perspectives a way of thinking about the relationship between capital and the news media which avoided oversimplistic 'transmission belt' models. News media texts did not simply relay the propaganda of the powerful. Rather, they often contained elements of competing frameworks and perspectives but they also contained textual devices which allocated more 'authority' or 'legitimacy' to interpretations based upon the ideological frameworks of the powerful. These studies suggested that news texts were not ideologically sealed: there *were* opportunities for subordinate voices to be heard, if only in disjointed and fragmentary ways. While retaining an insistence upon the centrality of the power relations associated with capital, these approaches were able to acknowledge the more open, pluralistic nature of the news media which some of the cruder instrumental political–economic accounts had difficulty in accounting for.

While the Gramscian and hegemonic approach has proved highly influential and has played a large part in the development of cultural studies as a discipline, it is not without its critics. Some suggested that an emphasis upon the power of dominant ideologies in maintaining social order, as opposed to plain economic compulsion, could be rather overdone (Abercrombie et al., 1980). More importantly for the purposes of this book was another critical point: the strategy of commencing with the text was chosen in order to avoid reductionism but this meant that researchers frequently ended up trying to make inferences about the social relationships involved in the production of texts from the content – a rather problematic form of inquiry (Elliott, 1981). Far better, it was argued, to go out and investigate these relationships, particularly as the conclusion that news texts were complex and often articulated more than one competing discourse, prompted questions about how those competing discourses arrived in the text. What sources of information did journalists use? What organisations were active in promoting particular frameworks or 'ways of understanding'? How was authority lent to particular frameworks or 'ways of understanding' within the news production process? Now it was certainly true that some work within the Gramscian/hegemonic approach made a start at exploring these questions. This is where the model of *primary definition* outlined in 'Policing the Crisis' comes in (Hall et al., 1978). Before exploring the contours of 'law and order' news, Hall and his colleagues do begin by reviewing the sociology of news production. The explanation for the ability of the powerful to primarily define news in terms of their preferred agendas was identified in terms of the pressures of news deadlines and the inclination of journalists to regard non-official sources as lower in the 'hierarchy of credibility' (Hall et al., 1978). However, the disadvantaged position of non-official sources was simply taken as given rather than established through empirical enquiry. Many of the researchers working with the Gramscian/hegemonic approach chose to look at the other end of the 'encoding–decoding' process, asking questions about how audiences made sense of the primary or secondary definitions embedded in media texts, and it was really left for the 'second wave' of researchers at the Glasgow University Media Group, during the 1990s, to pursue questions about power and the organisations contesting the news arena (for example, Miller et al., 1998; Philo, 1999).

Must political economy always 'reduce' complex social relationships and collapse into economic reductionism? Not necessarily. A more sophisticated political economy, combining an understanding of both the instrumental and the structural dimensions of power has long ploughed a sometimes unfashionable furrow to good effect (for example, Golding and Murdock, 1977, 1991; Garnham, 1979; Mosco, 1996). Rather than producing an essentialist or reductionist account, a sophisticated political economy, 'takes an explicitly non-reductionist and over-determined or multiply determined approach' to communication (Mosco, 1996: 5). What Mosco has in mind is an analysis which acknowledges, to quote Golding and Murdock, 'the interplay between economic organisation and political, social and cultural life' (1991: 18). In other words, a political economy should not start simply with the specification of economic interests but rather should understand even 'economic processes' as thoroughly penetrated and shaped by the political and cultural. However, what a sophisticated political economy does insist upon is the point that the interplay between economic, political and cultural practices and structures provides the context – the opportunities and constraints – within which actors struggle to mobilise material *and* symbolic resources. Golding and Murdock (1991) and Mosco (1996) both draw upon the idea of structuration to describe the dynamic process through which action is constrained by structure but equally how cultural or political practices modify structures. Structural constraints apply to all the actors involved including the powerful. Approaches that explore only the instrumental dimension find it difficult to explain, for example, why occasionally it is the powerful themselves, despite their instrumental connections, who suffer at the hands of the news media. To understand why even right of centre newspapers sometimes turn on Conservative ministers or large corporations, we need to consider market strategies, the competitive nature of news publishing and their interplay with editorial policy, not to mention the organic political relations certain papers develop with particular political parties.

It is in this context that I would like to place the sociology of news sources. Mosco argues that political economy helps to avoid the pitfall of too media-centred an approach to political communication (1996: 71). Similarly, Golding and Murdock (1977) stress the importance of placing the study of the mass media in the context of wider structures of inequality and power, but the danger of media-centrism was also the starting point for Schlesinger's call for a sociology of news sources (1990). Part of a political economic account must surely be an analysis of the way in which groups and organisations mobilise symbolic and material resources in order to try to secure access to the news encoding process. This kind of analysis has to combine an understanding of the instrumental and the structural; of the media strategies which groups may consciously formulate and the relationships with journalists which are consciously negotiated but equally the *wider* political and economic structures that limit or promote information flows and distribute material or symbolic advantages to certain groups rather than others. A sociology of news sources must acknowledge the degrees of openness in the news production processes in most European societies and the US. This means acknowledging the evidence which pluralist accounts provide of the competition and contestation in the news encoding process, without accepting the pluralist theoretical framework, with its unwarranted faith in the efficacy of political norms and its reluctance to really get to grips with the structures of dominance associated with capital or the extent to which news encoding is still highly gendered and racialised.[6]

The Modern and the 'Postmodern'

All the theories discussed up to this point have their roots in the work of theorists coming to terms with the political, social and economic structures of the modern age. However, for a number of important theorists, the rapid changes that have occurred in the use of information and communication technologies, the explosion in popular culture and the associated regimes of commodification, the associated changes in the occupational structures and the production relations of 'late modern' or 'postmodern' societies, all demand a break with traditional 'modernist theory' and the development of theoretical frameworks which place these developments at the centre of analysis.

Some of these changes are particularly relevant for a discussion of news sources and information flows. To begin with, there are now many more channels for political communication: not only do we live in an era of multi-channel broadcasting but there is more broadcasting on the traditional terrestrial channels, nationally and locally, with morning, lunch-time and afternoon slots all demanding to be filled with 'content'. Newspapers survive, sometimes thrive, but are coming to terms with the new communication age by integrating their print products with web pages and other electronic services. In this sense, we do live in a 'media-saturated age' and this presents more opportunities and new challenges to both news sources and journalists. Secondly, the rise of new communication technologies and global communication systems means that there has been a vast increase in information for those with the necessary resources to secure access to it. Thirdly, as theories of the postmodern emphasise, the production and exchange of signs and symbolic systems represents a vitally important sector in late modern/postmodern economies. The consequences of this are plain to see in the political arena. Election campaigns are fought out in the broadcasting studios of the land. Politicians hire 'appearance experts' and parties invest huge resources in the politics of communication and symbolism. Spin doctors now occupy positions at the core of every party and *how* things are presented often appears to be more important than *what* the policy is. These tendencies are reproduced beyond the confines of party politics. Public and private organisations now feel the need to hire press officers or public relations consultants and even marginal campaigning groups now try to develop more sophisticated media strategies, often exploiting new communication technologies and investing more thought in mobilising symbolic resources. For some postmodern theorists this all means that signs or symbols have been wrenched from their denotational contexts: images no longer refer to 'real things' but circulate in a symbolic universe autonomous from the 'real'. A political leader may be a 'fake' but it is how this 'fakeness' is constructed that counts.

Discourse, Knowledge and Governmentalities

Against the background of these changes, there has been a turn in social theory towards some influential alternative ways of conceptualising the social. Foucault, of course, has been a huge influence and a comprehensive discussion of his ideas is beyond the scope of this chapter. However, three Foucauldian themes have a particular relevance. Foucault understands power as both repressive and simultaneously an energising force with unpredictable effects (1984). Power is not simply exerted by one dominant group over a subordinate group but, through the discourses and forms of knowledge which bind the powerful and subordinate together, it positions both. Foucault, of course, resists essentialist models of power. Power cannot be 'controlled' by capital or any other 'essential' structure. Rather, it runs through the discourses and categories of knowledge which bind particular power-networks together, with unpredictable consequences. This is a fruitful theme when we explore the history of attempts to control and manage information flows because it reminds us that the powerful do not always manage information flows in the way intended. As we have seen above, governments may try to 'manage the news' only to find that leaks from within have undermined their strategy; 'whistle-blowers' can be the bane of powerful corporations, and the porosity of trade union executives is greatly welcomed by labour correspondents.

However, Foucault offers a second important theme in his later work on 'governmentality', by which he means an ensemble of 'institutions, procedures, analyses . . . reflections . . . calculations and tactics' (1979b: 20), through which particular regimes administer and govern. Governmentality brings with it particular ways of thinking about the issues and problems it is appropriate for government and public administration to address (Miller and Rose, 1993: 76). Indeed, from this point of view the discourses and categories of knowledge associated with particular governmentalities actually organise the architecture of the state. A department of 'health' emerges when government first begins to think about 'administering' a population's health; a department for the environment grows and expands its role as environmental discourses begin to shape government. The ministries in Britain dealing with 'labour', 'industry' or 'economic affairs' emerged as the discourses of economic management and the 'post-war settlement' ran through political thinking in the middle of the twentieth century (Emmison, 1983; Miller and Rose, 1993). Such new ways of thinking, in turn, stimulate changes in the organisation of news journalism and the relations between journalists and news sources (Manning, 1999). Some specialisms in journalism rise and others fall, with important consequences for news sources, as the architecture of the state is redesigned and senior editors in news organisations think through changing governmentalities (see Chapters 5 and 6).

Here, however, a third important issue associated with Foucault and theories of discourse has to be considered. Is 'social reality' constituted by the discourses through which we think, or is there an interplay between our discourses and ideas on the one hand, and an external social reality on the other? Following Foucault and Derrida, discourse theory suggests that 'social reality' is constituted through language: we socially construct our social world as we understand it through discourse. A *crude* materialist, on the other hand, might insist that dominant discourses merely reflect an external social reality. However, we might wish to suggest a more complex position. To return to the examples above, is the architecture of the state *only* a product of the discourses or governmentalities of the era, or rather, should we understand the structure of the state as being constituted by the interplay between *both* discourse and external social realities? In other words, to understand complex social practices, such as news journalism, news source activity or government, do we need to explore *only* the kinds of discourses which organise these practices, or should we also take into account an externally constituted social reality?

News Discourse and the Postmodern

In moving from 'archaeology' to 'genealogy', Foucault was, of course, signalling a move towards a position that *did* consider the complex interplay between discursive and non-discursive practices; between discourse and institutional power. And, despite Habermas's critique (1983), Foucault was not comfortable with the idea that his work marked the shift towards postmodernist theorising (Simons, 1995: 110). Nevertheless, discourse theory has become intertwined with postmodernist thinking, with significant implications for our understanding of news and news sources. A distinction needs to be made between the position that the concept 'postmodern' can be employed to describe and analyse the important changes in social, political and cultural formations described at the beginning of this section (for example, Jameson, 1984), from the more extravagant Baudrillardian accounts of postmodern society. Baudrillard and those adapting his ideas (for example, Poster, 1990) extend the thrust of discourse theory in a way that tempts the sociologist of news sources but at a cost. Baudrillard, of course, suggests that one of the distinctive features of the postmodern world is the centrality of the mass media and the importance of symbolic codes. This is why we have to abandon 'essentialising' social theories such as Marxism (Baudrillard, 1975, 1981). We now live in a world in which signs are detached from referents, a world in which the agencies of signification generate a stream of simulacra and the economic and cultural implode together, as signification rather than manufacture becomes the principle economic activity. In the modern era, it was still possible for the observer to assess the relationship between the sign and the referent, or between the media representation and the 'reality' it described. In the hyperreal postmodern world, the distinction between image and reality collapses, because in our media-saturated world it is not possible to 'step outside' the discourses, codes and cultural scripts continually recycled through the media (Baudrillard, 1983). Similarly, Poster (1990) argues that once we move from oral and written communication to a culture in which electronic communication predominates – 'the mode of information' – we are confronted by permanent uncertainty because the relationship between the streams of electronic information, or simulations, which flow all around us, and any notion of 'the real', is entirely precarious and unstable.

It is tempting to embrace this vision in approaching news and news sources. There are now so many news media outlets and so many political organisations seeking to hijack the various symbolic codes, or patterns of signification, to suit their media strategies. There is more political information communicated via the news media than ever before and yet, paradoxically, one can feel less informed about what is 'really going on'. When current affairs documentaries turn out to have been faked, or the guests on daytime television discussion shows are later revealed to be professional actors, it is tempting to relinquish all hope of evading the simulated. For some discourse theorists this is the postmodern conclusion that media studies should embrace. Stuart Allan, as we have seen, condemns earlier modernist media sociology for depending hopelessly upon 'empiricist notions of "reality"' (1995: 129). Too much time has been spent in the naïve attempt to demonstrate 'news bias' by tracing the 'gap' between news content and alternative measures of 'reality' (for example, official statistics or eyewitness accounts). For Allan, these kinds of attempts are epistemologically doomed for two reasons. First, they assume the possibility of objectivity – that if journalists were not 'biased' they could be 'objective'. Allan draws upon Tuchman's famous study to argue that journalists never produce 'objective' accounts of the world but rather accounts which 'balance' one socially constructed version of events against another (Tuchman, 1972). Secondly, Allan argues that earlier modernist analyses of news language assumed that readers would recognise a 'unitary meaning' in the news text – that the meaning of a news report would be interpreted in the same way by most news audiences. Allan draws upon discourse theory to suggest that there is no such order in the meaning of news texts and, indeed, there are always a multiplicity of possible interpretations as news audiences engage with news texts in an infinite number of ways. This is the Baudrillardian vision of a de-centred, chaotic world of multiple signification in which no 'essential' meaning or, indeed, social order can be found. Rather than attempt in futile fashion to gauge news media coverage against 'reality', we should turn our attention to the news texts themselves and the 'will to facticity' embedded within. In other words, we should focus upon the textual devices which operate to secure the authority of the various 'truth claims' in the text (Allan, 1995: 131).

Conclusions: Returning to the 'Real'

Allan's argument is seductive but it has its problems. First, while Tuchman (1972) employed a phenomenological perspective to demonstrate the ways in which news was constructed through the social practices of news journalism, she held back from Allan's epistemological leap. It is one thing to suggest that the news is socially constructed (very few media sociologists would disagree with this proposition) but it is quite another to suggest that we should abandon the task of placing news text production in a wider social context. While all measures of social reality are, in one sense, inscribed by discourse, if we do not attempt to relate news media accounts to alternative versions or assessments, we are abandoning the hope that the news media can in any way be held to account – by academic researchers or anybody else. In 1989, the *Sun* claimed that the Hillsborough disaster, in which nearly one hundred Liverpool soccer fans were crushed to death, was caused by drunken and rowdy behaviour on the part of the fans themselves. The subsequent report arising from the disaster indicated that serious errors were made in the stewarding of the match. Is an analysis of the *Sun*'s version of the events against competing alternative accounts really a futile exercise? The fact that the circulation of the *Sun* plummeted in Liverpool following the paper's coverage suggests that sometimes a more unitary, mutually agreed reading of news media texts by news audiences is possible.

Secondly, the great contribution that recent postmodern and discourse theory has made is in warning us against the dangers of employing 'essentialist' modes of explanation. The need to be sensitive to the multiple determinations and interplays which make up most aspects of social reality, including news production, is a welcome reminder. However, it is possible to develop an analysis that traces the ordering of social practices and relates these to a theory of dominance and structure. As Stuart Hall has recently commented:

> But while I have learned a great deal from Foucault in this sense about the relation between knowledge and power, I don't see how you can retain the notion of 'resistance', as he does, without facing questions about the constitution of dominance in ideology. . . . If Foucault is to prevent the regime of truth from collapsing into a synonym for the dominant ideology, he has to recognize that there are different regimes of truth in the social formation. And these are not simply 'plural' – they define an ideological field of force. There are subordinated regimes of truth which make sense, which have some plausibility for, subordinated subjects, while not being part of the dominant episteme. (Hall, 1996: 136)

After all, Stuart Allan suggests that there are 'hierarchies of definitional power' to be explored within the news text (1995: 131). Unless we begin to consider the news encoding processes and news source strategies associated with the production of a news text, and the power relations underpinning these, the 'hierarchies of definitional power' are left in a vacuum, located in the text but lacking a social context. Allan is sensitive to this point, and suggests that we can read news texts for evidence of 'a complex matrix of power struggles being played out at the level of the *naturalization* and *depoliticization* of truth claims.' But here, we return to the difficulties inherent in trying to make inferences about social practices or power relations from the evidence of media texts alone, rather than actually studying the encoding process itself. When we return to studying the news encoding process and the practices of news sources, we cannot avoid acknowledging certain structures which allocate dominance or authority to particular groups. This is why postmodern theorisations will only take the sociology of news and news sources so far. There has certainly been an explosion in the number and intensity of the information flows circulating in society but there is also some control and some order in the way they enter both the public and private domains. The task of a sociology of news and news sources is to trace the sources of order and control without reducing or essentialising a complex social reality.

Golding and Murdock locate political economy within a critical perspective which,

> . . . assumes a realist conception of the phenomena it studies, in the simple sense that the theoretical constructs it works with exist in the real world, they are not merely phenomenal. For this reason, critical analysis is centrally concerned with questions of action and structure, in an attempt to discern the real constraints which shape the lives and opportunities of real actors in the real world. In this sense critical theory is also materialist, in its focus on the interaction of people with their material environment and its further preoccupation with the unequal command over material resources and the consequences of such inequality for the nature of the symbolic environment.
>
> Second, critical analysis is historically located. It is specifically interested in the investigation and description of late capitalism. . . . This historical anchoring of

critical analysis is distinct from any approach which is essentialist, detached from the specifics of historical time and place. (1991:17)

In the remaining chapters of this book I will try to place the sociology of news sources in this kind of epistemological and theoretical framework. Central to the study of news sources is an understanding of the way in which both structures and dynamic social practices shape the flows of information generated by news source activity and the needs of news organisations. In this sense, such information flows are examples of structuration. The power relations shaping information flows between news sources and news organisations involve both instrumental and structural dimensions but their analysis has to be located in specific historical contexts. The empirical investigation of such specific contexts is an important part of a sociology of news sources but not its sole activity. Alongside this is the task of trying to describe and understand those structural dimensions of power, within the news encoding process, which are only 'visible in their consequences'.

Notes

1. Indeed, Curran (1996) develops a historical account of post-war media theory which treats all approaches as variants of either 'liberal' or 'radical' functionalism. This helps to underline just how frequently theoretical approaches consciously draw upon or 'lapse' into functionalist modes of explanation (institutions are 'explained' in terms of their functional contribution) but has the disadvantage of rather understating some important theoretical differences too.

2. Honourable exceptions include studies of 'resource-poor' community groups and campaigning organisations in the USA. See, for example, Goldenberg (1975) or Palentz and Entman (1981).

3. The classic discussions include Bachrach and Baratz (1962), Lukes (1974) and Schattschneider (1960).

4. The familiar examples of Marx's writing usually cited in this context are 'The Eighteenth Brumaire of Louis Bonaparte' and 'The Civil War in France', both in Marx and Engels (1968).

5. The term 'neo-Marxist' is used for the reason that several approaches discussed here are not explicitly 'Marxist' but draw largely upon Marxist modes of analyses while also recognising that Marx alone is not enough. In particular there is an anxiety to avoid economic and class reductionist forms of analysis and a desire to acknowledge other autonomous power relationships.

6. It is for this reason that the term 'radical pluralist' employed by some writers (for example, Davis, 2000: 175) does not seem to me to be a useful description for approaches that study the competitive activity of news sources in the light of an analysis of the highly unequal distribution of material and symbolic communicative resources. Both sophisticated political-economic and Gramscian hegemony models recognise that there is a degree of openness in news encoding, albeit across a highly uneven playing field. One serious omission from this chapter is a discussion of the theoretical approaches dealing with the racialised and gendered nature of news encoding and production. These issues are dealt with in Chapter 3 but in another bigger book these theoretical frameworks would be given the fuller treatment they warrant.

3 Journalists and News Production

Press officers and public relations staff will often comment that one of the essential attributes for doing their kind of work effectively is a good understanding of how news journalists do their job and the pressures or constraints associated with 'making the news'. After all, to place a story in the news media, or influence an emerging news media agenda, source organisations need an understanding of the news values which guide journalists in their selection of particular news items and an awareness of the rhythms or routines that characterise the workings of mainstream news organisations. Accordingly, this chapter explores the ways in which news organisations manage the processes through which information is gathered and transformed into news and the pressures that encourage journalists to follow familiar patterns of newsmaking.

Making News in a News Factory?

Journalists still often reveal a fondness for the idea that their work is about faithfully reflecting 'what happens out there' to their audiences; one still hears journalists describing their 'mission to explain' or their achievements in 'opening a window upon the world.' In contrast, even a cursory glance at the academic literature which reports fieldwork undertaken by researchers examining news organisations, both in Europe and the USA, will reveal dozens of books and papers with titles such as 'Making the News', 'The Manufacture of News', or 'Putting Reality Together'. While these titles have been produced by academic researchers drawing upon a number of quite distinct theoretical approaches, from political economy through organisational theory to social constructionism, they all agree that far from merely mirroring 'what happens in the world', the practice of news journalism involves a process of manufacture or fabrication. This is not to suggest that journalists deliberately fabricate stories or lie. Rather, it is to point out that the production of news each day, each week or on a rolling 24-hour basis, involves the routine gathering and assembling of certain constituent elements which are then fashioned to construct or fabricate an account of the particular news events.

Some of the earliest attempts by outside academic on-lookers to research and describe news production focused upon the work of key decision-makers in the process. Thus, in D.M. White's famous early example, it is the sub-editor who is understood as occupying a pivotal role as a 'gatekeeper' selecting certain stories but spiking others. The thrust of the analysis is directed towards explaining the decision-making process, as a psychology of news selection (White, 1950). One early objection to accounts which looked only at the psychological disposition of particular subeditors was that journalists operating in a variety of news organisations appeared to be guided by the *same* selection criteria. This encouraged researchers to move beyond individual psychology to consider the organisational pressures at play. As news deadlines approached, for example, the more discriminating the selection procedure for news stories in every newsroom appeared to become, irrespective of individual disposition (Geiber, 1956). In the Langs' case study of an early American television outside broadcast, attention moves to the technological dimension, as each camera location is understood as a selection decision in itself (Lang and Lang, 1953). So organisational pressures and technological determinants were added to the psychological traits of news editors in a growing list, compiled by academics, of reasons why news media representations of reality were imperfect distortions, rather than perfect reflections of reality.

In the next two decades, fieldwork and academic analysis moved from considerations of individual bias in selection decisions to the concept of organisational bias arising through the production process. News organisations came to be understood as functioning bureaucracies or factories with given 'inputs' and 'outputs', organisational rhythms, an insatiable appetite for fresh raw material or information of a particular kind, staffed by personnel trained or socialised to work according to standardised rules and practices. As the authors of one of the most comprehensive studies of television news production put it:

> Our description suggests broadcast journalism is by no means the random reaction to random events. On the contrary, it is a highly regulated and routine process of manufacturing a cultural product on an electronic production line. In stages of planning, gathering, selection and production broadcast news is moulded by the demands of composing order and organisation within a daily cycle. The news is made, and like any other product it carries the marks of the technical and organisational structure from which it emerges. (Golding and Elliott, 1979: 137)

This kind of approach regards two fond elements of journalistic folklore with a sceptical eye. First, many accounts of news production written by journalists themselves – particularly editors – dwell upon the skills, qualities and 'nose for news' of particular, heroic individuals.[1] This is a media version of the great men of history thesis. The difficulty with this approach, as Peter Golding neatly puts it, is that 'there is an awful lot of history and not many great men' (Golding, 1981: 65). To explain both the complexity of the news production process and the extent to which common features can be found in remarkably diverse news organisations, it is necessary to look beyond the qualities of particular individuals, to consider institutional and organisational routines and their place in the wider political–economic environment. Secondly, this prompts the questioning of another orthodoxy in journalism, concerning the importance of enterprise and creativity. The romantic image of the investigative reporter, as portrayed in films such as *All the President's Men*, mixing guts and grit to uncover the truth, or the feature writer deploying a creative muse to enliven the text, is treated equally sceptically. Much, often most, of what appears in daily newspapers or within our television news broadcasts is the product of neither enterprise nor creativity but of routine procedures of information gathering and processing. This is why, as Golding and Elliott put it, 'news changes very little when the individuals who make it are changed' (1979: 207). Indeed, the opportunities for the injection of enterprise or creativity appear to be diminishing in a multi-channel broadcasting era in which the growing number of news broadcasting operations generates an ever-growing appetite for news copy as raw material. MacGregor estimates that the aggregate output of British and trans-European television news, including terrestrial channels, together with Sky News, CNN, Euronews, NBC Superchannel, and Live TV, adds up to over 100 hours of news output in any 24-hour period (MacGregor, 1997: 24) – and that does not include the recently established BBC 24 rolling news service. Given this voracious appetite, it is hard to imagine how journalists could do anything other than bow to the imperative of routine news copy production.

However, some accounts suggest that the scope for such enterprise or initiative should not be underestimated. Tunstall (1993), for example, in a recent study of television news and current affairs producers, reports a significant degree of autonomy for news workers in this particular sphere of news production. Similarly, Jacobs (1996) argues that within the constraints of structure and bureaucratic routine inherent in mainstream news production, there remains scope for the interpretative skills of news journalists to make a difference. Jacobs bases this claim upon a case study of an American local television news team operating in Los Angeles. As we shall see below, some commentators have argued that news organisation executives have used both the introduction of new information technologies and the progressive casualisation of news workers to secure increases in productivity, and that this, in turn, has further routinised and standardised news production dynamics. Nevertheless, Jacobs concludes that the reverse has occurred in his case study. The local Los Angeles television station certainly hired freelance 'stringers' on a casual basis, to trim costs on staffing, and placed a growing reliance upon computer simulations and computer-assisted recycling of video library footage. However, Jacobs reports that this created more scope for the 'interpretative work' of journalists: first, because the use of such technologies depended crucially upon 'the way news workers saw the world' and their ability to utilise such technologies to create meaningful narratives; and secondly, because the use of 'stringers' to film news video clips involved the fostering of relationships of trust and shared reflexive understanding with the favoured freelancers (1996: 378–81).

Simon Cottle makes very similar arguments about the importance of news formats. The difficulty with the news factory analogy is that whereas in the era of mass production a car production line or sausage factory really did churn out the same standardised product day after day, the output of news organisations varies in a complex number of ways depending particularly upon the framing of news information in a variety of formats, constructed to suit the reception needs of particular news audiences (Cottle, 1993, 1995). For viewers of Britain's Live TV cable channel the news may be delivered in truncated tabloid 'bits' with the assistance of somebody dressed as a 'news bunny' giving 'good news' a thumbs-up sign, while on *Channel 4 News* a much more sobre approach provides extended coverage and analysis for the duration of one hour. So the format in which news is packaged makes an important difference to the kind of output that emerges from the news organisation and the construction of a particular news format will, in turn, involve a complex series of decisions in which journalists and editors draw upon their understanding of particular audience needs and also upon their skills in relating news genres to those needs.

In short, there is a danger that in envisaging the practice of news journalism as a production process, shaped by bureaucratic routines and organisational imperatives, we underestimate the extent to which particular journalists *do* make a difference. Editorial experience, journalistic flair and the 'grit' of the investigative reporter clearly have their place. This is, of course, an excellent example of a classic problem in sociological theory. To what extent can social actors, in this case journalists, shape the social environment in which they interact, and to what extent is their capacity to choose and act delimited by social structures and institutional practices? The answer, in practice, is likely to depend upon the kind of news organisation and the particular news specialism in question. As we shall see, the extent of exposure to commercial market signals, the pressures generated by organisational imperatives and deadlines, the level of managerial supervision, and interaction with routine sources of news will all vary in ways dependent upon particular empirical circumstances.

There are two further problems associated with the production line analogy which should be noted before the discussion moves on. It certainly sensitises us to issues of hierarchy, routine and organisational dynamics, but this can also be rather misleading if it distracts attention from the moments when the production line machine fails to work smoothly. For example, while news organisations may function fairly efficiently most of the time they are also often characterised by high levels of internal tension generated by personal rivalry, inter-departmental feuding and moral disagreements about the application of news values (Williams and Miller, 1998: 155). Further to this, as several critics have argued (MacGregor, 1997: 71), there is a danger that the production line analogy is used to describe but not explain. In other words, after having described how organisational imperatives impact upon news journalism, it is still necessary to take a step back and ask questions about why news organisations are constituted in such a way that these organisational pressures inexorably arise.

In asking these kinds of questions our attention is drawn away from the internal environment of the newspaper or broadcasting newsroom, to the external political-economic environment in which news organisations operate. Studies of news production can be rather media-centric at the cost of failing to appreciate the importance of external variables in the news production process. These include differences in the political influence and credibility of news sources and their capacity to control information (see Chapters 5 and 6), or the importance of particular structures of ownership and control (see Chapter 4), together with the market-driven nature of much news communication, and also, the extent to which the broader ideological climate may shape the thinking of journalists, editors, and news sources alike (MacGregor, 1997: 68–71).

Organisational Dynamics and the Pressure of Deadlines

Having noted the dangers in applying the factory or production line analogy in an overdeterministic way, it remains the case that the insights provided by the production field studies of the 1970s and 1980s remain as pertinent today as ever. Indeed, though some like Jacobs above may disagree, generally the organisational pressures encouraging the routinisation and standardisation of news journalism are more intense now than ever before. Above all, it is the cycle of news deadlines that drives the journalists' routine within a news organisation, whether this be a daily newspaper, a nightly television current affairs show, or an hourly radio news bulletin. Each form of news output may function to a different cyclical rhythm but it is this, more than anything else, which shapes how each news worker goes about her or his work, and which determines both the constraints and opportunities of the job. In other words, most news journalists and news workers have to meet deadlines as a matter of routine, and they will develop a number of techniques and organisational practices in order to accommodate this imperative. This is where human agency meets social structure. To adapt a phrase, journalists may make their own news but they do not make it just as they please under conditions chosen by themselves but under circumstances directly encountered, given and determined by the rhythm of the news organisation.

Philip Schlesinger's study of the BBC radio newsroom still provides one of the best illustrations of this point two decades on. Schlesinger noted that for BBC radio news journalists, time was experienced in two ways. Much of the rhythm of the radio newsroom was governed by the routine delimitation or parcelling of time into the tasks required to be completed before the deadline specified by each news bulletin, but sometimes time was also experienced as something overpowering when staff rushed to fill up the final news slots before a broadcast, or when a late story suddenly broke. Thus, according to Schlesinger, BBC journalists oscillated between being 'controllers' and 'victims' of time, although they rather enjoyed the excitement involved in being 'victimised' by time because it was felt that this was 'what true newsmen feel in coping with an erratic force' (Schlesinger, 1978: 86). It was this experience which provided much of the interest of the job and nourished the more romantic image of journalism as an event-driven occupation. However, despite the last-minute changes in the running order of items and the rushed scramble in the newsroom during the final hour before broadcast, Schlesinger emphasises that for most of the time news production was managed and ordered. This was achieved by ensuring as much predictability was built into the news-gathering process as possible.

> In general, production is far from chaotic at anything other than a superficial level. Its rationale is to aim at control and prediction, while those who work the system celebrate its relatively rare contingencies. Indeed, there is a strange irony in the last-minute rush to fill the slot. Mostly, the intake of news items occurs during the last hour by design, as the later they arrive the more immediate they are. This means that anxious newsmen are working a system that can only exacerbate their anxieties. The contingencies are in fact created by the newsday cycle itself, and those values which stress immediacy. (Schlesinger, 1978: 87)

So the frenetic scramble to meet the deadline is part of the routine and many of the other practices of news journalism can be understood as measures designed to ensure that fresh supplies of information are fashioned into news copy in time to meet each deadline as it rolls around.

One way of building certainty and control into the news production process is to establish stable relationships with outside institutions and agencies which can be relied upon to provide the kind of information that can easily be fashioned into news copy. This, in turn, produces two tendencies in news journalism. The first has important consequences for the politics of news sources. The pressure of news deadlines and the importance of obtaining information rich in news values, encourages a dependency upon official sources, whether they be government departments, sources associated with parliaments and the formal policy-making process, the police or the other state social control agencies. If nothing else, all these institutions are likely to be newsworthy precisely because they are powerful and they affect the daily lives of news audiences in innumerable ways. The extent to which this may privilege the powerful in a routine and systematic way, with regard to the struggle over news agendas, is a question that has already prompted more than two decades' worth of research into the nature of relations between official sources and journalists (for example, Tunstall, 1971; Sigal, 1973; Chibnall, 1977; Fishman, 1980; Cockerall et al., 1984; Ericson et al., 1989) and the extent to which the less well positioned, politically marginal can compete (Anderson, 1993; Schlesinger and Tumber, 1994; Manning, 1998). This, of course, is one of the major themes of this book, and one to which we shall return.

The second way in which news organisations secure a routine source of copy to meet the news imperatives of time and space is to turn to the news agencies which supply news copy as a commodity. With staffing costs regularly being trimmed, the temptation for news editors is to turn to agency copy more frequently, particularly for foreign news where the costs of maintaining large numbers of foreign correspondents has become prohibitive for many news organisations. The four dominant global news agencies at present are Agence France-Presse, World Television News, Associated Press and Reuters, with the latter two supplying both print and broadcasting news media (Boyd-Barrett, 1998: 19). In addition, there is Eurovision, through which the participating European television organisations exchange film material (Cohen et al., 1996). While in the future it is possible that other potential global agencies (for example, the Chinese Xinhua agency) will challenge the dominant position of the present global players, Boyd-Barrett draws our attention to the location of these agencies, which are all based in the most prosperous, Western countries of the world. Agency copy can certainly be edited or reworked in a variety of ways and Cohen confirms that the same television footage supplied via Eurovision is often used to construct quite diverse interpretative frameworks for news audiences in different European countries. Nevertheless, agency copy will inevitably reflect, at the very least, initial selection decisions, news values and news frames associated with the commodification of news information in Western societies. Even within Eurovision, it is the larger partners from the more powerful Western European countries that tend to dominate decision-making (Cohen et al., 1996: 54). The danger is that this will encourage a homogeneity in foreign news reporting and, perhaps, some aspects of domestic news as well, because coverage will frequently reflect the selections and news values of this handful of global agencies (Gurevitch et al., 1991; Patterson, 1998). This is not to suggest that the globally dominant news agencies entirely control the production of non-domestic reporting. First, the middle-ranking agencies and some 'retail outlets', including CNN, Sky News and NBC, provide significant competition. Secondly, the 'big four' agencies have to meet the needs of their customers and thus a 'bi-directional agenda setting effect' is produced (Patterson, 1998: 83). Nevertheless, according to observers such as Patterson and Gurevitch, precisely because the big news agencies are at pains to demonstrate that their copy is 'impartial' and 'objective' (two concepts which warrant further scrutiny below), the application of common 'objective' journalistic practices and 'professional' procedures frequently results in news copy with very similar characteristics.

The growing importance of news agencies has complex implications for campaigning groups and lobbying organisations seeking to secure access to news media arenas. The news agencies themselves are clearly 'targets' for news media work. Political élites, other official sources, pressure groups and campaigning organisations are likely to send video or press releases and briefing materials to the news agencies. They may also attempt to establish stable relationships with some of the specialist correspondents working for news agencies. There are both opportunities and constraints for news sources here. On the one hand, given the progressive globalisation of information systems, including the main news agencies, if a source is successful in securing access through one of the agencies, then it is possible that its message will be rapidly circulated globally, providing it has a news value that will appeal beyond a single domestic audience. On the other hand, whereas correspondents working for domestic news organisations, particularly the quality newspapers, may welcome the background briefing and contextual information that news sources can often supply, the journalists working for news agencies are likely to put speed at a premium (Patterson, 1998: 93). Although accuracy and authority are certainly important, it is the rapidity with which information can be distributed that secures reputation and contracts for the main news agencies. Provision of contextual detail is a little less important unless it concerns certain specialist areas such as financial intelligence where some agencies provide commercial research and data services (for example, Reuters). This means that pressure groups and campaigning organisations often have fewer bargaining chips in their dealings with news agency journalists.

Building Certainty into the News Production Process

If news journalism involves a routine state of high anxiety as daily deadlines approach, there are ways in which this tension can be managed, beyond a reliance upon familiar, reliable sources. As far as possible news is planned in advance. 'Helpful' news sources with a sophisticated grasp of how news journalism works can assist in this tension management. Official sources, members of political élites, and media-wise pressure groups, for example, may release documents or briefing materials days or weeks in advance of an announcement or launch, with an embargo upon publication until a specified date. This allows the news sources to ensure that opportunities for publicity are maximised and gives journalists time to absorb information and frame the story. Conversely, sources may choose to refrain from releasing briefing materials in advance to ensure that journalists have as little time as possible to digest information and draw conclusions that are unpalatable. A notorious example of the latter practice was the Thatcher government's release of the 1979 Black Report at the very last minute on the eve of a Bank Holiday without prior briefing. Journalists had very little time to absorb complex statistical evidence charting the close relationship between social class, deprivation, ill health and mortality in Britain. This report, commissioned by the previous Labour government, was not welcomed by the new administration and its findings were shelved. Through shrewd news management, front-page publicity was kept to a minimum.

However, the pre-planning of news coverage takes a more bureaucratised form through the use of the news diary, which is central to the running of every news organisation. The news diary represents a schedule of forthcoming events that will warrant reporting in the near future. This allows journalists to be allocated to particular stories, the key news aspects of the event to be agreed, and item space or time provisionally allotted. It will be composed from a variety of sources – press releases and briefing documents sent to the newsroom, an editorial review of the future political calendar, clippings and notes about previous patterns of coverage, suggestions made at editorial conferences – and it will offer several time horizons simultaneously, including a weekly, monthly and even an annual perspective. The main news diary for any news organisation is reviewed weekly at an editorial conference involving senior staff but particular teams of specialist correspondents (political, crime, home affairs, etc.) may use their own informal news diaries in conjunction with the main editorial diary. This is how predictability is built into the news production process.

> The diary is a key document in any news office. It records predictable events that automatically merit coverage by their unquestionable public importance. It is also a register of less significant events vying for inclusion in the 'automatic' category. In a sense production of the diary is news production in advance, except that it is based upon mere knowledge that events will occur not on observation of them unfolding. The diary is the implicit script of news. (Golding and Elliott, 1979: 93)

There is a tendency in some news organisations for a more centralised system of line management to be introduced which encourages a greater bureaucratisation of news production. At the BBC in London, for example, the Future Events Unit now operates as a specialised department, performing the functions of the news diary for all sections of BBC news (MacGregor, 1997: 192). Journalists often reveal an ambivalent attitude towards the 'diary system'. On the one hand, news production in its present frenetic form probably could not work without it; on the other, the news diary rather undermines a vision of journalism as the practice of recording the sudden, dramatic or unexpected.

Two decades ago, Golding and Elliott found journalists a little disturbed by the implications of the news diary system. One fear was that it would stifle journalistic enterprise and investigative reporting (1979: 93). If anything, the dangers in this respect are greater now. This is because in many news organisations the cycle of deadline and copy submission has grown ever faster, encouraging an even greater reliance upon the techniques employed to manage the pressure. It is clear, for example, that throughout Europe, as new and more efficient print technologies have been introduced, so newspapers have reacted by introducing earlier deadlines for more daily editions in an effort to secure a competitive advantage (Kuhn, 1995: 43). Similarly, in broadcasting, the proliferation of radio and television channels has intensified competition, placing journalists under even more pressure to meet deadlines ahead of rivals. As Nicholas Jones, a BBC political correspondent, explains, with the introduction of continuous, 'rolling' news formats, journalists must find ways of 'freshening up' stories that have already emerged, even if there have not really been any major developments. Equally, the competition to be 'first' encourages journalists to trim if not cut the corners of professional practice. The standard 'two separate sources rule' for corroborating stories, for example, was hastily abandoned by American journalists scrambling to get details into the public domain of President Clinton's encounters with the young White House aide, Monica Lewinsky.

Significantly, according to Jones, this 'production line journalism' is likely to give more opportunities to those news sources which understand that the ever growing appetite of rolling news services offers a void to be filled (Jones, 1995: 127). However, some news sources will be better placed than others to take advantage of the huge increase in the broadcast news media appetite for material. Those which can deploy more material and symbolic resources are likely to seize the lion's share of new opportunities to secure access to the news media. For example, in Britain, with the increase in news channels and news formats there has been a corresponding increase in political coverage. This has largely centred around the political élites located at Westminster. Millbank, a new purpose-built series of studios and editing suites occupied by the main news organisations, including the BBC, ITV and Sky, is located adjacent to Parliament which conveniently allows members of the main political parties to simply walk across the road to deliver interviews and briefings. In general, then, political élites are well positioned to take advantage of the growing broadcast news void by providing potential news copy or what Gandy (1982) calls 'information subsidies'. More sophisticated and well-resourced pressure groups such as Greenpeace can sometimes employ the same strategy and the diminishing real cost of new media technologies allows some campaigning groups to supply well-produced video news releases, almost as finished items. Nevertheless, the mainstream political process exerts a gravitational pull for political journalism in most European countries and the US, which affords the political élites a routine advantage in the scramble to satisfy political news media appetites. As Mancini (1993) describes in a study of the relationship between Italian political élites and correspondents, the already exclusive and introverted interaction between political élites and political correspondents may become even more intense and inward-looking as both parties respond to the increasing media appetite for political information. In this atmosphere of heightened interaction and faster news cycles, there is little time for sustained investigative reporting. Instead, new angles on stories are secured through human interest themes, exclusive interviews with élite members, or speculative interpretation offered by other élite members or authoritative commentators. In these circumstance, it may be harder rather than easier for sources outside the political mainstream to break in.

Formats and Opportunities

In short then, the older field studies of news production processes which stressed the importance of understanding organisational rhythms, dynamics and imperatives (for example, Epstein, 1973; Schlesinger, 1978; Golding and Elliott, 1979) still have enormous relevance. One cannot begin to fully comprehend the nature of the news that is offered to audiences unless one understands the centrality of time and space, deadlines, and resource management within the news organisation. Bound up with these issues is the question of news format. Clearly, different formats offer greater or more limited opportunities to include contextual detail and analysis. Journalists working for popular or tabloid newspapers frequently claim that, contrary to popular belief, it is more challenging to unpick and describe the complexity of events in the compressed space of a popular newspaper. As one medical reporter working for a British popular paper put it:

> We've got to be a lot more careful. We are putting it in a nutshell, in a smaller space. It is actually more difficult writing for a tabloid than it is writing for one of the heavies where you can go on and give chapter and verse in a way you can't here because it is going to get cut for space. (Quoted in Williams and Miller, 1998: 153)

As we have seen, one reservation that is sometimes expressed about the 'production line' analogy in discussions of news media is that it underestimates the possibilities for variation associated with distinct formats or news genres. Formats are never neutral in their ideological implications. Newspapers usually issue 'style books' to journalists in order to ensure that all copy is written to a distinctive style and format associated with particular papers but these also, in effect, produce an ideological as well as presentational 'house style' (Cameron, 1996). In television too, particular news formats have particular ideological implications. Cottle (1995) distinguishes the 'expansive', 'the limited' and the 'restricted'. The 'restricted' format involves the newsdesk report delivered by a journalist with little or no input from alternative 'voices' and thus reproduces a version of events framed exclusively in terms of the journalist's values. The 'limited' format may include pre-recorded video clips of interviews with other 'voices' but it is only in the studio interview or 'expansive' format that there are to be found significant opportunities for alternative or critical voices to contribute to a discursive treatment of news issues. As Cottle comments, 'in the context of social contest, conflict and struggle news formats play a critical role in either enabling or disabling the range of viewpoints and discourses sustained by vying social interests' (1995: 279). The introduction of electronic news-gathering and video has encouraged television news journalism to 'visualise' news formats in new ways, abandoning the live studio interview format in favour of on-the-spot reporting away from the studio which brings the double advantage, for news editors, of greater 'immediacy' and significant savings in studio production costs (Cottle, 1995: 281). The cost, of course, is paid in terms of less discursive news treatments and fewer opportunities for a wider range of news sources to inject critical or oppositional voices.

News Selection

A discussion of the process through which particular news items are selected for publication and others rejected involves, at the same time, a statement of the most obvious and immediately comprehensible and, at another level, a consideration of rather more complex issues concerning the ways in which taken-for-granted pictures of the world or largely unquestioned ideological assumptions help all of us, including journalists, to make sense of complex, often ambiguous events. On one level, all that we need to know is that journalists learn to select items which they think will sell news – stories involving sex, violence, the unusual and the sensational. These are ubiquitous news values, at least in Western Europe and the USA. On another more complex level, we need to acknowledge that journalists select stories that already 'make sense' in terms of their knowledge and experience. In other words, stories are frequently selected because they can be fitted into the 'inferential frameworks' which experienced journalists have already acquired in the course of their work (Lang and Lang, 1955). These 'inferential frameworks' may evolve or be modified over time but at any given moment they influence both the selection of news stories and the way in which the particular news ingredients of the story – the bits of information to be included – are assembled.

In the 'classic' discussion of the selection process Galtung and Ruge (1973) use radio transmission as a metaphor to illuminate the news selection process. If all the potential news events that occur in the world are understood as radio signals then news organisations can be regarded as radio receivers that are tuned to particular frequencies. Different news organisations will operate according to different frequencies. Given this metaphor, a series of propositions follow. First, 'the more similar the frequency of the event is to the frequency of the news medium, the more probable that it will be recorded as news by the news medium' (1973: 63). In other words, news organisations operating to a daily or faster news cycle will select sudden or dramatic 'events' but are less likely to select news stories that deal with gradual, unfolding processes. The latter do not suit the frequency of the news organisation operating to a daily cycle. Thus, events which occur over a long time span will go unrecorded unless they reach a dramatic climax. The causes of famine, for example, are complex and long-standing. Daily news organisations are less likely to consider such stories until 'suddenly' starving refugees appear in camps (Philo and Lamb, 1986).

Secondly, the amplitude of signals is an important factor. In other words, the 'bigger' the story the more likely it is to be picked up and selected by news organisations. However, the size or importance will be assessed by culturally specific criteria or the degree of 'cultural proximity' (Galtung and Ruge, 1973: 64). In other words, it is assumed that viewers and listeners are likely to be more interested in domestic news rather than news that happens in more remote parts of the world. This produces a curious moral calculus through which cultural proximity rather than proportions of human misery determine television running orders and the length of a news report. As the former editor of the British *Observer* newspaper puts it:

> There is a perfectly rational explanation for all this, of course – the usual conjunction of market forces and market research. Editors from Los Angeles to London believe that the news which shifts copies across counters is the news with immediate relevance to the punters. Your life, your stories. A small rail crash in Halifax beats a big one in Hanover. . . . A rail crash in Hyderabad is no more than a brief. (Preston, 1998)

In a study of the news selection practices operated at Eurovision, the agency that acts as a clearing house providing 'raw' video footage for eight European national television news organisations, Cohen and his colleagues found that television news editors throughout Europe were likely not only to prioritise the domestic over the foreign, but also to operate a process of 'domestication' for the foreign stories which they did select (Cohen et al., 1996: 74–86). Through a daily news conference, editors working on behalf of each of the news organisations involved would make their selections. Almost half the items selected during Cohen and his colleagues' fieldwork were primarily domestic from the point of view of the country concerned. A further 20 per cent were 'combined' in that they had both domestic and foreign implications (often dealing with international politics), and a third selected were exclusively 'foreign'. However, the latter were often utilised in a way which gave them a 'special localised or domestic slant' (1996: 85). Thus, for example, news of Italian election results were reported through German, French and Belgian television services in the context of news of 'our neighbours'. Similarly, BBC news, while less ethnocentric than some stations, still framed stories of conditions in Palestinian refugee camps in terms of the experiences of an English doctor working for an aid organisation. The danger, of course, is that a rather Eurocentric if not ethnocentric picture of global affairs is produced. The senior BBC foreign affairs correspondent, John Simpson, complained recently:

> We have to get away from the idea that only five subjects and twenty countries are interesting. We ought to swing around so we're not just focusing on the things we already know about. . . . I do not want this country to go into the ever-tightening cycle of the United States where they know less, they are told less, and so the broadcasters want to tell them less. (Quoted in Brown, 1998: 5)

There is certainly a danger that a pattern of diminishing coverage of 'other' cultures and countries in anything but a news bite, snapshot fashion, based upon low expectations of audience interest, fails in an educative role, and encourages further audience disenchantment with non-domestic reporting. Yet the forces which encourage ethnocentric news selection are powerful. The increased exposure of most newsrooms to the winds of the competitive market is one factor but the assumptions about the world and the nature of journalism, made by journalists in the course of their work, and which become institutionalised as taken-for-granted professional practices, are equally important. These reinforce, in complex ways, the impact of commercial pressures. As Galtung and Ruge note, journalists search for events that are 'meaningful' and of 'relevance'. The more culturally distant events are, the less 'meaningful' and the less newsworthy they often appear (1973: 64).

Galtung and Ruge suggest that for events to become news stories they must also satisfy the requirement of consonance. Journalists are guided in the selection process by a 'mental pre-image' (Galtung and Ruge, 1973: 64) of what is likely to happen. Events that are explicable because they are consonant with journalists' expectations are more likely to be selected, but by the same token the unexpected is likely to be regarded as news, providing journalists can make sense of it in terms of their basic working assumptions or 'inferential structures'; events have to be 'unexpected but within the meaningful and consonant' (1973: 65) to become newsworthy. Financial news has grown in importance in the eyes of news editors as share ownership and personal finance markets have expanded in recent decades. Stock prices may rise according to expectations or drop suddenly against predictions. Either possibility will be regarded as news and will be rendered meaningful in terms of journalists' knowledge and understanding of how financial markets work. In contrast, political turbulence in an Islamic state may be predictable or unexpected but, either way, deemed un-newsworthy because for European or US news editors, frequently lacking a sophisticated understanding of Islamic politics, such news is both culturally distant and not immediately 'understandable' in terms of their mental maps or inferential structures (Conway, 1997).

New Values – Universal and Particular

Although journalists are inclined to favour that which is culturally familiar, evidence suggests that many of the news values with which they work are, if not universal, certainly common to most newsrooms in Europe and the USA. The dramatic, the immediate, sudden events, stories with human interest angles, and stories that can be constructed around personalities are all likely to interest most Western print and broadcast news editors. Comparative studies of newsrooms located in various parts of the world confirm that despite differences in culture and social formation, tried and tested subjects such as news of political élites and powerful people, sex, crime, law and order are common favourites among news editors. Equally, stories that offer strong possibilities for 'visuals' will be favoured, particularly, of course, in television news (Golding and Elliott, 1979; Cohen et al., 1996).[2] On the other hand, it is also clear that beyond this 'tried and tested' list, there are differences in approach that are associated with the cultural context in which news values are applied. In their study of Eurovision, Cohen and his colleagues found important differences in the way the same raw video footage was utilised to construct stories between the television newsrooms of different countries (1996: 60). Equally, the historically specific is important. The 'mood of the times' at particular historical moments is important in influencing decisions editors make about which news items are selected and how they are constructed. Jan Ekecrantz, for example, explored the interplay between newspaper texts and particular historical contexts through a sample of Swedish newspaper content. In doing this, the embeddedness of news values in the context of particular social and political circumstances is very well illustrated. Ekecrantz (1997) found that in 1927 the themes of modernity, technological fascination and national grandeur guided the selection of items. Thus, there were frequent stories of boats being built and launched, Swedish business successes in different parts of the world, and the impact of new ideas in different fields. By 1955, the arrival of 'the People's Home' era – the Swedish social democratic equivalent of the New Deal in the United States or the post-war Welfare State in Britain – clearly impresses itself upon the kinds of stories that are selected. According to Ekecrantz, by this time Swedish newspapers embraced a public service role which involved placing less emphasis upon partisan politics and more upon post-war consensual values. Stories that served as metaphors for the values of 'the People's Home' became much more frequent. Thus, there were numerous items concerning construction, road building and new bridges – each reflecting a mood of progress achieved not only through physical construction but social intervention as well. Items that served as metaphors for social integration and cross-class co-operation became popular, but equally, items that illustrated continuing problems of social isolation or remaining class division were frequent. An item about a young couple from different class backgrounds who resorted to court action in order to secure the right to marry despite their parents' objections became the story of a successful class alliance. Stories frequently described instances of co-operation between institutions and social groups. However, by 1987, the selection of news items suggests a rather different understanding of society, not as a cohesive 'web of communicating and negotiating actors' but as 'an abstract system, with negative and unforseeable effects on [all] individuals' (Ekecrantz, 1997: 407). Rather than 'co-operation', 'afflict', 'damage' and 'malfunction' became some of the most frequently used words in items reflecting perceived crises both in the physical environment and the social democratic consensus. Typical news items concerned the evidence of pollution in lakes, fields and farming systems and the impact of cutbacks in social provision. Two decades on, accumulating evidence of environmental degradation and crises in public provision had made their mark in the process of news selection.

Evidence that particular themes or types of story are associated with specific historical periods is not confined to Sweden. The rise and fall of particular news themes is also the story of the changing fortunes of particular specialisms in news journalism. British crime reporters believed their 'golden age' occurred in the 1950s, when editors believed there was a strong public appetite for news of 'classic' English murders (Chibnall, 1977: 63–8). Sadly, for crime reporters if not for the victims of miscarriages of justice, with the abolition of the death penalty some of the 'drama' in reporting murder was removed. Nevertheless, crime is certainly still part of the staple diet for most newsrooms if not always 'front-page' copy. The period of the British 'post-war settlement' and neo-corporatist politics was also a period in which there was a huge newsroom appetite for industrial relations stories. Again, this changed with the arrival of the Thatcher government in 1979, and the progressive political marginalisation of trade unions. More recently, the fortunes of health, education and financial correspondents have risen as editors have perceived public interests to become more preoccupied with aspects of consumption rather than production (Parsons, 1989; Negrine, 1993;

Manning, 1998). The importance of the changing fortunes of particular news specialisms will be discussed further below.

Dumbing Down?

Significantly, Ekecrantz (1997) believed that recent trends revealed evidence of the growing importance of market criteria in news selection even in Sweden where a strong regulatory framework had been constructed to promote non-market-driven media goals. Certainly, some correspondents complain that there is pressure to emphasise the sensational more in order to sell the news, even in mainstream political reporting – hence the succession of scandal, corruption and sleaze stories that have characterised political reporting in some European countries and the USA (Jones, 1995: 10). The ambulance-chasing style of television reporting is also a response to growing market pressures. Jacobs (1996) reports that the local US television station in his case study employed seven vans and four helicopters in its daily search for the emergency spectacle. Amongst some journalists and commentators there is growing concern that this represents a 'dumbing down' or 'lowering of standards' in news journalism. Ian Jack, an experienced British foreign correspondent and former newspaper editor, has recently expressed the fear that market pressures are compelling all branches of news journalism to embrace popular, tabloid news values:

> Britain's popular press has had a shrewd sense of its mass audience since the days of Lord Northcliffe, but that sense now infects every newspaper and television bulletin; in an unforgiving market, all of them perceive the need to be more popular and therefore, more dramatic, playful, and 'human'. A sort of warmth has been achieved at the expense of credibility and trust. (Jack, 1998:3)

John Pilger, with a reputation for fierce campaigning journalism, mourns the disappearance of the form of popular journalism with a social conscience, once associated with papers such as Britain's *Daily Mirror*. At its best during the 1960s and 1970s, Pilger argues, the *Daily Mirror* found a style that combined popular news values with a serious commitment to social justice, 'expressed in the campaigns that touched the lives of millions and articulated, perhaps for the first time in the mass media, how their lives were lived' (Pilger, 1997). For Pilger, newspapers such as the *Mirror* have failed because they have chosen to follow Ruper Murdoch's papers down-market towards a news diet composed mainly of trivia, sex and show business gossip. Walter Cronkite, the famous former US anchor man for *CBS News,* has recently denounced US television news for 'targeting the lowest common denominator among potential viewers' with 'tabloid news values and schlock broadcasts' (Cronkite, 1997), while Jon Snow, the presenter of Britain's *Channel 4 News*, fears that British television news is in danger of following the American example towards a diet of 'flash infotainment' in place of serious news journalism (Snow, 1997). The Campaign for Quality Television, a campaigning group made up of British television professionals, has recently produced a report charting the decline in serious televison documentary journalism and in its place the rise of 'docu-soaps' – fly-on-the-wall accounts of ordinary peoples' lives which are cheap to make and generate high viewing figures but which rarely deal with serious issues of domestic politics or foreign affairs (Campaign for Quality Television, 1998).

It is tempting to attribute evidence of a lowering of standards simply to 'market pressures' but there is a danger of oversimplification here. Undoubtedly, the deregulation of news media markets in many European countries and the USA, has intensified competition between news outlets and encouraged an appetite for more sensational items in the newsrooms (Jones, 1995: 10), but this does not necessarily mean that the deregulated market mechanism provides the best measure of what news audiences 'really want'. What is critical is *how* news organisations respond to market competition and the organisational strategies which they employ. Very large numbers have responded by cutting costs, particularly staff and journalists, which clearly does undermine their capacity to undertake serious, investigative journalism, and by emphasising more strongly popular news values. However, this is not necessarily the only strategy for survival. In Britain there is some evidence that while some serious or 'quality' newspapers may be moving more down-market with a greater emphasis upon sport, celebrity and the sensational, at the same time, some popular papers may be moving back up-market. After a decade or more in which Britain's *Daily Mirror* clearly did chase Rupert Murdoch's *Sun* newspaper further and further down-market, recently it has tried to revive a more serious, campaigning style of journalism in an effort to appeal to a growing middle-income readership. Also, research conducted by the BBC and Channel 5 in Britain suggests that while audiences may be dissatisfied with aspects of conventional television news, further moves in the direction of gimmicky or sensational tabloid approaches might be unwelcome.[3]

There is a view advanced by some journalists and academics that an increasing emphasis upon popular or tabloid news values and commercial imperatives is to be welcomed, on the grounds that such a pattern makes the news more accessible. A movement down-market should not be interpreted as 'dumbing down' but, on the contrary, as a democratisation of news formats which, in the past, betrayed a cultural élitism. Not surprisingly, the editor of Rupert Murdoch's *The Times* newspaper has been an enthusiastic supporter of this view (Stothard, 1997) but academic versions of the same position can also be found (Connell, 1991). Certainly, it is the case that as news organisations adjust to more intense competitive market pressures, the consequences in terms of editorial policy may still provide opportunities for serious and investigative news journalism. However, in an interesting study of the impact of such forces upon the Norwegian press, Eide (1997) shows that the intensification of market pressures encourages only certain forms of serious, investigative journalism. The biggest-selling Norwegian paper *Verdens Gang*, for example, grew out of the resistance movement of the Second World War in a similar fashion to France's *Le Monde*, as an élite, liberal paper. In the course of the last three decades, however, it has evolved into a tabloid paper but not of the variety familiar to Britain's *Sun* readers. Rather it blends élitism and populism through what Eide describes as 'service and campaign journalism' (1997: 176). Readers are addressed in their private capacities as 'consumers, clients and private persons' rather than citizens. Coverage of the formal political process has not disappeared but the main thrust of campaigning journalism is directed towards consumer rights, health issues, travel advice and lifestyle information. Very similar patterns can be detected in newspapers around Europe. Indeed, the *Daily Mirror*'s move up-market has been based upon a very similar strategy. Given the importance of consumption and lifestyle issues for most members of news audiences at the end of twentieth century, this emphasis is understandable – but there is a cost. As Eide, following Sparks (1992), concludes, there is a danger that a journalism which primarily addresses the news audience as individual consumers, substitutes a 'lurking populism' for an analysis of the social totality and a 'proper understanding of politics and society' (1997: 179). The structures of power, authority and wealth which are at the root of so many of the pleasures and opportunities but also constraints and miseries experienced by the individual in the late, modern world are rendered, at best, only partially visible by a journalism of consumption and lifestyle.

Implications for Sources

What are the implications of this discussion of news production and news values for the organisations and social groups seeking to secure access to the news media? First, organisations and social groups seeking to secure access to the mainstream news media arena are much more likely to be successful if they understand the rhythms of news organisations and the values that guide news selection, and can find ways of expressing their agenda in these terms. This may mean, for example, finding a human interest news peg around which other elements of a political message may be hung or offering to journalists a 'personality' with which a campaigning issue can be associated. Secondly, given the event-driven nature of news reporting, it may also mean conceding that complex aspects or analysis of the underlying causes of a particular problem may simply not interest the news media. For example, Greenpeace scored significant success in using the late 1980s British 'seal plague' as a way of raising questions about ocean pollution. This was sudden, dramatic and involved 'cuddly animals'. Securing news media interest in debates over the long-term economics of energy production and future investment proved considerably more difficult (Anderson, 1993). The price of securing media access is to accept the news media inclination to simplify the complex (or ignore it) and to 'individualise' (Cottle, 1993) what are, in reality, often structural problems. Inevitably, staff with responsibilities for news media work within campaigning organisations frequently report having to tailor the content of the messages they present to journalists in the light of dominant news values and production processes (Chapman and Lupton, 1994: 31–4; Manning, 1998; Miller and Williams, 1998). In effect, this represents a process of incorporation; the different news media can provide opportunities to reach thousands, if not millions of members of news audiences, but this normally involves compromise in terms of the kind of message that is presented to the news arena.

Objectivity and Hierarchy

In Western Europe and the USA, journalism emerged as a professional practice in the nineteenth century and was powerfully influenced by the same empiricist currents flowing through the natural and social sciences during this period. Indeed, many of the conventions and structures of traditional news journalism rest upon the belief that 'facts' are always distinguishable from 'values'. Hence, the traditional distinction (now increasingly blurred in some newspapers) between 'news sections' and 'editorial opinion', and the divisions in professional practice between reporting and feature writing (Golding, 1981). Although most social scientists would now accept that knowledge of the social and political world is always constructed through social practices, journalists in their news-gathering work continue to be impressed by the apparent superiority of 'factual knowledge' which seems uncontaminated by values (Phillips, 1977; Schlesinger, 1980; Fenton et al., 1997).

However, by now it should be clear that given the organisational pressures, selection processes and source strategies which contribute to news production, news can never be 'objective' in the sense of being uninfluenced by the processes that make it. Indeed, much of the material journalists work with in producing news items is thoroughly contaminated with values, partial descriptions and professional spin. It is more appropriate, therefore, to regard 'objectivity' and 'impartiality' as labels that journalists use to refer to the sets of rules which guide their professional practice (Golding and Elliott, 1979: 208). In other words, 'objectivity' is not something that journalists can achieve in the sense of producing value-free and comprehensive accounts of 'real' events; rather, the term, in this context, describes a set of practices that journalists can *defend* as objective. This argument was first developed by Gaye Tuchman (1972) in her famous article, 'Objectivity as a Strategic Ritual'. Tuchman draws upon phenomenological or social constructionist theory to explore the claims made by journalists that the news they produce is 'objective'. She defines a ritual as 'a routine procedure which has relatively little or only tangential relevance to the end sought' (1972: 661) and argues that journalists' rituals can never obtain the 'objectivity' which they are intended to do. Rather, they are practices that help journalists to construct an account of reality that can be justified in the name of 'objectivity'. Journalists are caught between competing pressures. On the one hand, they must produce copy as quickly as possible in order to meet deadlines, beat rivals and get news out onto the streets. On the other hand, they are always aware of the dangers in producing 'inaccurate' copy, which include not merely professional opprobrium if they get 'facts' wrong but, at worst, an expensive libel case. Given the pressure of time, journalists employ a set of techniques or 'rituals' to guard against such dangers. These include 'the presentation of all possibilities', or ensuring that one party's version of the 'truth' is balanced against other competing versions of the 'truth'. While a journalist may not have time to confirm that what one senior politician says is true, 'objectivity' can be claimed for the news item if one politician's account is balanced by others. In other words, journalists claim objectivity by faithfully reporting what other people say. Tuchman suggests that further techniques are employed in the writing of copy to strengthen these claims: quotation marks are used 'judiciously' to signal the distance between the news subject's account and the journalist's detached neutrality; supporting evidence may be included in the form of other people's judgements; and careful attention is given to the sequencing or ordering of material, with the most 'important' information included at the beginning of the report (1972: 665–71). However, none of these techniques ensures that what is contained in the news report is the 'objective truth'. Rather, what is ensured, at best, is 'balance' between the competing truth claims of the different parties involved.

There is a strong phenomenological or ethnomethodological (see Chapter 2) influence in the work of Tuchman and similar researchers (for example, Molotoch and Lester, 1974). This theoretical approach understands the social world not as a domain of existence 'out there' but simply as a continuous and infinite series of practices through which social actors 'make sense' of things. There are clearly some advantages in examining the practices or 'assembly' techniques of journalists carefully. Soloski (1989), for example, makes the point that the objectivity rituals Tuchman describes not only serve as a defence against anticipated external attack but also help news organisations to exercise social control over their own journalists. More formal or rigid mechanisms of control are difficult to apply in organisations which have to allow their personnel considerable day-to-day autonomy. Inculcating 'professional' values and practices, such as a commitment to the ritual of objectivity, help to maintain informal social control within the news organisation.

The phenomenological or ethnomethodological perspectives of two decades ago anticipate the arguments associated with some postmodernist approaches of the last decade. As discussed in Chapter 2, the Baudrillardian influence has encouraged a new generation of media scholars to understand news making as discourse or textual practice in which news workers, or journalists, inscribe tests with a 'will to facticity' (Allan, 1995: 131). In other words, journalists include within the news texts they write a variety of textual devices which help to sustain the claim that they are 'factual' or 'objective'. Older, 'modernist' and 'empiricist' research is taken to task for naïvely attempting to assess the 'gap' between the journalists' construction of reality and other 'objective' measures of reality (Allan, 1995: 129). Since such independent measures of reality are themselves problematic, being constituted as value-laden discourses rather than objective accounts, the best course of action, so it is argued, is to concentrate upon exploring the devices within news texts which seek to claim a 'facticity', and the related question of the extent to which audiences embrace or negotiate the work of such devices.

Undoubtedly, the socially constructed nature of news texts has to be acknowledged and both the older phenomenological and more recent post-modernist work performs a valuable service in assisting us to do this. However, it is one thing to point to the socially constructed nature of news texts and the problematic nature of other measures of reality; it is quite another to arrive at a position in which the verification procedures of journalism are no longer regarded as important. In acknowledging the socially constructed nature of news texts we should not absolve journalists of the responsibilities of which, perhaps, they should be continually reminded, assuming that the circulation of accurate political and social information is a prerequisite for a healthy democracy. Two recent controversies in television news and current affairs illustrate this very well. The British television company Carlton has recently been reprimanded by the regulatory authority, the ITC, for failing to spot that some of the documentaries it commissioned from independent production companies were fakes, using actors to 'reconstruct' realistic (but not real) sequences of events involving topics such as drug smuggling. Audiences were encouraged to believe that they were watching 'real' drug smugglers operating in Colombia. Other 'fake' current affairs programmes have included an 'interview' with Fidel Castro which was actually pieced together from old film clips, a fly-on-the-wall account of petty criminals, and most recently, the revelation that numerous guests on daytime studio discussion shows were hired to play the part of people with, usually, titillating personal problems.[4] In a broadcasting market in which former public service organisations are placing a growing reliance upon small, independent production companies that face strong temptations to 'cut corners' to fulfil contracts, these controversies are likely to recur. Plainly, here, the verification procedures of journalists and the relationship between representation and the real are of vital importance.

A second controversy illustrates the same point. Recently, some journalists working in broadcasting have complained about the statutory obligations to maintain due balance and impartiality, incumbent upon public service channels in many European countries, which they believe stifle the potential of a more stimulating but polemic and explicitly committed investigative journalism. Given the 'impossibility' of ever achieving real objectivity in television news and current affairs, so the argument runs, would it not be better to introduce a new magazine style containing explicitly partisan journalism from a variety of perspectives?[5] In the light of Tuchman's work, it is tempting to accept such arguments as a means of escaping the sometimes rather stale formats which shape television news and current affairs. However, once again, the danger is that in acknowledging the inevitably socially constructed nature of news, the importance of verification or 'the honourable behaviour' of 'serious, careful, honest, journalism' (Martha Gellhorn, quoted in McDonald, 1998) is forgotten. As Lichtenberg (1991) argues, it is not a commitment to objective journalism that produces the formulaic juxtaposition of the same 'balanced' sources in orthodox news reports but, rather, the inability of journalists to escape the pressures of the production process which encourage routine dependence upon the usual, routine voices within political élites. Even if wholly objective journalism is difficult and, perhaps, impossible to achieve in *particular* circumstances (such as daily news production), there remains an obligation to try to produce accounts of the world based upon a consideration of all available evidence, assessed in as disinterested a way as possible. In this sense, the distance between good journalism and social science is less than is sometimes assumed. As Lichtenberg concludes, 'we cannot get along without assuming both the possibility and the value of objectivity' (1991: 230).

Tuchman's argument is important in one further respect. The 'balance' that journalists offer as an implicit substitute for objectivity is important because it affords the access which news sources may seek to exploit in order to secure news media coverage. In other words, as journalists construct their copy they may turn to campaigning organisations and pressure groups for alternative views or quotes to 'balance' the truth claims of official sources, political élites and other 'authoritative voices'. However, not all sources are regarded as 'authoritative'. Journalists usually assume a 'hierarchy of credibility' (Becker, 1972), with sources close to government being regarded as more credible than the more politically marginal or the more politically militant. This seems to apply in policy arenas ranging from health and sexuality (Miller and Williams, 1998), to environmental activism (Lowe and Morrison, 1984) and labour movement politics (Manning, 1998). This, of course, has important implications for our understanding of the relationship between the news media and power, and will be discussed in considerably more detail in Chapters 5 and 6.

Journalists and Sources: Background, Specialisation and Interaction

News journalists in Europe, the USA and elsewhere continue to be drawn from mainly middle class and educated élite backgrounds (Henningham, 1995; Cohen et al., 1996: 7). Daily national journalism in Europe and the USA has not quite become a graduate entry only occupation but the trend is moving in this direction. Evidence suggests that news journalism is also gendered as well as class stratified. In Britain, for example, the senior positions in newspapers and magazines continue to be occupied more frequently by men (Women in Journalism, 1998), with 'hard news' specialisms such as politics being particularly male dominated, while women find more opportunities in 'soft news' specialisms located further down the status ladder, such as health and education (Williams and Miller, 1998: 156). Differences in status between men and women in journalism are matched by concomitant differences in rewards. There is some evidence of a narrowing of the gap in pay for younger male and female journalists, but older men continue to enjoy better prospects than older women in terms of both advancement and pay (Bielby and Bielby, 1992; Women in Journalism, 1998).

By 1995, only 20 per cent of senior executive positions inside the BBC were taken by women (10 per cent below target), and only 32 per cent of middle management and senior professional positions were occupied by women (BBC, 1995: 97). Three years later, further progress had been made, with women occupying 29 per cent of senior BBC positions and 36 per cent of middle management posts (BBC, 1998: 82). Nevertheless, there remains a significant gap. The record of ITV companies is worse, with many companies unable even to produce data on senior appointments (ITC, 1996).

The gendered nature of news production is important not merely in terms of natural justice but also because it may affect the patterns of interaction between sources and journalists and the way in which news is represented. A very masculine culture and atmosphere can emerge if both the routine sources of information and the specialist correspondents gathering that information are usually men. A study of coverage during the 1997 British General Election found that in a sample of one week's television news output, 80 per cent was produced by male political journalists and only 16 per cent of the political actors featured were women (Fawcett Society, 1997). It is likely that the under-representation of women in formal politics and their under-representation in political media are mutually reinforcing patterns (Holland, 1998). According to one account of the behaviour of the press pack following the Prime Minister on the 1997 General Election campaign trail, with only two female reporters on board, the atmosphere was 'that of a minor stag party' (Coles, 1997: 4). A similar masculine culture has dominated reporting and relationships between sources and journalists on the labour and industrial beat for decades in Britain (Manning, 1998). The contrast with the USA where women have made more significant progress in developing careers in mainstream political reporting is notable (Coles, 1997). The suspicion is that a mutually shared masculine culture involving sources and journalists will encourage a particular way of looking at the world and reinforce particular 'masculine' assumptions or inferential structures shaping journalism. A concentration upon the 'cut and thrust' and individual gladiatorial contests of personality politics might, arguably, be one consequence of a 'masculinised' inferential structure. However, some theorists are critical of the view that there exists an 'essential' difference between male and female news agendas. As Liesbet van Zoonen (1998) argues, the growing importance of 'softer' lifestyle, health and personal journalism rather than traditional 'hard' news is not a consequence of more women entering journalism. Rather, the rise of 'soft' news categories is a market-driven phenomenon as newspapers compete more with magazines, and it is this which is encouraging the recruitment of women.

The under-representation of ethnic minorities in national news journalism is even more pronounced. In Britain, both main terrestrial television organisations are committed to monitoring and promoting equal opportunities in recruitment but are currently failing to meet their own targets. A little under 8 per cent of BBC staff have been currently recruited from ethnic minority backgrounds, while independent television companies vary in their figures from as few as just 1 per cent or less (Channel, Grampian, Border) to a more honourable 9.7 per cent at Channel 4; overall, ITV manages to currently recruit merely 3.7 per cent of its staff from ethnic minority backgrounds (BBC, 1995; ITC, 1996; European Institute for the Media, 1998). Recent data on recruitment within the newspaper industry are difficult to obtain, as are figures on ethnic recruitment into senior positions in broadcasting. Critics suggest that perhaps fewer than a dozen non-white journalists work for Britain's national newspapers (Ainley, 1998; Younge, 1999). Out of 63 editors of mainstream papers, not one is black (Benjamin, 1995: 58). Elsewhere, particularly in the USA, more progress has been made (Gandy, 1998: 145–9). The whiteness of the newsroom and the news beats is important because the absence of a more diverse and pluralistic occupational culture makes it more likely that some of the assumptions made by journalists in attempting to make sense of what happens 'out there' will reflect the taken-for-granted notions of a white and middle class perspective and will be left unscrutinised. The dangers in this respect will be all the greater because patterns of occupational socialisation in journalism are likely to be powerful, given the demands of the work routine and the pressure to internalise the culture of the newsroom (Gandy, 1998: 98).

The gender, class background and whiteness of the newsroom make a difference to the patterns of interaction between journalists on the various specialist beats and news sources. For example, organisations seeking to represent the interests and news agendas of ethnic minority communities will find their task that much harder if specialist correspondents lack appropriate cultural knowledge and understanding of contextual detail. A mutual cultural familiarity will be of assistance to news sources seeking to foster regular exchange relationships with journalists. Some evidence suggests that journalists often lean slightly to the liberal left in terms of political and social outlook (Tunstall, 1971; Manning, 1998: 238–43) which might encourage politically marginal groups, but evidence also points to an ingrained scepticism about all political doctrines which, among a younger generation working in more rigidly controlled and hierarchical newsrooms, can slide into a more conformist apathy (Henningham, 1995; MacGregor, 1997:5 2). From the perspective of the politically marginal seeking access to the mainstream news media, on balance, recent changes in the social profile and occupational cultures of journalism do not offer many more grounds for optimism.

As Tunstall (1971) noted, correspondents will relate to each other both as competitors and as colleagues. There are numerous ways in which journalists from rival organisations can assist each other on a day-to-day basis and frequently informal beat rules emerge governing how co-operation should be regulated. Thus, correspondents on the same beat but working for rival organisations, may acknowledge informal obligations to routinely confer together to clarify quotes or statements which may have been supplied at a press conference; ideas about the significance of particular stories may be swapped, or information about coming developments pooled. At the same time, the informal beat rules also permit correspondents as competitors to keep exclusive information or 'scoops' to themselves. In the past, informal co-operation between rival correspondents included participation in 'rings' which were based upon an agreed division of labour usually involving two or three journalists working for news organisations positioned in different sectors of the market and, therefore, not in direct competition (Manning, 1998: 249–51):

> There was co-operation at the basic level of, if you couldn't go to a news conference or you had to go somewhere else someone would cover for you or swap information. In the old days without screens . . . the information gathering process was a lot more laborious and there was so much to cover. Therefore, we would contact each other by phone to exchange basic information. But exclusives you kept to yourself. . . . (Labour correspondent, quoted in Manning, 1998: 250)

Such systematised arrangements are less common now, partly because they are frowned upon by editors and partly because correspondents now spend less time out and about on their beats. Nevertheless, the patterns of co-operation and competition between specialist correspondents are understood by sophisticated news sources and can be exploited to the latter's advantage. On the one hand, the offer of an 'exclusive' can sometimes be used as a powerful lever to ensure publication in a favoured paper; on the other, information or 'intelligence' can be disseminated via the informal system of contacts to ensure all specialist correspondents have an opportunity to discuss and digest it, if that is the source's objective.

The rise and fall of particular specialisms in national journalism play an important part in determining patterns of access for social groups positioned beyond the mainstream of Westminster politics. Of course, the growing importance of particular specialisms is, in part, a function of wider changes in the political and economic environment, but the rise of some branches of journalism and the fall of others determines the categories of knowledge that organise news texts and promote or limit opportunities for competing news sources (Manning, 1999). For example, during the last decade the fortunes of British financial, health and education correspondents have all prospered, while the labour and industrial beat enjoyed a 'golden age' during the 1960s and 1970s but is now in almost terminal decline.

Most specialist branches of news journalism have an association to represent their interests and formalise some of the patterns of co-operation discussed above. The oldest in Britain, of course, is the Westminster Lobby, formed in 1884 to 'organise' the accreditation of journalists enjoying access at the Palace of Westminster (Cockerall et al., 1984: 35). Since then, the Labour and Industrial Correspondents' Group emerged in the 1930s; the Crime Reporters Association was established in 1947; the Education Correspondents' Group was formed in the early 1960s; and the Medical Journalists' Association was established in 1967.[6] While, for example, the Medical Journalists' Association has grown from strength to strength and now numbers over 300 members, the Labour and Industrial Group's membership has declined from approximately 150 at its peak in the 1970s, to less than 50 today – a consequence of the changing editorial priorities of national news organisations as trade unions suffered progressive political marginalisation at the hands of hostile central governments (Manning, 1998).

This is one of the ways in which governments indirectly influence the ease of access to the news media enjoyed by news sources. In making decisions about the allocation of staff to particular beats, senior editorial staff will consider a number of factors including their reading of growing or diminishing interests among news audiences, 'the mood of the times' and the volume of 'good stories' likely to be generated in any specialist area; the orientation of government can also make a big difference. The environmental news beat grew in the 1970s as news organisations began to understand 'the environment' as a coherent news category for the first time (Lacey and Longman, 1993: 208) but it was not until, in a famous speech, Mrs Thatcher endorsed public anxieties about environmental problems that the fortunes of environmental correspondents as a specialist group really began to improve in terms of status and the politics of the newsroom (Anderson, 1991: 462). It was the exclusion of labour correspondents from the key information flows associated with government that encouraged news editors to attach less importance to the labour and industrial beat after 1979 (Manning, 1999). This is important for news sources because the existence of a group of specialist correspondents who share a degree of common knowledge and expertise with a particular source group can be a great help. Also, specialist journalists are likely to have an appetite for the kind of contextual knowledge that campaigning sources may be able to exploit in developing exchange relationships with correspondents (see Chapters 5 and 6).

News Technology and the Impact of Electronic News-gathering

> I believe another guilty party in this drama is the tape recorder. Before it was invented the job was done well with only three elements: the notebook, fool-proof ethics and a pair of ears with which we reporters listened to what sources were telling us. . . . The tape recorder listens, repeats – like a digital parrot – but it does not think. It is loyal but it does not have a heart; and, in the end, the literal version it will have captured will never be as trustworthy as that kept by the journalist who pays attention to the real words of the interlocutor and, at the same time, evaluates and qualifies them from his own knowledge and experience. (Marquez, 1997)

Journalists, like many people in most occupations, can find the arrival of new technology in the workplace a threatening and dismaying experience. If for one Nobel Prize winning writer, it is the tape recorder that diminishes the quality of journalism and erases professional skills, for other critics it is the introduction of electronic news-gathering systems (ENGs) that represents the greatest threat. On the other side of the fence, 'techno-optimists' in journalism believe that new information technologies will allow journalists to hold the powerful to account more effectively than traditional news practices. What both the 'pessimists' and the 'techno-optimists' sometimes forget is that it is not the technology as such which makes the difference but the social relationships through which it is deployed (Williams, 1974). New information technologies can be used to provide more contextual information and better-informed journalism, or they can be used to cut staffing costs, or to compete in a race against rival news organisations to circulate bits of news at an ever faster rate.

All branches of news journalism have benefited from information technologies which now allow the rapid deployment and storage of vast quantities of information but it is, perhaps, in broadcasting that these technologies have made the greatest difference in recent years. Here, the replacement of film by video, and the arrival of relatively cheap satellite communication systems, have helped television news organisations to accelerate dramatically the speed of news-gathering. As little as 20 years ago, foreign correspondents working for television had to air freight their film back to the newsroom, which often took several days, and write a 'voice-over' to accompany the film without the benefit of actually seeing what the camera crew had shot (MacGregor, 1997: 177–80). The use of video avoids the delay in processing film and portable ENG video editing equipment now allows items to be shot, edited and sent back to news organisations as finished reports, via satellite links. Since the first use of satellites for news communication in 1962, satellite time has become cheaper and more readily available, but commercial electronic communication services now make it possible for news broadcasters to deploy their own mobile satellite trucks in the field, thus even avoiding the need to book time on one of the traditional satellite systems. For print journalists, the speed of communication has been similarly accelerated, as correspondents can file copy from anywhere in the world, providing they have a satellite telephone link ('satphone'), a fax or a laptop computer.

The use of digital storage and communication systems further accelerates this process by allowing the integration of electronic news-gathering with electronic databases and computer networks. This is the technological infrastructure that now supports the arrival of 24-hour rolling news services. CNN has pioneered the 24-hour news service since it started in 1980, creating a global market for its services by using the latest electronic communication systems to broadcast instantaneous pictures and reports from the locations of disasters, plane crashes, war zones, the collapse of the Berlin Wall and the storming of parliament in Moscow. Competitors in Europe such as Sky News and now News 24, a BBC rolling news service, hope to exploit the possibilities digital technology offers, and to run news operations with significantly reduced staffing. When working properly, the BBC's Electronic News Production System should allow television news to be produced with just two, rather than eight, staff in the control room (Brown, 1997: 3).

The rapid development of Internet services also has implications for news journalism. The Internet and access to electronic databases may provide an additional resource for news journalists but the Internet will also compel news journalists to embrace change in two further senses. First, as a growing number of high- and middle-income families across Europe and the USA can now access the Internet,[7] the roles of newspapers and television as retailers of information are potentially threatened. In June 1997, for example, NASA chose to put the first pictures beamed back from the Mars space probe on its website, thereby providing instant access for 200 million people. Political leaders can now, if they wish, deliver interactive press conferences not merely to a few dozen members of the correspondents' lobby but to millions of Net users. Political élites can attempt to circumnavigate the editorial and evaluative functions of the news media by placing information on their websites, as in the case of the Starr report dealing with the allegations against President Clinton. Rather than compete with the Internet, many news organisations have attempted to utilise it. Journalists now frequently access the Net to obtain information as quickly as possible, just like other members of the public. Most newspapers in the UK, for example, published versions of the Starr report which they had themselves downloaded.

Secondly, journalists can go to websites provided by competing news sources in order to secure quotes and briefing material in much the same way as more traditional routes. Thirdly, some news organisations are beginning to harness the power of the Net to supplement services and information for news audiences. The BBC, for example, is now making extensive use of the Net to supplement broadcast information or integrate conventional terrestrial broadcasting with simultaneous transmission via its websites. Similarly, some newspapers now signal to their readers that background briefing material for certain news items can be found at their websites, or they may publish whole editions on the net. The main global news agencies provide similar interactive services via the Net (Boyd-Barrett, 1997: 135). And, of course, some news organisations are now signing deals with Internet service providers to provide free or cheap access for their audiences.

According to the more optimistic interpretations, it is unlikely that news journalism will ever be supplanted by the proliferation of new information channels, even if the Net can carry instantaneous pictures and information from multiple sources. Bardoel (1996), for example, suggests that the sheer volume of information now spilling into the public domain, paradoxically, makes news journalism more vital, simply because without a filtering system to sift and evaluate the quality of information, news audiences will be overwhelmed. This need will encourage new forms of journalism and new journalistic skills to emerge. A more 'instrumental' journalism will transform journalists into 'information brokers' drawing on a variety of journalistic, graphic and database skills to supply particular clients with information relevant to their concerns (Bardoel, 1996: 296–9). As Bardoel seems to acknowledge, this is not an altogether reassuring picture of the future. It implies a fragmentation, even collapse, of the public sphere and a transformation of public journalism (together with public service broadcasting) into a segmented, commercially driven information industry, addressing the needs of segmented markets rather than news audiences.

For the 'ultra-techno-optimists', however, ENG combined with Internet and database search facilities will usher in a new era of investigative journalism, through which crusading journalists will hold political élites and remote corporations to account. Koch, for example, believes that on-line data services will transform both the content of journalism and the relationship between journalists and their sources. Journalists will no longer depend upon briefings from official sources because they will enjoy access to 'information equal to or greater than that possessed by the public officials they are interviewing' (1991: xxiii). Indeed, journalists will able to hold the political élite to account by checking their 'truth claims' against 'impartial' electronic data (1991: 320). Many of the older specialist beats, Koch suggests, will simply become redundant as journalists gather information of a superior quality electronically, via database searches and the net. Indeed, the ease of access to specialist information will mean that it will no longer be necessary to employ specialist correspondents. Rather, journalists will become multi-skilled or multi-knowlegeable, working on diverse assignments according to their particular interests and the needs of the news organisation. Even the narrative structure of news journalism will be transformed because the old conventions referring to 'balance' between sources will no longer be applicable if journalists construct their reports using material gathered through their own electronic enterprise in searching databases. This, in turn, will help to restore the credibility of news organisations, too closely associated with political élites for too long. A second benefit for news organisations will be found in the emergence of a secondary market for recycled news, stored electronically by news organisations (Koch, 1991: 305). The current availability of annual editions of quality newspapers on CD-ROM confirms at least the accuracy of this prediction.

However, 'techno-pessimists' read the developments in ENG and the intermeshing of news journalism with globalised Internet information systems rather differently. Faster news reporting does not necessarily mean a journalism of enhanced quality. A long-standing criticism of CNN and other rolling television news services is that they accentuate the event-driven nature of much news reporting, at the expense of analysis and contextual evaluation. Katz argues that the CNN rolling 'live' format eliminates the editor:

> Rather than collecting information and trying to make sense of it in time for the evening news broadcast, the CNN ideal is to do simultaneous, almost-live editing, or better yet, no editing at all. CNN journalism almost wants to be wrong. (Katz, 1992: 9)

Certainly, the rush to provide instantaneous news can lead to corners being cut. A desire to be first pushed NBC in the USA to suspend the 'two-source' rule and place the uncorroborated Monica Lewinsky tape on its website, thus precipitating the scandal that rocked the Clinton Presidency in 1998.

With the speed at which 24-hour news stations operate it is difficult to observe the conventional rules regarding the verification of sources and this, in turn, increases the danger that erroneous reports will be circulated and widely published. The spread of electronic news-gathering means that deadlines for copy are brought forward, as news organisations can publish more editions of papers and provide more frequent broadcast bulletins. The danger is that some of the most important procedures in producing authoritative news journalism – gathering background or contextual information, verification from independent sources, and informed analysis or evaluation – are likely to be the first casualties when news deadlines accelerate. This appears to be the case not only for rolling news services but for conventional print and broadcast news through Europe, as well as the USA (Jones, 1995: 11; Kuhn, 1995: 43). A news service driven by the desire for instantaneous reporting will value less the knowledge and range of contacts acquired by specialist correspondents working in particular fields. For the pessimists, there is a danger that these technological innovations will de-skill journalists; that they will become little more than office-bound information processers, 'reduced to just a cog in an ever widening "information machine"' (Bardoel, 1996: 288).

Electronic news systems allow journalists in the newsroom to almost instantly integrate news copy with graphics, images and data retrieved from digital libraries. The introduction of ENS has allowed the BBC, for example, to develop a 'bi-media' policy in which television and radio news functions are integrated. BBC journalists now file reports for use in both media, producing savings in production costs but, the critics suggest, at the price of a deterioration in the quality of the journalism.[8] Once the initial decision to invest in expensive technology such as ENS has been made, there is an ever growing pressure to use the technology frequently in order to secure the efficiency savings that 'justify' the decision in the first place. As a consequence, professional criteria of news journalism are subordinated to the concerns of the budget and efficiency measures. And managers can become fascinated with new gadgets (MacGregor, 1997: 186–99). With ENS and ENG technology, relatively expensive live studio interviews, which Cottle argues offer more openings for groups or individuals seeking to contest dominant news frames (1995: 278), become a less attractive option for television producers. The arrival of ENS in the newsroom may reinforce other pressures (discussed in Chapter 4) which are compelling journalists to spend more time behind their desks, rather than out and about on the news beat. A 'telephonic culture' (Manning, 1998: 262) may develop between specialist correspondents and regular news sources on some beats but, overall, a more event-driven, electronically based news journalism is unlikely to prove fertile soil for the growth of delicate 'exchange relationships' between journalists and the more politically marginal organisations seeking access to the public arenas supported by the news media. Journalists may become 'multi-skilled' in handling ENS-based news production but there is a danger that this will be at the expense of the knowledge and range of source relationships necessary to produce journalism with contextual depth. This, in turn, will hardly promote the vitality of the public sphere or the opportunities for a diverse range of news sources to present their agendas in the news domain.

Notes

1. There are a huge number of memoirs, biographies and autobiographies. See, for example, accounts by the newspaper barons of the inter-war period, such as Beaverbrook (undated) or Camrose (1947). Good examples from the post-war period in Britain include Cudlipp (1953), Hetherington (1981) and Lamb (1989). For examples in broadcasting, see Goldie (1977) or Bell (1994).

2. MacGregor points to the impact of the merger of radio and television news operations at the BBC – John Birt's bi-media strategy – as one instance where visual news values appear to be declining in importance (1997: 142).

3. See 'BBC Seeks to Unravel the Paradox of TV News', *The Guardian*, 1 October 1998, p. 4. See also Preston (1998).

4. For example, see 'Fake TV: the Cuban Connection', *The Guardian*, 9 June 1998; 'Vanessa Show Faked', *Daily Mirror*, 11 February 1999; and 'Trisha is Faked Too', *Daily Mirror*, 12 February 1999.

5. For a discussion of these arguments written by a leading television news journalist, see McDonald (1998).

6. See, Manning (1998: 170); Chibnall (1977: 50); and Williams and Miller (1998: 148).

7. Analysts Goldman Sachs estimate that over 70 per cent of households in Western Europe will be on-line by 2007. Numbers are currently increasing by 10,000 per day (Doward, 1999).

8. There has been considerable concern among BBC news journalists about the move to bi-media production based upon the new Electronic News Production System. All journalists involved in the production of BBC Radio 4 news and current affairs wrote a letter outlining their concerns to the BBC Board of Governors (see 'Staff of Radio Four in revolt over technology', *The Guardian*, 20 October 1998). At the time of writing, rumours suggesting that Greg Dyke, the new Director General of the BBC, was planning to review the bi-media strategy had begun to circulate.

4 Proprietors, Corporations and Politicians

If we are to understand what determines the opportunities open to news sources to shape news agendas, we have to understand how certain institutions and structures regulate the flows of news information. In exploring this question we are also examining the features and processes beyond the newsroom which represent the political and economic environment in which news organisations operate. This chapter considers questions of power associated with the ownership of news organisations and the consequences for news information circulation of the positioning of news organisations in competitive markets.

For most modernist mass communication theories, developed in the pre- or immediate post-war era, there are two big threats to the free circulation of ideas and information in the public domain. Pluralists, radicals, Marxists or neo-Marxists may be more or less sanguine regarding the capacity of the market to support the free flow of news information but all are agreed that the power that is associated with the ownership of media capital represents at least a *potential* threat to this circulation of ideas. All are also agreed that there is an inherent tension in the relationship between political élites and journalists. Given the importance of news communication for political success, most politicians will experience a powerful temptation to attempt to steer the political communication process to their advantage. The more powerful they are, the more compelling this temptation and the more likely that they will succeed, at least part of the time. The formidable array of formal and informal levers for exerting influence or direct control over news publishing and broadcasting which the state possesses casts a long shadow over the routine dealings between political élites and media élites.

Ownership and Power

There is little doubt that for newspapers, at least, proprietors have often had a powerful influence in shaping the character of the paper and the culture of the newsroom. This, in turn, has important consequences for the strategies employed by those groups interacting with news journalists. As we know, campaigning groups frequently distinguish those news organisations with which they feel most comfortable working, from those regarded with a degree of wariness (Manning, 1998; Miller and Williams, 1998). It is, perhaps, more than mere coincidence that those newspapers least trusted by news sources are frequently those owned by powerful proprietors with sharply defined moral or political agendas. Such powerful proprietors are also in the habit of forging close connections with political élites in government and this has further implications for the ways in which information is circulated in the public domain.

Such interconnections which relate proprietors, political élites and journalists within networks of power represent a fundamentally important dimension of the political and economic environment for news sources. As Graham Murdock (1982) suggested almost 20 years ago, it is possible to understand the relations of power which organise the production of news in terms of two dimensions: the instrumental and the structural. The instrumental dimension refers to power that is expressed through intentional action. The analysts of instrumental power, or power in *action*, focus upon 'the way in which people, acting either individually or collectively, persuade or coerce others into complying with their demands or wishes. They concentrate on identifying the key allocative controllers and examining how they promote their own interests, ideas and policies' (Murdock, 1982: 124). In other words, the interconnections or power networks involving journalists, political élites and proprietors represent the instrumental dimension through which power in news media production can be traced. It is not difficult to identify many of the interconnections that allow proprietors to *intentionally* influence both journalists and members of political élites using the authority associated with ownership of media enterprises. However, according to Murdock, 'structural analysis looks beyond intentional action to examine the limits of choice and the pressures upon decision-making.' Analysis along this dimension may involve a 'focus on the ways in which the policies and operations of corporations are limited by and circumscribed by the general dynamics of media industries and capitalist economics' (1982: 124).

In other words, the political and economic environments within which all news media operate are made up of both the power networks through which social actors intentionally seek to shape processes *and* the structures that place constraints upon proprietors, corporations, editors, journalists and politicians alike. For example, proprietors may have certain editorial interests or inclinations and editors may wish to shape newspapers in their own image but these impulses will usually be subordinated to, or at least circumscribed by, the inevitable dependence of all newspapers upon advertising revenue. The choices that are made and the editorial policies adopted can only be selected within these limits. News organisations that ignore the structural imperatives of the political and economic environment jeopardise their long-term survival chances or risk being absorbed by rival organisations. While some researchers have spent much of their time either meticulously tracing the instrumental interconnections of media power webs (for example, Mills, 1956; Milliband, 1973; Hollingsworth, 1986; Chippindale and Franks, 1991) or, analysing the structural pressures of the market, advertising dependencies, regulatory frameworks and so on (for example, Hirsch and Gordon,

1975; Garnham, 1979; Veljanovski, 1989), Murdock is anxious to emphasise that these two types of approach are compatible and complementary. Each is necessary for a full understanding of the nature of the political and economic environments and the nature of the power relations that produce news.

The proposition that rich and powerful individuals use their wealth in order to purchase news media outlets which are then employed, in turn, to further consolidate their power and wealth, is hardly novel. Through the 150 years of newspaper publishing for mass markets in Europe and the USA, such individuals frequently rise up, sometimes disappearing with death or bankruptcy, but sometimes founding family dynasties which continue to the present day. In France during the 1930s, a wealthy textile manufacturer, Jean Prouvost, built a media empire around an evening paper *Paris Soir*, the weekly *Marie Claire*, the magazine *Match* and eventually the prestigious daily *Le Figaro*. The Hugenberg press empire dominated news publishing in pre-war Germany. Alfred Hugenberg reinvested capital accumulated through steel production, in newspaper and magazine publishing, news agencies, advertising and film-making. Hugenberg's papers waged a reactionary conservative campaign against Weimer democracy and expressed a sympathy for Nazi politics. Indeed, Hugenberg became Minister for Economics in Hitler's first cabinet of 1933 (Kleinsteuber and Peters, 1991). In England, one of the early examples is provided by Alfred Harmsworth who spotted a gap in the newspaper market in the late nineteenth century, with the growth of the literate lower middle class, the first beneficiaries of the 1870 Education Act. Harmsworth had already made considerable profits through weekly magazines but the *Daily Mail* proved to be a huge financial success. This success was based upon a new market strategy: a low retail price subsidised by a high volume of advertising revenue, combined with plenty of competitions, prizes and promotional gimmicks. Within the first four years, the *Daily Mail* was selling almost one million copies a day, underlining the potential profits to be made from a new mass market. This provided the platform for the construction of a family empire: Alfred's brother, Lord Rothermere, took over the running of the *Daily Mirror* after its initial launch in 1903 proved a failure, and Lester Harmsworth, the third brother, acquired a large string of local and regional publications. This formed the basis for the Amalgamated Press group which, with titles including *The Times*, *Daily Mail*, *London Evening News*, *Daily Mirror*, *Daily Record* and *Sunday Pictorial*, achieved a dominant position in British newspaper publishing during the inter-war period, after Alfred died in 1922.

Northcliffe and Rothermere are regarded as two of the leading press barons of the inter-war period. A third is Lord Beaverbrook, who secured the controlling interest in the *Daily Express* for £17,500 during the First World War and subsequently added the *Sunday Express* and *London Evening Standard*. With the Berry brothers, enobled as Lords Kelmsey and Camrose, the press barons of this era owned nearly one in two of every national and local daily paper sold in Britain (Curran and Seaton, 1997: 44).

Two points are worth noting here. First, Northcliffe, Rothermere and Beaverbrook represented a new, more active and interventionist style of proprietor in England, one who was much less inclined to respect conventions concerning editorial independence. Northcliffe interfered in all aspects of his papers, from layout design to the staffing of the classified advertisements department; both he and Beaverbrook hired and fired with relish. The press barons rarely hesitated in imposing their decidedly right-wing views and personal preoccupations upon most, though not all, of their papers. The campaign which Beaverbrook and Northcliffe unleashed in their newspapers against 'waste' in public expenditure during the period between 1918 and 1922 would make even the most hawkish modern disciple of New Right economics blanch. Both Beaverbrook and the Harmsworths broke ranks with the Conservative Party at certain moments during the 1920s and 1930s. Rothermere enjoyed some success in sponsoring Anti-Waste League candidates in a series of by-elections in 1921, while both Beaverbrook and Rothermere supported the United Empire Party in a protest directed against Conservative Party foreign policy in 1930. Naturally, their newspapers went with them. By the mid-1930s, Rothermere's politics had shifted decidedly further to the right, with both the *Daily Mail* and the *Daily Mirror* producing glowing tributes to Mosley's Fascist blackshirts. At the same time, all the press barons of this era were commercial newspaper men; they hired journalists with professional and commercial skills, not those who might make the mistake of placing the elegance of a political or literary idea before the need to sell papers. As one of the Berry brothers and owner of the *Daily Telegraph* put it, 'more than one newspaper has been ruined by putting a brilliant writer in the editor's chair' (Camrose, 1947: 8).

The second point to note is the extent to which political and media élites were enmeshed and interconnected during this period. This is well demonstrated by the fact that Beaverbrook, the Berry brothers and two of the three Harmsworths were enobled. Some lords may receive their peerages for good works or services to the nation, others by virtue of their political value to governments and prime ministers. What is certain is that once ensconced in the House of Lords, the media barons of the 1920s and 1930s enjoyed access to the most important political channels. However, to be enobled one usually has to already occupy a position of political significance. Beaverbrook, for example, had spun his political networks through the Conservative Party long before receiving his peerage. Having made his fortune through property and steel in Canada in the first decade of the century, Beaverbrook settled in England determined to accumulate political power to match his wealth. He became a Conservative MP in 1910, helped his friend and fellow Canadian Bonar Law to seize the leadership of the Conservative Party in 1911, and played a significant part in the 'coup' that replaced Asquith with Lloyd George as Prime Minister in 1916. The fact that the *Daily Express* had swung strongly behind Bonar Law's leadership campaign in 1911 did not escape the notice of Beaverbrook's rivals within the Conservative Party (Driberg, 1956: 79).

Clearly, then, it is not difficult to draw ample evidence from history to illustrate the instrumental dimension of power that characterises relations between media and political élites. Nevertheless, for several commentators (Curran and Seaton, 1997; Williams, 1998), the press barons of the inter-war period were less successful when seeking to directly intervene in the political process. Their political campaigns disturbed the silt at the bottom of the political pool but achieved little more; their capacity to directly change public opinion over particular issues should not be overestimated. After all, the United Empire Party quickly petered out, and support for Mosley's black-shirts never amounted to much beyond a minority of the disaffected and particular members of the Royal Family. However, their indirect influence was more significant in cultivating a climate in which it was more difficult to circulate radical or transformative ideas in the public arena. The press barons pioneered the editorial position of the 'common man', a political 'common sense' which was all the more powerful in its conservatism precisely because it claimed an independence or detachment from mainstream political parties. As Beaverbrook explained,

> The *Daily Express*, while its sympathies are undoubtedly Conservative, has preferred to maintain a complete independence and to support or resist politicians in so far as their policies do not conform to what it believes to be the public interest. It has created a point of view of its own, stands consistently by it, and subjects all proposals to this test.
>
> The *Daily Express* believes in freedom and equality of opportunity for all British subjects. It is against every kind of privilege, prejudice and restriction. It is in favour of all that makes for the liberty of the human spirit to express itself through hard work and sane enjoyment. It opposes all kind of government controls whether they take the form of a Socialist bureaucracy trying to manage our business for us or of a kill-joy administration trying to ration our amusements. (Beaverbrook, undated)

This was, indeed, a powerful formula for success and one that has a striking contemporary resonance. A Conservatism that is represented as anti-establishment and in tune with the aspirations of the people; opposed to government controls, or 'interference', and in favour of hard work and hard play (or 'sane amusement'); and willing to take on the establishment on behalf of the average reader, could easily be mistaken for the contemporary marketing strategy at the *Sun* and one or two other right-wing English tabloid papers.

The press barons of the inter-war era exercised an absolute instrumental power within their news organisations. That some journalists with differing political persuasions sometimes prospered under their patronage (for example, Michael Foot, a distinguished left-wing Labour Party leader, was taken under Beaverbrook's wing as a young journalist) only serves to illustrate the indulgence of the press barons, rather than their fair mindedness. In their dealings with political agents beyond their newspaper offices, the instrumental power of the barons was rather more circumscribed but significant enough for only the rashest among political élites not to take their views and interests into account in their strategic reckoning. After all, it was Baldwin, a Conservative Prime Minister, who complained that the press barons 'enjoyed power without responsibility'. For a while, in the two decades following the Second World War, it was sometimes suggested that the era of the press barons was finished; that either more hard-nosed commercialism or the maturing of liberal values within the political culture of Western democracies, or perhaps a combination of the two, would prevent for ever more, the emergence of a new generation of politically driven, autocratic press barons (Koss, 1973; Whale, 1977). This was partly because during this period in the USA and Britain, and a little later in France and other Western European countries, there emerged robust public service broadcasting systems which, liberal optimists hoped, would provide a counterbalance to the influence of newspaper publishing empires.

Even before the era of media deregulation, these hopes were rather overblown. The press barons of the inter-war period did not dissolve their empires but left them to their sons; with Sir Max Aitkin, for example, taking charge of the Express Groups and Vere Harmsworth succeeding his father, Lord Rothermere, at what was now Associated Newspapers. More significantly, a new cohort of press barons emerged in the 1970s and 1980s. It is sometimes suggested that figures such as Rupert Murdoch, Robert Maxwell and Conrad Black are qualitatively different in kind to the press barons of the earlier era because for modern proprietors it is, above all, profit or the bottom line, rather than idiosyncratic political interests which drive their decision-making (Koss, 1973). The promiscuity of Murdoch's papers around the world in bed-hopping between political parties is frequently cited as evidence of a man driven purely by profit rather than political principle. As one former *Sunday Times* editor said, 'Murdoch is something of a serial adulterer when it comes to politicians. He dumps Prime Ministers as casually as he dumps editors' (Neil, 1998). However, this is to oversimplify the complexity of the political and economic environment and to misread the strategies of the media barons in both eras.

Politics and Economics

Beaverbrook, Northcliffe and Rothermere may have pursued some causes which, viewed in a contemporary light, appear bizarre, but in doing so they were careful not to jeopardise the long-term profitability of their companies. On the contrary, their incessant political networking was integral to the commercial success of their organisations. Equally, while Murdoch has a reputation for hard-nosed commercialism, it is the political affiliation of his papers, not their politics, which may on occasion change. In other words, Murdoch's papers may switch parties, and prime ministers, but they are much more faithful to Murdoch's political vision. The 'good society' is one in which labour markets are flexible and deregulated as far as possible, corporate investment opportunities are promoted and corporate liabilities minimised, social policy is driven by a conservative morality, but individuals are encouraged to enjoy 'freedom' and 'fun' through consumption. Murdoch also backs 'winners', which partly explains why the *Sun* abandoned the British Conservative Party at the 1997 General Election.

For the media and political élites in Britain, the importance of the *Sun*'s conversion could not be overestimated. Throughout the 1980s, the *Sun* not only provided staunch support for the Conservatives, and particularly Mrs Thatcher's style of leadership, but most significantly appeared to provide a crucially important channel of political communication through which the Conservatives could reach skilled working class voters – the psephological Holy Grail for party strategists. Previous Labour Party leaders had bitterly blamed the *Sun*'s hostile coverage for the Labour Party's poor results throughout the 1980s. The editor of the *Sun* in 1997, Stuart Higgins, explained his newspaper's conversion in the following terms:

> Imagine the nightmare scenario for us on election day with Labour having the landslide they had and us being on the wrong side. It would have had commercial *and* journalistic impact. It would have been a complete nightmare, going against everything we think the Sun stands for, i.e. popular opinion. . . . The two great reservations we had with Blair, and continue to have, were Europe and the unions. We've been in the vanguard of the fight against European interference. . . . What we did was stifle their [the *Daily Mirror* – the *Sun*'s main rival at the popular end of the market] potential for growth. But our switching to Labour wasn't to win sales. It was because we wanted to be in step with our own readership. (Quoted in Greenslade, 1998: 2)

This captures very well, the complex mix of commercial, editorial and political considerations involved in the articulation of the *Sun*'s political stance. Above all, the paper seeks to consolidate the 'organic' relationship it has fostered with its readership; it must be in step with, not lagging behind, the understandings and aspirations of *Sun* readers. However, as Higgins emphasises, this is not simply about sales. Upon the preservation of the paper's credibility with its readers depends not only its commercial prosperity but also its ability to articulate effectively the particular blend of right-wing politics and neo-classical liberal economics which is Murdoch's vision. As Stuart Higgins confirms, the paper remains implacably hostile to organised labour and steadfastly Eurosceptic.

The other news media within the News Corporation empire follow similar patterns. Commercial criteria and political values are inextricably bound together. Even the Chinese government of the 1990s is not entirely out of step with Murdoch's political prescription, though it is, perhaps, in his dealings here that Murdoch has been at his most pragmatic, which is hardly surprising given the potential profits to be made from television markets in the far east. The conclusion to draw, then, is that political and commercial criteria cannot be untangled when we try to understand the position of the powerful media proprietors such as Rupert Murdoch. It is rare to find a newspaper proprietor whose politics are likely to damage the commercial interests of their organisation and newspaper proprietors with a principled commitment to labour movement values and the revival of trade unions are few and far between.

Contemporary Proprietors and Global Empires

What *is* new about the position of contemporary media proprietors is the extent to which their ambitions are global. This is related to the loosening of the regulatory controls for media corporations during the 1980s and early 1990s in most Western European countries, the USA, and elsewhere, which has made it significantly easier to extend corporate interests across national borders and through different media sectors. It is also related to the technological changes that have encouraged a rapid growth in types of media, from digital broadcasting to the Internet, promoting new opportunities for corporate investment. No study of the instrumental dimension of media power could be complete without a consideration of Rupert Murdoch and News Corporation, the global parent company that nurtures his many local operations.

As is well known, Murdoch inherited a single newspaper title from his father in the early 1950s, and after building a highly profitable stable of papers in Australia, he moved into the English market, acquiring the *Sun* in the early 1960s, the *News of the World* in the late 1960s, *The Times* and *Sunday Times* in 1981, and *Today* in 1987. He became an American citizen in order to build his US interests which now include the fourth US national television network, Fox Broadcasting, Twentieth Century Fox (movies), the *New York Post*, and the publisher HarperCollins. With the merger of Sky and its rival, BSB, in 1990, Murdoch secured a dominant position with regard to satellite broadcasting in Britain and his satellite interests then expanded across the globe as far as Hong Kong, where the acquisition of Star TV afforded a gateway to China and the potentially huge markets in the Far East. News Corporation owns major newspaper, television, film and publishing interests around the world: in aggregate Murdoch's papers have the highest global daily circulation, and the spread of 'Rupert's footprint' across the world makes News Corporation a truly transnational company.

In terms of the instrumental dimension of power, the breadth and depth of News Corporation interests affords Murdoch three distinct sets of opportunities for promoting and frequently securing his interests. Each of these, in turn, has implications for the ways in which information flows are directed and the nature of the information that journalists and news sources can exchange. First, Murdock can exercise authority internally within his media and news organisations. Given the diverse and globalised nature of his interests, Murdoch cannot maintain a regime of daily intervention within each of his news organisations in the manner of the old press barons but he ensures that his editors and senior executives understand in very clear terms what is required. With most of his papers, Murdoch has been highly interventionist in approach, dictating style, tone and format; encouraging certain kinds of story; forging an editorial stance in tune with his politics; and appointing people who broadly share his views. Both editors who resisted and lost, such as Harold Evans, and those who bought into the Murdoch vision and thus lasted longer, such as Andrew Neil, report that in the daily routine of running a Murdoch paper one somehow sensed his presence, even when he was actually thousands of miles away (Evans, 1983; Neil, 1996). The editorial 'no-go zones' at Murdoch papers, associated with commercially sensitive topics such as the record of the Chinese government, are well established within the organisational culture. Experienced journalists working for Murdoch news organisations are unlikely to expend much time in trying to persuade news desks to run with these kinds of stories (Young, 1998).

Secondly, the size and perceived political significance of the Murdoch empire opens political doors and allows him to foster contacts with political élites. Political élites cannot afford to ignore the significance of the Murdoch press. In Britain alone, News International controls approximately 37.5 per cent of total daily and Sunday circulation.[1] This does not mean that News Corporation interests are automatically expressed in government. The recent decision of the Blair government to block News International's bid for Manchester United Football Club illustrates this. But it does mean that political élites will tolerate and sometimes encourage a dialogue with News Corporation. Tony Blair, of course, travelled half-way around the world in order to make a New Labour presentation to News Corporation before winning the 1997 General Election in Britain. It was Blair who, reportedly, lobbied the Italian Prime Minister on News Corporation's behalf and critics have interpreted the British government's reluctance to accept a legislative amendment from the House of Lords designed to outlaw 'predatory pricing', one of Murdoch's favourite tactics to employ against rivals (see below), as a measure of the extent to which he enjoys influence within the Blair administration.[2] During the 1980s, Murdoch enjoyed particularly close relations with the Conservative Thatcher government; despite its earlier incarnation as a left-of-centre tabloid, under Murdoch the *Sun* became one of Mrs Thatchers' most ardent supporters, and Murdoch himself enjoyed frequent visits to Number 10 and the premier's weekend retreat at Chequers. Despite widespread public controversy, News Corporation interests enjoyed a rather comfortable ride in Britain during the Thatcher years (King, 1998); News International's acquisitions were not referred under competition law to the Office of Fair Trading, and Sky was allowed to evade both competition law and the regulatory framework for terrestrial broadcasting because its satellite was not regarded as 'British'.

Discussions around legislative and policy matters are sometimes facilitated by the exchange of people, as well as ideas. Tim Allen, for example, who came to prominence as one of Tony Blair's communications advisors, left government to head up Corporate Communications at Sky in June 1998. Murdoch has reportedly been reluctant to become formally integrated within political establishments in the manner of the old press barons but such positions, being nationally defined, are of less value to press barons who operate across the global stage. If the observation of one journalist at the 1998

European Audiovisual Conference is at all accurate, Murdoch has no need for formal links: 'Those who witnessed three government ministers, Robin Cook, Chris Smith, and Mark Fisher swarming around Murdock during post-prandial coffee . . . will have been left in no doubt as to who wears the trousers in the Murdoch/Labour relationship' (Bell, 1998: 5).

A third set of opportunities illustrate the way in which political and economic structures not only exert their own constraints but may also generate further moments in which power can be consciously exercised to secure commercial objectives. Thus, for example, News Corporation can exploit its structural position as one of the biggest global media conglomerates, to eliminate or damage competitors. 'Predatory pricing' or the deliberate sale of newspapers at very low retail prices in order to weaken rivals is a strategy which Murdoch has employed on more than one occasion. The scale of the economic and financial resources at the disposal of News Corporation make it a formidable enemy in this kind of war. *The Times* has been at the forefront in these circulation and price wars, its targets in Britain being its closest rivals in the broadsheet sector, the *Daily Telegraph* and the *Independent*. News International has been able to absorb huge losses in employing these tactics: at one stage it was estimated that 80p was being lost on every Saturday copy of *The Times* (Greenslade, 1998: 7) and while the *Daily Telegraph* has been able to fight back quite effectively, the price war almost mortally wounded the already ailing *Independent*. Losses of approximately £70 million over a year at *The Times* have been sustained through cross-subsidisation from more profitable sectors of the News Corporation empire. Precisely the same strategy was employed in the early years of Sky, large losses being sustained until the only rival in the sector hauled up the white flag (Chippindale and Franks, 1991), and with Sky's recent decision to give digital set-top boxes away to new customers it appears that the same approach is being used once more to see off digital rivals such as ONdigital and cable operators. Only corporations with huge resources can afford to deploy these kinds of aggressive market strategies – the satellite war between Sky and BSB is reported to have cost £1.2 billion and this only lasted seven months.[3]

The majority of national newspaper titles in Britain belong to media conglomerates boasting prominent individual proprietors, or chief executives (see Table 4.1). While News Corporation and Murdoch cast the longest shadow across the news production stage in England (four titles and approximately 37.5 per cent of daily and Sunday newspaper circulation), the Telegraph titles are owned by Conrad Black, a Canadian millionaire with newspaper, extraction and other global industrial assets; the two Express titles are now owned by Lord Hollick's United News and Media/MAI group, which also includes the Anglia and Meridian television franchises among other things; the *Financial Times* is controlled by the large leisure and media conglomerate Pearson; and the Independent titles are now exclusively in the hands of Tony O'Reilly, whose wealth is derived from Irish newspapers and processed foods. Only *The Guardian* and *The Observer* are obvious exceptions, being owned and administered by the Scott Trust, while Mirror Group

Newspapers (to whom the nation owes a special debt for the late, lamented cable channel Live TV) was owned and very much controlled by Robert Maxwell before his death resulted in ownership of the group passing to the financial institutions which acted as creditors.

To summarise, power exists within the political and economic environment of news production in complex ways. Where proprietors and their senior executives choose to exercise power intentionally or instrumentally they usually do so in terms of three kinds of opportunity: they may exercise power internally to ensure that their news organisations produce news formats or editorial regimes of which they approve; they may exercise and accumulate power externally through their exchanges with political élites; and they may consciously

TABLE 4.1

Newspaper	Parent company	Circulation	% of total circulation	Prominent shareholder
The Sun	New International	3,746,376		Rupert
Times	New International	744,490		Murdoch
Sunday Times	New International	1,402,210		
News of the World	New International	4,176,409		
	Total	10,069,485	37.53%	
Daily Mirror	Trinity Mirror	2,331,101		Sir Victor
Sunday Mirror	Trinity Mirror	1,964,659		Blank
The People	Trinity Mirror	1,645,822		
Daily Record	Trinity Mirror	654,556		
	Total	6,596,138	24.58%	
Daily Mail	Associated Newspapers	2,336,587		Harmsworth Family
Mail on Sunday	Associated Newspapers	2,219,225		
	Total	4,555,812	16.98%	
The Express	United News and Media/MAI	1,099,830		Lord
Express on Sunday	United News and Media/MAI	988,720		Hollick
	Total	2,088,550	7.79%	
Daily Telegraph	Hollinger	1,046,813		Conrad
Sunday Telegraph	Hollinger	825,678		Black
	Total	1,872,491	6.96%	
The Guardian	Guardian Media Group	402,182		
The Observer	Guardian Media Group	402,484		
	Total	804,666	3.00%	
Independent		224,494		Tony
Independent on Sunday		251,409		O'Reilly
	Total	475,903	1.78%	
The Financial Times	Pearson	368,384	1.38%	
Total daily and Sunday circulation		26,831,429		

Based upon audited circulation figures for April 1999

exploit the advantages which acrue with the structural positions of their organisations to further consolidate resources, or undermine rivals. Of course, instrumental power describes the *capacity* to utilise the various levers or decision-making processes through which power is translated (Lukes, 1974), but this capacity may not always be exploited. For example, in contrast to his father, Vere Harmsworth, the third Viscount Rothermere, was often content to delegate the running of the *Daily Mail* and Associated Newspapers to his editors, although under his chairmanship, the parent company Daily Mail and General Trust grew into a £1.2 billion media conglomerate. A preference for delegation and an agreeable flat in Paris should not be allowed to disguise a real capacity to intervene in all aspects of news production.

Other Beasts in the Jungle

It is because News Corporation is one of the biggest transnational corporations that Rupert Murdock illustrates so clearly the distinct dimensions of instrumental power. However, the political and economic environments within which news sources spin and journalists weave are inhabited by many other powerful news proprietors who also enjoy the capacity to exercise instrumental power in the directions identified above. Some enjoy a global presence, while others operate in local contexts. In Germany, the Axel Springer Group dominates the newspaper market, owning the only national daily tabloid or 'boulevardzeitungen', *BILD* (daily circulation 4.5 million), the more heavyweight *Die Welt*, *Bild am Sonntag* and *Welt am Sonntag* which are the main national Sunday papers, 90 local or regional titles, 30 publishing companies, four television stations and seven radio stations. The Springer Group controls approximately 23 per cent of the newspaper market (Kleinsteuber, 1997: 83). The political disposition of a news organisation is informed by several influences: its market strategy and the importance of securing a regular audience or readership, developments in national or regional politics, and its internal culture and tradition, among other things. Nevertheless, the interests and preferences of a proprietor are often decisive. The newspapers owned by the Springer Group owe much of their tone and perspective to the sharply right-wing politics of their original proprietor, Axel Springer, who pursued the role of a Cold War warrior to combat the spread of socialism in the 1950s and 1960s (Humphreys, 1996: 81). While Axel Springer died in 1985, his politics enjoy an afterlife through the Springer Group titles.

In France, Hersant played a similar role in building a large and powerful newspaper grouping (although the structure of ownership is less concentrated than in many other European countries) and in ensuring that similarly right-of-centre political perspectives were articulated through these channels. Like Murdoch, Hersant's commercial and political goals were inseparable: control over economic resources was exploited to accumulate political influence which, in turn, opened up further commercial opportunities, while Hersant newspapers always projected a consistent, right-of-centre perspective.

It was his influence among the French political élite, particularly amicable relations with President Giscard d'Estaing and Prime Minister Chirac, which allowed Hersant to circumnavigate the 1944 press ordinance intended as a measure to prevent the concentration of newspaper ownership. In purchasing *France-Soir*, *L'Aurore* and *Le Figaro* in 1975/76, Hersant infringed these regulations and did so once again when, after having gained control of 30 per cent of the circulation of the daily press, he took a controlling interest in the La Cinq television channel in 1987. Nevertheless, repeated attempts by journalists' trade unions and even the socialist majority in the 1984 National Assembly to impose regulatory curbs upon his interests failed because they could not counter the political and commercial strength of Hersant's Socpresse group of papers. As with Murdoch in Britain, rival political leaders, including Chirac and Giscard D'Estaing, jostled for Hersant's favour, while key personnel such as Michel d'Ornano left government to take up positions within Hersant companies (Tunstall and Palmer, 1991: 142–5).

In Italy, industrial and financial capital has long been entwined with news media interests. The Agnelli family, owners of Fiat, Juventus Football Club and a vast network of companies, have owned the leading daily *La Stampa* since the 1920s. By the early 1980s, Gianni Agnelli, nicknamed the 'the Lawyer', had built the Rizzoli-Corrieri newspaper and magazine group (including the dailies *Il Corriere della Sera* and *La Gazzetta dello Sport*), together with the prestigious daily *La Republica*, into Italy's largest news conglomerate, with approximately 21 per cent of newspaper circulation (Mazzoleni, 1997: 131). Similarly, de Benedetti ('the Engineer'), owner of the controlling interest in Olivetti, moved from technical and industrial interests to buy *L'Espreso* and merge this news magazine with Mondadori to form a large media conglomerate with newspaper, magazine and radio interests in 1988. In each case, newspapers were purchased as much for the political influence with which they were associated as much for their profitability (Mazzoleni, 1991: 174–80). Silvio Berlusconi, the third and most notorious of Italy's 'media moguls', has been able to exploit the dramatic relaxation of the regulatory environment since 1979 to build a media empire, Finivest, which controls three national television channels (enjoying with the public service RAI a duopolistic reach of 90 per cent of the mainstream television audience), interests in other European broadcasting enterprises, publishing, football and sport concerns, together with financial and property investments. In contrast to the pre-war English press barons, Berlusconi was successful, albeit temporarily, in using his news media interests to promote his own political ambitions. Berlusconi filled the vacuum left by the collapse of the traditional party political system during the 'political revolution' of the early 1990s, to found a new political party, Forza Italy, enrol all his employees as members, and mobilise the full force of his television channels in campaigning to win the 1994 General Election. Berlusconi's first premiership was only a few months old before he became embroiled in allegations of corruption. Nevertheless, he has continued to mobilise his media assets to political advantage. Before the 1995 regional elections, Forza Italy had 136 advertising spots on three Finivest television channels in just one week and, to underline the point that political and commercial objectives are often entwined in the case of media corporations, in June 1995 the full force of the Finivest television advertising was once again mobilised to fight media anti-trust proposals in a national referendum. The referendum result was a success for Berlusconi (Statham, 1996: 523).

Media Corporations and Conglomeration

It is easy to become distracted by the colourful and flamboyant antics of some of the more powerful media proprietors. Tunstall and Palmer, for example, define the 'media moguls' of their study in terms of three characteristics: 'media moguls' own and operate media companies in 'a personal and eccentric style'; they will have built their empires, rather than inheriting them; and they will be 'politically involved', through the political networks they establish, the campaigns they promote and the extent to which they mobilise political resources to overcome regulatory obstacles to commercial expansion (1991: 105–8). Undoubtedly, the political involvement of media proprietors, their capacity to act and influence along the instrumental dimension of media power, is a notable feature of their presence in the political–economic environment, as the discussion above has tried to illustrate.

However, there are some problems associated with this kind of approach. First, as Tunstall and Palmer concede, there are a number of powerful media proprietors who do not fit the definition. Some, such as the Rothermeres, have inherited their media empires and thus, in Tunstall and Palmer's terms can only be considered 'crown princes', rather than full 'media moguls'. This, in itself, seems a little eccentric, given that the Rothermeres' Daily Mail and General Trust is one of the most significant media conglomerates in Britain and one which, with its historic connection to the Conservative Party, has played a very significant political role in recent decades. Secondly, not all 'media moguls' necessarily run their organisations in an eccentric style. Rupert Murdoch, for example, does not shy away from personal publicity but certainly does not court it either, other than for commercial reasons, and by all accounts administers his business empire with a ruthless efficiency rather than personal idiosyncracy. Thirdly, a 'hands on' personal style is not necessarily an essential feature of the media proprietorial phenomenon either. Some media proprietors with enormous *potential* power to intervene within their business empires and elsewhere, choose to permit their editors and executives routine autonomy, only intervening at critical moments when strategic decisions are to be made. Again, Vere Harmsworth (the third Viscount Rothermere) illustrated this very well: although in every sense a 'newspaper man', he was quite prepared to allow Sir David English routine editorial autonomy at the *Daily Mail* because he knew that Sir David shared both his political and commercial philosophies.

In short, the 'personal qualities approach', in stressing eccentricities of behaviour and personal struggles towards power, risks losing sight of some of the more fundamental features of the position of media proprietors. First and foremost, media proprietors derive their potential power from the ownership and mobilisation capital located in media, financial and industrial sectors of local and often global markets. Secondly, while leadership styles, editorial philosophies and personal qualities may widely vary, all are conditioned by the interplay of commercial and political strategies deployed by media companies to ensure organisational survival in the face of competition from rival media enterprises.

In short, while the eccentricities and idiosyncracies of particular 'media moguls' are often remarkable and worthy of study in terms of the rich variety of factors that shape the human personality, what underpins all their circumstances, circumscribes their opportunities and conditions their decision-making, is the logic of media capital. This point, in turn, prompts a return to the *structural* dimension of power highlighted at the beginning of this chapter. Some of the most powerful media corporations in late capitalist societies are not owned by particular individuals but by groups of investors, sometimes made up of combinations or alliances of shareholders including banks, financial institutions and other media companies. In France, for example, two large multi-media corporations, Agence Havas (the privatised news agency) and Hachette, along with Hersant, dominate French communication and media sectors. Hachette began as a company publishing books in the first half of the nineteenth century, entered newspaper publishing in the late nineteenth century and now has interests in book and newspaper distribution (37 per cent of turnover), newspaper publishing (34 per cent of turnover), broadcasting and advertising (7 per cent), and a variety of weekly and monthly magazines, including the top television listings weekly (Kuhn, 1995: 236). Through a network of interlocking directorships, Hachette is also associated with Matra, a civilian and military communications technology company, and Publications Fillipacchi, another large print media company (Euromedia, 1992: 64). Similarly, Havas was created in the 1830s as an international news agency, regulated by the French state. With privatisation in 1987, it has diversified and now owns a controlling interest in the television channel Canal Plus, a majority shareholding in CLT which owns Radio Luxembourg and other television interests, together with major shareholdings in advertising, free newspapers, Audiofina (audio-visual production), tourism and publishing (Kuhn, 1995: 236). By entering into an alliance with the telecommunications group Alcatel Alsthom, Havas now owns Generale Occidentale, with interests in video rentals, cable, media and publishing houses, and has become 'the fifth largest media organisation in the world after Time-Warner, Disney, Bertelsmann and Murdoch' (Machill, 1998: 442).

Based in Germany, Bertelsmann is now a huge transnational media conglomerate, controlling over 100 separate companies with interests in magazine and journal publishing, including the popular current affairs weekly *Stern*, books, music, film and audio-visual production (Humphreys, 1994: 86). Through its ownership of the publishing company Gruner Jahr, Bertelsmann now controls 3.8 per cent of daily newspaper circulation (Euromedia, 1992: 83). Its broadcasting interests include three German mainstream television channels and the pay-TV channel Premiere. Through these broadcasting interests, Bertelsmann is associated with the French Canal Plus (shareholders in Premiere) and the large German regional newspaper group Westdeutsche Allgemeine Zeitung (WAZ). Through the merger of its German mainstream television companies with the main broadcasting company in Luxembourg (Compagnie Luxembourgeoise de Telediffusion), Bertelsmann has the largest broadcasting reach across Europe, with 19 television and 23 radio stations (Euromedia, 1997: 88).

In other words, some of the most important changes occurring are to do with the *structure* of ownership of news media organisations and the implications for news production of the *structure* of news markets. The trend in media industries across Europe and the USA is for media companies to acquire interests in diverse fields of media production and other forms of commercial activity. This process of conglomeration has important implications for the way in which news is commodified and distributed through news markets. Commodification is the way in which news is packaged and sold to news audiences. Thus, in addition to analysing the consequences for news production of the inclinations and strategies of proprietors (the instrumental dimension of power), we also need to be aware of the constraints and imperatives determined by the structure of ownership and the process of commodification.

TNCs, Structures and Commodification

According to supporters of free market economics, the free news media market unregulated will 'naturally' generate a diverse range of editorial perspectives in news products and continuous innovation in style and technique (see, for example, Adam Smith Institute, 1984; Veljanovski, 1989). Critics from a variety of perspectives are rather more sceptical. They suggest that rather than offering limitless possibilities guided only by the desires of the consumer, constraints and pressures associated with the structures of production and the market-place limit, rather than promote, the diversity of editorial perspectives and types of news approach available.

As we have seen in the cases of News Corporation, Havas, Hachette and Bertelsmann, newspapers and news broadcasting stations in Europe and the USA, are increasingly likely to be owned by larger media corporations. The biggest of these, such as News Corporation, Bertelsmann, Time-Warner and Disney, are truly transnational in structure in the sense that they 'maintain facilities in more than one country' and 'plan their operations and investments in a multi-country perspective' (Herman and McChesney, 1997: 13).[4] In other words, while the origins of particular transnational companies may be rooted in particular locations within nation states, they no longer owe an allegiance to these. Rather, investment decisions will be made according to the criteria of opportunity and profit maximisation. The term 'transnational' is used in preference to 'global corporation' on the grounds that the economic activity of these very large corporations is not evenly distributed around the globe (Sreberny-Mohammadi et al., 1997: xix). On the contrary, the distribution of media and communication technology is highly unequal. For example, according to a recent United Nations report, in the USA and many parts of Western Europe there are over 50 telephone lines per 100 people, while in much of Africa, Bangladesh, Haiti and Afghanistan, for example, the figure is less than one telephone line per 100 people (quoted in Denny, 1999).

It is possible to cite particular international companies that have put profit before nation in any decade of the twentieth century. However, in the last two decades of the twentieth century three factors have contributed to the rise of media TNCs as distinctive phenomena. First, the rise of TNCs in the last two decades has coincided with the triumph of neo-classical economic liberalism as the defining policy framework embraced by the most powerful trading nations and key global financial institutions. The influence of the IMF, the World Bank and, since its creation in 1993, the World Trade Organisation has been to promote liberalisation of trade, the opening up of markets, and a strong antipathy towards economic regulation, in most areas of economic activity where powerful corporations perceive an advantage to be gained. News has always been a commodity to trade but, in the past, the exchange of news information through international markets was circumscribed by the power of particular nation states – the 'big four' wire-based international news agencies grew through the colonial expansion of particular Western nation states in the nineteenth century (Boyd-Barrett, 1997). Now, given the powerful forces seeking to promote liberalisation and the weakening of national government controls, the drive towards global cultural commodification, including news production, has significantly accelerated. Companies such as CNN, World Wide Television and Visnews, which deal in news, either wholesale or retail, across international frontiers, now represent very significant opportunities for TNCs. CNN, for example, is now owned by Time-Warner.

Secondly, TNCs can exert political pressure within nation states to encourage further deregulation in media markets and to erode support for public service broadcasting systems. Rupert Murdoch's use of *The Times* in Britain as a platform to launch critical attacks upon the BBC is just one example. While the continuing popular support for public service institutions in some countries has confounded critics and surprised supporters, there is no doubt that it is now much harder to sustain a political defence against the appeal of multi-channel commercial options and the apparent 'inevitability' of market solutions (Blumler, 1992a; Herman and McChesney, 1997: 46). Thirdly, the last two decades have seen the arrival of a significant set of new communication technologies, including satellite, cable and now digital broadcasting, together with relatively cheap personal computers and Internet services, to offer important new market opportunities for TNCs to enter.

The crucial point to note here is that while the endeavours of particular entrepreneurs and corporate heads have certainly played their part – Ted Turner, for example, gambled on the idea of a rolling cable news service and made CNN a huge success – the power of the large media corporations and

TNCs is derived from their *structural* location and the opportunities that are associated with such locations. For example, large media corporations often benefit from opportunities and efficiencies generated through vertical or horizontal integration. When two large corporations merge operations, significant savings can be made in terms of plant, facilities, labour costs and administration. As Herman and McChesney argue, it is the logic of the market that is driving companies towards merger to achieve a larger critical mass and associated economies of scale (1997: 53). At the 'mega-size' level, the $19 billion merger of Disney with ABC, one of the 'big four' US TV networks in 1995, afforded both economies of scale and new commercial tie-ups – opportunities to market Disney products on television and to provide ABC with access to the Disney back-catalogue. At a lower tier on the media corporation ladder, the successive merger of Britain's ITV franchise companies in the mid-1990s was driven by the same logic. Granada secured a controlling interest in Yorkshire, Tyne Tees and London Weekend Television; Carlton purchased Central and West Country Television; Scottish Media merged with Grampian; and United News and Media now owns Meridian, Anglia and 20 per cent of HTV, to put alongside interests in Channel 5, digital television and the Express Newspaper Group. Now Carlton and Granada are partners in ONdigital which seeks to compete with Sky for the emerging digital broadcasting market.

Vertical integration (the merging of companies involved at different stages of the production and distribution process) often permits greater control and security in the market-place together with further opportunities for profit-making. A classic example in this respect is provided by News Corporation where interests in television and film production (Fox Studios) provide material for distribution via Fox Television in the USA and Sky in Europe, with marketing and promotional opportunities provided through print media, including News International papers in Britain, newspaper and TV listings publications in the USA, and, occasionally, a tie-up with the publishers, HarperCollins, also owned by News Corporation. As we have already seen, an additional advantage in achieving a critical mass in media markets is that it affords the fire power required to fight the kind of battles against rivals which News Corporation has engaged in over the years. The history of News Corporation also illustrates a further advantage of size: large transnational corporations often find it easier to evade or minimise the impact of state regulation. A requirement that independent directors be appointed to the board was hardly an onerous requirement for Murdoch when he purchased Times Newspapers, and in every other instance British governments chose to turn a blind eye to Murdoch acquisitions. The two most recent Royal Commissions on the Press (1962, 1977) acknowledged that competition was likely to lead to a diminishing number of newspaper titles but were reluctant to forcefully argue a case for robust regulation and the 1996 Broadcasting Act has made it significantly easier for patterns of cross-ownership between broadcasting and print media to develop (Curran, 1997: 290–7). The European Commission has found it equally difficult to regulate the activity of transnational media corporations, choosing instead to actively encourage the growth of large 'European' media companies to counter the influence of non-European rivals (Morley and Robins, 1995: 17; Hirsch and Petersen, 1998: 213–14).

In some instances the process of conglomeration (corporations acquiring interests in diverse economic sectors) can produce dis-economies of scale – some corporations simply get too big or too unwieldy to manage. The British corporation Pearson, for example, has recently sold off a number of media and leisure interests, including Madame Tussauds, the Westminster Press, a 9.75 per cent stake in BSkyB, satellite, software and financial data companies, in order to concentrate upon 'core' media activities (Bell, 1999). There is also some evidence to suggest that as some corporations choose to farm out certain production or administrative functions to independent companies, some media production will become 'vertically dis-integrated' (Sreberny-Mohammadi et al., 1997: xxv). However, the overall benefits in terms of control, stability and profit maximisation provided by horizontal and vertical integration make it likely that patterns of merger and acquisition through media sectors, including news production, will continue. In other words, the logic of the market will continue to encourage the concentration of ownership through which a fewer number of large corporations swallow smaller operations, and extend their interests through further media sectors and beyond. As Humphreys writes with regard to European press concentration: 'The main point, however, is that press concentration has its own dynamic effect; the strong grow at the expense of weaker competitors. They do so because they enjoy competitive advantages: economies of scale, higher profitability, and, by virtue of this, increased borrowing power' (1996: 68).

Concentration of ownership and a diminishing number of news outlets (particularly newspapers) does not necessarily mean less competition; the media giants may fight even more furiously for survival. However, it does mean that political diversity is likely to diminish as the number of separate media companies with particular histories and organisational cultures declines.

The Structure of News Markets and Political Diversity

In considering the issue of media markets and political diversity, the relationship between the instrumental and the structural dimensions of power is crucial. Along the instrumental dimension, we have seen that proprietors may choose to impose particular political regimes at some or all of their newspapers. The direct imposition of such political regimes with regard to broadcasting organisations is often more problematic because of statutory public service requirements for balance in political reporting. Clearly, however, there are also structural reasons why the diversity of political perspectives represented by news organisations may be constrained. A tendency towards a concentration of ownership in news media is one example, produced by the logic of the market as much as the will of any particular entrepreneur. In some European countries – the Netherlands, Sweden and Norway are examples – systems of state intervention help to counter the logic of concentration by subsidising particular newspaper titles. Nevertheless, the point remains that the market has a tendency to limit rather than promote diversity of ownership.

Secondly, the start-up costs involved in news media production necessarily limit the number and nature of new entrants to the news markets. Only those possessing large amounts of capital, or with access to those mobilising large sums of capital, will be able to contemplate starting a newspaper given the huge costs involved. Thirdly, in newspaper publishing particularly, the effect of advertising revenue is to further distort and constrain the range of editorial perspectives and political positions represented. After steady growth through the 1980s, advertising revenues contracted in some news media markets in the early 1990s and television has begun to erode the large share of advertising revenues enjoyed by newspapers in much of Europe. Nevertheless, advertising continues to contribute between 50 per cent and 75 per cent of newspaper profits in all Western European countries (De Bens and Østbye, 1998: 19). In Germany, for example, where newspapers typically derive 60 per cent of their income from advertising, this dependency has further exacerbated the trend towards the concentration of ownership because larger newspaper groups with bigger slices of readership are more attractive to advertisers (Humphreys, 1994: 79–81). Smaller newspaper groups become particularly vulnerable to take-overs in times of recession when advertising revenues decline. Newspapers with quality or broadsheet formats are likely to be particularly dependent upon advertising revenue because their circulation figures and retail revenue are likely to be much lower than popular or tabloid papers. However, dependence upon advertising revenue brings its own market logic which places significant constraints upon editorial strategy. Advertisers are likely to pay more for access to high- and middle-income readers and audiences. In the past, left-of-centre papers have floundered because advertisers have associated left or socialist editorial positions with lower-income, working class readers (Curran, 1978). It is this problem which has always proved the major obstacle to the British Labour movement achieving its ambition of promoting a daily paper with a left–socialist editorial stance to replace the *Daily Herald*, which finally collapsed in 1964 despite still selling over one million copies each day. In France, for example, in 1988 while the up-market *Le Figaro* generated over 70 per cent of its income from advertising, the firmly left *L'Humanité* secured only 11.5 per cent from the same source (Kuhn, 1995: 39). Critics have pointed out that the logic of advertising works in the same way to disadvantage the ethnic minority press in Europe and the US (Wilson and Gutierrez, 1995: 19–30) and to limit the extent to which non-white cultural and political perspectives are represented through broadcasting (Gandy, 1998: 123–7). This is not the consequence of the preferences of particular individuals; rather, it is the *structure* of the advertising market which produces a tendency to disadvantage the subordinate and to privilege the powerful.

Finally, we can see in the continuing patterns of privatisation, marketisation (the greater use of market mechanisms in public sector provision) and the weakening of traditional public service values a further example of market logics unfolding, accelerated by structural pressures. As Humphreys (1996: 301) suggests, while the political hue of particular governments produced important local variations, the trend towards deregulation or 'liberal re-regulation' (Siune et al., 1992: 4) is driven by the pressure of media markets to expand across national frontiers and the rate of technological innovation which has fuelled transnational corporate expansion. Governments of all political persuasions (in France, for example, it was the socialist administration of the early 1980s which initiated the policy of commercial liberalisation and deregulation in broadcasting; see Kuhn, 1995: 166–73) have felt compelled to loosen regulatory frameworks, weaken public service obligations in Europe and elsewhere in order to 'go with the flow' and ensure that their media and communication industries are in shape to compete.

Why should such patterns concern us? The answer is that such trends, driven by commercial imperatives and market structures, impact upon the range and nature of political discourses sustained by news media. Format and news genre are at stake (Cottle, 1995). The opportunities for a diverse range of news sources, groups and organisations to encode their ideas, shape agendas and exert some control over news information flows depend, in part, upon what kind of news and current affairs broadcasting is sustained by the market and what kinds of newspapers survive. While the quantity of news reporting and current affairs discussion may be expanding as broadcasting channels proliferate through deregulation and technological innovation, evidence from around Europe suggests that deregulation and marketisation encourage more popular, or populist, forms of news broadcasting but make it more difficult to sustain the depth of current affairs discussion (Blumler, 1992a; Pfetsch, 1996; Statham, 1996; Ferrell-Lowe and Alm, 1997). It is also now clear that competition in newspaper markets does not necessarily produce greater diversity or product differentiation. In Britain, for example, it was claimed by free market adherents a decade ago that greater flexibility in news labour markets and the associated benefits in terms of the application of new production technologies would soon permit a flowering of new titles to cater for every niche in the news market. These hopes were temporarily sustained with the arrival of new national dailies including *The Independent*, *The Correspondent* and *Today*, and Sunday titles, *News on Sunday*, *Sunday Correspondent* and *Independent on Sunday*. However, from this list only the Independent titles have survived, and these only barely. The trend towards a diminishing number of titles owned by a smaller number of large companies appears to have reasserted itself because competition usually favours the large and securely established. If anything, competition in newspaper markets across Europe seems to encourage a cautious product imitation in which rivals mimic rather than innovate, leading to 'increased standardisation of both the cultural content and the format of modern [European] newspapers' (Humphreys, 1996: 73).

Evidence also suggests that more intense competition in newspaper markets often encourages a softening of hard news values with a greater reliance upon show business, celebrity and human interest stories and, crucially for the theme of this book, that news sources will need to adapt to these more popular news values in order to secure coverage (Love, 1990; Ekecrantz, 1997; Eide, 1997). The danger, of course, is that in adapting, campaigning groups are compelled to compromise the coherence and, perhaps, the radicalism of their message. Eide (1997) charts the transformation since 1966 of the Norwegian daily *Verdens Gang*, from an élite liberal paper to a popular daily tabloid selling in supermarkets. Eide argues that this transformation is associated with the emergence of the consumer society and the growing importance of issues of lifestyle and consumption for readers. The paper 'addresses its readers in their capacity as consumers, clients and private persons – more so than in their capacity as citizens' (1997: 177). There is a campaigning journalism to be found in the paper but it is directed at 'lifeworld' issues, not the 'systemworld', as Eide puts it. The reader is not provided with a picture of how social system failures or features of the social structure have produced problems for the citizen as a member of particular communities and society as a whole; rather, social, political and environmental issues are individualised or not addressed at all. Campaigns are mobilised around the difficulties which individuals may experience as consumers and private persons, in shopping, obtaining health care, or choosing forms of transport. Editorial shifts of these kind, driven by market pressures and commercial strategy, have profound consequences for campaigning groups and political actors. While certain opportunities for building newsworthy agendas may be opened up, the possibilities for developing macro-wide critiques of aspects of society as a whole, and for rendering visible the social or public nature of private troubles, are severely diminished.

Instrumental and Structural Dimensions of Power and the Flow of News Information

By now it is possible to summarise why an understanding of the way in which power works along both instrumental and structural dimensions is necessary in analysing the circulation of news information flows between news media and other features of the political–economic environment in which news media and news sources are located. Certain constraints and certain opportunities for information flows to accelerate are generated structurally. Access to capital is a prerequisite for entry and survival in news markets. This, in itself, is a powerful exclusionary mechanism, defining which groups and which interests will enjoy the capacity to produce and circulate news most easily. Patterns of concentration and conglomeration are generated by the logic of the market but function to consolidate control over news production within a diminishing number of very large corporations. The importance of advertising revenue for news organisations and the logic of the advertising market have further structural consequences for the circulation of news information because they further advantage certain kinds of newspaper and particular broadcasting formats to the disadvantage of others. We can understand these as structural phenomena in the sense that they are not necessarily the result of conscious choices made by powerful individuals. However, to complete the picture we have to acknowledge that such structural pressures may make certain outcomes more likely and others less likely but they do not finally determine the nature of information flows and news production. Proprietors, editors, journalists and, indeed, press officers working for subordinate groups and organisations, will react to the limitations and opportunities afforded by the logic of the news market and its structural features. They will formulate strategies to achieve objectives and make choices; those in advantageous positions will seek to exercise power to secure their interests. As we have seen, news media proprietors are particularly well placed to do this.

Structural pressure and instrumental choice interact and frequently produce mutually reinforcing effects. For example, while we have seen that the consequences of the logic of advertising markets is to make it rather more difficult for left-of-centre publications to survive, we also know that advertisers can sometimes also exercise influence along the instrumental dimension of power when editorial decisions about feature articles or comment columns are being made (Curran, 1978; Miller and Reilly, 1993: 32). The results of the combination of structural pressures and instrumental action are not to privilege the powerful in every instance, nor, obviously, to produce a uniform, right-of-centre news discourse. There is variety in political commentary and definition in most news markets; there are some opportunities for critical, environmental and left political perspectives to be articulated, particularly through weekly publications and non-mainstream broadcasting and sometimes even within the mainstream. Bertelsmann, for example, continues to publish the left-of-centre magazine *Stern* because it taps a profitable niche and, as we have seen, in some European countries regulatory mechanisms secure more diversity in newspaper publishing than the market would otherwise support. An interesting recent example is provided by *Daily Express* in Britain. It was f-ormerly a trade union baiting, left bashing, right-wing daily paper, but since being purchased by Lord Hollick, a Labour-supporting peer and major shareholder in the United News and Media conglomerate, the *Express* seems to be moving towards the centre ground. Its relationship with the Conservative Party seems a little more detached. The question arises, how much is this a consequence of the new proprietor's political preferences, or, given the paper's steady decline in circulation over recent years, an attempt to reposition itself in the market-place with an eye to younger 'New Labour' supporting readers? Commercial and political impulses may, once again, mutually reinforce each other. Yet there are clear limits to the range and nature of political discourses that can be sustained in most news markets: right-of-centre, pro-market discourses usually find healthier and more robust channels for circulation, while discourses that fundamentally challenge systemic aspects of the market and the interests of capital often struggle to find equivalent outlets.

The Corporate Drive for Profit and Routine Journalism

One final consequence of present structures of ownership and control has yet to be discussed in this chapter and that is the impact of corporate strategies for media workers, and journalists in particular. The experience of the English newspaper industry since 1987 provides a demonstration of what has already occurred in the US newspaper industry (Hickey, 1998) and what is increasingly likely to happen throughout Europe wherever newspapers are owned by corporations seeking to drive costs down and push profits up.

Since the late 1980s there has been a remorseless drive to push down costs in the English national newspaper industry which has had important implications for staffing, investment in investigative journalism and the professional autonomy of journalists. There are several factors at work here but underlying this process is the determination of media corporations to maximise the profits to be secured from the commodification of news. While some commentators regard the 1987 Wapping Dispute as a defining moment, Wapping is perhaps best understood as the result of the conjunction of three developments. First, the Thatcher administration had already taken several steps to weaken trade union power, including the outlawing of secondary picketing and the toleration of historically high levels of unemployment. Employers were encouraged by government to take a much tougher stance on industrial relations throughout industry. In retrospect, we can understand the mid-1980s as the time in which both regional and national employers in the newspaper industry began an offensive against print and media unions (Gall, 1993, 1997). Secondly, the print and production technology that would allow newspaper employers to strip out an entire occupational tier of compositers and print workers was already available and, in some instances, already installed. Effective union action had prevented the full exploitation of this technology up to the late 1980s. However, in the new industrial relations climate fostered by the Thatcher government it was perhaps only a matter of time before one or more employers seized the moment to demand the efficiencies and savings in labour costs which this new production technology promised. Thirdly, the 1984–85 Coal Dispute had already set a precedent in terms of the use of state power to discipline and suppress striking workers locked in a protracted dispute. During the 1987 Wapping Dispute, Murdoch and News International managed to dispense with one print workforce, hire another, shift newspaper production from Fleet Street to Wapping, and present the journalists working for News International papers with the stark choice: 'cross the Wapping picket line or be sacked'.

Following Wapping, resistance to rationalisation among both print workers and journalists in the English newspaper industry has been, at best, sporadic and ineffective. All the leading titles have relocated away from Fleet Street to new headquarters distributed at intervals along the Thames. The consequences for both journalism and the strategies of news sources are significant. With weakened unions in some newsrooms and entirely non-unionised staff in others, employers have been able to force through both cuts in staffing and more 'efficient' working practices. The arrival of new technology has not only eroded print jobs but in the newsroom electronic news-gathering systems have permitted rationalisation and more 'efficient' work regimes for journalists too (Koch, 1991: 307–8). One consequence is that journalists depend more upon electronic information gathering – by telephone, fax and e-mail – and less upon direct interaction with news sources. In short, they are often more desk-bound.

The combination of tougher work regimes and the dispersal of newspapers away from Fleet Street has broken up the informal networks of contacts between journalists which served as an exchange system in which bits of gossip, specialist intelligence and job opportunities could be traded (Waterhouse, 1995). A younger generation of journalists are unlikely to mourn the passing of this micro social system but older journalists frequently complain that its loss has contributed to a decline in the quality of journalism because contemporary desk-bound specialists simply do not have the time or opportunities to 'chew things over' with colleagues.

> In the old days we were all within half a mile of each other and we would all drink in the same pub – the upstairs bar of the Cheshire Cheese. . . . After Wapping everything was destroyed . . . you're tied to a screen. A new generation don't know what it was like, what they've lost. . . . (Quoted in Manning, 1998: 243)

The drive to push down costs encourages generalisation rather than specialisation in journalism and erodes the professional culture which emphasised expertise and specialist knowledge in particular fields (see Chapter 3). Journalists both in Britain and the USA now publicly express fears about the future of specialist news reporting and investigative journalism (Hickey, 1998; Jack, 1998). Specialist and investigative reporting is expensive. Days spent away from the computer terminal are often regarded as 'unproductive' by senior managers, even if they allow more informed copy to be submitted. Inevitably these kinds of work regimes threaten the 'relative autonomy' of journalists. In broadcasting journalism there are parallel pressures. Cuts in the staffing of news and current affairs at both BBC and ITN are examples of a broader trend throughout Europe and the USA (Machill, 1998: 438). Pressure to deliver ratings threatens the programming spaces formerly reserved for 'serious' current affairs, while marketisation strategies have encouraged a greater reliance upon independent production companies, lacking a track record in methodical investigative reporting.

For 'non-official' news sources struggling to secure access to news agendas the implications of these patterns are contradictory. According to some commentators, the tough work regimes and desk-bound nature of news journalism can encourage a dependency upon public relations sources and press officers who can supply 'ready made copy' (Michie, 1998: 35). Staff cuts in the newsroom encourage an appetite for 'information subsidies' (Gandy, 1982). However, this is not necessarily an unqualified 'good thing' for news sources associated with the subordinate or politically marginalised. There are advantages to be gained from developing 'exchange relationships' with specialist correspondents (see Chapters 6 and 7) but the delicate balance of obligations and entitlements bound up in such exchange relationships are less likely to evolve when news sources find themselves communicating mainly with generalist rather than specialist reporters and by electronic system, rather than face to face. There is some evidence that exchange relationships can emerge through a 'telephonic culture' in which press officers for campaigning groups deal mainly with journalists by telephone (Manning, 1998: 262; Miller and Williams, 1998: 132) but there is no doubt that rationalisation and staff cuts in the newsroom diminish the opportunities for vibrant exchange relations between journalists and the more politically marginal groups to develop.

Of course, there are dangers in swallowing 'golden age' myths both about Fleet Street and the professionalism or independence of journalists in previous decades. Nevertheless, we should not lose sight of the connection between these recent changes in the practice of journalism and the emerging structures of ownership in news media. As news organisations become 'parts' of much larger TNCs or media conglomerates, senior executives grow ever more aware of the need to deliver profits at the end of each financial year. The challenge for journalists is to find ways in which an informed news journalism can still be delivered within the constraints set by this process of intensified commodification. The challenge for news sources is to manage information flows in ways that can open up parts of the news agenda so that their voices can be heard. In this, as we shall in the following chapter, the politically powerful have very considerable advantages.

Notes

1. This figure is based upon ABC circulation figures as at April 1999. Critics point out that newspaper circulation is an imperfect measure of audience reach because it does not take into account other media interests associated with a company, such as broadcasting, nor the point that the total number of purchasers of a media product may be less than the number who are exposed to its message. If media concentration is measured by more complicated indicators such as revenue volumes, aggregated newspaper and broadcasting audiences, or a combination of the two, then News International is second to the BBC in terms of market share (Robinson, 1995).

2. See 'Blair helped Murdoch bid' and 'Sleeping with a Tiger' by Michael White, both in *The Guardian*, 30 March 1998. Also, 'Peers Question Motives of Ministers in Press Price War', *The Guardian*, 10 February 1998.

3. *The Observer*, 2nd August 1998, Business Section, Media, p. 7.

4. Herman and McChesney (1997) reject the arguments of those who suggest that TNCs are still largely rooted in particular nation states (see, for example, Hirst and Thompson, 1996). Herman and McChesney argue that while TNCs may locate their headquarters in a particular country and even continue to undertake the largest proportion of their business within that country, none the less, if commercial criteria conflict with national allegiances with regard to investment decisions or profit maximisation, it is the former rather than the latter which take precedence.

5 Political Elites, the State and Categories of Knowledge

This chapter explores the capacity of the state to regulate news information flows in a variety of ways, and the practices of political élites in attempting to direct information in particular directions. The previous chapter distinguished between two dimensions of power, the instrumental and the structural. It was suggested that in order to draw a comprehensive picture of the ways in which news information flows were sustained and controlled, it was necessary to explore not only the deliberate (instrumental) exercise of proprietorial power and managerial authority within the newsroom but also the way in which market structures and economic pressures constrained and defined how news information was commodified. The same assumption underpins this chapter. Along the instrumental dimension we can identify members of political élites – government ministers, party politicians, civil servants, spin doctors and party workers – who enjoy the capacity to exercise a significant degree of control over the information flows which sustain news journalism. We can understand these political élite members as *actors* exercising a degree of choice in the strategies they select for information control.

We can distinguish two kinds of instrumental action, the promotional and the restrictive (Franklin, 1994: 76). A number of commentators have pointed to what is sometimes termed the 'promotional culture' which characterises party politics in the USA, Britain and, increasingly, other Western European countries too. What is being referred to here is the extent to which party politicians and political élites now prioritise the use of marketing, public relations and advertising techniques in 'selling' politics. In other words, political élites now invest substantial resources and much political effort in 'promoting' particular information flows, via marketing, advertising and, of course, attempting to 'manage' the networks of formal and informal contacts with news journalists. At the same time, there are also a number – in Britain, an alarmingly high number – of mechanisms at the disposal of political élites for the purpose of closing down, or restricting, information flows which may undermine their strategies or precipitate unpalatable political embarrassments. Restrictive mechanisms include resort to law and the application of formal censorship, but also the various informal techniques that are applied to 'discourage' journalists from publicly pursuing inconvenient lines of inquiry.

However, political élites can never 'promote' or 'restrict' information flows entirely at their own convenience. To begin with, political élites are characterised by external competition and internal conflict. Mainstream political parties not only compete for votes but struggle for media attention – in many ways their lifeblood. At the same time, within governments ministers engage in personal rivalries, while their departments of state squabble over administrative turf and resources. These external and internal tensions often make the overall political management of information flows more problematic, as rivals and factions leak information to further their campaigns. Moving beyond the instrumental dimension, there is another sense in which information flows are constrained by forces beyond the intentions of particular political actors. Information flows between political élites and news journalists are largely channelled and structured through the architecture of the state, or the particular arrangements of departments assembled by governments (Manning, 1999). The architecture of the state at any given historical moment is, of course, in part a product of conscious decisions taken by political leaders. Prime ministers in Britain, for example, sometimes take the opportunity to create new departments or merge existing ones. However, at another level, we can understand the architecture of the state as reflecting less consciously articulated assumptions about 'the economy', 'the polity' and 'the way the world works'. In other words, the way in which government departments are constructed is partly a product of administrative discourses or taken-for-granted ideological assumptions which underpin policy-making at a 'deep' level. The shape of the state in Britain, for example, began to change as Keynesian and interventionist approaches achieved a hegemonic position among policy-makers in the mid-twentieth century. This, in turn, was intimately bound up with the emergence of administrative discourses or 'governmentalities' concerning 'the economy' and 'industry' (Emmison, 1983; Miller and Rose, 1993). Yet, the emergence of such ideas or discourses about the economy and industry are responses to complex social and economic structural developments. So the architecture of the state, through which many political information flows are channelled, is simultaneously both a result of political choice and a product of 'deeper', more complex forces governing the emergence of dominant discourses within particular political–economic environments.

The Centralised Public Relations State in Britain

Many commentators agree that despite recent government measures intended to devolve certain powers to the regions, the last two decades have witnessed a progressive centralisation of control within the British state and nowhere is that more evident than in the case of information management and supply. The management of information has, of course, always been a preoccupation of government, and while that function was traditionally undertaken by civil servants, the distinction between 'public information' and 'party propaganda' was always a difficult one to sustain. The British government established measures for managing information flows using accredited correspondents during the First World War (Knightley, 1989: 94–5). Even at this stage it was difficult to untangle the political interests of Asquith, and later Lloyd George, in presenting their policies in the best possible light, from the national interest in 'maintaining morale' during a national crisis. Staff with responsibility for press liaison were attached to some ministries during the 1920s. By 1932 a press liaison officer was appointed to the Prime Minister's staff and by the mid-1930s most ministries 'in daily contact with the mass of the public' had established 'information divisions' to handle press and publicity work (Ogilvy-Webb, 1965: 54).

At first these were primarily designed to act as defensive filters, shielding ministers and senior officials from intrusive journalists. However, by the outbreak of the Second World War, the government's information strategies, directed through the Ministry of Information, demonstrated the proactive potential of the state information machine. Far from merely filtering journalists' enquiries and issuing instructions on the proper use of gas masks, the Ministry mounted a sustained campaign to win hearts and minds, not only by meticulously censoring military reports but by offering in a variety of ways, from radio talks by J.B. Priestley to films and news journalism, a vision of the 'good society' for which the sacrifices of war would be worthwhile. In the post-war period, while certain propaganda and information control functions were wound down, most of the activities of the Ministry of Information were devolved into the relevant peacetime ministries, or the newly created Central Office of Information (Tulloch, 1993).

The post-war settlement included as an integral element, the assumption that an interventionist state could promote a variety of initiatives to reform and improve civil society. Government management of information for the public good was widely regarded as a 'natural' part of this process. Throughout this period the distinction between government information (neutral) and political party propaganda was officially maintained, though in practice the lines were blurred. The Civil Service grade of Information Officer, established at the end of the Second World War, was based upon an understanding of the role of government press officer as a 'neutral' disseminator of information providing a public service. Public money, so it was argued, should not be spent in ways which served the propaganda purposes of political parties rather than the public interest. Despite the obvious difficulties in practice, the organisational culture of information officers within the Civil Service formally continues to be based upon this distinction. Explicitly political work is officially regarded as properly belonging to the sphere of privately funded political assistants and researchers, not civil servants. This is clearly laid down in the Whitehall Red Book which provides a professional code of conduct for civil servants.

While acknowledging that the line was always a fine one, critics insist that 1979 represents a turning point because under Mrs Thatcher's premiership the distinction between public and party interest became well and truly blurred (Cockerall et al., 1984; Golding, 1992). This was, in part, a consequence of the privatisation programmes of the mid-1980s which included huge advertising and public relations campaigns in an effort to capture the public's imagination and ensure successful share flotations but, of course, given the intimate association between privatisation policies and Mrs Thatcher's administration in this era, such expenditure was as much about selling 'Thatcherism' as informing the public (Philo, 1995). Indeed, the government's investment in public relations and media work of all kinds grew tenfold in little more than a decade so that by 1988 only Unilever and Proctor & Gamble spent more on advertising than the government, and by the beginning of the 1990s the government had actually outstripped the corporate sector (Golding, 1992: 507; Scammell, 1995: 3). Mrs Thatcher is sometimes credited with importing political marketing techniques from the USA for the first time and there is no doubt that under her leadership the Conservative Party prioritised the integration of policy, strategy and political presentation with a new intensity. This had profound implications for the management of information flows between government and journalists.

Under Mrs Thatcher, power, including control over key information flows, was further centralised within the Cabinet Office and the Prime Ministers' private office (Dunleavy, 1990). Bernard Ingham, Mrs Thatcher's press secretary, was eventually given an enhanced role as head of the entire Government Information Service. This meant that the press officers attached to each department of state or ministry had to co-ordinate their work through Ingham. John Major's Conservative administration appeared to place a little less emphasis upon information control and news management (the roles of Prime Minister's Press Secretary and Head of the Government Information Service were disentangled once again) but the Conservatives became so embroiled in 'sleaze allegations' that no amount of spin doctor wizardry was likely to save them. Crucially, Major lost the support of normally faithful Conservative newspapers (see below).

With the arrival of Tony Blair and 'New Labour' in office, the emphasis upon information control, news management and centralisation has, if anything, increased. Blair has taken steps to further strengthen the authority of the Cabinet Office under his direct influence and this quite explicitly includes control of information flows. The Mountfield Report was commissioned to consider how best to 'modernise' the Government Information Service and its recommendations included, among other things, the creation of a new Strategic Communications Unit, staffed by both civil servants and special political advisors, to work directly under Alistair Campbell, the Prime Minister's Press Secretary (Mountfield Report, 1997). In response to its mauling at the hands of tabloid papers sympathetic to Mrs Thatcher in the 1980s, the Labour Party ploughed very significant resources into building a slick political communications team which, with a US-style 'instant rebuttal unit', could simply out-gun the opposition by the time of the 1997 General Election. This very heavy emphasis upon 'presentation' has naturally continued in government. The steady growth in government advertising has continued too – £9 million being spent in television advertising for the New

Deal initiative alone. The new Labour government spent £105 million on advertising in 1998/99 (beating Mrs Thatcher's previous record of £104 million spent promoting the privatisation share issues in 1986/87),[1] with advertising campaigns promoting government policies in health, education, energy supply and the Millenium Dome (Garrett, 1998). While it is true that a large proportion of this budget has been devoted to campaigns which *are* in the public interest, such as the advertising designed to alert organisations to the danger of the Millenium bug, it also remains the case that all such public information campaigns have a party political as well as administrative function.

In an unprecedented purge, 8 out of 18 Heads of Information within the Government Information Service (GIS) have resigned in little more than a year, to be replaced by appointees approved by the Prime Minister and his press secretary; the number of special advisors with political rather than public service briefs has doubled; and Alistair Campbell has instructed information officers to be more proactive in communicating Labour's political message. As one former civil servant commented:

> It is very frightening actually, because with an unwritten constitution we have these various checks and balances and one of the cherished elements in all that was that the government in power could not use the fact that it was in power to peddle its own party ideals to remain in power. There was the notion of the neutrality of the GIS based on a mission to inform and a duty to tell the truth; and not just the good bits; all that's under threat. (quoted in Franklin, 1998)

Two caveats need to be made here. First, governments can never supply 'neutral' information; despite the culture of the Whitehall Red Book the provision of 'government information' will in any age be a political process. Choices regarding the kind of information, its range, format and organisation will inevitably be political. Secondly, the process of more explicitly politicising the GIS was begun under Mrs Thatcher, hence the notorious changes in the calculation of unemployment rates, the disappearance of measures of poverty, and so on.

Nevertheless, for some critics, the centralisation of control over information, the tight reign which Number 10 exercises over the media work of Cabinet Ministers, and the aggressive stance adopted towards 'awkward' journalists, amount to a significant departure even from the days of Mrs Thatcher and her press secretary, Bernard Ingham.[2] Indeed, Alistair Campbell was hauled in front of the House of Commons Public Administration Select Committee once it emerged that he demanded the right to exercise control over every aspect of Cabinet Ministers' media work, from the articles they wrote for newspapers to their interviews on radio.[4] Fears voiced by opposition parties and commentators regarding the blurring of the division between civil servant and political advisor prompted Tony Blair to establish an enquiry into the role of spin doctors and the relationship between government representatives and the Westminster Lobby in the early months of the administration. However, this enquiry was headed by Campbell and Mandelson, at this time Blair's two most trusted spin doctors. Not surprisingly, the enquiry made little progress in exploring the extent to which the government exercised undue influence over the briefing and information channels available to journalists (MacAskill, 1997).

The controversy over the role of Alistair Campbell and other New Labour spin doctors is a familiar one. Bernard Ingham, Mrs Thatcher's press secretary, was regarded with a similar mixture of fear and loathing by both political opponents and members of the Conservative Cabinet. He, too, was highly partisan in his briefings on behalf of Thatcher – so much so that several papers withdrew their political correspondents in protest at one point. He was also criticised for allowing the distinction between public information and party propaganda to become blurred; of adopting an aggressive and bullying style towards journalists; and of exercising too much influence in a way which lacked accountability (Cockerall et al., 1984; Harris, 1990). Certain dissident Conservative Cabinet Ministers were convinced that they were the victims of unattributable Ingham briefings, calculated to weaken their positions. These familiar complaints are now levelled at Alistair Campbell. Political opponents, it is suggested, have been smeared using the system of off-the-record, unattributable briefings to journalists which underpins information flows between media and political élites (Sweeney, 1998).

While the complaints about Alistair Campbell's role are familiar, his civil service contract contains one novel feature. Prime ministerial press secretaries are normally employed on standard Civil Service contracts underlining their official role as disseminators of information, rather than propagandists, even if they have been recruited from outside government. Campbell, like Joe Haines, his predecessor as a Labour press secretary at Number 10 under Harold Wilson, was recruited from the ranks of newspaper journalists. He had been political editor on the *Daily Mirror* and later *Today*. On taking the post as the current Prime Minister's press secretary, Campbell has signed a standard contract which imposes Civil Service regulations except those clauses which deal with impartiality and objectivity.[4] This is a significant departure because it finally abandons the doctrine that the Prime Minister's press secretary should be merely a neutral conduit for information but it also means that the person exercising control at the top of the Government Information Service is not formally bound by professional obligations of detachment or impartiality.

Spin Doctors and their Arts

The term 'spin doctor' has only entered political discourse in the last two decades and its arrival is, in itself, an indication of the extent to which British politics has followed the USA in placing more and more emphasis upon presentation and communication to the point where political public relations has become a full-blown industry, employing thousands and generating turnover worth millions of dollars. Spin doctors may be formally employed as public servants, as is the case with Alistair Campbell; they may have a political responsibility for something quite different and yet, unofficially, practice the 'black arts' in a quasi-official manner, as Peter Mandelson did before he resigned his first Cabinet post; or spin doctors may be placed on the party pay-roll as party workers rather than public servants. Whatever their positions, if they are to be effective they must have a shrewd understanding of the political news media, the needs of journalists and the culture of particular news organisations, together with a thick skin and, to put it delicately, a forthright personality.

At the risk of oversimplifying, there are seven arts which the spin doctor must master. First, they must have a big appetite for monitoring news media output and must acquire the techniques needed in making their displeasure plain to journalists responsible for news copy that is deemed unacceptable. While journalists' complaints about bullying or intimidation are best regarded with a degree of scepticism (journalism is hardly an occupation for the faint-hearted or mild mannered), it is also the case that both Campbell and Bernard Ingham very quickly established reputations for dishing out toughly worded reprimands to correspondents whose stories had not met with their approval. Peter Mandelson was also widely regarded as a spin doctor who could intimidate, though in a rather more subtle and perhaps more menacing way. Campbell, on the other hand, has been known to insist upon squeezing himself alongside Tony Blair inside the tiny mobile radio studios designed for just interviewer and interviewee, in order to 'stare' at the interviewer (Jones, 1995: 132, and 167). The ultimate sanction for a press officer working on behalf of a political élite is to threaten to limit information flows or to re-direct such flows to new media outlets (Scammell, 1995: 275). This may, in part, be an empty threat – news media coverage is now a prerequisite for political success – but in recent months 'New Labour' spin doctors have sometimes talked darkly about preferring the tabloid to the broadsheet papers, or indeed, seeking out entirely new outlets among the leisure and domestic magazine sector, daytime television, or the ethnic minority press.

However, an enthusiasm for bullying and intimidating journalists is not enough and such tactics will not succeed, given the fairly hard-bitten disposition of most correspondents, unless journalists believe that they are in danger of losing something valuable. In other words, effective spin doctors must develop a reputation for supplying valuable news copy. A second art, therefore, is to be able to provide accurate information that journalists can trust. A third art is to understand how journalists like to frame political stories and the news values that may guide correspondents working for particular kinds of news organisation, broadsheet or tabloid paper, radio or television news station. A fourth art also follows from the second: effective spin doctors ensure that they are close to their political masters, and that journalists know that in being briefed by such a spin doctor they are being allowed a glimpse into the mind of the minister and the most recent deliberations of those at the top of the political edifice. Fifth, a good working knowledge of the politics of the newsroom is necessary, including the nature of the hierarchies that exist within news organisations and an understanding of which news editors enjoy the most authority in the editorial process. The best spin doctors have an authority which allows them to complain right to the top when necessary. Next comes availability: the age of the rolling news format has made journalists particularly value those press officers and sources who respond quickly to enquiries. Spin doctors must ensure that journalists can contact them easily and not only in office hours. With the proliferation of news outlets in the era of multi-channel, 24-hour broadcasting, journalists will be eager for any suggestion of a new angle on a current story or idea for a new lead. Finally, however, all this depends upon a tacit understanding of the exchanges which organise interaction between spin doctors and correspondents and an ability to foster enduring relationships. As a BBC political correspondent suggests,

> A spin doctor cannot hope to operate successfully without having first established a coterie of trusted reporters and other contacts. These journalists might move jobs and transfer between news outlets but relationships which have been built up over a period of years provide the surest foundation for skilful media management. (Jones, 1995: 123)

The crucial art for a spin doctor is to understand how to bargain with information: how much to release, when it should be released to optimise its value and what can be secured in return for the release of information. Journalists will value those press officers whom they come to trust sufficiently to be able to bounce ideas off or 'try out' new interpretations of developments. Although there are never any guarantees, spin doctors may hope that if journalists come to regard them as useful sources of 'insider' information, in return journalists may acknowledge certain tacit obligations regarding the way in which they construct their copy. Spin doctors may anticipate, for example, that while not serving simply as uncritical mouthpieces for spin doctors, correspondents enjoying the benefit of insider briefings should include in their selection of the most salient themes those identified by the spin doctor.

As we shall see in subsequent chapters, press officers working for a variety of campaigning groups and organisations may understand and practise these arts. What makes operators at Westminster, such as Campbell, Mandelson and Bernard Ingham, so formidable is that positioned as they are at the centre of government, they have more effective control over many information flows and, by virtue of their functions within government, have access to information that is immediately newsworthy. 'New Labour' has become notorious for its attempts to control information flows, to the point where it even requires its own Members of Parliament to carry electronic pagers directing them how to 'stay on message', though the origins of this preoccupation with message control can be found in Peter Mandelson's time as the party's communication officer during the 1980s. Mandelson established a system that required all interviews and media work to be authorised through his office. Centralised control of information flows was a most important feature of a party strategy that New Labour has simply consolidated in government. The more powerful an organisation, the more effectively it can usually exert control over information flows from within. All this means that in the competition to encode news agendas, spin doctors working for the powerful have some significant advantages.

The Limits of News Management

Spin doctors do not have it all their own way. 'Fire-fighting techniques' or damage limitation may be required if spin doctors are faced with the arrival of a damaging story in the public domain. One tried and tested technique, for example, is to spin a damaging story away from the substantive issue and towards the question of media coverage itself. Thus, for example, in 1987, Labour spin doctors were quite successful in turning potentially highly damaging *Sunday Times* allegations about links between its leadership and the Kremlin into speculation regarding the motives of the newspaper in publishing the story (Jones, 1995: 137). More recently, the Conservative Party tried to shift the focus from allegations in *The Times* concerning the personal finances of the party treasurer Michael Ashcroft towards the question of whether or not the newspaper passed documents to a back-bench Labour MP. Most recently, a story highly damaging to the present New Labour government, in which an eminent doctor and Labour peer went on record as saying that the government was actually spending less in real terms on the National Health Service than the previous Conservative government, 'mutated' during the day into an argument over whether or not the doctor had commented upon the Prime Minister's wife's birth plan during the same interview. It was an example which some commentators believed had Alistair Campbell's fingerprints all over it. These fire-fighting techniques sometimes betray a hint of desperation but they are more likely to work when applied by powerful organisations commanding a measure of political authority.

Press officers or spin doctors working on behalf of political élites hold the strongest hands in the news management game and yet journalists are not passive partners but active negotiators in their dealings with political élites. Politicians sometimes make media 'gaffs' which journalists seize upon despite the best efforts of their political advisors or media minders, while at other times correspondents can sometimes 'work a story up' by exploiting the dynamic that exists between media and political élites. In 1997, Frank Dobson, newly installed Minister for Health in the new Labour government, candidly refused to rule out a consideration of health charges in a forthcoming departmental review. Within minutes political correspondents worked the story up to front-page significance by securing comments and quotes from political rivals and organisations representing health professionals, all happy to co-operate with a story that served their own agendas (Wintour and

Mills, 1997). In certain circumstances journalists can work with much more limited raw materials, passing on a scrap of unsubstantiated information to a member of a political élite who will then be approached by another correspondent hoping that a quote may be solicited. Nicholas Jones, BBC political correspondent, describes the process as follows: 'Working in reverse order to a team of pickpockets, one journalist will pass on information and then another will speak to the person who received it in the hope of teasing out the required news line in the form of a quote' (Jones, 1995: 224).

Above all else, the power of press officers and spin doctors operating on behalf of political élites is constrained by the *porosity* of the political structures within which they work. In other words, the capacity of press officers working within government to control the channels through which information flows from the inside to the outside world will depend upon specific political and historical circumstances. Press officers spin most effectively in situations where journalists are most dependent upon them. In circumstances where journalists can obtain alternative versions and interpretations, or more comprehensive background 'contextual information' from other sources, the authority of the spin doctor is diminished in proportion. To take a simple example, governments can consolidate the power of the spin doctors working on their behalf if strict discipline is maintained by ministers and most information arriving in the public domain, either on record or off record, is channelled through official press officers. On the other hand, if cabinets are politically divided or government departments are engaged in turf wars or other rivalries, which is often the case, such tensions and feuds are likely to generate multiple information flows for journalists, as one faction briefs or counter-briefs correspondents against another. The Wilson cabinets of the 1960s were remarkable for both personal rivalries and interdepartmental feuds generating a stream of non-attributable briefings to the advantage of political and industrial correspondents (Manning, 1999: 326); conflicts between the information officers working within different departments undermined the government's news management work in the early years of the Thatcher government (Scammell, 1995: 184); while tensions between ministers and back-benchers crucially weakened the Conservative governments's media work with regard to the 'poll tax' in the late 1980s (Deacon and Golding, 1994). Ironically, conflicts between leading spin doctors can sometimes generate their own unauthorised information flows, as in the case of the turf war between Bernard Ingham, Thatcher's press secretary, and Tim Bell, one of Thatcher's favoured advisors (Scammell, 1995: 186–7), or the tension between Peter Mandelson, David Hill and Alistair Campbell, the three main architects of the communication strategy adopted by 'New Labour' (Jones, 1995: 169–70).

To summarise, the news media workers and spin doctors working on behalf of political élites enjoy very considerable advantages in the struggle around the definition of political issues and events, but their power is proportional to the extent to which they can exert control over the various channels through which information flows from government to the outside.

And in this respect, while they may exhort members of political élites to maintain discipline and resist the temptation to engage in turf wars, this advice is not always taken. While the examples to illustrate this section have been taken from recent British political history, the same principles apply in Europe and the USA.

Does a Promotional Culture Promote Democracy?

There is a popular stereotype of the spin doctor as a shadowy figure, applying 'dark arts' for machiavellian purposes, which is frequently peddled by journalists although often the very same journalists are the main beneficiaries of such 'dark arts'. However, while the popular assessment of spin doctors may be critical, some recent liberal and pluralist commentators have mounted a defence. Some estimates suggest that between half and three-quarters of political news copy has its origins in the work of spin doctors and official sources (see, for example, Sigal, 1973; Althiede and Johnson, 1980; Fishman, 1980; Turk, 1986). The growing importance of presentation and communication in politics is regarded by some as one illustration of the broader movement towards a 'promotional culture' in which a growing proportion of daily life is constructed around the marketing, advertising and lifestyle discourses of the consumer society. It is certainly not the case that all political commentators regard this development with apprehension. Scammell (1995), for example, insists that in this era of 'designer politics' the democratic process will be strengthened in significant ways. Scammell reflects an apprehension about ideologically driven politics which is characteristic of American liberal–pluralist political theory. If party manifestos are constructed around more sensitive measures of public concerns and aspirations, as opposed to political ideologies and traditions, this may be no bad thing. If spin doctors allow parties and politicians to communicate more effectively with political audiences this may strengthen rather than undermine the democratic process. An emphasis upon style, presentation and image will assist in the process of making politics meaningful to a public beyond the activists.

In other words, a consumer-orientated designer politics actually allows a break to be made with older élitist models which assume that the policy process must be driven by politicians and 'experts', who then seek a retrospective mandate from the political public. Scammell believes that a new concern for political marketing allows the traditional élite-dominated policy process to be reversed. Parties do not necessarily abandon core values, and political marketing 'rarely picks the details of policies', but it can set the parameters and suggest 'the stance and tone of policy', and recommend 'shifts of emphasis to play up or down parts of the already selected programme' (1995: 10). Underpinning this position is a distinction between marketing and propaganda: 'Marketing's unique contribution is the strategic concern with what the market (electorate) wants and what it will bear. . . .

Propaganda, especially in situations of state monopoly, tends to begin with the premise that the product is sacrosanct, while public opinion is malleable and can be won over to the propagandists' cause' (1995: 8–9).

Propaganda is coercive and unyielding. It implies relations of domination and subordination. Political marketing, on the other hand, according to Scammell, affords a more sophisticated and sensitive combination of communication channels between political actors and electorate. Scammell's argument includes a stout defence of the role of political spin doctors and the lobby system that organises their relations with journalists (see below). While she acknowledges some excesses on the part of some spin doctors, their overall contribution to the process of political marketing is benign. In short, while the quality of some of the information generated might be questionable, without political advertising, public relations and spin doctoring, the supply of political information to the electorate would be much diminished. Scammell does express some reservations. The use of political marketing should be judicious; in the USA, Scammell concedes, an over-reliance upon marketing, not merely to campaign but as an integral element of the routine decision-making process, has led to an over-cautious blandness in politics (1995: 277). On the other hand, Scammell insists that it is possible to get the political balance right and points to Mrs Thatcher as an example of how to achieve this, allowing public relations to temper but not dictate the thrust of policy.

This argument touches upon the fundamental questions raised in Chapter 1 about the contribution that mass media and political communication channels should make to a healthy democracy. If, for Scammell, the growing use of political public relations, on balance, strengthens the relationship between political élites and electorate, for other critics there are more troubling aspects to the growing importance of political impression management. For some, there are dangers in the growth of a new class of political communication expert, as a core fraction of the political élite, extremely powerful and yet unaccountable because they rarely stand for elected office. Their influence induces in the polity a sense of permanent electioneering, distorting policy-making, encouraging bad government and a slavish devotion to public opinion rather than what is right (Sabato, 1981; Blumenthal, 1982; O'Shaugnessey, 1990). These are responses to what could be described as the American condition of public relations politics, although a pessimistic reading of developments might suggest that these features are a likely future outcome in British and West European politics, too.

Another fundamental problem which Scammell acknowledges but rather brushes over is the tension between the political élite and party activists inherent in the 'public relations model'. There are certainly signs that this problem is already manifesting itself in British politics. As we have seen, effective news management and spin doctoring require maximum control of the channels through which news information flows from within an organisation to the outside environment. In the context of organised party politics this, in turn, implies a significant shift towards greater centralised control and a diminution of the role of ordinary party members and activists. If all members of a party, from back-bench MPs to local activists, are to remain 'on message', singing from the same song sheet, then this must be co-ordinated from the centre. This, of course, is one of the most important features of 'New Labour' – a determination on the part of the leadership to wrest control of both policy-making *and* presentation away from rank and file party members. The length of the Labour Party's period in opposition was enough to subdue many party activists before the 1997 General Election success. Now in office, it is very likely that resistance to the centralisation process from within the party will be more visible and vocal. There is a paradox in this which Foucault would certainly relish – the exertion of power generating its own resistance. The New Labour project to manage the news by attempting to orchestrate more directly what party members say in public may engineer its own difficulties, as ordinary party activists open up unauthorised channels to the news media through which to express their opposition. There is an inherent tendency towards leakiness within most political parties, characterised as they are by factionalism, personal rivalry and ideological differences. Only the most centralised and authoritarian internal power structures can hope to keep the lid on for very long.

A further key issue concerns the content of political communication in the era of the spin doctor and again this relates to fundamental questions of theory and philosophy. The era of political marketing and the spin doctor brings also the era of the political sound bite. Political marketing implies more than simply market research and 'effective communication'. Spin doctors are primarily concerned about presentation and image rather than coherence and internal rigour in argument. Quality and rationality are rather problematic terms to use in relation to political discourse at the best of times. It would be foolish to claim that in some previous golden age of political communication, the engagement between politicians and public was characterised by wholly rational debate and a scrupulous concern for the truth. Nevertheless, some commentators do sense a qualitative change of some kind in the nature of political discourse in the era of television campaigning and more intensive news management. Some fear that the skills of political debate have been degraded. Some question whether the processes through which the rigour and coherence of political arguments are tested, remain as vigorous today as in previous eras (Jones, 1993; Franklin, 1994). Some fear that mud slinging will increasingly replace debate over the merits of particular policy options (Hall-Jamieson, 1992). The extent to which the contemporary configuration of media institutions, markets and public relations organisations can sustain a public sphere for rational political debate is, as we have seen, one of the central preoccupations in the writings of Habermas (Chapter 1). Does political marketing and the work of spin doctors really facilitate rational political communication and encourage more informed debate involving political élites and citizens, or do these developments erode and undermine rational political dialogue? On the other hand, for some critics, given that all discourses express power, social interests and the struggle for domination, to mourn for the loss of rationality in political communication is to mourn for the loss of an illusionary ideal.

The Lobby System

We have already noted that the British state began to employ information officers to deal with press enquiries within the larger ministries in the years between the First and Second World Wars. This put in place an infrastructure that would allow the practices and relationships of the prototype Westminster Lobby to be extended beyond Parliament to the various departments of state. The Westminster Lobby represents one of the earliest mechanisms for controlling the flow of news information to the advantage of political and media élites. It is based upon the formal sanction of closure and exclusion, combined with the more subtle exchange relations which typically characterise interaction between news sources and specialist correspondents. In other words, through the relationships of the lobby political élites may seek both to promote certain information flows and to restrict others.

Security fears precipitated by the rise of Irish nationalism in the 1880s prompted a system of access restrictions and accreditation to be introduced at Westminster. When the names of parliamentary reporters and accredited political journalists were added to the list of those enjoying access to the Members Lobby in 1884, the Westminster Lobby was, in effect, created (Cockerell et al., 1985: 34–5). It has evolved into a non-official but highly formalised system of information exchange which offers some significant benefits for participants but which, none the less, is also characterised by inherent tensions. Correspondents who are members of the Lobby enjoy privileged access to the 'backstage' of the House of Commons, being able to mix with Members of Parliament in the corridors and numerous bars at Westminster. A considerable amount of political gossip can be acquired by simply 'being there', though much of it may be of a non-attributable, 'don't quote my name but . . .' basis. Perhaps more importantly, members of the lobby are briefed by the Prime Minister's press secretary in the morning and again in the afternoon each day. They will also be briefed daily by officials working for the main opposition parties, and perhaps also by other Cabinet Ministers.

The key to understanding how the lobby system works is the set of semi-formalised rules which govern relationships between journalists who are members of the lobby and politicians. Above all else, journalists must acknowledge the distinction between on- and off-record briefings. A huge volume of information is traded at Westminster on the basis of non-attributable briefings. The reporting euphemisms that are now familiar clichés indicate the frequency with which political correspondents have drawn upon the lobby as a source of off-the-record information. While 'the mood at Westminster last night . . .' might refer to off-record soundings taken among back-bench MPs frequenting the bars before a vote, 'sources close to the

Prime Minister' will now be recognised not only by journalists and politicians but by large sections of the public, as a reference to the Prime Minister's press secretary, thanks to the various public accounts of the work of the lobby.

For the political élite the advantages of the lobby system are obvious, though disgruntled government representatives sometimes talk darkly of by-passing the system. First, it allows official announcements to be rapidly circulated to all the main news media outlets, and secondly, it also allows more politically delicate information to be placed in the public domain but in a way that ensures distance between the item of information and its source. Thirdly, in the exchange relations which characterise interaction between political and media élites, the lobby system allows particular politicians to earn some credit with their contacts in the political media. Correspondents will come to value a 'good source' at Westminster; they will certainly be more willing to listen to someone who has proved a good contact in the past and just may be of help if there is some kind of 'media emergency' in the future.

From the journalists' point of view the benefits of the lobby system are more problematic and from time to time, some political correspondents do indeed renounce the lobby system, calling for greater transparency in information distribution. The advantages from the correspondents' point of view usually prove too tempting in the end and such protests are often short-lived. The primary advantage of the system for journalists is that it affords a regular and routine supply of information, some of it of a high quality in terms of contextual detail and intelligence. Political correspondents will very much value a press secretary such as Bernard Ingham, for Margaret Thatcher, or Alistair Campbell, for Tony Blair, who enjoy the ear of the Prime Minister and can provide genuine insights into the process of government. The gossip gathered around Parliament can also prove invaluable and unreliable in equal measure. Secondly, the Westminster Lobby also evolved into a professional association for political correspondents. Even when it officially did not exist, it actually operated with a formal constitution and rule book, elected officers, held an AGM each year, and organised various social activities through the year. As a professional association it could represent the interests of political correspondents in discussions about procedures and arrangements with the Sergeant at Arms at Westminster and with the political élite. Thirdly, as is the case with most specialist correspondents, members of the Westminster Lobby find themselves to be both competitors and colleagues (Tunstall, 1971). Thus, while they will be anxious to scoop their rivals with an exclusive where possible, they will more routinely consult with colleagues over the significance or likely outcome of particular political events, discuss ideas for news angles, and to a certain extent pool information.

If the Westminster Lobby is the prototype, the 'mini-lobbies' which have evolved around the main departments of state are structured in much the same way, and across Europe, exchange relations between political élites and journalists have evolved along similar lines though not necessarily in such a formalised set of arrangements. In France, for example, in recent years government has come to rely more upon the informal briefing arrangements established at the Elysée (Presidential staff) and Matignon (Prime Ministerial staff), as Havas, formerly the official state news agency, developed an independent commercial role (Kuhn, 1995: 66–7). In Italy, while there is less reliance upon formal briefings provided by political press secretaries, precisely the same informal exchange relationships operate around the *palazzi del potere*, or 'power palaces', such as the Chamber of Deputies – 'the most important place for parliamentary and political news production in Italy' (Mancini, 1993: 35). Here, journalists spend a great deal of time discussing political interpretations with colleagues and mixing with politicians according to a mutually agreed set of informal rules, in much the same way as the Westminster Lobby. While formal press releases may be issued, 'topics which make the news are based more on confidential talk, information supplied by a political friend and gossip' (Mancini, 1993: 35). Relations between politicians and political correspondents in other Western European countries are structured in terms of very similar normative obligations (Esaiasson and Moring, 1994; Humphreys, 1996: 50).

Supporters of the lobby system, including Scammell (1995: 188–200), argue that without it, the volume of political information arriving in the public domain would be diminished and that, in any case, lobby practices are impossible to abolish given the mutual interdependence of media and political élites. Far better, such supporters insist, for there to be a formal lobby arrangement which at least ensures that all major news organisations are represented, than for there to be an informal system whereby only those journalists favoured by the political élite are the beneficiaries of off-the-record briefings. However, some critics of the lobby system, including academics, journalists and even one or two politicians, have called for either fundamental reform or absolute abolition (Williams, 1946; Cockerell et al., 1985; Hennesey and Bevins, 1990). In the mid-1980s both *The Guardian* and *The Independent* withdrew their political correspondents from lobby membership but these protests did not last very long. The main thrust of the critique is that the lobby system encourages journalists to become dependent upon political élites in a way which permits the latter to secure too great a degree of control over the way in which information arrives in the public domain. A system that is based so heavily upon non-attributable briefings means that the political élite are not held to account for the quality of the information they supply. One ex-member of the lobby describes it in the following terms: 'Ghastly . . . I loathed the lobby system, like a battery hen, like a Strasbourg goose, someone stuffs a bloody great tube down your neck and pumps you full of information' (Simpson, 1998: 4).

For Scammell, the power of particular press secretaries, such as Bernard Ingham, in manipulating the lobby has been exaggerated, while the Lobby itself has made an effort to make its workings more transparent in recent years. Even journalists most critical of lobby practices still welcome individual off-record briefings. At least the lobby system, Scammell argues, ensures that journalists working for less prestigious regional news organisations benefit from the information flows that inevitably emerge from within the political élite (1995: 193–200).

The problem with the debate set in these terms, between critics of the Lobby such as Hennesey and Simpson on the one hand, and its pragmatic supporters such as Scammell on the other, is that it looks at the Lobby only as a self-contained mechanism, and not as one institution within a wider, more complex system of information control. And yet, as we have seen, the state now affords government and political élites a variety of promotional and restrictive mechanisms with which to regulate the flows of information into the public domain. The lobby system needs to be placed in the context both of the rise of the 'public relations state' discussed above, and the range of formal mechanisms which the state can employ to regulate information dissemination. It is to the latter that we now turn.

Censorship and Mechanisms of Restrictive Control

The British state possesses a formidable machinery with which to restrict or suppress inconvenient information flows. Far from following a path towards liberalisation, if anything, the inclination of the British state has been towards the more authoritarian in recent decades. The Thatcher government introduced several legislative measures which significantly strengthened the power of the state in its dealings with journalists. Mrs Thatcher appeared to attach little importance to the concerns of civil rights campaigners. The pressure group Charter 88 was established in 1988 to campaign both for liberal constitutional reform and to reverse what appeared to be a growing authoritarianism in the state's orientation to the news media. However, those who hoped that a more liberal climate might emerge under subsequent administrations, particularly 'New Labour', have not had their expectations fulfilled.

Keane provides a list of ways in which the state intervenes to restrict the information flows supplying the news media in modern democracies, as follows: the use of a variety of 'emergency powers' to exert pre- or post-publication pressure upon journalists, including everything from bullying to arrest and document seizure; 'armed secrecy', including phone tapping and clandestine activities directed against media personnel; and the use of deliberate disinformation techniques, or 'lying', to shield the activity of government from public scrutiny (Keane, 1991: 94–107). Franklin (1994) draws our attention to the more subtle ways in which the British government can exert pressure in particular news sectors. The Home Secretary's role in the appointment of BBC governors is one example; the series of government-initiated reviews of the role of the BBC and its sources of funding provides another. While BBC producers and journalists are perhaps unlikely to consciously avoid contentious issues during the period of a review, more senior personnel within the organisation will be unlikely to wish to court controversy, or antagonise ministers (Franklin, 1994: 75–82).

All governments interfere in news production and, in doing so, most governments are likely to confuse national or defence concerns with their own political interests. However, their scope for doing so and the extent to which they are successful will depend upon the configuration of legislative arrangements and security mechanisms available to the state. While state structures in most Western societies are likely to share a number of familiar purposes to do with social control, ideological reproduction and the protection of powerful interests, there are also important differences in political culture and climate which produce distinctive approaches to questions concerning the relationship between government and news media (Gurevitch and Blumler, 1977). In Britain, successive governments have been reluctant to intervene in order to regulate the workings of media markets, or to interfere much in the processes of acquisition and merger that have allowed media conglomerates to grow, and yet British governments appear to have rather fewer qualms when it comes to exercising mechanisms of censorship to control inconvenient *content* from arriving in the public domain (Curran and Seaton, 1997: 298–332). In some other parts of Europe, at least it can be said that, historically, governments approached both forms of intervention with an equal determination.

The most well known formal mechanism within the British state's armoury is the notorious Official Secrets Act which was enacted in 1911 on the eve of the First World War. Ironically, the pretext for this measure was a national panic encouraged by the press about German spies roaming the country. Section 2 of the original Act made it illegal for anyone who had 'signed the Act' to pass on classified government information of *any* kind to another person, including journalists. The inclusive nature of the old Act meant that it could be applied to any government official, from a high-ranking civil servant in the Ministry of Defence to a museum keeper or postman. The draconian nature of the Act, allowing the government to prosecute in relation to any government information classified under its provision, from defence secrets to army laundry lists, was increasingly criticised by those who believed that it would be used by governments not to protect national security but prevent publication of what was politically embarrassing. In the period after 1945, despite the atmosphere of the Cold War, the number of prosecutions declined. The Act was even criticised by liberal sections of the judiciary. However, in the 1980s this trend was reversed. The Thatcher government, in particular, appeared to have few liberal scruples about using the full range of legislative and informal mechanisms available to exercise control over information flows to the public domain. Controversy over the Thatcher government's commitment to Cruise and Trident nuclear weapons and the outbreak of the Falklands War in 1982, accelerated this drive to control. A series of high-profile prosecutions under the Act ensued. Sarah Tisdall, a junior civil servant, was convicted and jailed in 1983 for leaking a memo which confirmed that American cruise missiles had arrived in the country much earlier than the government was prepared to admit. A year later, Clive Ponting, a senior civil servant, was acquited by a jury, after pleading a public interest defence, after he had leaked details that discredited Mrs Thatcher's public account of the events leading to the sinking of the Argentinian battleship, the *Belgrano*. Further setbacks, including the publication in Australia of *Spycatcher*, the highly embarrassing memoirs of a former MI5 agent, and huge public controversy when police raided the offices of BBC Scotland to seize the tapes of a programme due to be broadcast about the Zircon satellite, persuaded the Thatcher government that reform of the Act was necessary.

The reform which was enacted in 1989 was presented as a liberalising measure because it defined more precisely the nature of the information governed by the legislation. In practice, quite the opposite was the case. The terms of the Act remain so vague that almost any information which the government chooses can still be deemed relevant to the Act, and most significantly, the Act extends its application to *anyone* who handles information classified under its provisions. This means that not only government employees but members of the public and journalists can be imprisoned if they handle classified information. This is an extremely powerful deterrent for journalists contemplating the investigation of matters which the government might wish to keep out of the public domain. While prosecutions under the Act may be infrequent, its effect in terms of encouraging a more pernicious process of self-censorship within the newsroom should not be underestimated.

Mrs Thatcher's government also introduced the 1984 Police and Criminal Evidence Act (PACE). This included sections which significantly extended the power of the police to seize information in the hands of journalists. In the three years following its enactment, over 2000 applications were made by the police under its terms to search for and seize material held by journalists (Costigan, 1996: 231). The 1989 Prevention of Terrorism Act (PTA) and certain provisions in the 1997 Police Act further enhance the power of the police to seize material held by journalists and broadcasting organisations, while the Criminal Justice Act obliges journalists to divulge their sources to the police if it can be demonstrated that such information is relevant to a criminal investigation. In these circumstances, sources may think twice before spilling the beans to a journalist. Both Channel 4 and the American television network ABC have been subject to action under the PTA to compel journalists to hand information and material to the police. Recently the police have begun to use the PACE Act to secure access to the data files of Internet service providers and organisations undertaking electronic journalism (Campbell, 1998).

The combination of legislative measures at the disposal of the British state for the purposes of controlling information are formidable but one very recent development provides some grounds for more liberal optimism. An attempt by the Special Branch to compel two British newspapers to hand over material relating to allegations of security service incompetence made by David Shayler, a former MI6 officer, spectacularly failed. Having sought a judicial review, *The Observer* and *The Guardian* successfully argued that such police action was in breach of Article 10 of the European Convention on Human Rights. In an important ruling Lord Justice Judge concurred with the newspapers' case and, indeed, remarked that many of the rights claimed by the papers were already enshrined in English common law. According to one

Observer journalist this represented 'the most ringing defence of freedom of expression heard in an English courtroom for many years' (Bright, 2000: 18). Whether this really does represent a landmark ruling remains to be seen but it does serve to remind us that the state in late, modern capitalist societies is not a monolithic edifice and usually contains within its institutions both repressive and more progressive currents.

The defence- or 'D-notice' system is not enshrined in law but may be all the more important because of this. Once again, this mechanism emerged in 1912, just before the First World War, in order to manage the flow of military information to the public domain. After the Second World War, newspaper editors voluntarily agreed to continue with the system and it now not only applies to military material but to matters of 'domestic terrorism' too, which might cover anything from the war in Northern Ireland to information about animal rights activists or direct action environmental groups. A Cabinet sub-committee known as the Services Press and Broadcasting Committee, consisting of Ministry of Defence civil servants, representatives from the armed forces, security services and 'reliable' senior figures in journalism (usually newspaper and broadcasting senior editors), meets annually to review a set of standing D-notices, which provide guidance to editors as to what should or should not be revealed in news items. In the past, the secretary of the D-notice committee might write to individual editors to 'provide guidance' over particular stories. Editors are not under any formal or legal obligation to observe the guidance provided by the D-notice committee but it is understood that it would be most unwise not to do so. No other state in Western Europe has such an elaborate, informal system at its convenience for the purpose of regulating the flow of 'sensitive' information to the public domain. While PACE, the PTA and the other measures mentioned above are most potent in exerting control before publication, the laws of libel, sedition and blasphemy are, of course, available to members of the political élite and their deterrent effect should not be underestimated.

While newspapers have irritated and embarrassed British governments at regular intervals throughout their history, it has not been considered necessary for government to exercise a direct control within the production process. However, partly because in the period before the Second World War broadcasting appeared to be a qualitatively more powerful system of mass communication, the British state chose to exercise a much more direct degree of control at the stage of production. The British Broadcasting Corporation was established by charter as the monopoly supplier of radio and later television services in 1926. Although the BBC lost its monopoly in 1956, its charter continues to be subject to periodic review by Parliament and the framework within which the commercial terrestrial channels operate is also determined by government. Through first the Home Secretary and now the Minister for Culture, Media and Sport, the government oversees the appointment of governors of the BBC and determines the composition of the Independent Television Commission which regulates the commercial terrestrial sector. Ministers have considerable powers to intervene in exceptional circumstances in the content of programme making: the ban imposed between 1988 and 1994 on the real voices of those associated with paramilitary organisations in Northern Ireland was one example. The television coverage of Parliament itself is governed by very specific rules permitting 'talking head' and 'wide-angle' shots but forbidding shots panning across the chamber to reveal the number of empty seats. Even if an exceptional disturbance breaks out, the camera must resist the temptation to switch away from the Member addressing the chamber. Both the BBC and the independent television sector are required by law to maintain due balance and impartiality and to meet specific (though, following the 1990 Broadcasting Act, diluted) public service obligations in their programming. In short, if minded to, the British government has considerable powers to intervene both in strategic policy and appointment issues.

Freedom of Information, Privacy and Rights of Reply

The movement of the state towards a more authoritarian stance on issues of public information and the role of the news media was strongly associated with Thatcherism. Some supporters of 'New Labour' anticipated a new era and a change of emphasis on these issues with a change of government. So far, the evidence is mixed. In opposition, the 'New Labour' front-bench had strongly criticised the culture of secrecy and information manipulation associated with government. A new law modelled on the US Freedom of Information Act was promised to allow citizens, including journalists, access to government files and records. In office, 'New Labour' appears a little more nervous about relinquishing the controls previous governments exercised over information flows, and its first attempts to draft a Freedom of Information Act were widely condemned for weighting the provisions heavily in favour of the state rather than the public interest. Injunctions have been served on former security service personnel to prevent information about MI5 and MI6 reaching the public domain in cases highly reminiscent of the *Spycatcher* episode during Mrs Thatcher's period in office. While Tony Blair and other leading members of the Cabinet voted against Mrs Thatcher's toughening of the Official Secrets Act in 1989, in government 'New Labour' appears to find it rather more useful and rather less of a threat to civil liberties. While Labour was highly critical of the Conservative government's use of Public Interest Immunity Certificates ('gagging orders' signed by a government minister) to prevent government documents being used as evidence in court, and thereby entering the public domain, 'New Labour' in government has in a two-year period issued 50, compared to the 30 issued in the last two years of the Conservative government.[5] The promised Freedom of Information Act is about to be submitted to Parliament but is likely to disappoint those campaigning for significant liberalisation because it proposes to allow government huge areas of discretion regarding what information is released.

It is certainly the case that political élites in most European states have paused before granting entirely unfettered public access to government information and public documents. Nevertheless, the balance struck between public interest and national security (or political self-preservation) has frequently been secured in a way that affords at least some rights for journalists in securing access to government information. Indeed, in Austria, the Netherlands, Norway and Sweden there is an express constitutional right affording public access to government documents. The state has to establish a public interest case *not* to disclose. In France, a freedom of information act affords public access in principle but specifies particular exemptions, while in Germany the *Land* press laws afford right of access for journalists, together with a public interest defence for publishers. In Spain, freedom of information is implicit in the design of the constitution (Humphreys, 1996: 55). In the USA, perhaps the most formally open country in terms of public information, the 1966 Freedom of Information Act has been amended over the last two decades through a series of 'sunshine laws', so that the public now enjoys access not only to documents dealing with final policy decisions but even papers dealing with policy deliberations – something the British Civil Service has stoutly resisted. The catch is that, in practice, it often takes months or even years for the American government bureaucracies to yield up their secrets (McGuire, 1999).

Inevitably, in devising a regulatory framework for the circulation of information by news media, there is a difficulty in trying to untangle the public interest from the interests of the powerful. It may be in the public interest to support the right of a free press to expose the private wrong-doing of a member of a political élite, but is it in the public interest for the press to expose, for salacious purposes, the private life of an ordinary member of the public, or that of a show business personality? In the USA, the balance struck has been firmly on the libertarian side, with the news media declaring open season on the sex life of the President, not to mention many other prominent politicians, as well as show business stars and 'ordinary people' with 'extraordinary stories'. In Western Europe, the balance has largely been secured in a way that affords the ordinary citizen's privacy some measure of protection while, as we have seen, granting journalists the right to obtain information from governments providing it is in the public interest for such information to be released.

While a British journalist is trained to write every paragraph of copy with an eye to the libel laws, in the USA the First Amendment guarantees a freedom of the press which tends to minimise the threat to news organisations posed by libel actions. In the USA it is necessary to prove that a news organisation acted with malice or recklessness in publishing information before a libel case can succeed. In a number of European countries, more finely tuned regulatory frameworks governing individual privacy or a statutory right to reply, offer an alternative to libel laws which can easily become a gagging tool for the wealthy. In France, for example, legislation designed to protect the privacy of the individual against public exposure through the media, has meant that, for the most part, politicians can conduct affairs of business or the heart free from the doorstepping attention of the paparazzi. In addition, the 1881 law on press freedom does permit the state to take action against newspapers publishing items that might 'damage' the President or public authorities, but this power, while applied with regularity during the De Gaulle era, carries a political cost in terms of loss of public prestige which contemporary French political élites are a little more reluctant to pay. Less visible, informal pressures are politically preferable.

In most other Western European countries, there exists some kind of framework to regulate the relationship between news media and the private citizen. In Norway, privacy invasions are subject to criminal law; in the Netherlands and Austria these matters are subject to civil law; while in Sweden a press council regulates a voluntary system, which in contrast to Britain's voluntary Press Complaints Commission, is widely regarded as providing effective redress for citizens (Humphreys, 1996: 58). Germany, too, has a right to privacy supported by criminal law and all these countries provide either voluntary or legally enforceable 'rights of reply' for citizens who have suffered media misrepresentation.

In Germany, the political fall-out from the 1962 'Spiegal affair' had a long-term impact in the post-war period, making it significantly more difficult for powerful institutions or individuals to be seen seeking to impinge upon press freedom. Humphreys describes this episode as Germany's Magna Carta (1996: 49). The news magazine *Spiegal* had published details of planned NATO military manoeuvres in an article critical of West German defence policy. The government reacted by raiding the magazine's offices, seizing files, and charging both the author and publisher with high treason. However, the ensuing public outcry and support for the magazine provided by other newspapers eventually compelled the German government to climb down. In the aftermath of the Spiegal affair, the legislative protection afforded to newspapers in West Germany's press Acts was significantly strengthened (Humphreys, 1994: 72–4). In contrast, in Britain, as one British newspaper editor put it, 'Our libel laws are almost perfectly designed to protect a powerful person with a modest talent for the plausible lie' (Rusbridger, 1997). The huge costs of fighting a libel case through the English courts mean that it is pretty much a prerogative of the rich and powerful. Merely the threat of a libel action can sometimes be sufficient to deter publication: several journalists possessed information indicating that Robert Maxwell's financial empire was built on shaky foundations but found their news organisations reluctant to challenge such an enthusiastic issuer of writs. It required a huge stroke of luck for Rusbridger's own newspaper, *The Guardian*, to successfully defend itself against a potentially very expensive libel action, although the allegations it published concerning former Conservative Minister Jonathan Aitken proved to be entirely true. Aitken denied receiving illicit cash payments and perks, including a weekend in Paris, while in ministerial office. It was only because the hotel concerned went into receivership that the crucial invoices became available to the defence (Rusbridger, 1997). Aitken was later convicted for perjury.

In the United Kingdom, while the Press Complaints Commission can uphold complaints made by individuals about their treatment at the hands of the news media, there is neither a statutory nor a voluntary framework to provide either privacy protection or a right of reply. The Press Complaints Commission is funded by the newspaper industry and, while governments have exerted political pressure to encourage a more rigourous approach, critics suggest that it inevitably lacks the teeth that a statutory and independent body might possess.

In short, it is difficult not to draw the conclusion that in the United Kingdom, the arrangements made to protect ordinary people who lack the means to fight expensive libel actions are relatively weak in comparison to those in other Western European countries, while the state possesses a formidable arsenal of weapons for the purposes of restricting inconvenient information flows. However, this is not the whole story. A strong state with an extensive potential capacity to control news information flows does not necessarily imply that such restrictive controls are effective. For some commentators, Britain offers a paradox in that its state possesses some of the most elaborate mechanisms for exerting control over news information in the non-totalitarian world, and yet, in this climate, the culture of investigative journalism remains vigorous (Humphreys, 1996: 47). It is, after all, possible that the potential exercise of such power in itself stimulates a resistance among some journalists. Secondly, some commentators (for example, Seymour-Ure, 1991; Humphreys, 1996) point to the inefficiencies inherent within the apparatus of government. Political élites and the government departments they control are frequently 'leaky'. As we have seen, many 'leaks' are sanctioned by spin doctors or political élite members, but not all. Unauthorised leaks can sometimes emerge despite the best efforts of the state personnel responsible for policing information flows. Thirdly, we should not overlook the proliferation of new media channels which are more difficult for the state to exercise formal control over. Live radio phone-ins provide one example. Mrs Thatcher was once famously trapped by a housewife from Portsmouth during a live phone-in with the result that the inconsistencies in the official version of the sinking of the Argentinian battleship *Belgrano* were publicly exposed. More recently, train drivers and rail staff rang British radio news phone-ins to challenge Railtrack accounts of its safety procedures following two London rail disasters. Perhaps most importantly, the growth of the Internet has provided a means of news communication which nation states find almost impossible to restrict. Given the length of time it requires to obtain an injunction against a particular website and the speed at which information can be copied and circulated to a multitude of sites around the Net, beyond the reach of any particular nation state, the mechanisms of restrictive control exercised by particular governments can appear rather ineffective. The failure of the British government in 1999 to prevent a list of 117 MI6 agents being published on the Internet provides an obvious example of the way in which the globalisation of news communication systems can undermine nationally based controls.

Broadcasting: To Enforce, Persuade or Bully?

The occupational socialisation and formal training that journalists receive ensures that they pay close attention to the legal implications of copy as they construct it. Yet, as we have seen, even in Britain where the formal restrictive mechanisms are quite formidable, the state can never be entirely sure of its capacity to formally restrict or regulate information flows, and the political costs involved in being *seen* to attempt to formally control can be significant. Often, informal political pressure – critics might use the term bullying – has been a preferred option for political élites. In Britain this has particularly been the case with regard to broadcasting. The BBC is bound by its charter which is periodically reviewed and renewed by government, while the relevant minister can exercise formal influence through the appointment of governors, the determination of the funding mechanism (at present, the licence fee), and in rare cases of 'national security' through a power to intervene in programming. In the terrestrial commercial sector, government regulates on the basis of the legislative framework established by, for example, the 1990 Broadcasting Act. One of the regulatory obligations frequently laid upon broadcasting organisations is to maintain political balance and impartiality. In Britain both the BBC and the commercial television companies are obliged by law to do this; in Italy an official regulator, the Guarantor, has the power to fine television stations which fail to operate a system of normative self-regulation with regard to balance; in Germany a more decentralised system allows representation by political parties and 'socially significant groups' on regulatory boards with responsibility for balance and content on particular channels; while in France control and regulation were exercised directly by the state until 1982 when the *Haute Autorite de l'Audiovisuel* was established as a quasi-independent regulatory body (Humphreys, 1996; Statham, 1996).

While there is, therefore, a variety of formal relationships between state and broadcasting organisations in Europe, critics argue that it is often informal pressure that is more significant in allowing political élites to exercise influence over broadcasting. In Western democracies there are limits to the extent to which governments can be *seen* to exercise formal control over broadcasting without precipitating a political crisis. However, more subtle mechanisms may still be available. Britain is often cited as a prime example of how this may work, though there is plenty of evidence that similar political pressures are exerted in other parts of Europe (Statham, 1996: 520). The BBC was, from its creation in 1926, constituted as a public corporation, rather than a state-controlled broadcasting organisation, and this allowed it to operate with a certain 'relative autonomy'. Nevertheless, the BBC has certainly been subjected to periodic but intense informal pressures, particularly during periods of war or national crisis. This pressure can be exerted in a variety of ways which can range from quiet behind-scenes arm twisting, to veiled threats regarding future funding, and loud public controversies over 'bias' or a lack of 'patriotism' involving the press, as well as agitated back-bench MPs. During the

1980s, the Thatcher administration, back-bench Conservative MPs and their allies in the right-wing press mounted a series of attacks upon the BBC and, less frequently, the ITV companies, for what was regarded as disloyal or irresponsible coverage of the Falklands War, the war in Northern Ireland, and the issue of nuclear disarmament (Negrine, 1994:100–18). This created a climate in which it took a pretty tough-minded producer to approve coverage of topics that were likely to further enrage the government. Older studies of the internal culture of the BBC have shown that such political controversies have certainly induced a greater caution in the approach of editors and managers in the past (Schlesinger, 1978; Tracey, 1978). Things have not changed very much under New Labour. Only nine months into New Labour's first administration, Alistair Campbell was already voicing public criticisms of the BBC as 'over-staffed and dumbed down'; he complained loudly and publicly over the way in which certain ministers were interviewed on the BBC Radio 4 *Today* programme; and in a way highly reminiscent of the 1980s, a collection of ministers joined Campbell in roundly condemning television coverage of the NATO bombing in Serbia.[6] In particular, John Simpson, the BBC's correspondent in Belgrade, was denounced as undertaking propaganda work for the Serbian enemy because he filed a series of reports describing the destruction and consequences for civilians. In 1986, the BBC's Kate Adie was accused of doing exactly the same by the Conservative government when she reported the bombing of Gaddafi's palace in Lybia. When governments turn up the heat around news organisations they can be confident that while they may not succeed in preventing all unpalatable coverage, such informal political pressure will at least make news editors and managers think particularly carefully before approving news items that are likely to bring a fresh wave of political controversy.

Categories of Knowledge

A final theme needs to be briefly aired before this chapter is complete. We have explored the ways in which political élites and the personnel who command the state can deploy resources to promote particular information flows, and the strategies both formal and informal which they can employ to restrict or regulate information flows. In the previous chapter, a distinction was made between the instrumental and structural dimensions through which power flows. The strategies discussed so far in this chapter all depend, of course, upon intent or the conscious exercise of instrumental power. There is also a way in which information flows are opened up, channelled or terminated that is not associated with deliberate political decision-making or the instrumental strategies of particular political élites but, rather, concerns what Foucault has referred to as 'governmentality'. By this Foucault is referring to the ensemble of 'institutions, procedures, analyses . . . reflections . . . calculations and tactics' (1979a: 20) that characterise the overall approach or 'way of thinking' of a government. This is usually shaped by more than simply the vote motive and the day-to-day cut and thrust of party politics. The 'way of thinking' which characterises a government will, in part, reflect dominant ideological frameworks, ways of thinking about society, assumptions made about technical knowledge, visions of the 'good society', and so on, which are not necessarily consciously spelt out but nevertheless guide the general orientation of government. Such 'ways of thinking' will include partly taken-for-granted assumptions about what kinds of problems it is appropriate for governments to address.

During the 1930s, for example, a complex interplay of factors helped to set in motion a process which eventually culminated in the emergence of a new 'way of thinking' or form of 'governmentality' with the regard to industrial policy in the post-war period. These included, among others, the growing influence of Keynes, the optimism of modernism and a confidence in the use of technical knowledge to bring about social change, the political forces associated with mass unemployment, not to mention the necessity of interventionist planning during the Second World War. Drawing upon Foucault and Althusser, Emmison (1983) has argued that during this period a new discourse about 'the economy' emerged, a way of thinking and talking about the economy as a 'thing' or 'object' of government policy. Indeed, the category of 'industry' as a discourse was similarly constituted during the same period (Miller and Rose, 1993) and the evidence of the emergence of such discourses or forms of 'governmentality' is to be found in the establishment of new departments of state to deal with the various sectors of industry and economic activity, in the period before and after the war.

There is an important relationship between forms of 'governmentality' and the categories of knowledge which underpin the division of labour in national journalism. Newspapers began to appoint specialist labour and industrial correspondents at much the same time as the emergence of the form of governmentality that directed the state towards a more interventionist approach to economic and industrial issues. By 1937, it is clear that a coherent specialist group of labour and industrial correspondents working a news beat which included the bigger trade union headquarters, the TUC and key government industries was flourishing. While the revival of the labour movement and the outbreak of several high-profile industrial disputes, such as the 1937 'Coronation Bus Strike', helped to heighten the interest of news editors in labour and industrial copy, it was the professionalisation of information supply within departments of government that really permitted and stimulated the growth of industrial journalism because it ensured a *routine* supply of information likely to provide news copy (Manning, 1998, 1999). By 1935, all the ministries 'in daily contact with the mass of the public', had established information divisions with full-time press officers (Ogilvy-Webb, 1965). The Ministry of Labour, and to a lesser extent the departments dealing with such matters as transport, aviation and technology, generated significant information flows for industrial correspondents.

This, of course, does not in itself explain why news organisations developed an increased appetite for labour and industrial copy. The explanation is twofold. The increasing supply of industrial news copy emerging from government in the late 1930s and 1940s was a necessary but not sufficient condition. Certainly, because governments are powerful they are also newsworthy, which lends government information a saliency in the minds of news editors that other sources may lack, but more importantly, news editors and journalists, as much as members of political élites, are likely to be influenced by newly emerging discourses or forms of 'governmentality'. While there were many critics among both political élites and newspaper editors, the notion of a more active state, guided by technocratic principles, intervening in 'the economy' and 'industry' to promote growth and consensual industrial relations, began to chime with the mood of the times and thus become embedded as part of the 'world view' of many, if not all, editors and 'opinion leaders', as well as political élites. Attaching greater weight to labour and industrial news followed naturally, particularly as one consequence of the new consensualism was a greater proximity between government and 'the two sides of industry'. Equally, the renunciation of the post-war settlement, technocratic planning, and the interventionist state, with the arrival of the Thatcher administrations, had equally profound consequences for the division of labour in news journalism and the editorial perspectives of those exercising control within news organisations. A new scepticism about the value of consensual labour relations and industrial intervention was shared by Thatcher and the editors of several key newspapers; as the unions were politically marginalised and excluded from government, so labour and industrial correspondents found that their news editors were re-evaluating the value of their copy and their status in terms of the hierarchy of specialisms.

Since 1979 the fortunes of labour and industrial correspondents in national journalism have continued to decline. This was certainly, in part, a reflection of the emasculation of trade unions and the decline in news copy about 'strikes', but it was also a reflection of a rather deeper shift in the frameworks and assumptions underpinning the outlooks of many editors and managers within news organisations. The Thatcher administrations projected a new vision of the world in which trade unions played little or no part, 'industrial relations issues' were a thing of the past, and the role of government was to actively encourage the unleashing of market forces through society. This new 'way of thinking' had a powerful influence upon many editors, and not only those in charge of right-wing papers. Thatcher's re-modelling of the state (the winding down of interventionist activities at departments such as Employment and Trade, the selling of public utilities, and the refusal to involve government in industrial disputes) reinforced this shift in the outlook of editors and journalists because it produced a severe reduction in the flow of information from government departments to labour and industrial journalists. They were no longer able to offer such good copy to their editors. It seemed as if the important agendas had moved on and left labour and industrial journalists behind (Manning, 1998 and 1999). The drive towards de-recognition and de-unionisation in many news organisations, themselves, only served to reinforce further the 'received wisdom' that trade union stories were somehow out of date (Gall, 1997).

As is so often the case, one group's misfortune is another's opportunity. These crucial changes in the 'ways of thinking' promoted by government and the re-structuring of the architecture of the state which reflected these new assumptions, produced a rapid and dramatic improvement in the fortunes of other news specialisms. For example, financial journalists, consumer affairs and media correspondents all benefited; all found a growing appetite for their copy and a greater willingness on the part of news organisations to recruit additional staff to these desks, as editors 'sensed' that their readers were more interested in share issues and campaigns to privatise public utilities, than in shop-floor politics. The more nimble-footed among labour and industrial correspondents began to widen their briefs to include things such as the work of the new bodies established to regulate the newly privatised utilities.

Here, then, is an example of the way in which government, through its capacity to organise the architecture of the state, and the part it plays in promoting particular 'ways of thinking', can have an important impact upon the categories of knowledge that inform the specialisms in news journalism. There are other examples to illustrate the point. Education correspondents benefited from the growing importance of education as a political issue through the 1960s when Wilson's Labour administration placed comprehensivisation at the heart of its technocratic discourse of 'modernisation'. Medical correspondents have found their specialism broadened and redefined as 'health', reflecting the growing political importance not only of NHS reform but also of the wider change in public understanding of 'health issues', including complimentary treatments. The fortunes of some rise, the fortunes of others diminish, as the composition and political nature of government changes. This, of course, is not a one-way process. Governments do not usually get elected unless they can somehow harness the 'mood of the times' to their own agendas; the popular ideologies and outlooks of the day, which are themselves reflections of ordinary people's experiences and reactions to the political and economic environments in which they live and work, have a profound influence upon the various 'governmentalities' that emerge. Nevertheless, in understanding the way in which information flows between political élites and news organisations are opened up, sustained or suppressed, we need to be aware not only of the level of instrumental action through which political actors, spin doctors and journalists deliberately and consciously bargain, negotiate and struggle for the capacity to define meaning, but also of a distinct dimension through which rather deeper processes of ideological, political and economic change shift the discourses or 'ways of thinking' that sustain the key categories of knowledge in journalism.

Notes

1. Annual Accounts of the Central Office of Information, 1998/99.
2. See, for example, Bob Franklin's lettter to *The Guardian* newspaper, 4 June 1998.
3. 'Campbell Dodges Tory Fire with Special Job Clause', *The Guardian*, 2 April 1998.
4. 'Campbell Faces Commons Grilling', *The Guardian*, 31 March 1998.
5. Figures obtained from four departments of state by *The Guardian* using the Open Government Code of Practice, 20 July 1999, front page.
6. See, 'Whitehall in Spin over Lack of Public Support', *The Guardian*, 20 February 1998, p. 12. See also Hattersley (1998), Friedland (1998) and Dugdale (1999).

6 Considering the Powerful and the Politically Marginal

In Chapter 3 we examined the role of journalists in the production of news, and in Chapters 4 and 5 we looked at some of the most important external constraints upon the news production process, including the structure of ownership and control within which news organisations operate, the influence of the political élites and the ever present 'shadow' of the state. Now our attention turns to those organisations beyond government which for a variety of reasons seek to shape the production of news, or influence the news agenda, through their interaction with news journalists and news organisations. However, as we shall see, the culture, news values and practices of journalists described in Chapter 3, and the constraints or imperatives of the news environment described in Chapters 4 and 5, have a crucial bearing upon the kind of news opportunities that arise for such organisations.

Although this book aims to provide a comprehensive account of the news production process and the broad constraints that impinge upon the work of journalists, a central preoccupation is with the issue of *access* to the news media. As was suggested in Chapter 1, the degree of success enjoyed by organisations beyond government in presenting their interpretations and analyses in the public domain, via the news media, is both an important indicator of the health of the democratic process and one important guide to the distribution of power in society. In short, the health and vitality of the *public sphere* depends upon the success of a diverse range of political groups and organisations in submitting their arguments and evidence to the news media.

Why should groups or organisations beyond the formal boundaries of government wish to secure access to the news media? As we shall see, particular objectives and strategies are contingent upon the specific political circumstances in which groups find themselves. Nevertheless, the following are among the more common reasons for organisations beyond government to develop news media strategies. For organisations enjoying a realistic expectation that government ministers will take their policy agendas seriously, the news media can sometimes serve as a useful alternative channel to the conventional lobbying routes through Whitehall and the departments of state; for other organisations a more generalised appeal to 'public opinion' via the news media may assist in attempts to secure the attention of government for the first time. However, news media strategies can represent far more than merely a set of techniques through which organisations can talk to government by proxy. News media strategies are frequently employed to assist in recruitment campaigns for new members or to communicate messages to existing ones. Information may be placed in the public domain via the news media to undermine the position of a rival organisation or to weaken the position of an internal rival within the same organisation. The intended target audience for news media work may vary in size from 'the general public', a particular social group or segment of the public, an organisation's membership, a set of employers, the government, a particular minister, or a very particular group of two or three 'key' individual opinion leaders. As Miller and Williams comment, 'the complexity of public relations politics is in the myriad of agendas and audiences which the strategists may try to influence' (1998: 123).

Primary Definition and the Politically Marginal

All this may appear rather bewildering. In circumstances of such complexity, with such a diverse range of political objectives and media strategies, is it possible to discern any patterns or common features upon which to draw generalisations about the relationship between news sources and the process of news production? This chapter will try to demonstrate that it is, indeed, possible to determine some continuities and consistencies in a complex and rapidly changing field and that these are bound up with the capacity or inability of organisations to mobilise material and symbolic resources, and to exert control over the flows of information which may emerge from within their internal environments. In short, the long-term or overall success or failure of news media strategies is *usually* related to the structures of power in society and the unequal distribution of material and symbolic resources. This is precisely what is at stake in the debate over primary definition discussed in more detail in Chapter 1. For Hall and his colleagues, official news sources and those institutions closely associated with the capitalist state routinely set the terms of the news agenda, or primarily defined the news, not as a consequence of conspiracy but because news journalists, working within the constraints of a pressurised news production process, identified them as 'authoritative sources' or 'accredited witnesses' (Hall et al., 1978: 58). It was this proposition that provided the key to understanding the ideological nature of news coverage. News coverage privileged the interpretations of the powerful – particularly those articulating the interests of capital – not through conspiracy or conscious design but because the hierarchy of credibility perceived by journalists reflected the structures of power in society.

As we have seen, the critics of the concept in its original formulation suggest that it is flawed both theoretically and empirically; that it is too rigid in its attempt to distinguish those institutions with the capacity to primarily define the news from those without; that it rests upon an ahistorical model which cannot explain changes over time in the distribution of opportunities to primarily define; and that empirically it can be demonstrated that organisations such as non-official sources or marginal political groups can successfully set the agenda, or primarily define, in particular policy arenas (Schlesinger, 1990; Anderson, 1993; Miller and Williams, 1993; Schlesinger and Tumber, 1994). However, while Schlesinger is critical of the way in which 'structuralists' have employed the concept of primary definition, he also makes it clear that he does not advocate a pluralist model (see Chapters 1 and 2) in which power is understood as diffuse, and routine access to the news media is believed to be liberally distributed throughout society. On the contrary, he insists that an empirical exploration of the media opportunities available to a variety of potential news sources can still be conducted 'from within a theory of dominance' (1990: 63). Schlesinger is quite clear about the value of retaining a model that describes the ways in which powerfully dominant groups in society can exploit their control of material and symbolic resources to secure more frequent access to the news media. To develop this point a little further, such an investigation of the relative effectiveness of news media strategies of the politically marginal can enrich a 'theory of dominance' rather than undermine it. By exploring the ways in which the less powerful can mobilise their material and symbolic resources to secure *some* media opportunities, a great deal can be learnt both about the institutionalised disadvantages with which they have to contend and about the routine advantages enjoyed by the powerful.

Locating the Politically Marginal

Up to this point we have referred to those organisations beyond government but have not attempted a more precise description of those news sources that are not regarded as 'official'. If we abandon the distinction between 'primary' and 'secondary' definers of news altogether, as some critics wish, then perhaps it is not necessary to distinguish between the powerful and powerless in the competition between news sources. However, if we believe that inequalities in access to the news media between competing news sources *are* significant, then we need to devise a means of charting or describing the distribution of those inequalities. For Schlesinger, this is part of the empirical investigation to which the sociology of journalism should turn its attention (1990: 69). In other words, it is through actually investigating the politics of news agenda setting and the strategies employed by competing news sources, that we can chart the degrees of access enjoyed by particular organisations and groups.

While Schlesinger is critical of the rigidity he finds in Hall et al.'s model of primary definition, none the less his preference for the retention of a 'theory of dominance' does imply a structure with some kind of permanence – a structure that consistently grants to the powerful more opportunities for news interventions. The task then is to think through what such a structure might look like, and there is more than one body of literature to which we can turn. As described in Chapter 3, the sociology of journalism and news production has long distinguished between 'official' and 'non-official sources'.

Official sources, associated with the apparatus of government and the state, enjoy crucial advantages in the competition for news access because given the organisational pressures of ever tightening deadlines which journalists face and the expectation that they will deliver newsworthy copy, treating official sources as a routine first port of call becomes an organisational expedient (Sigal, 1973; Altheide and Johnson, 1980; Fishman, 1980; Cottle, 1993), while the exchanges between official sources and specialist correspondents encourages the development of a shared culture into which both parties are assimilated (Chibnall, 1977; Cockerall et al., 1984). All these studies assume a highly significant divide between the 'official' and the 'unofficial' but tell us little more about the possible differences *among* non-official sources. And yet, the relative advantages or disadvantages faced by non-official sources and their differing media strategies remained a neglected theme in media research because research approaches tended to suffer from a 'media-centrism' (Schlesinger, 1990: 62) which placed journalists and news organisations rather than their external sources in the forefront of the investigation (Ericson et al., 1989: 24). Both Shell and Greenpeace, for example, are formally unattached to government and are, in this respect, both unofficial sources, yet a 'theory of dominance' might suggest that the experience of each as a potential news source might be quite different. The concept of primary definition as originally formulated within an approach owing a large debt to Althusser and Gramsci (see Chapter 2) would certainly locate large transnational capitalist corporations, such as Shell, in a category shared with the other primary definers, rather than among the less powerful groups only successful in offering secondary definitions.

So we need a model that allows an exploration of the relative differences between non-official sources while, at the same time acknowledging the fundamental advantages enjoyed by official agencies. In Chapter 2 we noted that traditional pluralism and pressure group theory had generated a series of attempts to characterise the nature and activity of political organisations beyond government through the construction of typologies based upon distinctions between sectional interest groups and promotional groups (Potter, 1961: 25), or economic and non-economic organisations (Moran, 1983: 123). These approaches are helpful in that they prompt questions about the ways in which material and symbolic resources are used to achieve particular objectives, but we have noted that such typologies have largely been abandoned because they encourage an exclusive focus upon the resources and behaviour of pressure groups rather than the relationship between pressure groups and the state (Smith, 1993: 2). For our purposes they are less helpful because in assuming that pressure groups will identify the government and departments of state as their main campaigning targets, such typologies betray a 'state-centrism' which ignores the importance of the news media as a primary target in their own right (Manning, 1998: 14–15).

However, more recent models offer more potential. Grant (1990) distinguishes between 'insider groups' which enjoy regular access to government departments and 'outsiders' who are denied such privileged access. Grant further subdivides 'insider groups' into 'prisoners', dependent upon government for a variety of reasons, and 'low profile' and 'high profile' insiders. 'Low profile' groups are content to work behind the scenes in the committee rooms and corridors of government while 'high profile' groups are prepared to break cover by engaging with the news media to focus public attention upon their agendas. Grant acknowledges the dynamic and fluid nature of pressure group politics in a way not recognised in the earliest applications of the concept of primary definition. Thus, he subdivides 'outsiders' into 'potential insiders', 'outsiders by necessity' and 'ideological outsiders'. While the latter two kinds of pressure group will remain on the outside, either because they lack the political skills and understanding required to engage in dialogue with government or because they choose to remain on the outside for ideological reasons, Grant's typology acknowledges the possibility that some pressure groups can come in from the cold and secure a place on the inside with routine access to government. Though Grant does not discuss the implications for the politics of news sources, it is plausible to suggest that by moving 'inside', groups may secure a stronger position in the struggle to primarily define news events. By implication, other unfortunate groups may lose their insider status if the political climate changes, and with it opportunities to shape the process of primary definition.

Critics suggest that Grant's typology fails to pay sufficient attention to the ways in which successful or influential pressure groups can 'colonise' government departments in a way that fractures the coherence of the state. In other words, influential insider groups may develop alliances with civil servants, state personnel and even ministers, to form 'policy communities' that may compete against other departments of state and their 'policy communities' (Richardson and Jordan, 1985). For example, the National Farmers' Union enjoyed unrivalled access within the Ministry of Agriculture, Food and Fisheries (MAFF) for almost four decades after the Second World War (Self and Storing, 1974; Smith, 1991). For some observers of pressure politics, particularly those in the United States, such 'policy communities' are best described as 'iron triangles' involving elected political representatives, civil servants and pressure or policy groups (Peters, 1986). Each party in the triangular relationship is dependent upon the other two to secure policy objectives. The pressure group needs access to government but can 'deliver' members and lend political legitimacy to government proposals. Whether an 'iron triangle' or a 'policy community', the significant point for our purposes is the implication that particular pressure groups, or 'non-official sources' in the eyes of news media researchers, can develop relationships within departments of state, and with elected representatives, characterised by high degrees of stability and closure. In other words, such relations are more or less permanent and exclusive; access is closed to other potentially interested political groups and agencies. As we shall see later, this has significant implications for the study of the politics of news sources because 'closure' also suggests a capacity to control information flows to the outside world, including the news media, and perhaps a more powerful ability to primarily define.

In practice, power in policy-making may be rather more decentralised and disaggregated than the 'iron triangle' image suggests (Rhodes and Marsh, 1992: 8). For example, the National Farmers' Union was unable to prevent the opening up of the food and health policy arena to other significant interests despite its powerful presence within MAFF (Smith, 1991). The opening up or fragmentation of the food policy community also had important implications in terms of the politics of news sources and control of the information flows entering the public sphere. In a sense, when a policy community fragments, opportunities to primarily define the news are at least temporarily fragmented too. Certainly, with conflicting messages being generated by the main interest groups in the food and agricultural communities in the 1990s as food scares proliferated, news audiences grew increasingly sceptical of almost all the main interpretative frameworks on offer, frequently choosing instead to attempt to pick their way through the morass of information (Reilly, 1999).

Given the apparent diversity in degrees of stability and of openness or closure to be found within some of the policy sectors clustering around government, political theorists now frequently present a continuum that has 'policy communities' at one end and 'issue networks' at the other (Rhodes, 1988; Smith, 1993). While 'policy communities' are characterised by a limited number of members, a shared set of policy values among participants, a small number of decision-making centres, and a high degree of closure which may exclude Parliament as well as the press, the most extreme 'issue networks' will be characterised by a plurality of participants moving in and out of the network, multiple decision-making centres, and explicit conflict between those with competing policy objectives. Policy network theorists suggest that policy-making in most areas can be plotted somewhere along this continuum between the closed community and the issue network. It is tempting to suggest that the capacity to shape the news agenda and possibilities for the powerful to primarily define the news, are similarly distributed.

Using Pressure Group Theory in the Sociology of Journalism

How can these attempts to model the policy-making process help us to distinguish between the various non-official sources at work in seeking access to the news media? The authors of these pressure group typologies have been taken to task by some researchers in the sociology of journalism (perhaps rather unfairly in the case of Grant[1]) who insist that sharper distinctions have to be drawn between 'protest organisations that exist beyond the bounds of vested corporate and state influence' (Deacon, 1996: 178), such as Greenpeace International or organisations representing the economically marginalised, and corporate and professional sector organisations, representing industrial, financial, retail or professional interests. Deacon provides three reasons why these different groups should not be lumped together. First, corporate and professional organisations occupy a more prominent position in the eyes of journalists because 'economic and industrial issues are among the most perennially news-worthy topics for the media'. Secondly, some non-official organisations such as trade unions 'experience dissimilar levels of media hostility' because their working class affiliations 'tend to place them in opposition to the dominant value system'; and thirdly, journalists make distinctions between groups they see as axe grinders or 'advocates', and neutral experts or 'arbiters' (Deacon, 1996: 178–9). According to Deacon, voluntary or protest groups have a better chance of persuading journalists to understand them as 'arbiters' or experts in particular policy fields.

Undoubtedly Deacon is right in calling for 'more precision' in the analysis of non-official sources (1996: 180) but it is possible to tease out a number of promising suggestions from the literature which may help us to approach the variety of non-official news sources with the precision that Deacon requires. First, both the 'insider–outsider model' and the 'policy community–issue network' continuum suggest that normative obligations regulate interaction between participants within the policy-making process. Grant, for example, suggests that to maintain their inside access to government, 'insider groups' must be circumspect in their dealings with the mass media. Even 'high profile insiders' recognise that if they make life too uncomfortable for governments through public criticism and campaigning, they may pay the price by losing their insider status (Grant, 1990). Similarly, Rhodes argues that the opportunity to consult in policy-making is subject to accepting the 'rules of the game' (Rhodes, 1988). By implication also, those 'outsider' groups hoping to move inside have to be aware of the limitations this may place upon the kind of news media strategies they can employ. In the HIV/health policy arena, for example, the Terrence Higgins Trust is more circumspect than it might otherwise be in developing news media strategies because it knows that its relationship with central government (including some funding) might be endangered if it jeopardised its 'responsible' image (Miller and Williams, 1998: 127). As Grant notes, some groups may choose to remain 'ideological outsiders' because this may allow more scope for public campaigning, including more critical news media work. Extending Grant's typology a little further, some groups may lack not only the political skills and understanding to approach the lobbying process (his 'outsiders by necessity') but may also lack the cultural capital or media know-how to develop the sophisticated news media strategies required to enter the news media arena.

Secondly, following from this point, both the insider–outsider and policy network models imply that the media environment as well the formal political environment has to be taken into consideration when assessing the position of particular campaigning or policy groups. Indeed, it is possible that the kind of exchanges that occur between such groups and the news media play some part, at least, in forming the character of the policy network. Given the high degree of sensitivity to media coverage that characterises most modern political élites (Golding, 1990; Franklin, 1994), it is hardly contentious to suggest that considerations of actual or potential news media coverage must loom large in many policy dialogues and most participant strategies.

Thirdly, both Grant's approach and that of Rhodes, Smith and others, point to the importance of the exchange of resources. As Smith argues, '[Policy] Networks exist where there is some exchange of resources between state and groups. This can range from a limited exchange of information to the institutionalisation of a group in the policy process' (1993: 7). What is important here is the suggestion that information and perhaps other symbolic resources such as 'credibility' or 'legitimacy' can operate as commodities to be controlled, exchanged and exploited or 'cashed in'. For example, the capacity of the chemical industry to control and mobilise information that is of value to government but not readily accessible through alternative sources awards it very significant political advantages (Grant et al., 1988). Similarly, Smith argues that those with command over expertise and knowledge in the health policy sector can exploit this ownership of information to secure significant advantages in the policy process (1993: 10). Equally, both the capacity or inability to determine when and how information is placed in the public domain is one important way in which differences in power and position between non-official sources can be described. As we have already touched upon in Chapter 3 and as we shall discuss further in this chapter, the control and exchange of information and other symbolic resources plays a crucial part in the dealings between news sources and news organisations. One of the important characteristics of powerful institutions and organisations, those with a greater capacity to primarily define news agendas on a regular and routine basis, is the capacity to control the release of information in the overlapping but distinct political and media environments. This is hardly an original proposition in its own right (see, for example, Ericson et al., 1989). However, placed in the context of the debates over policy processes it acquires an enhanced significance. For example, one preoccupation of researchers employing the policy community/issue network model has to been to trace and explain shifts along the continuum from closed policy community to looser, more open issue network and vice versa. Placed in a fresh context such shifts can be understood to be intimately bound up with changes in the capacity to control information and release information that has an 'exchange value'. A closed policy community can maintain closure only so long as it can retain control of the flow of relevant information arriving in the political and media environments. The power of participants and the degree of closure weakens to the extent that participants fail to determine the timing and nature of information released into the public domain and the extent to which rival 'outsider' organisations can exert control over flows of information with value to, for example, journalists or other agencies in the public sphere.

A fourth point follows: non-official sources placed in a particularly disadvantaged position will be those who cannot control information flows from within their own organisations. As we shall see in the following chapter, those institutions such as trade unions whose organisational culture and history emphasises internal democracy, relative openness in decision-making but also political factionalism, are also inherently 'leaky'. Information pours out of such organisations in ways which can often undermine the strategy and power of their leaderships (Manning, 1998). In contrast, while whistle-blowers do sometimes emerge, one indication of the power of large corporations and other institutions, including NHS Trusts and even universities, is their relatively non-porous nature. Senior managers employ a variety of formal and informal sanctions to exert routine control over the flows of information that emerge from such organisations.

Fifthly, Hall et al. (1978: 57–8) argued that primary definers were regarded by journalists as authoritative sources, placed higher in a hierarchy of credibility than competing secondary definers, by virtue either of their position as political 'representatives of the people' or because of their 'recognised' knowledge as impartial experts. Subsequently, a large body of literature has evolved which explores the ways in which journalists attempt to distinguish the 'authoritative' from the less credible in various policy arenas including welfare policy (Golding and Middleton, 1982), environmental issues (Anderson, 1993), crime and justice (Schlesinger and Tumber, 1994), the debate over Mrs Thatcher's 'poll tax' (Deacon and Golding, 1994), community campaigning (Goldenberg, 1975) and AIDS (Williams and Miller, 1998). The possession of 'authority' or 'credibility' is, of course, intimately bound up with access to the dialogues of the policy process in and around government. To return to Grant's typology, 'insider groups' are more likely to be regarded as 'authoritative' by journalists precisely because they are believed to be closer to the decision-making process and privy to more information with currency than 'outsider groups'. And yet, acquiring an 'authoritative' status in news coverage can help organisations secure or preserve an insider position. In other words, the most politically adept organisations can exploit the interplay between political and media environments to strengthen their positions. On the other hand, many of Grant's 'outsiders' are doubly disadvantaged. Rather than exploit a virtuous interplay between political and media environments, they face an uneasy dilemma. As outsiders they lack the authority that would immediately command the attention of journalists. One option might be to resort to publicity stunts or the politics of the spectacular. These kinds of media strategies may generate short-term publicity but at the expense of infringing 'the rules of the game' which regulate the conduct of relations between groups and government, and at the risk of further political marginalisation, if the news media represent their behaviour as 'extremist' (Gitlin, 1980; Greenberg, 1985). Cultivated notoriety is a double-edged sword: it may purchase short-term access to the media but at the expense of long-term political marginalisation.

This is one of the great dilemmas faced by politically marginal non-official sources and it often involves making difficult decisions not only about media strategy and lobbying technique but about political agenda too. For the politically marginal, the cost of moving towards the 'inside' is not merely the selection of a less extravagant media strategy but sometimes a dilution of political objectives also. Thus, for example, even in the 1960s and early 1970s when the campaigns to address issues of poverty and social justice in Britain were at their highest tide, groups such as the Child Poverty Action Group and Shelter were careful to publicly and politically distance themselves from more militant campaigning groups, such as the National Claimants Union or the various squatting movements (Whitely and Winyard, 1983: 35–6; Seyd, 1975: 426). In this era, both the CPAG and Shelter integrated media strategy and political agenda to construct a 'moderate' voice of pressure politics in contrast to more 'extremist' political movements. Similarly, the new generation of environmentalist groups which emerged in the 1960s faced precisely the same dilemma. The use of high profile spectacular stunts generated publicity but encouraged both journalists and policy-makers to categorise them as irresponsible and lacking in authority (Greenberg, 1985). As we shall see, it has taken organisations such as Friends of the Earth and Greenpeace considerable effort in adjusting political and media strategies, in order to accumulate more political capital and this can still be very easily eroded (Rose, 1998).

For some, including Grant's 'outsiders by necessity', there is no choice. Their political agendas and membership characteristics may consign them to the margins in the eyes of policy-makers and journalists, whether they like it or not. Of course, these are likely to be the groups organised by the most politically marginalised, those placed in the most disadvantaged positions in terms of political and communication resources. In contrast, some forms of militancy carry far fewer penalties. The National Farmers' Union, as militant as any campaigning group in its promotion of the interests of the agricultural industry, enjoyed both a very secure political position on the inside and generous news media treatment for almost four decades in the post-war period, despite its uncompromising stance (Smith, 1991).

Decision-making and Non-decision-making: Adding Structure and Ideology to the Analysis

So, a number of fruitful lines of enquiry are suggested when the sociology of journalism is integrated with the literature on pressure groups and the policy process. However, much of the pressure group and policy process literature is based upon a case study approach, heavily indebted to pluralism in terms of theory and methodology (see Chapter 2). There are two familiar but important limitations associated with this approach. First, the behaviourist and empiricist assumptions underpinning traditional post-war pluralism encourage a conceptualisation of power in terms of manifest, observable decisions. Formal decision-making processes can be easily documented – even quantified – and therefore appeal to those social scientists who believe that research should engage only with the observable and measurable. However, there are other dimensions to the exercise of power which are less amenable to empirical observation but none the less highly significant. Power is also exercised when institutions cultivate an organisational culture that makes it difficult to raise particular issues in the first place. In other words, there is a dimension of non-decision-making in which the powerful can use institutional and cultural resources to discourage the emergence of certain issues into decision-making forums (Bachrach and Baratz, 1962; Lukes, 1974). This point is of great relevance for the study of the politics of news sources too. As suggested above, some of the most powerful news sources are those which can exert effective control over the flow of information entering particular arenas of the public sphere. Such power cannot easily be understood through empirical observation because it is not exerted in the domain of manifest decision-making, but rather through the organisational cultures of institutions which can discourage internal debate and which possess the *potential* to punish 'whistle-blowers'. Such institutions or organisations may also enjoy the power to discourage other institutions from supplying the news media with information. The prosperity of the network of financial institutions in the City depends as much upon mutually recognised restrictions over the release of financially sensitive information (Newman, 1984; Parsons, 1989), as it does upon the occasional 'leaks' which may send share prices up or down. The financial difficulties of the tycoon Robert Maxwell were widely known among both financial institutions and financial journalists long before he disappeared over the side of his boat, but no one chose to place details of his financial affairs in the news media. Equally, as we shall see in Chapter 7, news coverage of the recent salmonella and BSE food scares in Britain was crucially shaped by non-decision-making processes within the Ministry of Agriculture, Food and Fisheries (MAFF). In other words, in anticipation of the interests of farmers and food producers but not necessarily through any process of direct lobbying on the part of the latter, certain information possessed by MAFF was not released into the public domain at the height of the news coverage and only emerged several years later.[2] The mere prospect of tangling with large transnational corporations, such as MacDonalds, has been sufficient to persuade broadcasting organisations, newspapers, trade unions and even the Vegetarian Society to refrain from placing critical information in the public domain (Michie, 1998: 94). Following Bachrach and Baratz (1962) we can say that powerful news sources can exercise power along a dimension that refers to non-decision-making, while the less powerful may lack the institutional authority to exercise significant influence in this way.

An important caveat should be inserted at this point. The powerful may *attempt* to exert control over information flows either through explicit decision-making or by fostering an institutional culture that discourages political communication, but this process may involve negotiation and compromise. Both policy and news agendas may evolve through a complex of negotiations involving powerful and less powerful forces. The Health Education Authority, for example, might sometimes encourage journalists to pursue themes or lines of enquiry by putting them in touch with non-official sources, if it felt that its relationship with government proscribed a media initiative in its own right (Miller and Williams, 1998: 128), while similarly at the Home Office civil servants might sometimes unofficially assist pressure groups to develop media campaigns against criminal justice policies which were officially embraced but which were not welcomed within the department (Schlesinger and Tumber,

1994: 72). The negotiated character of many political and news media agendas has to be acknowledged in any theoretical framework. What this implies, of course, is that 'success' or 'influence' in applying media strategies cannot simply be measured in terms of the public profile of the most visible groups (Miller and Williams, 1998: 127). What may appear in print may conceal a complexity of behind-the-scenes exchanges in information among interested sources, both official and unofficial.

The second limitation in the conceptualisation of power associated with traditional pluralism follows from the first. An emphasis upon observable decision-making within a case study approach encourages a neglect of structure, ideology and the interests of the state, as the context in which decision- or non-decision-making occurs (Smith, 1993: 27). This is what Lukes (1974) has called 'the third dimension of power' underpinning decision-making and non-decision-making. Crenson's 'classic' study of the 'un-politics of air pollution' (1971) makes this point very well. In a 'one company town', dependent upon a single large steel mill for its prosperity, a powerful US steel corporation exerted influence over the news agenda simply through its presence in the community. Too many interests depended upon the company for discussion of issues potentially damaging to its interests even to surface in public debate, let alone appear in the pages of the local paper. It was the structural position of the corporation within the community and its associated ideological power, rather than any specific decision-making process, which explained its capacity to shape news agendas.

At a broader level, one cannot begin to understand the power of the leading financial institutions within the United Kingdom without considering the history of the City and its role in financing and administering the British Empire. It is this which explains why the City enjoys such strategic economic power and why the British government is compelled to acknowledge its interests (Moran, 1984; Smith, 1993: 4). By the same token, the 'legitimacy' of the role of the City in government and the 'inevitability' of the City as a key feature of the economic landscape are taken for granted as axiomatic in much news journalism (Hutton, 1996: 23). As Smith argues, the greatest difficulty for traditional pluralism originates from its attempt to 'understand business as just another interest group' when, in fact, the material and symbolic resources at the disposal of capital and the functional position business occupies in providing employment for people and wealth for the economy allows its representatives to 'establish institutionalised relations with government which are more intense, of greater duration and of a higher quality than those of most other groups' (Smith, 1993: 27). Such relations also confer advantages in the politics of news sources – access to information of value to journalists, news significance acquired through proximity to government, symbolic resources such as 'respectability', and so on.

Approaches within the policy and pressure group literature which still employ a pluralist grounded methodology, focusing upon actors and explicit decision without considering structured inequalities in the distribution of material and symbolic resources, are likely to seriously underestimate the full significance of media work in the exercise of power. Simply asking members of political élites, for example, whether or not media coverage has strongly influenced their decision-making is unlikely to yield profound results. Not surprisingly, most say 'no' (Kingdon, 1984). Similarly, noting the dissatisfaction of the Chemical Industries Association with news coverage of industrial issues is not an adequate investigation of the 'ideological pull' which capital may exert in news production, as Grant appears to believe, nor is it sufficient evidence to refute Marxist analyses of the role of the news media (Grant, 1987: 31–5).

Travelling from a rather different theoretical starting point, writers drawing upon the ideas of Foucault also point to the importance of government and the ideological environment. Again, power is understood as not being amenable to investigation in the terms proposed by traditional pluralism. For example, writers such as Emmison (1983) and Miller and Rose (1993) explore the ways in which particular discourses of government have promoted particular modes of government intervention. As we saw at the end of Chapter 5, as the discourses of 'economy' and 'industry' emerged in the period before the Second World War, so too did particular power relations associated with intervention and regulation. In turn, the 'industry' and 'economic' news beats for national news journalism grew, bringing with them particular opportunities for new sources (Manning, 1999). The critical shifts in 'governmentality', to use Foucault's terminology (1979a), from interventionist to neo-liberal during the Thatcher administration, coincided with a decline in certain news beats (e.g. industrial) and the rise of others (e.g. financial). Such changes bring about very important shifts in the range of opportunities available to particular non-official or marginal groups for news media work.

Finally, then, we can say that the powerful may exercise influence in the news encoding process, not merely at the moment when explicit decisions are made about the release information into the public sphere (dimension one) but also continually, as the non-decision-making 'silent agenda setting' process ensures that certain potential information flows never emerge (dimension two). By virtue of history and structural location, powerful organisations may display an ideological 'gravitational pull' which is reflected in news coverage and underpins the working practices of journalists (dimension three). In contrast, politically marginal groups are disadvantaged in terms of each of these three dimensions of power. This is not to suggest that politically marginal groups cannot secure some significant successes. As we shall see, the interaction between news sources and news organisations involves a process of negotiation, bluff and bargaining, the outcome of which can never be predicted with absolute certainty. Skill and experience in mobilising resources and applying news media strategies can make a difference, even for the most marginalised groups. Nevertheless, the broad contours of the division between the powerful and the marginal in the politics of news sources are described in these terms.

Figure 6.1 provides a graphical summary of the theoretical framework employed to explore the diversity of positions that non-official news sources find themselves in. A continuum between 'insiders' and the most politically

INSIDER GROUPS	POLITICALLY MARGINAL GROUPS
←...... Degrees of political marginalisation ......→	
More political and cultural capital	Less political and cultural capital
'Quiet dialogue with government' as option	Publicity and the 'politics of spectacle' as main option
News interest associated with insider status	News interest associated with 'notoriety'
Opportunities to exploit the virtuous interaction between political and media environments	Fewer such opportunities
'Authority'/higher position in hierarchy of credibility	Less 'authority'/lower position in hierarchy of credibility
Opportunities to shape processes of primary definition	Fewer such opportunities
Possession of information with 'exchange value' for correspondents	Lack of information with 'exchange value' for correspondents
Greater ability to control information flows emerging from within organisation	Inability to control information emerging from within
Greater 'bargaining power' when dealing with journalists	Less bargaining power when dealing with journalists
Concentration of material and resources	Limited access to material and symbolic resources
Capacity to influence decision-making and non-decision-making processes in other organisations by virtue of structural position and capacity to mobilise material and symbolic resources	Disadvantaged structural position. Insufficient command over material and symbolic resources to influence decision/non-decision-making

CONTEXT FOR THE POLITICS OF NEWS SOURCES PROVIDED BY:

NEWS PRODUCTION PROCESSES

SYMBOLIC ENVIRONMENT (IDEOLOGICAL CLIMATE)

INEQUALITIES IN THE DISTRIBUTION OF MATERIAL AND SYMBOLIC RESOURCES

POLITICAL AND ECONOMIC ENVIRONMENT

FIGURE 6.1 *Non-official sources: degrees of political marginalisation and media power*

marginalised suggests two important points. First, that there is not a simple dichotomous division between the powerful and the powerless but rather a variety of positions for non-official sources along the continuum, determined by their command over the resources and opportunities identified. Secondly, that the politics of news sources is dynamic; the positions of particular non-official sources may change over time. As their command over the resources and opportunities identified grows or diminishes, so their position on the continuum between the more powerful and the politically marginalised will change. However, Fig. 6.1 also emphasises that the situation is by no means entirely fluid either. The processes of news production, and the ideological structures and political–economic forces which provide the context both for political activity and media representation, ensure that the politics of news sources is also characterised by relative stability. Politically marginal news sources may struggle to improve their position through effective news media work and the skilful mobilisation of resources but their prospects of moving further along the continuum towards the powerful may be limited and their command of an improved position always precarious. In contrast, powerful non-official news sources, by virtue of their position in relation to ideological structures and political economic forces are far more (although never entirely) secure.

The Skills of News Media Work

In Chapter 3 the production of news was discussed from the journalists' perspective. From that discussion it is possible to deduce what some of the essential elements in successful news media work for non-official sources are likely to be. As every press officer will confirm, effective news media work starts with an understanding of how the diverse news media operate and what their distinct needs may be. As we have seen, news journalism is a pressurised occupation. Particularly for those staff working in daily, regional or local news, a combination of ever advancing deadlines and growing workloads means that easy access to sources for information and comment is vitally important. An effective press officer working for either official or non-official news sources will make sure that all key journalists have instant 24-hour access to a press officer or representative of their organisation. For large organisations this can be arranged on a rota basis. The incoming New Labour government reportedly caused consternation among some government information officers by establishing new rostas for Civil Service press officers, with more evening and weekend duties. For smaller organisations, with limited resources and staffing, an emphasis upon availability may mean releasing home telephone numbers and being prepared to respond to press enquiries at any time of the day or night and every week-end. It also means being well briefed, anticipating likely lines of enquiry and ensuring that the organisation has at least some kind of comment to make. As one trade union press officer puts it: 'So the key to it is professionalism and being there right at the beginning, knowing what you want to say and knowing what snags you may face . . . what questions journalists may ask, the things the *Sun* may write about, etc.'[3]

Charlie Whelan who, until his high profile departure in February 1999, was employed by the Chancellor of the Exchequer to handle media work, secured this position on the basis of a dazzling career as a trade union press officer. Armed with a mobile phone and a cheerful willingness to be contacted at any time of the day or night, Charlie Whelan rose from the relative obscurity of the AEU office at Ford, Dagenham, to become one of the most well-regarded union press officers on the labour and industrial beat. Describing this earlier career, one labour correspondent commented: 'Charlie's brilliant . . . he's switched on to what we need and most of the time he can provide an immediate answer. Bill Jordan and Gavin Laird [President and General Secretary of the AEU] trust him, so there's no wasting time.'[4] Convincing journalists that one knows the mind of the key decision-makers within the organisation and, in that sense, can speak with 'authority' is a huge advantage. These 'bread and butter' points hold for any press and media work on behalf of non-official sources, from groups campaigning within the 'poverty lobby' (Seyd, 1976; Wilson, 1984), to community activism (Goldenberg, 1975), health campaigning (Wallack et al., 1993), and environmentalism (Rose, 1998).

A second cardinal point is to distinguish between types of news media, recognising the opportunities and limitations of each. Given the ideological and circulation-driven inclinations of the tabloid press in Britain, it would be foolish to approach *The Guardian* and the *Sun* in precisely the same way. For trade union press officers, a degree of circumspection was sensible when dealing with enquiries from the *Sun*. As one union press officer commented:

> We have an A service and a B service . . . the B service is what the *Sun* get. They don't contact us to confirm a story, they only contact us to get some kind of quote that will land the union in the shit. They're never looking for positive stories, so we deal with them honestly and give them anything they want, we send them faxes, press releases, etc., but we don't give them anything else. I mean we don't phone the *Sun* industrial editor and say 'check that – you might find something interesting in that.'[5]

Similarly, the Terence Higgins Trust will deal with the *Sun*'s enquiries but will resist any proactive news media work with them (Miller and Williams, 1998: 130). Most non-official sources will categorise journalists into 'sympathetic' or 'hostile' categories on the basis of experience and their knowledge of the politics within particular issue arenas (for example, Wilson, 1984: 80–90; Miller and Williams, 1998: 131). Similarly, the more effective non-official news sources will be aware of the opportunities that local contexts can generate for securing access to regional and local media. Thus, during the campaign against the 'poll tax' a more diverse range of dissenting voices (trade unionists, voluntary organisations, anti-poll tax federations, etc.) were consistently prominent in local, as opposed to national, coverage (Deacon and Golding, 1994: 142). Trade union press officers often target local media with information concerning, for example, local job losses or hospital closures (Manning, 1998: 141–3) and environmental groups often score significant success by wrapping environmental themes around local issues (Anderson, 1997: 132).

Two problems occur in using local media. First, news sources cannot depend upon any shared contextual understanding when briefing local reporters: few local news media organisations, either in print or broadcasting, can afford to employ correspondents with specialist knowledge of particular policy areas. Secondly, the diversity of local news media and their close relationships to particular localities, are threatened by a combination of changes in ownership and marketing strategies, the declining vitality of local government as more power is transferred to central government, and the arrival of new technologies with new production routines (Franklin and Murphy, 1991). This may mean that local news media prove less fertile for non-official or politically marginal sources in coming years.

Equally important is an understanding of the relationship between message, media and target audience; in other words, the set of relationships which marketing experts would describe as the 'marketing mix'. If government ministers and key policy-makers are the key targets for messages about resource allocation, then quality newspapers provide an obvious channel (Miller and Williams, 1998: 129). Union press officers may wish to 'reach' employers, business élites or other trade union leaders, in which case the *Financial Times* often provides a useful medium (Manning, 1998: 135). Greenpeace, in contrast, with an appetite for visual stunts and an investment in sophisticated video production technology, consistently targets popular television news with the aim of communicating to the broadest possible audience (Rose, 1998).

It is one thing to understand which news media to target; it is quite another to have the ability to create copy that will be of interest to journalists. Thus, the textbook account of public relations will stress the importance of grasping the news values which guide the interests and selection criteria of particular journalists. Undoubtedly, this is an important aspect of news media work for non-official sources. One trade union press officer commented: 'I don't just release any old story because somebody wants me to. I will judge what is the story which is going to be used [by the news media], if its going to be used we go . . . and ninety nine times out of a hundred I'm right.'[6] For non-official sources with complicated political or technical points to make, there is a craft in translating such points into popular journalism: 'We understand what national journalists want because that's our background, too, and we're in a position to angle our material for them.'[7]

Media and communication work, or public relations broadly defined, has become a large industry in its own right and many of the larger non-official news sources can afford to employ professional communicators, recruited either from journalism or from more specialist corporate communications backgrounds. This can sometimes generate an inner tension within news source organisations. In my own study of trade union press officers I found important differences between those recruited from backgrounds in journalism or corporate communications, and those recruited from within the trade union movement. Those coming from a background in professional communications were more likely to prioritise journalistic criteria in the communication process and to justify their work through appeals to professionalism or concepts drawn from communication theory. In contrast, those recruited from within trade union organisations often attached rather more importance to the values and political principles of their trade union backgrounds. This was a difference of emphasis rather than distinct philosophy in the main: former journalists frequently worked for trade unions because of their political commitments and most union press officers recruited from within the ranks recognised the need to operate in a 'professional way'. Nevertheless, in many politically marginal organisations there is a potential tension between the desire to unfold a politically coherent argument, and the need to engage with the requirements of the news media and fashion 'stories' in terms of conventional news values and news frames. Within the environmentalist organisations, for example, there have been tensions between those committed to greater use of the news media, and those activists determined that this should not be at the cost of diluting direct action campaigning (Greenberg, 1985: 353; Gamson and Wolfsfeld, 1993), and similar dilemmas face organisations campaigning over gay rights (Miller and Williams, 1998: 130). For a 'modernising' trade union media officer, from a background in corporate communications, traditional trade union culture represented an impediment to effective communication. The task was to:

> . . . cut through the way trade unions sometimes speak. Trade union speak is a language all of its own, and part of our job is to make sure it's turned into a language people understand when they're eating their tea in front of the telly. Some of us don't have the twenty years experience [of trade unionism] but what we do have are the skills to make that twenty years mean something.[8]

Trade union officers recruited from within the ranks of the labour movement were sometimes a little more hesitant before subordinating union custom and culture to the demands of the news media, although one union press officer took a rather iconoclastic view of both traditional trade unionism and the professional 'expertise' of the communication industry. When I asked him how he translated trade union issues into popular journalism, he simply said, 'It's easy. My old granny could do it! I just write pieces as I would like to read them in the newspaper!'[9] This was Charlie Whelan, interviewed while still working as press officer at the Amalgamated Union of Engineering Workers, and before he was appointed to his position as media spokesman for the Chancellor of Exchequer. This rather glosses over the potential tension that may exist between the political interpretations developed by politically marginal groups and the news media strategies which they select. For example, trade unionists may believe that in order to understand the meaning of industrial disputes, they must be placed in the context of complex histories of institutional tensions or even analyses that place deeper structural relations between capital and labour in the foreground. This kind of approach will hardly generate the kind of copy that journalists will happily fashion into 'stories'. Rather, an approach which emphasises the immediacy of events and 'individualises' industrial disputes in terms of personalities and the drama of conflict is more likely to strike a chord with correspondents. Equally, environmentalist groups may want to point to the complex and long-term socio-economic processes underpinning 'natural disasters' but mainstream news values encourage journalists to focus upon immediacy, drama and human interest angles. The temptation for politically marginal groups is to find human interest angles associated with their agendas for journalists to work on, and to present arguments in individualised ways with sensational or dramatic aspects. Yet, the danger is that the coherence of the political analysis is lost in the effort to secure media access. This is the problem of news media incorporation – something we shall return to later in this chapter and in Chapter 7.

What the Public Relations Model Leaves Out

Much of what has been said so far could be gleaned from any of the 'how to do it' public relations textbooks currently on the market. However, textbook accounts of public relations are usually seriously flawed for two reasons. First, they present an over-mechanical account of the public relations process which ignores the crucial *social* dimension of the relationship between news sources and news media; a relationship based upon negotiation and the exchange of information often within the terms of an implicitly agreed normative framework. Secondly, textbook accounts usually gloss over the significance of inequalities in the possession and control of symbolic and material communicative resources. Even the effective application of 'textbook' public relations procedures is dependent upon the possession of sufficient resources to make press officers or media representatives easily accessible to enquiring journalists.

In part, the miners lost the news media war during the 1984 Coal Strike because, despite the best efforts of Arthur Scargill on television, the Coal Board and the government simply out-gunned the National Union of Mineworkers. Leaving aside government information officers, the Coal Board hired more than 20 press officers during the strike to ensure that journalists could easily obtain those notorious figures on numbers abandoning the strike and returning to work (Jones, 1986). In its attempt to rebut those figures, the NUM depended upon one officer who had to combine media work with a number of other responsibilities, and the telegenic qualities of its President. Of course, the reasons why the NUM lost both the propaganda war and the strike go deeper than this (Winterton and Winterton, 1989; Milne, 1994).

Nevertheless, it provides one example of the way in which corporate wealth can be translated into 'PR clout'. A more recent illustration is provided in Miller and Williams' account of the competition between news sources in the 'AIDS news' arena: while the Department of Health regularly allocated over £1 million to its public relations activities in the late 1980s and early 1990s, the Terence Higgins Trust formally spent nothing and in practice depended upon the best efforts of one or two staff or volunteers (1998: 124–6).

The command of significant communication resources is not, of course, entirely monopolised by the corporate sector. Greenpeace, for example, runs over 30 offices around the world, and Greenpeace Communications, a division of Greenpeace International based in Amsterdam, controls a sophisticated television and video production studio, complete with its own film archive and the very latest in editing suites, not to mention a digital sound studio (Anderson, 1997: 85). The Greenpeace press desk operates around the clock. Indeed, some argue that the rapid rate of innovation in communication technology will reduce the costs of entry to regional and even global communications systems for dissenting groups and non-governmental organisations (Dowmunt, 1993; Sreberny-Mohammadi and Mohammadi, 1994). However, it remains the case that command over material resources is a huge advantage in the fight to win access to the news media and secure a preferred agenda. As Miller and Williams comment: 'Access to a secure financial base is a key resource for any organisation which wants to pursue particular aims and affects their ability to allocate separate budgets to campaigning or information work. . . . The lack of financial resources imposes clear limits on the kinds of informational strategies it is possible to launch' (1998: 124).

Orthodox textbook accounts of public relations usually devote little space to the distribution of symbolic resources either, other than to refer readers to examples of 'corporate branding' and related marketing processes. Symbolic resources include a wide variety of non-material resources which may be exploited to enhance the impact of communication but, crucially for the purposes of this discussion, they can specifically assist non-official sources in their efforts to negotiate with journalists and gain access to news coverage. Greenpeace, for example, have exploited the British public's long-standing sympathy for animals, most famously in its use of whales and seals in a variety of advertisements and publicity campaigns. At critical times, the resonances associated with such symbols can be used to convince journalists to follow particular stories, such as the 'seal plague' of the late 1980s (Anderson, 1993).

According to Gamson and Modigliani (1989), shrewdly constructed news media strategies can tap into deeply entrenched cultural themes or 'symbolic packages' which are established as part of contemporary folklore, or what Barthes would describe as modern 'myths' (Barthes, 1973). As Gamson and Modigliani show, nuclear power can be represented in terms of several symbolic packages, each with quite distinct but powerful sets of cultural resonances. A symbolic package based around the theme of 'progress' invited the public to understand nuclear power in the context of familiar themes of scientific advances, human progress, technological benefits, and so on. Anti-nuclear protesters offered several alternative symbolic packages constructed around equally familiar cultural themes, including the dangers of an irresponsible or unaccountable science (a theme perhaps first explored by Mary Shelley), the need for 'natural solutions' to modern problems, and the remoteness of corporate power. Similarly, trade unions organising ambulance drivers were able to exploit the cultural resonances associated with the popular public image of nurses – selfless compassion, caring devotion, etc. – so that in the words of one union press officer, ambulance workers involved in a protracted dispute were represented in some newspapers as 'angels with blue flashing lights' and 'mercy men' rather than 'militant' trade unionists (Manning, 1998: 328).

Opportunities to mobilise appropriate symbolic packages are valuable in themselves. However, they can be doubly useful because they encourage news media interest and suggest potential news frames to journalists which may generate positive coverage. As Gamson and Modigliani suggest, 'A package's resonances, we argue, facilitate the work of sponsors [news sources] by tuning the ears of journalists to its symbolism. They add prominence to packages by amplifying the effect of sponsor activities and media practices' (1989: 6). In other words, in their daily work in constructing and processing news copy, journalists have to be sensitive to issues or events which chime with particular beliefs and themes embedded in popular culture. News sources which can wrap their agendas or interpretations around such themes are more likely to attract their interest.

However, one weakness in Gamson and Modigliani's analysis is that questions about the relationship between symbolic packages and power are largely left unexplored. For Gamson and Modigliani, the shifting dominance of particular symbolic packages is attributed entirely to 'a combination of cultural resonances, sponsor activities, and a successful fit with media norms and practices' (1989: 9). Does this mean that one sponsor's activities or media strategies stand just as good a chance as any other, providing there is media fit and appropriate cultural resonances? This overlooks the point that certain cultural resonances have a stronger ideological significance than others; some have a history in popular culture as old as modernity while others are rather more ephemeral. We know, for example, that racist and patriarchal ideologies have a long and deep-rooted history in Western culture; that cultural themes which distinguish the 'deserving' from the 'undeserving' poor (Golding and Middleton, 1982), the 'militant minority' from the 'moderate majority' (Thompson, 1970), or 'wild hooligans' from 'law abiding citizens' (Pearson, 1983) provide ideological motifs, intimately connected with the interests of the powerful and the maintenance of the status quo. Gamson and Modigliani, then, are quite right in identifying symbolic packages as resources which offer opportunities for 'sponsor activity' but we need to remember that such symbolic packages are not all equivalent – some have greater durability and ideological power than others – and that 'sponsors' do not enjoy equality of opportunity in their competitive efforts to mobilise them. The devil may not have all the best tunes but governments, corporations and powerful agencies can frequently 'play' some of the most resonant cultural themes to their advantage.

Consideration of the relationship between symbolic packages and power leads us back to the issue of 'authority' and the hierarchy of credibility. The association of particular symbolic packages with certain news sources has important implications for the way in which journalists assess news source credibility. News sources which articulate symbolic packages constructed around technical arguments may strengthen their credibility in the eyes of journalists and specialist correspondents if the data and arguments are judged reliable. While Friends of the Earth have engaged in plenty of publicity stunts over the years, they have also attempted to support their press and media work with detailed technical arguments and environmental research (Greenberg, 1985). Similarly, in its heyday in England during the late 1960s and early 1970s, the Child Poverty Action Group acquired a reputation for its technical expertise regarding social policy and the benefit system – something that distinguished it somewhat from Shelter. At that time, Shelter emphasised rather more the 'politics of spectacle', based upon the director Des Wilson's barnstorming campaigns and publicity stunts (Seyd, 1975, 1976).

The possession of expertise helps news sources to rise up the hierarchy of credibility in the eyes of journalists and helps to ensure that they become regular points of contact on specialist correspondents' beats. Journalists remain at most times sceptical of news sources which they regard as 'axe grinders' or 'advocates' to use Deacon and Golding's phrase (1994: 15). For example, one campaigner in the 'AIDS news' arena explained that while his professional status as a doctor lent credibility to his work as a news source in the eyes of journalists, he felt this had subsequently been undermined by his identification by journalists as 'slightly liberal' (Miller and Williams, 1998: 126). However, journalists often need to acquire technical information rapidly and despite their expectation that 'advocates' may put a spin upon information, they may turn to them not only for 'comment' but also background knowledge, provided that the symbolic packages, or discourses, associated with such news sources and the political strategies employed by them are not perceived to be 'extremist' or 'outrageous'. From the journalists' perspective, a judgement has to be made between trust or suspicion at each stage in the process of interaction with sources (Mancini, 1993). Sources which can represent themselves as 'trustworthy' have an advantage, even if it is recognised that their status as political actors will colour their communicative work.

Once again, however, we return to the issue of power, resources and the differences between politically marginal groups. The politics of news sources illustrates as clearly as any other topic how the capacity of the powerful to communicate more frequently and effectively than the politically marginal, is contingent upon the interplay of symbolic and material resources. Those non-official sources enjoying sufficient command over material resources to fund research and data gathering exercises will find it much easier to make their claims to expertise appear plausible. Equally, those groups in regular contact with central government and policy-makers on the 'inside', are more likely to be perceived by journalists as 'credible' sources. In turn, securing a place on the 'inside' in relation to government is partly dependent upon the kind of symbolic packages which non-official sources choose to exploit. The Terrence Higgins Trust, for example, has been circumspect in its articulation of liberal moral and sexual codes precisely because it has been aware of the influence of moral conservative organisations within the Thatcher and Major administrations and the danger that its funding from government might be jeopardised (Miller and Williams, 1998: 127). It is through the interplay of material and symbolic resources that power is exerted.

For the more politically marginal, without 'insider status' and fewer material resources, the situation can appear rather bleak. Goldenberg, in his study of 'resource-poor', politically marginal community groups in Boston, concluded that while 'status, officiality, knowledge, and money' were in short supply, such groups could still mobilise alternative resources, such as 'size, legitimacy and credibility' in their efforts to generate news media coverage (1975: 47). In other words, journalists would take an interest in groups which could demonstrate that they 'spoke' for a substantial body of local opinion. However, while gaining access to the press once was easily achieved through stunts and the politics of spectacle, the real problem for resource-poor groups was in securing 'continuing access' (1975: 145). Resource-rich groups could mobilise command over political, symbolic and material resources to initiate and sustain media contacts. Given four resource-poor groups and three newspapers in Goldenberg's study, only three out of the possible twelve 'interactions' became 'regularised' (1975: 137). In some cases, the politically marginal groups lacked even the cultural capital or media understanding to begin to identify which journalists might be useful contacts. Where 'regularised contact' was established between groups and particular journalists, this was because these politically marginal groups had something to 'bargain' with. Put simply, such groups had the skills to deal with journalists in terms of 'exchanges'. Exclusive interviews with community or political leaders, or information with a high 'value' in terms of political context were 'commodities' with value. In return, journalists wrote stories which at least acknowledged the interpretative frameworks or agendas submitted by these 'resource-poor' groups.

There are opportunities, then, for politically marginal, non-official sources to provide the 'information subsidies' (Gandy, 1982) which news journalists find of value and which can be traded in the exchange relationships that often emerge between specialist correspondents and regular news sources. However, proximity to power is a great advantage in obtaining information of interest to journalists. As Deacon and Golding put it, the 'power to create and distribute meaning still resides with centres of material and political power' (1994: 203). The concluding section of this chapter explores what this actually means for powerful corporate communicators. Politically marginal news sources will be considered in Chapter 7.

Corporate Communicators

Corporate news media work is almost as old as modernity itself. Even in the 1840s and 1850s, the European railway companies discovered the double-edged nature of the emerging modern communication systems, as newspapers both helped to publicise the advantages of the new railway routes as they spread across the countryside and simultaneously aired public fears about the risks of railway travel. However, formalised systems of corporate public relations developed as the modern corporations of the early twentieth century evolved into bureaucratic organisations. In Britain, it was Pilkingtons, the glass manufacturer, who first established an internal public relations department in 1928, followed close on its heels by ICI in 1930. In the post-war period, the in-house public relations department became a common feature of corporate life, as it had done in the USA a decade earlier, introduced, in the words of the Unilever department, 'to protect, maintain and develop the good name of Unilever inside and outside business by all legitimate means' (Newman, 1984: 236). One sharp stimulus to the growth of corporate public relations in Britain was the threat posed by the programmes of post-war nationalisation. The familiar 'Mr Cube' was first conscripted by Tate & Lyle into its public relations campaign to ward off the threatened nationalisation of the sugar industry (Ball and Millard, 1986: 68); an equally anxious ICI mounted a sustained public relations battle against nationalisation in the late 1950s and an estimated one and a half million pounds at 1959 prices was spent by the corporate sector as a whole on anti-nationalisation public relations work in the run up to the 1959 General Election (Finer, 1966: 89–90).

Throughout the following two decades corporate public relations activity steadily grew, but it was the arrival of Mrs Thatcher in office following the General Election of 1979 that really accelerated its development. Michael Edwards, in his role as Chief Executive at British Leyland, had already demonstrated how corporate public relations could be used simultaneously to raise the external profile of a flagging company and to re-route internal channels of communication in a way which by-passed trade union officials (Jones, 1986). Now Mrs Thatcher applied public relations techniques to the selling of politics with a ruthless and unprecedented intensity. The Thatcher administration's style set the tone for the 1980s. What Saatchi & Saatchi and Tim Bell appeared to be able to do for Mrs Thatcher, the corporations fondly hoped could be done for business in both industrial and financial sectors. In the former, much corporate public relations activity was engaged in legitimating the steps taken by managements determined to push home the advantages Thatcher's employment law reforms appeared to hand them in their struggles with organised labour (Jones, 1986; Wickens, 1987). It was the public relations department at British Steel which suggested that employees could be persuaded to warmly embrace the news of mass redundancies with the catchy slogan, 'Ride the Fear Stimulus' (Cayford, 1985).

The 1980s also saw a transformation in the activity of financial markets in Britain and elsewhere, as global financial trading grew, market practices were deregulated and governments like Mrs Thatcher's set about the process of privatising state assets. This had several important implications for corporate public relations. First, the sale of public utilities and state assets involved a very considerable expenditure in public relations as well as advertising, which helped to fuel the public relations boom of the 1980s (Golding, 1992). Secondly, the related rise in shareholding among the public helped to stimulate a growth in financial journalism not only in specialist publications but in daily newspapers and broadcasting which has continued, albeit with a minor dip during the recession of the early 1990s, to the present (Newman, 1984; Tumber, 1993). The intensification in news media interest compelled financial institutions and publicly quoted companies to take public relations and news media work more seriously whether they liked it or not. Thirdly, a more competitive market, more volatile trading with the deregulation of the Stock Exchange, and the more persistent danger of take-over as institutional investors put dividends before continuity, have meant that the placing of financially sensitive information in the public domain can have very significant consequences, requiring very careful presentation, or equally well thought through responses to media enquiries (Newman, 1984; Parsons, 1989). News media coverage of the performance of publicly quoted companies can play an important part in representing 'market judgements' or 'market fears' (Warner and Molotoch, 1993). Inevitably, attempting to influence the way in which 'market perceptions' are constructed through news coverage has become an important part of corporate activity. Finally, developments outside the boardroom lent an added urgency to the proliferation of corporate public relations. From the 1960s onwards, environmentalists, health campaigners, civil rights activists and consumer organisations had begun to place corporate targets in their sights with increasing persistence. Corporations had to learn how to deal with hostile publicity campaigns and to develop public relations 'fire-fighting techniques' for those occasions when noxious gases leaked from a plant or oil tankers deposited environmental catastrophes in the oceans. Listed public relations companies have grown from 46 in 1967, to 2,700 in 1997 and in-house departments from 720 to 6,500 in the same period (Michie, 1998: 12). Michie estimates that there is roughly one PR person for every two journalists in Britain.

Corporations and 'Bad Publicity'

Despite the potential communicative power concentrated in the hands of the corporate sector, it remains the case that businesses and corporations are often suspicious of the news media, frequently inclined to believe that their conduct is misrepresented by journalists, and occasionally prone to make claims about the existence of an 'anti-business culture' among media élites (Grant, 1987: 32; Drier, 1988; Hoge, 1988; Tumber, 1993). It is sometimes argued that the social and educational background of creative and media élites does, indeed, foster a liberal or left-wing hostility towards commerce and corporate life (Lichter and Rothman, 1988). However, given the growing integration of news media enterprises with other corporate processes of commodification, and the more rigorous application of business imperatives within the newsroom in recent years (see Chapter 4), this argument now appears less plausible. Although older journalists are tempted to hark back to a 'golden age' before the bottom line came to dominate the culture and practices of the newsroom, earlier sociological studies of news journalism suggest that few journalists were insulated from the organisational pressures of 'revenue goals' even in 'halcyon days of old', let alone in the era of the corporate newsroom. In other words, news journalists are as immersed in a corporate culture as many employees and subject to the same imperatives of the bottom line.

Nevertheless, there are instances in which business and corporate organisations appear extremely uncomfortable in the news media spotlight and there are several reasons why. Consumer issues are regarded as having stronger news values now, than in earlier decades. Several newspapers run weekly columns in which teams of reporters pursue readers complaints against particular companies in relation to their products or services. Television pioneered this approach for many years on Ester Rantzens' *That's Life* programme. Its successor, BBC 1's *Watchdog* has proved such a thorn in the side of corporate flesh that reportedly a high level delegation of senior executives from ten of the largest British companies, including Dixons, Airtours, Ford, British Telecom, Hotpoint and Procter & Gamble, have co-ordinated a joint campaign to persuade BBC governors to bring the programme to heel.[10] Secondly, corporations operating in particular sectors are more likely to experience bad publicity because of the nature of the way in which they secure their profits. As we shall see below, the environmental consequences of the activities of certain corporations involved in, for example, oil and extractive industries are likely to have a high profile. When things go wrong in industries such as food processing, health and medical care, transport and energy the same point applies. Thirdly, as discussed in Chapter 3, stories which have 'consonance' or longevity, or which strike a chord with the public in the view of journalists, can sometimes cause considerable prolonged embarrassment in the corporate world. The large salary increases and bonus payments awarded to 'fat cats' in the boardroom and the profits made by the senior managers of privatised utilities have provided some British newspapers with a continuing news frame in recent years. As Tumber notes, major fraud and white-collar crime in the City, together with sex scandals associated with leading executives or entrepreneurs, contain many of the ingredients specified by mainstream news values (1993: 350–1). It would be surprising if the frauds at Guinness, BCCI, County Natwest and more recently Barings were ignored, given the sums involved and the colourful personalities. According to Tumber, the British tabloid or 'red top' papers were the most likely to devote coverage to these themes, followed by *The Guardian*.

In the past, an additional factor has been the ineptitude of many corporations in making the most of their communicative assets. Not only have senior executives occasionally scored spectacular media own-goals (Gerald Ratner's widely reported public admission that much of what was sold in his jewellery shops was 'crap' provides one example) but in the past corporations have often failed to cultivate relationships with specialist news correspondents. Certainly, industrial and economic correspondents were critical of the apparent lack of effort invested in anticipating their requirements for information and stories which had news value (Adeney, 1983) and often cited unions or nationalised industries as more useful sources of commercial information (MORI, 1993). Until recently, few senior executives in the corporate world would have included news media skills in their job descriptions and few were much good at dealing with journalists. One study of the financial press in the United States found that corporate executives were quoted as infrequently as union officials, even in articles dealing with the performance of their own companies (Warner and Molotoch, 1993: 173).

The recent huge investment in corporate public relations work is, in part, a recognition that in the past the corporate world has failed to grasp the importance of public presentation. There is now a much more widespread appreciation of the point that corporations operate in a media-sensitive environment. This has included investment in training executives to deal with media crisis management, or what is sometimes called 'fire-fighting'. Large corporations such as Procter & Gamble issue 'crisis management manuals' to all staff in their public relations and communications departments, and organise news media exercises in which freelance journalists are hired to play the parts of reporters from CNN, or even more fearsome, researchers for the dreaded BBC *Watchdog* television programme (Armstrong, 1998).

Corporate Power and Communication

Despite the public relations gaffs, unwelcome headlines about corporate salaries, and damaging publicity surrounding particular incidents, it remains the case that corporations and the communications agencies working on behalf of capital, enjoy significant advantages when they compete in the news media arena against politically marginal news sources. There are four institutional mechanisms through which corporate public relations and news media work is sustained. As we have seen, the larger corporations began to develop in-house public relations departments in large numbers in the post-war period and now in-house work is often supplemented with, or replaced by, the services provided by consultancies. For those who subscribe to the 'dumbing down of news' thesis discussed in Chapter 3, the erosion of standards of investigation in journalism, combined with additional pressure upon journalists to deliver productivity, has encouraged a greater willingness on the part of newsrooms to accept copy based upon material submitted by public relations teams (Baistow, 1985; Michie, 1998: 35). In addition to the departments and agencies dealing specifically with public relations, the representative organisations and trade associations contribute to the news media work of capital. In Britain, the Confederation of Industry (CBI) placed less emphasis upon media work when its position 'inside' government was secure, but now attaches much more importance to publicly representing business through the news media (Grant, 1990). The Institute of Directors now regularly makes news media interventions, while other trade associations, such as the Road Haulage Federation, the Chemical Industries Association and the increasingly prominent Retail Consortium, representing the interests of the big supermarkets, are all now more news media active than in previous decades.

In addition to companies, consultancies and representative organisations, there exist a number of 'front organisations' which can fulfil several public relations functions. They can be used to lend an air of neutrality and technical detachment to messages that are actually intimately associated with the commercial interests of particular companies or economic sectors but they also provide a convenient device permitting corporate interests to disseminate messages they do not wish to be directly associated with. Perhaps one of the most notorious is FOREST– the Freedom Organisation for the Right to Enjoy Smoking Tobacco. Forest campaigns against 'tobacco censorship' and 'health fascists' in an effort to promote freedom for smokers, but is, of course, funded almost entirely by the tobacco industry. Its notoriety probably undermines its attempts to convince the general public of the 'scientific complexities of the smoking debate' and journalists are certain to receive their press releases or public relations copy with a high degree of scepticism. However, other 'front organisations' develop a rather less contentious public discourse and may therefore experience more success in their attempts to appropriate an image of technical detachment. The British Nutrition Foundation, for example, seems like just the organisation to which both journalists and the wider public could turn to for reliable information on diet and nutrition – an arbiter rather than an advocate, to use Deacon and Golding's distinction (see above) – unless one suspected that its dependence upon the food processing industry for a large proportion of its funding might colour its interpretation of available data. The British Genetic Study Unit may have mobilised the discourses of 'science' and 'genetics' in discussions of birth control but actually represented the interests of London Rubber Industries (Wooton, 1978: 19), while the British Road Haulage Federation has revealed over the years an admirable sense of civic duty in quietly supporting a number of by-pass campaigns and road-friendly local pressure groups (Ball and Millard, 1986: 68).

The oldest 'front' organisations representing capital and corporate interests emerged in the pre-war era. The Economic League was formed in 1919 and has devoted itself to 'the preservation of personal freedom and free enterprise', and the opposition of 'all subversive forces . . . that seek to undermine the security of Britain and British industry' (Nugent, 1979: 78). This has required the League to compile blacklists of such subversives – largely active trade unionists and members of the labour movement. Another organisation, Aims for Industry, was founded during the Second World War in anticipation of the dangers that nationalisation programmes might pose for British capital. Funding for such campaigning was supplied by companies and the corporate sector. Historically, both organisations managed to combine a low public profile with feverish rates of activity in terms of news media work. In 1948, the Economic League claimed to have initiated 25,300 column inches of press copy in its campaign against the enemies of business (Finer, 1966: 85). Just how much influence such organisations have actually had with journalists is difficult to judge. Certainly, it is hard to find evidence of any sustained relationships with the specialist correspondents covering labour and industrial affairs in the post-war period (Manning, 1998) but it is possible that the stream of briefing information produced by both organisations did have some influence in other areas of news journalism. With the arrival of Thatcher in office in 1979, much of the *raison d'être* for such organisations disappeared and the right-of-centre policy 'think tanks', such as the Institute of Economic Affairs and the Adam Smith Institute, enjoyed a much closer relationship with government. Nevertheless, front organisations for business and corporate interests continue to operate with the Economic League, for example, which now specialises more in compiling and marketing its lists of 'subversives' to interested companies.

Using the framework discussed at the beginning of this chapter, it is possible to point to a number of significant advantages which capital enjoys in its media work. For some companies, size and economic significance can make them inherently newsworthy, particularly if they operate in a sector which places them in the public eye. The privatised public utilities are likely to be regarded by industrial correspondents as essentially newsworthy for these reasons (Manning, 1998: 221). However, news values are complex. British Airways is big, hugely significant in economic terms, and looms large in the minds of the holidaying public, and yet it lacks something which its smaller rival, Virgin, possesses in abundance – a colourful, 'larger than life' personality at the head of the organisation. 'Personality' is, of course, a key news ingredient and stories that can be personalised are more likely to be selected by most news organisations. As one industrial editor put it, 'Quite often we like to personalise things. There's no such thing as Virgin Airways but there is Richard Branson's Virgin Airways . . . so that the individual becomes synonymous with the organisation.'[9]

Companies and corporations with high profile chief executives are likely to generate more coverage. A circular logic operates here, of course, through which each additional phase of news coverage of a corporate 'personality' further confirms the newsworthy status of the individual concerned. Consonance can operate as a virtuous as well as vicious circle for some news sources. However, few companies have the 'benefit' of a Branson-like personality to kick-start their news media work. What companies and representative organisations usually do have are significant material resources which can be translated into communicative activity and, if sufficiently economically significant, the political contacts associated with insider status and the membership of policy networks that will signal to journalists potential news significance. It has been argued above that the powerful have more opportunities to mobilise symbolic resources and exploit 'symbolic packages' or discourses to construct interpretative frameworks that work in their interests. Nevertheless, symbolic packages or discourses are 'slippery' and corporations have not always found it easy to push home and secure their favoured frameworks. A large 'responsible employer' creating 'wealth for the nation' can become 'a remote and unaccountable transnational' if it decides to close a factory and move out of town. Their advantages in terms of material resources (more press officers on the job, more information more rapidly disseminated) and economic and political significance will help in the deployment of symbolic resources but success is not guaranteed.

Corporate Control of Information Flows

However, corporations do enjoy a more permanent advantage in the battle to control and regulate information flows to the news media and the public domain. Whereas symbolic resources are 'slippery' and can be transmuted or inserted into alternative 'symbolic packages', control of valuable information is associated with the authority and corporate power exercised by capital in late modern societies. Here, capital can depend upon a more stable and permanent advantage providing the 'exchange relationships' which engage journalists and sources are understood. Once again, the ability to exert more or less effective control (few organisations can exert complete control) over the flow of information emerging from within the internal organisational environment explains a number of the significant advantages enjoyed by corporations and the representative organisations of capital. There are several reasons why corporations can exert very effective control in this way.

First, the recognition that corporations and public limited companies cannot avoid operating in a media-sensitive environment has encouraged many to tighten up and formalise organisational media practices. Executives and employees are now trained to channel all news media enquiries through one source, usually the corporate communications department or public relations consultancy. This provides 'increased gateway control' (Michie, 1998: 35). Secondly, in contrast to organisations such as trade unions, corporations can exert a number of formal and informal controls to prevent 'whistle-blowing' or 'leaking'. Employees may suffer formal sanctions, including the sack, if they do 'leak' information and many companies include 'gagging' clauses in employment contracts. In any case, the organisational culture fostered in many corporations will discourage the unauthorised release of information. Employees may fear that they will damage their company's, and therefore their own, prospects if they do 'leak'. Definitions of commercial sensitivity grow ever wider, and increasingly information is regarded as a corporate asset and not something to be freely released. Thirdly, while late capitalism remains intensely competitive in many sectors, among financial and corporate élites there is also a mutual recognition of shared interests which can also inhibit the free circulation of information. Comparisons between the world of politics and the corporate world suggest that leaking was significantly less frequent in the latter (Tiffen, 1989: 40; Tumber, 1993: 347). Leaking information that might promote the interests of the corporation by undermining the position of competitors or regulatory bodies is, however, rather more frequent (Michie, 1998: 110–11).

While business and financial élites exert a tighter control over the flow of business and financial information, journalists depend upon such 'contextual information' to write stories (see Chapter 3). In order to place immediate events in some kind of context and to assess the reliability of particular pieces of evidence, they need background information which may relate, for example, to the business plans of particular companies, the politics of the boardroom, the relationship between companies and particular clients, or the views of senior executives or other key players. This particularly applies to specialist correspondents dealing with financial or economic affairs but the point also applies to general reporters. Yet with staff cuts in news organisations and less time for investigative reporting, journalists become ever more dependent upon such tightly controlled corporate and financial élite sources. As one former City diary editor explains:

> Staff numbers in most City newsrooms have been slashed dramatically in cost-cutting exercises. This puts enormous pressure on the journalists that remain. If you don't produce X-hundred words a day, you're out. If you're away from your desk, people don't think you're out meeting contacts or doing research because there isn't time for much of that – they assume you're skiving. So you come to rely on a fairly small number of contacts who come to you – the PR people. (Quoted in Michie, 1998: 35)

As the amount of time available for background research diminishes and the complexity of business and financial issues increases, so the temptation for journalists to gather their 'contextual information' from corporate sources grows stronger. This argument should not be stretched too far. There remain many specialist correspondents who have worked a city desk for long enough to acquire the knowledge, and a sufficiently large contact book, to permit the cross-checking of sources and some intelligent detective work. Nevertheless, the opportunities for corporate and financial élite sources to influence news frameworks or agendas are growing significantly.

Corporate influence is also exercised in rather less subtle ways. Wealth can sometimes translate directly into communicative power. In a world in which there is a proliferation of media outlets and a widespread reflexive interest in media representation, the investment of material resources in one area of media production can often generate news interest on the part of journalists. Thus, the large biotechnology company Monsanto recently invested in a series of advertisements attempting to reassure the public about the 'non-hazardous' nature of genetically modified food, but this strategy, in itself, generated further news comment and news items (Armstrong, 1998). Similarly, advertisements that capture the public imagination – recent examples have included those for particular cars, brands of coffee and types of beer – have generated popular tabloid news interest, while the privatisation sell-offs of the 1980s, including the 'Tell Sid' advertising campaign for gas shares, produced similar news interest and displays of subeditorial ingenuity in reworking the popular advertising slogans of the campaigns.

Another tried and tested way of directly translating wealth into communicative power is by resorting to law or its threat. The English libel laws are particularly accommodating for those with sufficient money at their command not to be daunted by the prospect of entering the libel court. Often merely the threat of an action delivered on the headed notepaper of a top firm of solicitors with a litigious reputation is sufficient to make editors desist from pursuing particular stories. Notoriously, Robert Maxwell kept most of the financial journalists in Fleet Street at bay, including those whose pension funds he was raiding, through such litigious intimidation. However, it is not merely the rogues of the financial world but those positioned in the most respectable parts of the corporate sector who sometimes resort to such tactics. Recently the September/October 1998 issue of *The Ecologist* magazine was pulped by the printer days before it was due to be distributed.[11] The issue was devoted to the dangers of genetically modified crops and, in particular, the role of Monsanto, the American biotechnology company mentioned above. Although the printers had printed *The Ecologist* for 29 years, the firm severed all contact with the magazine while at the same time publicly denying that Monsanto had exerted any pressure. Significantly, when the magazine was finally printed, neither WH Smiths nor John Menzies would agree to distribute it, and in 1997 a television programme dealing with Monsanto milk hormone products was dropped by Fox TV in the United States at the last minute (Williams, 1998). Perhaps the pastmasters of the application of corporate clout to control news flows are McDonalds. As we have seen, news organisations as diverse as Channel 4, *The Guardian*, the *Independent* and the BBC, have all paused for thought after receiving communications from the lawyers at McDonalds.

Yet, it is patently not the case that the possession of such corporate clout *guarantees* control over news communication in every instance. The process of news production can never be hermetically sealed in a way that would ensure complete corporate control because journalists are committed to competitive careers which encourage a high degree of sensitivity to 'exclusives', news organisations are varied in type and goals, and the interests of media élites are frequently divergent from those of business and financial élites, even if all are locked into an economic system that commodifies for profit. Thus, paradoxically, the application of corporate clout in the form of litigious threats can often encourage precisely the kind of publicity a corporation seeks to stifle. Long may McDonalds have regretted the libel action it eventually won against the 'McLibel Two', as the case dragged on for year after year, periodically generating fresh news coverage which cast McDonalds in the role of corporate bully. Needless to say, the information which so antagonised McDonalds when it was distributed as a leaflet outside a McDonalds restaurant in London, became globally available on the McLibel website within weeks of the action commencing. Recently, Monsanto has also learnt that the alleged exercise of corporate clout to shut down news information flows can sometimes become an unwelcome news story in its own right, with the publicity generated by the pulping of *The Ecologist*.

Despite the enormous resources at the command of large companies, an assessment of the communicative power of capital is complex. Wealth can be translated into communicative power but it cannot guarantee that the message corporate organisations seek to communicate is received in precisely the way intended. Material resources can greatly assist the distribution and dissemination of the symbolic packages or discourses preferred by capital but cannot necessarily secure them. Corporate power can deter journalists in some instances and helps to tighten the control that corporations exert over the flow of information emerging into the news media environment, but it cannot prevent the quite frequent appearance of news themes which embarrass companies and prompt awkward questions about the legitimacy of corporate practice. The capacity of capital to exert communicative influence through its silent presence remains as strong today as it did when Crenson first began to explore the dimensions of non-decision-making nearly 30 years ago. Yet, it is rarely possible for obvious reasons to determine with any kind of precision what comes to be understood as 'off limits' in the news-gathering process. What we can say is that the news media environment in which corporations are positioned offers them normally favourable terrain. However, it is also a contested terrain. As Tumber puts it: 'The majority of business coverage is supportive, complimentary and consonant with the media's role in reproducing dominant ideology. However, the media are not entirely closed to critical comment. Recent work has suggested that a relatively open terrain of struggle may exist not accounted for by a one dimensional view of what constitutes a dominant ideology' (1993: 358).

Two factors make the terrain more problematic for business in recent years, according to Tumber. First, 'consumer and environmental groups' offer more critical alternative sources of information and news frames which capital is compelled to contest. Secondly, the news media, partly in order to legitimate their own authority and partly in response to the competitive nature of news production, are now more inclined to frame business stories in terms of conventional news values involving scandal, sex and abuses of power. The next stage in the discussion is to consider the competing efforts of these rival news sources in consumer and environmental politics. In doing so, we move from the centre of power in contemporary society to the political margins.

Notes

1. Grant's (1990) distinction between insiders and outsiders can surely accommodate the potential differences between large industrial producer groups and campaigning groups.
2. See 'BSE Safeguards Flouted', *The Guardian*, 10 October 1998, p. 1.
3. Interview conducted by the author, 31 July 1990. See also Manning (1998).

4. Interview conducted by the author, 7 July 1992. See also Manning (1998).
5. Interview conducted by the author, 6 March 1991. See also Manning (1998).
6. Interview conducted by the author, 6 June 1991. See also Manning (1998).
7. Interview conducted by the author, 6 March 1991. See also Manning (1998).
8. Interview conducted by the author, 21 June 1991. See also Manning (1998).
9. Interview conducted by the author, 24 July 1992. See also Manning (1998).
10. 'Vexed Business Elite to Hold Watchdog Meeting', *The Guardian*, 3 August 1998, p. 2.
11. 'Printers Pulp Monsanto Edition of Ecologist', *The Guardian*, 29 September 1998, p. 5.

7 News Media Politics and the Politically Marginal

Much of Chapter 6 was devoted to considering the advantages that the more powerful corporate and institutional news sources can wield in their struggles over news agendas. This chapter looks at those potential news sources which occupy the more politically marginalised positions, including trade unions, environmental pressure groups, and organisations campaigning in the health and social policy arenas. To return to the argument developed in the previous chapter, these are the groups with less command over material communication resources, and who may face greater difficulties in shaping news media agendas because of their distance from government or lower ranking on the 'hierarchy of credibility' for news correspondents. These groups are unlikely to be able to influence the non-decision-making dimension of news agenda formation by virtue of their political prominence or economic importance. Instead, they are likely to be more dependent upon the 'politics of spectacle' as a technique for securing coverage, and more dependent upon both the skilful use of 'symbolic packages' and the gains to be secured through fostering effective 'exchange relationships' with specialist correspondents. Accordingly, their vulnerability in the continuous struggles over the news agenda will be determined firstly, by the degree to which their 'symbolic packages' can be refused or displaced by those hostile to their interests, and secondly, but crucially, by the extent to which they are characterised by 'leakiness', or an inability to control the flows of information emerging from within their own organisational environments.

Trade Unions as Politically Marginal News Sources

When the concept of 'primary definition' was first formulated by Stuart Hall and his colleagues in the mid-1970s (Hall et al., 1978), the strength of the British trade union movement and the proximity of its leadership to government persuaded the authors to include the trade union élites as 'primary definers'. The ensuing political marginalisation of unions, not only in Britain but to a lesser extent throughout the advanced capitalist world (Edwards et al., 1986; Ferner and Hyman, 1992), has underlined the force of Schlesinger's critique – that an ahistorical understanding of primary definition will miss the processes through which the capacity to primarily define is eroded (see Chapters 1 and 6). Indeed, so marginal are trade unions to the formal political process in Britain today and so infrequently are industrial relations featured in news coverage compared to two decades earlier, that some might suggest a discussion of their potential as news sources is hardly warranted.

However, I think there are several good reasons for including such a discussion. The relationship between capital and labour still represents a fault line in contemporary capitalist societies; it is by no means the only fundamental relationship of domination and subordination but is one of the most important, generating conflicts involving the mobilisation of both material and symbolic resources. Trade unions have long played an important part in defending the interests of labour against capital but, paradoxically, trade union leaderships have also played a part in the continued reproduction of such patterns of subordination, being 'at one and the same time, part of the problem and part of the solution, a form of resistance to capitalism and a form of integration within capitalism' (Hyman, 1985: 123). Given the work of the news media in both reflecting and reproducing the most important patterns of domination and subordination in society, the heightened tensions and shifts in the balance of forces between capital and labour are always likely to find expression through the news media. In times of sharper tension, the reverberations arising from such conflicts will echo through news coverage, underlining just how strategically important the news media arena actually is. Few national industrial disputes are fought out without the deployment of news media strategies on either side (Jones, 1986; Manning, 1998). Charting the contours of news coverage of industrial relations was for a while an academic industry in itself. While some sceptics question the validity of the methodologies employed in these studies (Harrison, 1985; Cumberbatch et al., 1986), there is a huge volume of evidence which suggests that the representation of industrial relations in newspapers and broadcasting frequently undermined the legitimacy of trade unions, neglected the agendas which unions sought to place in the public domain, and that this pattern was repeated in Britain, the USA and other parts of Europe (see, for example, GUMG, 1976; Easthope, 1990; Puette, 1992).

Trade unions in most contemporary capitalist societies have, perhaps belatedly, recognised the importance of developing effective media and communication strategies in the last decade and it is not difficult to explain why. Apart from their experience of hostile news media coverage, membership levels are falling: in the United States union density has fallen to a mere 10 per cent in many occupational sectors, while in Britain levels of unionisation vary, remaining highest in professional occupations at around 50 per cent but descending to as low as 36 per cent in former union strongholds such as craft and engineering, and as low as 11 per cent in the growing service and retail sectors. In Britain and the USA, the difficulties unions have experienced in retaining membership levels have been compounded by tough employment laws severely constraining recognition and recruitment rights, although European Union law has in some ways strengthened individual employment rights (Edwards et al., 1992). For some, the reasons go even deeper than this. Theorists such as Offe (1985), Lash and Urry (1987) and Mulgan (1996), suggest that the structure of modern societies is changing fundamentally, driven by the twin forces of capitalist globalisation and compositional change in the occupational structure. In an era of global capitalist competition, so it is argued, the exercise of collective strength to protect workers' conditions is doomed to fail, and the days in which unions could consolidate their strength in large industrial plants have gone forever. This argument may be a little overstated. There is considerable empirical evidence to support the view that some, at least, of the downturn in union fortunes is bound up with more temporary phenomena associated with the business cycle and political climate rather than structural change (Kelly, 1990). Indeed, in Britain recruitment is just beginning to increase for the first time in two decades. Nevertheless, it is undoubtedly the case that unions have realised that they must find new sources of support and that they must reach out to workers in occupational sectors with very little tradition of union organisation. In part, this must involve finding new ways to 'speak' to groups frequently neglected by traditional unionism: part-time workers, women, young workers and the various ethnic minorities now making up large sections of the 'super-exploited' segments of late capitalist economies (Cunnison and Stageman, 1993). Women, for example, now make up nearly 40 per cent of the British TUC's membership and it is this evidence of change in the nature of potential membership which prompted the launch of the TUC's 'New Unionism' project in 1998 to reach the unorganised sectors of the British economy. The same forces have prompted trade unions in the USA and Western Europe to develop similar interests in news media work and communication strategies (Douglas, 1986; Waterman, 1990). The logic is captured well by one of the new breed of union media officer working for the GMB in Britain:

> Trade unions must inevitably find new ways of speaking to their members and their potential members. Twenty years ago you could probably recruit a hundred people by standing outside the factory gates at 5.30 am and handing out a few leaflets saying, 'That person in there is a bastard, you need us.' There are smaller units now; it is far more difficult trying to recruit two or three people working in a small office in Beaconsfield [a leafy suburb in South East England] than it used to be to recruit two or three hundred at the Camel Laird shipyard. Industry has changed and trade unions have to change with it, which means that your communication techniques have to change. More and more people get their information from television, radio, papers and magazines, and that means that there are becoming more and more important ways to communicate with any potential recruitment audience. (quoted in Manning, 1998: 38)

As we shall see, it is not only for recruitment purposes that unions now prioritise communication strategies and particularly work with the news media. Unions must not only 'speak' to new potential recruits but they must communicate effectively with their existing members to consolidate their support, and sometimes they must also appeal to the 'the force of public opinion'.

Given the erosion in their industrial strength and political relations with government, some trade unions embroiled in disputes with employers have begun to place more hope in news media work than in the traditional exercise of industrial muscle.

Communication Strategies in a Hostile Media Environment

For politically marginal groups operating in hostile news media environments, four distinct though not mutually exclusive communication strategies can be pursued and over the years trade unions have tried them all. The first strategy is based upon an analysis of the structure of media ownership which concludes that hostile coverage is associated with the interests of those companies and individuals which, either directly or indirectly, exert editorial influence through their command of media capital. In periods when the political climate has tolerated discussion of radical intervention in media markets, trade unions in Britain have called long and hard for reforms that would either place regulatory constraints upon media cross-ownership or would open up opportunities for unions to exercise a 'right of reply' against unfair coverage (Basnett and Goodman, 1977; TUC, 1979; Lennon, 1996). In France, Sweden and certain other European states, legislation affording some of these protections is already in place (Weymouth and Lamizet, 1996). In the USA, trade unions have restricted this kind of strategy to what could be called 'corporate outing', identifying the interlocking structures of corporate ownership which bind most of the news media to corporate capitalist interests and attempting to present this as an issue of public concern (Douglas, 1986: 46–8).

A second strategy involves by-passing the mainstream channels of news communication, either by use of advertising, sponsoring various forms of cultural production, or by establishing fully independent channels of news communication. Historically, American unions have been rather more ambitious than many of their European counterparts. After experiencing the familiar difficulties of those attempting to launch new newspapers with little capital in the first two decades of the twentieth century, the American Federation of Labor (AFL) established its own radio station in Chicago in 1926, followed by a number of individual union-funded local FM stations in the 1930s and 1940s (Douglas, 1986). As broadcasting costs rose and television became the dominant force in the post-war era, a number of American unions began to exploit the 'public service slots' available on national commercial television (Pomper, 1959). Trade unions in Europe have, in the main, depended upon the institutionalised links between left-wing or social democratic political parties and public broadcasting systems, as in Italy prior to deregulation, although local branches of the French CGT trade union confederation began to exploit the potential of pirate radio in the late 1970s and early 1980s (Kuhn, 1995: 98). American unions have, over the years, sponsored and even participated in Broadway musicals, mainstream films and theatre (Douglas, 1986). Unions in Western European states have been similarly involved in cultural production. In Britain, trade unions have traditionally been more conservative in terms of cultural strategy, although public sector unions, such as Unison, have an honourable record in sponsoring theatre with a labour movement theme. Unions in the USA, Britain and Western Europe have all used advertising in recent decades to either raise the positive profile of trade unionism in general or to campaign on particular issues (Puette, 1992; Douglas, 1986; TUC, 1985). The big advantage of advertising is, of course, the editorial control afforded to the unions; the big disadvantage is the cost involved, particularly with regard to broadcasting and national newspaper slots.

A third strategy could be described as 'media pressure politics'. Unions, like political parties and other pressure groups, have from time to time sought to exert pressure upon news media institutions by making news content and allegations of 'bias' political issues in their own right. Evidence of unfair treatment will be drawn to the attention of news organisations or occasionally submitted to official enquiries, such as the last Royal Commission on the Press in Britain (1977), and media monitoring exercises will sometimes be mounted to substantiate the criticisms. In the USA, the Labor Institute for Public Affairs, established in 1982 and funded by the AFL-CIO, has a specific brief for such work, while in Britain both the TUC and individual unions have employed similar strategies (Manning, 1998: 62–4). The problem with media monitoring exercises is that an increasingly media-literate public is no longer surprised by evidence of media injustice and journalists frequently just ignore them, although in the past they have caused some discomfort among media professionals when the evidence is compelling (Skirrow, 1980).

Of course, these strategies are by no means mutually exclusive, and there remains a fourth approach which trade unions are placing an increasing reliance upon. This can be described as 'accommodative' because rather than attempting to reform or by-pass existing means of news communication, this strategy emphasises the importance of working with the existing news media, making adjustments in institutional arrangements to accommodate the needs of news journalists. This represents an important departure because the labour movement in most Western European countries, and in the US, has traditionally regarded the news media with a great deal of suspicion. One union official famously described journalists as 'our enemies' front line troops'[1] and this view was widely shared by trade unionists who regarded the news media as inextricably bound up with the interests of capital. The view that unions could achieve more positive news coverage by taking steps to accommodate journalists, first found favour in the United States when Albert Zack was appointed as Director of Public Relations for the AFL-CIO in 1958, and in Britain when some white-collar unions appointed press officers in the 1950s and early 1960s. Unions organising in traditional manual and industrial sectors took very few steps to formally accommodate the needs of the news media until the early 1980s when the TUC Media Working Group published a series of policy documents encouraging individual unions to take news media work more seriously.[2] It was at this point that many more unions began to invest in the appointment of full-time press officers and the creation of departments with specific responsibilities for dealing with news media coverage. The result has been a noticeable improvement in the effectiveness of union media work as assessed from a journalist's point of view (Jones, 1995: 145).

However, just as trade unions in Western Europe and the United States turned towards the news media, the interest of national news organisations in industrial relations began to wane. The labour and industrial beat was for a period following the Second World War, one of the most prestigious for ambitious young journalists to cover. This reflected the centrality of formal industrial relations processes to the functioning of the state in an era of neo-corporatism. With the rise of neo-liberal governments in Britain, the United States and parts of Europe during the 1980s, and the ensuing marginalisation of unions, the importance of labour and industrial coverage declined in the eyes of news editors. Unions were no longer at the heart of the political process. Accordingly, the number of specialist correspondents working the labour beat declined. In Britain, numbers dropped from around 100 during the heyday of industrial coverage in the 1960s, to approximately 50 in the early 1990s (Manning, 1998: 217). In the United States, over a rather longer period of protracted decline, the figures fell from approximately 1,000 labour reporters in the 1940s to just 10 in the 1990s (Hoyt, 1984: 34–8; McChesney, 1997: 72). This underlines just one of many dilemmas for politically marginal groups seeking to employ news media strategies: there are so many variables over which they have little or no control and yet can have a crucial bearing upon the success or failure of the strategy. This is a point to which we shall return at the end of this chapter.

As is the case with particular politically marginal groups competing in any combination of political and media arenas, there are vast variations in the resourcing and organisation of news media work between trade unions. For example, the GMB in Britain has positioned itself at the forefront of modernising trends within the labour movement and, accordingly, has invested heavily in communication and media resources. A communications directorate has been established, working to an annually reviewed communication strategy, which in turn forms an integral part of the union's overall industrial and economic project. The director of communications and the staff with specific responsibilities for news media work have access to the most senior officers within the union which allows them to speak with 'authority' for the union. This means that media officers can usually respond quickly to journalists' enquiries without the need to refer upwards. The directorate is equipped with the latest in news media technology, Press Association monitors and electronic news communication systems, and invests in sophisticated media monitoring or 'clippings' services. This kind of heavy investment in news media work is much more familiar in American unions where a commitment to accommodative news work developed earlier and where the political culture has encouraged the growth of political public relations as an industry (Puette, 1992: 140–52).

While the GMB represents one extreme in British union communication work, there remain many unions, including some of the largest, which invest very much less in news media work. The AEU, which has now merged with the electricians to form a new union (the AEEU), was at the time of my own fieldwork in the early 1990s, only just beginning to take news media work seriously. It equipped a single press officer with a desk, a word processor and a Press Association monitor which had to be turned on sparingly for reasons of economy (Manning, 1998). Yet it was widely regarded as fast becoming one of the shining examples for news media work in the eyes of labour correspondents and others, because of the enthusiasm and skill of its press officer, Charlie Whelan, who was to rise to prominence, or notoriety, as 'spin doctor to the Chancellor' with the election of the new Labour government in 1997. What the AEU lacked in equipment and the material resourcing of communication work was compensated by the energy of Whelan, who maintained a highly interventionist, almost hyperactive, commitment to news media work. Labour correspondents had become accustomed to being phoned or paged by the AEU's press officer with suggestions for AEU-related stories, even when they were attending the conferences of other unions. Whelan could be described as a news media opportunist:

> . . . you can see what's on the news and something might come up that everybody else is doing and you think: F***, we've got no quote from the union on that. So I ring up and say, 'There's a quote from Gavin Laird [Union General Secretary] on that story', and nine times out of ten they'll add it in. (Charlie Whelan, quoted in Manning, 1998: 113)

However, this enthusiasm was tempered by a sound understanding of mainstream news values and an understanding that often it was better to 'keep one's powder dry', rather than pester journalists with stories that did not really have mainstream news interest. The point was, however, that Charlie Whelan frequently did have stories with such news interest because he was close to the leadership and in touch with the various political currents within the union and the industrial relations scene. As we saw in Chapter 5, labour correspondents described him as 'brilliant'. The chorus of dismay from journalists on Whelan's forced resignation from the New Labour government staff suggests that his flair for spinning the juiciest stories had not diminished in high office (Hennesey, 1999). Other trade unions with fewer material resources but high reputations among many journalists included the TGWU, where two overworked press officers serviced the news media needs of the huge, sprawling union, at that time still the largest in Britain. While they lacked the investment in material media resources to be found at the GMB, they were both former journalists who invested a great deal of time in maintaining links with former colleagues and drew upon their experience to relate union themes to mainstream news values.

By no means all unions had acquired a sophisticated grasp of news media work by the early 1990s: there remained several in my study which allocated neither material resources nor political energy to communications. Some remained deeply suspicious of the mass media; others simply did not believe that their unions were likely to generate many stories of national significance for journalists. However, what is important is the extent to which command over significant material resources was *not* a prerequisite for what labour correspondents would regard as effective news media work. While the GMB invested thousands of pounds in equipment, staffing and detailed planning, some journalists remained critical, even describing the strategy as 'over-flash'. What the GMB officers sometimes failed to provide for labour correspondents was what they valued more than anything – intelligence, or 'contextual information' to use the phrase employed by one former labour editor on *The Times* (Philip Bassett, quoted in Manning, 1998: 285). In other words, 'extra' bits of information about political undercurrents, likely developments, internal rivalries and so on – the information that would allow journalists to build an overall picture of events and place particular stories in wider contexts.[3] For labour correspondents, the most effective union press officers were those who were easy to contact and quick to respond, understood mainstream news values, could speak with 'authority' because they enjoyed the trust of their senior officers, but most crucially, were willing to foster what can be described as 'exchange relationships' with journalists. Labour correspondents were critical of unions who 'just belted on a press officer' but kept them 'permanently in the dark' (Manning, 1998: 284). The best union press officers were those who provided a little bit more; those who were close to the various political factions or decision-making centres within their unions, and could provide background briefing or the material for an interpretative piece of journalism. In other words, it was intelligence or 'contextual information' that served as the main bargaining chip which the more effective union press officers could play when fostering exchange relationships:

> I very desperately wanted a certain story placed in a certain newspaper three weeks ago . . . that is where it *had* to be, to be read by the people we wanted to influence. I mean it was a good story anyway so the paper would have taken it but I wanted to make sure that only that journalist got it, so in order to convince that person that they were getting something that was important to them, we provided additional information from other areas as well . . . and we serviced that story very, very thoroughly. Now the unwritten rule is that that person will help me with other stories as well. (Press officer for a large general union, quoted in Manning, 1998: 135)

There is, then, a complex relationship between industrial correspondents and union press officers, in which each side acknowledges certain rights and obligations. The latter are expected to recognise the needs of journalists: the criteria defining 'good copy', the importance of speed and accuracy in responding to enquiries, the value of an 'exclusive' to individual journalists, and above all, the nature of intelligence or 'contextual information'. In turn, press officers will hope that journalists will write 'balanced' accounts which at least acknowledge a union point of view and will at least listen to suggestions put to them for particular news items or features. By no means did every dialogue between labour correspondents and union media officers conform to this normative framework in every aspect. Nevertheless, most participants on the labour and industrial beat would recognise much of what is suggested here.

Union News Media Successes?

The obvious question to ask is whether trade unions, as politically marginal groups facing all the disadvantages in terms of the unequal distribution of material and symbolic resources discussed in Chapter 5, can use the exchange relationships that exist between union personnel and journalists to achieve more effective coverage of the agendas they seek to communicate? Do accommodative news media strategies work for unions? According to certain observers, trade unions have secured some notable successes in recent years through the application of accommodative news media strategies (Jones, 1986; Woolas, 1990; Milne, 1997). What follows are some illustrations of how unions have employed news media strategies within particular campaigns and some comments regarding the extent to which these can be described as 'successes'.

The 1989 Ambulance Dispute provides an interesting test of the potential of accommodative approaches for unions because it involved five unions with reputations as sophisticated exponents of news media work (Woolas, 1990). The unions concerned were NUPE, NALGO and COHSE (who subsequently merged to form Unison), together with the TGWU and the GMB. The fact that three of the unions involved were already in preliminary merger talks encouraged co-operation and an effective division of labour was agreed. NUPE took responsibility for all journalists' enquiries, COHSE concentrated upon parliamentary lobbying, and NALGO took responsibility for other aspects of the publicity process. In this way, all unions spoke with one voice and communication resources were exploited to maximum effect. Roger Poole, a NUPE officer with excellent television skills, was given responsibility for all broadcasting interviews; a union press officer was available to respond to media enquiries at all times, seven days a week; and the proactive dimension of the strategy concentrated upon appealing to human interest news values by arranging opportunities for journalists to travel with individual ambulance crews as they responded to emergency calls. The unions were determined not to go on strike but rather to operate an overtime ban. This would compel the government to admit that it had reneged on a previous agreement not to depend upon overtime working for the provision of emergency services and would avoid the damaging symbolism of 'strike action'. In other words, the industrial strategy of the unions was subordinated to the communication strategy.

To further assist the union cause, the Thatcher government had already run into some considerable political difficulties over its stewardship of Britain's National Health Service and there was considerable public sympathy for nurses and health workers, who were widely regarded as overworked but poorly paid. In short, if accommodative news media strategies were to prove successful for unions anywhere, it should be in circumstances such as these. The great danger the unions faced was that journalists would return to the news frames which dominated the reporting of British industrial relations during the 1970s, particularly the images of 'militant' public sector workers taking action to paralyse services and 'hold the public to ransom'.[4] One measure of success is the extent to which these old frames did not re-appear in news coverage, although this cannot be attributed entirely to union media work. The popularity of trade unions among the public was beginning to rise again in inverse proportion to Mrs Thatcher's determination to emasculate them. This probably featured in news editors' calculations about how to approach the dispute. Nevertheless, some early tabloid news coverage confirmed that there was a very real danger of the old news frames being taken off the shelf and dusted down. The fact that after this very early phase, news editors abandoned 'the militant public sector' news frame in favour of an approach that highlighted 'mercy men' and 'angels with blue flashing lights' (Manning, 1998: 316–57) underscores the effectiveness of the union approach.

In Britain, during the last decade, unions taking action in a number of sectors, including health, postal delivery, rail and air transport, have all prioritised news media work as an integral element in their overall strategies. The 1997 British Airways dispute provides another good example and there are some parallels to the 1989 Ambulance Dispute. Both involved workers in service industries engaged in a fight with a very large and powerful employer. Both sets of unions prioritised news media coverage as an essential part of an overall strategy and in both cases the unions sought to offer to the news media a set of 'symbolic packages' referring to the feminisation of trade union activity. In the case of the ambulance dispute, journalists were introduced to female drivers who 'struggled to make ends meet for their families on such low wages'; in the case of the British Airways dispute the image of air stewardesses on picket lines was too tempting for news photographers to resist. In each case, the union priority was to avoid traditional images of collective, masculine pickets jostling in a disorderly and threatening way. As one labour correspondent commented, 'Nothing better highlights women's emerging position in the trade union movement than last summer's British Airways cabin crew strikes, which were effectively run and won by women, comprehensively defying traditional union stereotypes' (Milne, 1998: 2).

Against the image of non-threatening, feminised strikers, the TGWU encouraged journalists to contrast a large and powerful corporation, bullying its workforce. Again, the similarities to the ambulance dispute are notable. Initially some news organisations, particularly right-inclined anti-union papers such as the *Sun* and the *Daily Mail*, endorsed some of the news themes offered by British Airways. Thus, there was considerable attention devoted to the 'perks' of life as a cabin crew member, while some papers began to investigate allegations that TGWU members had assaulted members of rival union organisations. Inevitably, some reports dwelt upon the inconvenience that might be caused to holidaymakers if the strikes persisted.[5]

However, these themes surfaced only briefly at the very beginning. The TGWU press office, staffed in the main by a single press officer, was able to establish a news framework in which the cabin crews were characterised as the underdogs locked in a battle with a giant corporation behaving like a 'nineteenth-century mill owner', bullying workers and denying workplace rights.[6] Andrew Murray, the TGWU press officer, describes the union's news media strategy in the following way:

> Bill Morris (TGWU President) said to me that the problem with transport disputes was that you could never win the public argument, and there is a certain amount of historical evidence to support that view because transport disputes do affect the public and, generally, this is seen as the responsibility of the people going on strike rather than the employer, but this was the first time that this did not happen. The majority of public opinion blamed British Airways for the situation . . . because it was defined as being about bullying. British Airways got up to all the old tricks . . . they said it was about high living air stewardesses, then they looked for a Red Robbo, a mindless militant figure, but they couldn't make up their minds who it was . . . they couldn't even decide who the demon figure was and so this never really played and in the end you had a situation where the *Sun*'s first editorial was a fire breathing attack on trade unions – greedy people junketing and that sort of thing – but the second editorial was a 'who's to blame for this, well we can't really say', and that's in the most anti-union section of the press, a shift from negative to neutral. And the quality press and even the Daily Mail [another paper with a traditional right-wing hostility to trade unions] were all running editorials about 'Brutish Airways' and the negative employee relations tactics . . . because the mind set had already been established and that was through working in advance not just with industrial correspondents but with city specialists and transport specialists, many of whom were willing to believe – and this reflects the general change in national climate – that a big, blue chip company was behaving badly.[7]

Murray, then, tried to set the agenda, or *primarily define* the key aspects of the dispute for journalists at the very outset, through detailed briefing. However, his success is surprising not only because it was secured through the pages of newspapers including those traditionally implacably hostile to trade unions, but because the disparity in communication resources between the TGWU and British Airways was so vast. The corporate communications division at British Airways employed a staff of 40; the union, having cut its press office staff by 50 per cent, employed just one man and his mobile phone. Several factors help to explain this news media success for the union.

As Murray is the first to acknowledge, the climate of public opinion had already grown more sympathetic to trade unions as their power was eroded through the 1980s, and news organisations were sensitive to this. Nevertheless, the TGWU still had to find a news media strategy that could make the best of these more favourable conditions. First, the very size of British Airways was, in some respects, a disadvantage. Andrew Murray was able to respond to press enquiries more rapidly precisely because the union organisational structure was more streamlined and its leadership had granted him considerable operational autonomy. Given the corporate culture within BA, its press and public relations staff were considerably more circumspect in dealing with journalists. As one labour editor pointed out, 'The TGWU has less of a chain of command and it's been light on its feet and able to respond to things quickly. They've also benefited from having Murray, who is a highly intelligent and articulate man' (Barry Clement, Labour Editor on the *Independent*, quoted in Milne, 1997: 3).

Secondly, the TGWU approach included a deft and humorous style in arranging photo opportunities and publicity angles. Thus, for example, in response to BA filming pickets, the union suggested that members with shares in the company might like to film shareholders at the annual general meeting. This generated considerable media attention and successfully underlined the point that BA were using intimidatory tactics against union members. Andrew Murray recognised that it was hardly credible to present the TGWU as a David locked in a struggle with a BA Goliath because the union had always been one of the largest in the country. However, it *was* credible to frame a struggle between the corporate Goliath and professional, middle class stewards and stewardesses in these terms: 'decent, normal professional people into whose hands you want to put your life when you go aboard an airline'.[8]

Thirdly, the BA corporate team made a number of serious misjudgements in terms of both industrial and communications strategy. The decision to issue letters to staff threatening to sack or sue played into the union's hands by appearing to confirm that BA was, indeed, a corporate bully. Despite its size, the BA communications team failed to always make a member of staff available to deal with media enquiries. BA denied that it had been filming pickets and was then forced to admit that it was, and a BA director fell into a trap laid by one of the TGWU negotiating team during a live BBC television *Newsnight* interview and appeared to agree to conciliation in front of millions of viewers. Even the air conditioning in the BA media centre broke down on the first day of the strike. As Andrew Murray commented, BA 'organised for a war that never happened', preparing for a set-piece confrontation along the lines of the battles between capital and labour a decade earlier. BA failed to understand that for the TGWU the news media contest was as important, if not more important, than what happened on the picket line.

A study of the Union of Communication Workers' campaign against the British government's plans to privatise the Royal Mail service in 1994 paints a similar picture (Davis, 2000). In this dispute, too, the union chose to prioritise a news media strategy over traditional industrial strategies. The idea was to make a 'positive case' for the retention of the postal service in the public sector based upon the benefits to the public, rather than referring to the possibility of industrial action or the concerns about job losses. This allowed the union to build a set of alliances with other interested campaigning groups including pensioners and consumers groups, together with opposition political parties and even a right-wing think-tank. Significantly, while the union was unable to match the communication resources of the government and Post Office managers, and was unable to match in quantitative terms the battle to make contributions to news articles, its alliances with other groups reaped dividends because these 'other' actors, or 'third party endorsements' made significant contributions to news reports and the flow of the debate (Davis, 2000: 180–3). The campaign is likely to have played a significant part in the government's decision to abandon the privatisation proposal.

Trade unions around the world are turning to news media work as a strategy to be employed during harsh times in which global forces are undermining the collective strength of organised labour within particular nations, and neo-liberal governments appear determined to administer the *coup de grâce*. In New Zealand, for example, a series of measures enacted by governments through the 1980s culminated in the 1991 Employment Contracts Act which denied all collectively negotiated employment rights. The response of the New Zealand Council of Trade Unions (CTU) was to prioritise a news media campaign because the weakening of union strength in the workplace and the configuration of political forces around the state meant that successful opposition to these measures through the exertion of traditional collective strength was unlikely to succeed (Scott, 1997). In Canada and the USA, unions are following a similar course (Puette, 1992; McChesney, 1997: 72). Communication strategies are likely to become increasingly important as the globalising tendencies of economic forces prompts trade unions to internationalise their campaigns (Waterman, 1990). Indeed, trade unions can now exploit the potential of global communication technologies, including the Internet, to communicate with each other, reach key target audiences and co-ordinate union activity on an international scale (Lee, 1996). The international campaign against the Multilateral Agreement on Investment (MAI) provides a timely illustration. The MAI proposals were strongly favoured by some of the most powerful transnational corporations because they would have compelled national governments to embrace neo-liberal market-driven policies in many key areas of economic and social policy. The Internet became a vital tool with which to circulate the necessary information on the implications of the MAI so that eventually over 600 unions and campaigning organisations, in dozens of countries, could begin to target nationally based news media, political élites and 'opinion leaders' (Vidal, 1999). Now over 1700 websites around the world, such as LabourNet or Cyber Picket Line, are permitting union activists to exchange information globally in a way that is quite unprecedented (Davies, 1998).[9]

There is a danger in presenting news media strategies as the great panacea for politically marginal groups. There are usually difficulties, dilemmas and costs associated with the use of such strategies and the experience of trade unions illustrates this well. To begin with, news media work is unlikely to provide a means for fundamentally transforming power relationships for any politically marginal group. Just as the poor will remain poor despite the best efforts of media-sophisticated pressure groups on their behalf, so trade unions will generally be placed in a subordinate position when confronting capital

· the media strategy employed. In the cases of two of the British ' disputes examined above, while the media strategies assisted the ... involved and helped to minimise the political damage that more hostile news coverage might potentially have done, in both cases the final outcome was not an unqualified industrial triumph. While securing some improvements for members, *real* concessions to management were made in the resolution of the conflicts. No amount of sophisticated media spin-doctoring will thwart a powerful neo-liberal government if it has determined to undermine the rights of organised labour, as in New Zealand. And trade unions are powerless to prevent the changing tide of news values which has turned against them, prompting news organisations to drastically reduce the number of industrial correspondents with specialist interests in labour relations (see Chapter 3).

Secondly, and following on from the previous point, more powerful organisations can usually deploy more media resources, more effectively, over the long term. The unions involved in the ambulance dispute stole a march on the employers and government at first, but after several months of protracted dispute, the latter had come to appreciate the importance of the news dimension and had deployed their forces more effectively. Thirdly, and crucially, one function of power is the capacity to exercise more effective control over the flow of information entering the public domain than the less powerful. Trade unions are classic illustrations of this point. Powerful corporations are better able to control their employees' contacts with journalists. Trade unions are inherently 'leaky' organisations; their organisational cultures are often highly politicised and factionalised; and branch, regional and national levels, and their histories of dissent, all mean that unions will routinely generate multiple information flows to which journalists can attend. During the golden era of the British industrial beat, in the 1960s and 1970s, labour correspondents would be briefed by the Communist Party supporting members of the NUM national executive in one pub and then cross the road to be briefed by the more right-wing members of the same executive in another pub. Much the same arrangements operated for a number of the larger unions. Even today, journalists know that often it is possible to by-pass a union press officer to gather off-the-record information from another source. The relatively short duration of the BA dispute (union members were only on strike for three days) meant that the TGWU leadership were able to hold their local branches in line and 'on message'. However, in the ambulance dispute the length of the campaign, which lasted nearly nine months, generated severe strains at a local level, with more militant branches calling for and taking unofficial action. This made it very difficult for the national officers to manage all the information flows that began to emerge from within the unions. Thus, despite the careful planning at a national level in order to present the dispute *not* as a strike, stories began to emerge about the possibility of unofficial strike action from sources at local branch level. The danger of the dispute being placed by journalists in the notorious 1979 'Winter of Discontent' news frame loomed large once again.

In Chapter 6 the problem of 'media incorporation' was introduced and this represents a final potential difficulty for trade unions. As we have seen, trade unions have recently placed a growing reliance upon accommodative strategies to secure access to the news media. They have accepted the 'imperatives' of news journalism, embraced popular news values, wrapped their arguments around stories with 'human interest' or 'a personality', and resigned themselves to the fact that a news editor's appetite is most likely to be whetted by the sudden and dramatic. Their press officers, often coming from backgrounds in journalism, frequently embrace the 'inevitability' of working with mainstream news values while acknowledging the associated constraints. The danger for politically marginal groups such as unions is that the adoption of accommodative strategies leads to 'media incorporation'. In other words, the message is trimmed to suit the purposes of the messenger. In the ambulance dispute, the coherence of the union position and its justice could only really be demonstrated by acknowledging the complexity of the detail. Stories that 'individualised' the dispute by concentrating upon human interest angles (for example, feature articles concentrating upon the 'heroic' efforts of particular crews or the struggle to make ends meet for workers' families) certainly appealed to public sympathy but failed to communicate coherently the heart of the union case. Media incorporation can have a further constraining effect: there is a temptation to smother the radicalism of a union agenda in an effort to satisfy mainstream news values and win the respect of journalists as a credible source. As one former labour commentator put it a long time ago, union leaders must be wary not to allow 'publicity about the worth of unions to be a substitute for worthy activity' (Pomper, 1959: 491). These are dangers rather than inevitable consequences.

Green Spin Doctors

The new generation of environmentalist groups which emerged in the 1960s and 1970s are often associated with a new emphasis upon campaigning through the mass media (Lowe and Morrison, 1984: 83; Greenberg, 1985; McCormick, 1991). In Britain, groups such as the Ramblers Association, the Town and Country Planning Association, and the Council for the Preservation of Rural England, represent a 'first generation' of environmentalist groups that emerged before the Second World War and, while sometimes resorting to direct action or civil disobedience as campaigning tactics, they did not necessarily place the mass media in the foreground of their campaigning work. The second generation of post-war campaigning groups were distinctive in two senses: first, with varying degrees of intensity, they all identified the mass media as a primary target for campaigning activity; and secondly, the emerging evidence of the scale of environmental threat prompted in many cases an international or global, rather than national, perspective. Greenpeace International is perhaps the prime example, being a truly global pressure group with a strong organisational presence in most European countries but with the capacity to sustain political activity and media-orientated campaigns around the world. Organisations such as Friends of the Earth and the World Wide Fund for Nature are similarly constituted (Anderson, 1997: 85).

Nevertheless, despite the breadth of their campaigning reach, most of the new generation of environmentalist groups have spent much of their political existence as politically marginal 'outsiders', which is one reason why they were the subject of some of the first studies to explore the possibilities for the less powerful to contest patterns of primary news definition with the powerful (Hansen, 1991; Anderson, 1991). In recent years, European governments have been compelled to acknowledge the political significance of 'green politics' and the pressing urgency of many environmental issues. Indeed, a centre-left and green coalition has controlled central government in Germany since 1998, while in Britain the Deputy Prime Minister has been given special responsibility for environmental issues, presiding over a 'super-ministry' that embraces both environmental and transport briefs. European governments may acknowledge that in certain circumstances the expertise and scientific research gathered by Greenpeace, Friends of the Earth and other organisations may contribute to the policy-making process. However, these developments do not herald a new era of insider access for environmental groups, but instead represent a partial and temporary opening of some doors to particular policy communities.

For much of the post-war period, environmentalist groups were denied access to the 'insider channels' within key departments of state such as agriculture or industry (Lowe et al., 1986). In the mid-1980s Greenberg found British civil servants still referring to Friends of the Earth as 'a bunch of kooks . . . who dressed up in funny costumes to gain publicity' (1985: 360). If the political influence of environmentalist groups has grown in the last decade, this is partly as a consequence of the increasing public support for environmental campaigns which, in turn, is partly contingent upon the success of the news media strategies deployed (Cox et al., 1986). Nevertheless, both at national government and European Union level, environmental groups struggle to penetrate the agricultural policy community, and fare only slightly better with regard to health, energy and industry (Smith, 1993; Greer, 1998). Smith, for example, identifies a set of institutional barriers which ensure that environmental campaigners remain on the outside: these include the shared dominant beliefs of the agricultural policy community integrating European farming interests, food producers and policy-makers and the associated 'rules of the game' informally governing how groups 'should' behave in seeking access to the policy community (Smith, 1993: 102). In Britain, for example, while the National Farmers' Union enjoys a statutory right to be consulted through the policy-making process, environmental and consumer groups do not. Although under growing political pressure to acknowledge a broader range of interests as environmental and food scares accumulate, the Directorate General VI of the European Commission and the Council of

Agricultural Ministers which have responsibility for many aspects of EC agricultural and environmental policy remain implacably closed to environmental groups (Smith, 1990).

Environmental Groups and News Journalism

The implications of the continuing political marginalisation of environmental groups are important for the politics of news sources. Without the regular, routine access to policy-making processes enjoyed by key producer interests (for example, industrial and chemical interests, farming and food producer lobbies) environmental groups are at a disadvantage in their dealings with specialist correspondents and journalists. First, they will not be privy to much of the 'intelligence', 'contextual information', rumour and speculation that is the currency of political correspondents. Secondly, as discussed in Chapter 6, insider status confers a higher position on the hierarchy of credibility with which journalists assess the standing of competing news sources. Although the food risk and environmental hazard scares of recent years have shaken public confidence in 'expert' or official pronouncements on various issues, from nuclear energy to genetically modified food, environmental organisations have had to invest a great deal of time and resources in developing their own research activity in order to make credible their own claims to speak with the authority of science when dealing with journalists (Eyerman and Jamison, 1989). And the 'authority' acquired in this way is easily dissolved, as the case of the Brent Spar demonstrates (see below).

A third point concerns the diverse nature of environmentalist groups. While Greenpeace International, Friends of the Earth and the WWFN are highly organised and integrated political agencies, there is a huge range of campaigning activity, mounted with contrasting degrees of formality and organisational cohesion, and associated with the emergence of 'new social movements' across Europe and the USA (Anderson, 1997: 90–104). Such activity ranges from hunt saboteurs attempting to disrupt British fox hunting, to German greens blocking nuclear fuel trains, Norwegian protestors picketing Downing Street in protest against radioactive emissions from British nuclear power stations, and the coalition of environmentalist, Third World and trade union activists who produced a truly 'global demonstration' outside the Seattle World Trade Organisation conference in November 1999. In the past, journalists have frequently succumbed to the temptation to demonise such forms of protest, representing those involved through the imagery associated with politics and lifestyles beyond the consensual norm (Cohen and Young, 1978). There is some evidence that this is changing and that it is harder for sections of the news media to demonise direct action environmental protestors because there is a perception shared by a number of news editors that public sentiments have changed. The case of Swampy, an English anti-roads protestor who risked life and limb by tunnelling under the proposed route of the A30 near Exeter, is a case in point. He emerged to become a temporary national hero. According to the editor of the tabloid *Sunday*

Mirror, the explanation lies both in the extent to which Swampy could be represented in terms of positive mainstream news values and in a sensitivity within the newsroom to perceived changes in the public mood:

> Swampy is great copy. He's called Swampy. He digs in the earth. He doesn't say very much because its actions not words. He doesn't go out to harm people. His hairstyle is like nothing on earth, and he has that slightly bemused but inoffensive look. . . . If he had a child it would be Son of Swampy. If he got married it would be Here Comes the Bride and Swampy, too.
>
> There is a constituency out there for the guy. The points he puts across deserve to be put across. For a fair number of our readers he was doing what they wanted to see done. He risked his life for what seemed to be a very precarious protest [arising from the danger of tunnel roof collapses]. It was not harmful. It was defiant. (Quoted in Bellos, 1997: 4)

The 'Swampy fever' which unfolded in the British media in the course of the next few days was unprecedented (Swampy was invited to do fashion shoots in *The Times* and quiz show appearances on television) and illustrates the ways in which environmental issues and a green political agenda could be positively represented in the news media. However, while patterns of news coverage overall may be changing, the disadvantages faced by environmental groups, as political outsiders, remain real enough.

These are compounded by a fourth point. In the arena of environmental news coverage, environmental organisations face some very well resourced opponents. Transnational corporations, particularly those most likely to be exposed to hostile coverage arising from their investment and production strategies, have grown increasingly concerned about 'green issues'. Oil companies such as Shell and BP, chemical companies such as ICI and Fisons, and biotech companies such as Monsanto, spend a great deal on 'greenwashing' their activities. This may involve supporting 'front organisations' such as the Global Climate Coalition, the Soil and Water Conservation Association, or the 'Business Council for Sustainable Development' – all environmental-friendly sounding organisations but actually funded by the corporate sector to promote their interests when environmental debates hot up in the news. It might even involve sponsoring books and academic critiques of environmentalism which sometimes also surface in the news when discussions of a 'green backlash' are topical (Michie, 1998: 81–9). Most large corporations, of course, also have their own public relations departments to support news media work. Shell annually spends around £20 million on advertising designed to improve its image rather than sell a particular product (Armstrong, 1998). And the lessons to be learnt from the difficulties of one corporation in grappling with the environmental agenda are quickly absorbed by another. Following Shell's difficulties over Brent Spar, BP has tried to turn the spotlight on Greenpeace, questioning its legitimacy and attempting to portray it as a wealthy but unaccountable and internally undemocratic 'Goliath', rather than an eco-friendly David (Bennie, 1998: 402–4). Very much the same themes – the unaccountability and irresponsibility of environmental pressure groups, their skilful and dangerous use of the media – are sometimes echoed in the news media work of governments and state officials. Alternatively, the corporations and governments may collude to encourage a 'silence' in news coverage, by deliberately not responding to environmentalist campaigns (Rose, 1998: 132, 204).

Given this formidable set of forces ranged against environmental groups it is hardly surprising that some commentators are pessimistic about their capacity to sustain an influence over the process of primary news definition in environmental coverage (Protess et al., 1991; Greer, 1998). Protess, for example, studied the interaction between pressure groups, journalists and policy-makers in relation to a set of health, environmental and crime issues in the United States, concluding that while the policy-making process was often influenced by dialogue between political élites and journalists, environmental and health campaigning organisations were largely excluded. Similarly, it is sometimes argued that the recent increase in the importance attached to environmental stories by news organisations is a product of changes in the attitudes of political élites, rather than the efforts of campaigning groups. It was when Mrs Thatcher, in a Prime Ministerial set speech, decreed that the environment was 'important' that British newsrooms really woke up (ITN science editor quoted in Love, 1990). Are the possibilities for effective news media work as restricted as this for environmental groups? Other commentators believe that the capacity of environmentalist groups to seize the initiative in agenda setting and either visibly (Anderson, 1997) or less directly (Hansen, 1993) shape the process of primary definition should not be underestimated. What news media strategies can be employed?

The News Media Strategies and the Social Construction of the Environment

Environmental organisations such as Friends of the Earth and Greenpeace share a common history in prioritising media campaigning but in the past there have been perceived differences in emphasis. While Friends of the Earth have always placed considerable importance upon the acquisition of accurate information and research evidence to support their claims to speak with 'authority' (Anderson, 1991: 472), Greenpeace has sometimes been criticised for placing more emphasis upon direct action, stunts, and the media coverage associated with a 'politics of spectacle' (Rucht, 1995: 71). In contrast to the experience of trade unions where a labour and industrial news beat had emerged in Britain before the Second World War and provided a convenient channel for briefing specialist correspondents, no comparable environmental beat existed during the 1960s and early 1970s, when the second generation of environmental groups emerged. Resort to stunts and spectacle represented one way of addressing this problem and to stimulate dialogue with news organisations (Hansen, 1993: 150). While Greenpeace continues to mount frequent direct action and spectacular campaigns, it too now invests very considerable sums in science and information gathering work. As we shall see below, however, some journalists retain a sceptical orientation towards Greenpeace briefings because in their view direct action campaigning is at odds with 'objectivity' and 'scientific detachment'.

Unlike trade unions which, as we have seen, have typically come to use accommodative news media strategies after periods in which their suspicion of the politics and economic interests of the news media encouraged attempts to reform, by-pass or ignore rather than accommodate the news media, environmental groups developed accommodative strategies from the outset. With the accumulation of greater resources over the years and the arrival of cheaper communication technologies, an organisation such as Greenpeace International can now produce its own television and video products, its own marketing and art work, its own website and global electronic communication materials. However, it is notable that on the whole, environmental organisations have not felt compelled to challenge the structure of ownership and control of the news media, or to mount campaigns to politicise the issue of news content bias with the same intensity as trade unions. This is partly explained by the differences in political culture associated with environmentalism and the labour movement. The influence of socialism within trade unions and the labour movement has always prompted questions about the power of capital and the privileges of ownership, but it may also reflect real differences in the experience of coverage and treatment at the hands of the press. Newspaper proprietors, for example, may not perceive environmentalists as such a direct threat to their own interests as trade unionists and, indeed, may acknowledge that their readers sometimes share environmental concerns. As Lowe and Morrison put it:

> Who, for example, other than the truly demented would, in principle, demand more air, water and noise pollution, the spillage of radioactive material, the despoilation of the countryside, or even the killing of seal pups, as a good thing in itself? What this means is that for journalists to be committed to the environmental cause does not itself seem tendentious, though such commitments may become controversial in specific instances – such as the sinking of a mine shaft at the expense of a local beauty spot – when the goal of environmental conservation is counterposed to economic and technological goals. (1984: 80)

By the early 1980s approximately half the environmental organisations operating in Britain had established their own media or press departments and a significant minority of those running such organisations came from media backgrounds (Lowe and Morrison, 1984: 84). Similar arrangements emerged as environmentalist organisations grew throughout Europe and the USA. In contrast to the recent history of trade union–media relations where trade union news strategies have been impeded by the contraction of the labour beat and the declining status of labour news, the media work of environmental organisations has been greatly assisted by the emergence of an environmental beat during the 1980s. During the early 1980s, first broadsheet, serious newspapers and later broadcasting organisations began to appoint specialist environmental correspondents (Lowe and Morrison, 1984: 83).

The rise and fall of particular news specialisms as categories of knowledge is related to complex political, economic and cultural forces (Manning, 1998). Changing public attitudes, the intervention of natural scientists in lending authority to the claims made by environmentalists, and the recognition on the part of political élites that such issues would have to be addressed all contributed to the sensitisation of news organisations (Anderson, 1991: 463–5) but the contribution of environmental organisations to this process should not be underestimated. Once an environmental beat began to grow, it was possible for environmental organisations to foster exchange relationships with a group of journalists who were likely at least to listen because their professional careers depended upon the rapid acquisition of pertinent environmental information. By no means have all news organisations appointed environment correspondents, nor do environmental organisations choose to deal exclusively with them – health, transport or science correspondents may offer better outlets for particular stories. Nevertheless, the emergence of an environmental beat has provided a stable channel through which those working for environmental organisations can attempt to utilise the norms and protocols of source–journalist relations to their advantage. In turn, this has allowed environmental organisations to rely a little less upon 'the politics of spectacle' in their attempts to secure access to the news arena. Rather than depending exclusively upon mounting publicity stunts to generate news interest, they can spend a little more time working through established contacts on the environmental beat (Anderson, 1991: 469).

In order to channel information to the public domain via news beats, environmental organisations have to frame their agendas in ways that will appeal to mainstream news values. Some commentators have assumed that this is an unproblematic exercise because potential environmental disasters have an inherent news interest and associated 'strong emotive and moralistic appeal' (Lowe and Morrison, 1984: 79). However, things may be a little more complicated. As Hansen (1993) and Anderson (1997) have argued, the 'environment' as a concept is socially constructed through its representation in the mass media; it does not contain any inherent features which make it 'obviously' newsworthy. Decisions made by editors and journalists are influenced by a number of complex processes which means that the newsworthyness of environmental issues cannot be taken for granted (see Chapter 3). Even Shell's decision to sink the Brent Spar in the North Sea, which eventually generated controversy around the world, was not immediately recognised by environmental correspondents as a newsworthy story (Rose, 1998: 138).

For environmental organisations, this underlines the importance of framing their agenda in terms of as many mainstream news values as possible. However, there are some inherent tensions in doing this. First, even the more institutionalised groups such as Greenpeace still display organisational cultures which, to a degree, reflect the values and ideology of the new social movements. Thus, for example, Greenpeace is reluctant to offer one spokesperson as a 'telegenic', media friendly personality to 'represent' the organisation, despite the appeal that 'personalities' have for the news media, because it retains an egalitarian organisational philosophy (Hansen, 1993: 167). There is a second, more profound problem in that a full explication of environmental issues would necessarily involve a description of long-term and gradual processes bound up largely with impersonal structural forces unfolding across a broad global canvas. Global warming, for example, is not sudden and dramatic (Anderson, 1991: 465). This, of course, does not translate into compelling news values in the eyes of mainstream journalists. However, organisations such as Greenpeace and Friends of the Earth have learnt to encode *parts* of their agenda in terms of the particular and local, the sudden and dramatic. Thus, for example, British environmental organisations wrapped a powerful message about ocean pollution around the story of a large number of seal deaths on the east coast (Anderson, 1991). Dying seals have strong visual and emotive appeal for mainstream news media. Similarly, the Italian environmental organisation Lega Ambiente connected a long-term concern about the production of waste to particular examples of corruption in political office – a topical theme in Italian media coverage of politics (Triandafyllidou, 1996), while Greenpeace International has used its 'direct action' stunts, including occupying off-shore oil installations and camping on Rockall, to make broad concerns about energy policy and waste disposal have immediacy and human interest in the eyes of European and US news journalists (Rose, 1998), and the Swedish Society for the Protection of Nature (SNF) used the topicality of controversial regional construction projects to insert elements of its concerns about energy and transport policies into media coverage (Gooch, 1996: 121). Environmental organisations are sensitive to the semiological dimension of news encoding, too. If attention to news values helps to secure interest in a particular story, then attention to the language in which a story is encoded can help to steer the audience towards a particular evaluation of issues. Thus, waste 'disposal' becomes 'dumping' and animal 'culls' become 'killings' (Bennie, 1998: 400). Exciting visuals, cuddly animals, daring stunts and human interest angles are all deployed with growing sophistication by environmental groups.

So the 'new' environmental organisations in Europe and the USA have been good at drawing upon mainstream news values to encode elements of their environmental agenda from the outset (in contrast to many trade unions which were very much more reluctant to embrace accommodative news strategies). And they have learnt to target particular news media with increasing accuracy, briefing 'serious' or broadsheet journalists for certain stories, 'popular' or tabloid papers for others, and television for stories with strong visual appeal (Lacey and Longman, 1993: 223). There are some differences in strategy and approach. Friends of the Earth are a little more pessimistic about the opportunities provided by television, preferring to concentrate upon the established beat among environmental and science newspaper correspondents; Greenpeace, on the other hand, are prioritising visual stories for television and popular journalism (Anderson, 1991: 470). There is some evidence that the former strategy actually generates more coverage (Hansen, 1993: 153).

Information Flows and the Environmental Beat

If the painstaking cultivation of journalistic contacts is more productive, this may be related to the importance of the exchange relationships that can be fostered on the environmental and science beats, between sources and journalists. Much television output is made up of 'one-off' current affairs and issue-orientated programmes, increasingly made these days by independent production companies without a particular commitment to environmental news. Environmental correspondents, however, working for newspapers or news broadcasting departments, have to obtain information from somewhere to produce their quota of news copy (Hansen, 1993: 160). This pressure is likely to sensitise them to the information flows generated by environmental groups. In other words, the dependence of specialist journalists upon 'contextual information' (information with particular political significance, generated by experts or authorities, or material that allows journalists to anticipate key developments, etc.) encourages environmental correspondents to be more receptive to the briefings provided by environmental organisations, providing the 'contextual information' supplied is credible and relevant. As Hansen comments, it is one thing to achieve short-term publicity through stunts and spectacle, it is quite another to achieve more permanent status as legitimate, authoritative sources (1993: 151). Organisations such as Friends of the Earth and Greenpeace can certainly enhance the currency of the information they offer to correspondents by relating it to ongoing political processes, either at a national or an international level (government white papers, treaty renewals, trade negotiations, etc.). In other words, they can attempt to insert elements of their own agendas into the mainstream news agendas associated with formal politics. They can act as a conduit for information leaked by insiders within other organisations, including British Nuclear Fuels, energy companies, European Commission officials, and national government civil servants, and they can generate news interest through the commissioning of opinion polls and surveys, or even resort to legal action as a way of generating media interest (Hansen, 1993: 172–3; Bennie, 1998: 399–400).

All these can be understood as strategies to enhance the value of the information which they supply to journalists. However, it is in the provision of scientific and technical data that environmental organisations often hope to offer correspondents the most valuable 'contextual information' (Hansen, 1993: 174; Bennie, 1998: 400). Few journalists working for mainstream news organisations have the time or expertise to research the technical aspects of environmental debates (Anderson, 1997: 128). This encourages a dependence upon sources that can provide and summarise such information, providing they appear authoritative. In earlier decades, government and industry were able to claim a monopoly on the provision of 'authoritative' technical data.

According to Hansen, Greenpeace and other environmental organisations had achieved a position of authority for their own research and intelligence material by the early 1990s. Almost a decade later Anderson seems to support this judgement (Anderson, 1997: 207). The problem, however, is that this is a fragile status, vulnerable to rapid erosion if things go wrong and that is precisely what happened in the case of Greenpeace's Brent Spar campaign.

The Case of the Brent Spar

For some researchers, the inherent qualities in the 'environment' as an issue will encourage a receptiveness on the part of journalists (Lowe and Morrison, 1984). However, other researchers found that the association of environmental groups with 'stunts' and 'direct action' produced a lingering image of political partisanship, making some journalists suspicious of environmental organisations and sceptical of their briefings (Linne, 1993). As the BBC science correspondent commented to Anderson a decade ago: 'I mean if scientists are fairly agreed that something serious is happening then I would take more notice of them than I would necessarily of an organisation like Greenpeace claiming something's happening because it doesn't quite have the authority of some other organisations or that conventional scientists have' (quoted in Anderson, 1991: 463).

At this time, 9 out of 12 journalists questioned by Anderson indicated that they were mistrustful of Greenpeace. If the investment in 'science' has helped environmental organisations to secure more credibility in the eyes of journalists over recent years, the Brent Spar episode suggests that a lingering scepticism very quickly reasserts itself and that traditional hierarchies of credibility are rapidly resurrected by some journalists. Shell's decision to abandon the plan to decommission and sink the Brent Spar in the summer of 1995 was regarded at first as a triumph for Greenpeace campaigning and its action in occupying the off-shore installation. However, this media and political success evaporated alarmingly when four months later Greenpeace admitted that it had overestimated the volume of toxic waste contained within the Spar storage tanks as a result of a simple error in sampling. Headlines in several newspapers and news bulletins echoed the *Daily Express*'s 'Dark Side of Greenpeace Do-gooders', while *The Times* and *Daily Telegraph* complained about Greenpeace's 'lies' (Rose, 1998: 148, 162). A number of senior journalists felt that they had been manipulated by Greenpeace and that their faith in the 'authority' of Greenpeace information had been misplaced. One commented: 'Our relationship is very tense; [Greenpeace] manipulated us and the agenda; we felt bounced quite significantly over Brent Spar. . . . We felt manipulated and could not put our own journalism into it. We have been very cautious since then'[10]

The erroneous waste estimate had not actually played a central part in the controversy because it had been produced by Greenpeace *after* the debate had taken off and publicity had triggered strong political reactions, together with organised public boycotts of Shell outlets in Germany, Scandinavia and other parts of Europe (Rose, 1998: 145). As a 'fire-fighting tactic', Greenpeace had immediately gone public as soon as it became clear that an error had been made. In this light, the reaction of some British news editors might be regarded as somewhat exaggerated, particularly as a number of errors made by Shell in its briefing material for news media were passed over.

What explains the intensity of the editorial reaction against Greenpeace? Ironically, part of the answer is related to the sophistication of the Greenpeace news strategy. In selecting an off-shore installation, Greenpeace had positioned itself in a way which afforded significant control of the key information flows to the media. With budget constraints exercising an increasing influence over editorial decisions, few news organisations originally believed that the issue warranted the expense involved in sending correspondents and film crews to the Spar. Accordingly, many news organisations relied heavily upon Greenpeace's own film footage and briefings when the controversy erupted. Thus, at least in the early phases of the story, Greenpeace had some very significant advantages in attempting to exercise control over the nature and flow of information entering the news arena. Conflict and tension is always likely to be generated in circumstances where one agency enjoys a near monopoly upon the supply of valuable information. Although the dependency of news organisations upon Greenpeace was a consequence of their own editorial and budgetary decisions, none the less it caused a resentment among senior journalists. Richard Sambrook, Head of Newsgathering at the BBC, complained at the 1995 Edinburgh Television Festival that Greenpeace had been 'pulling us by the nose', while David Lloyd (Senior Commissioning Editor at Channel 4 News and Current Affairs) argued:

> On Brent Spar we were bounced. This matters – we took great pains to represent Shell's side of the argument. By the time the broadcasters had tried to intervene on the scientific analysis, the story had been spun so far in Greenpeace's direction. . . . When we attempted to pull the story back, the pictures provided to us showed plucky helicopters riding a fusillade of water cannons [Shell used water cannons against Greenpeace protestors]. Try and write the analytical science into that to the advantage of the words. (Quoted in Rose, 1998: 158)

So, the very success of the Greenpeace strategy had damaged the relationship it enjoyed with journalists. Significantly, in the quotation above, David Lloyd of Channel 4 distinguishes between the Greenpeace argument and 'analytical science', – by September 1995 in the eyes of many senior journalists Greenpeace's appeals to science were discredited. BBC TV's 'News Review of the Year' summarised the episode as one in which 'the world discovered that Greenpeace had been wrong all along' (Rose, 1998: 165). Chris Rose, Campaigns Director at Greenpeace, believes that the haste with which senior editorial teams dismissed Greenpeace's science, was bound up with more complex issues because the main thrust of its analysis had never depended upon exactly 'how much' waste the Spar contained but, on the contrary, a rather more comprehensive analysis of the relative environmental costs involved in dumping or recycling materials. Rose argues that the Spar controversy merged with wider political anxieties shared by the Euro-sceptic sections of the British press and a growing backlash against environmental politics. In the two years following the Brent Spar controversy, both the BBC and Channel 4 in Britain commissioned documentaries that developed much wider and more hostile critiques of environmentalism. The Brent Spar episode came to represent, for some sections of the news media, an illustration of the dangers that arise when pressure group 'power' is allowed to distort an otherwise rational policy-making process (Bennie, 1998: 407). Even two years later, BBC's *Newsnight* introduced an unrelated item by saying: 'The disposal of the Brent Spar oil platform highlighted the difficulties of nations disposing of their industrial detritus. The environmental campaigners who played on European emotions against dumping in the Atlantic now acknowledge that they may have been wrong' (Rose, 1998: 168).

A pessimistic reading would suggest that the inferential frameworks (see Chapter 3) employed by journalists in trying to make sense of the world now repositioned Greenpeace and other environmentalist organisations in a former category, as less trustworthy sources guilty of allowing their politics to contaminate the quality of the information they supplied to the news media. However, the picture is not entirely bleak for Greenpeace. The MORI surveys of British journalists on the environmental beat suggest that its reputation has not been fatally damaged by the Spar episode. The most hostile views are more likely to be held at a higher level within news organisations, among editors, feature writers and senior staff. In 1995, 70 per cent of European journalists indicated that environmental pressure groups were 'very useful' sources of information, while only 33 per cent indicated that their own governments were; a mere 3 per cent thought that corporations were (Worcester, 1996).

Environmentalism, New Communication Technologies, and Exchange Relations

Underlying the critical reaction against Greenpeace was a further anxiety shared by broadcasting journalists about the growing importance of video news releases (VNRs). Greenpeace claims that it only infrequently uses VNRs because it more frequently supplies raw footage to broadcasting organisations, rather than an edited and finished product (Rose, 1998: 157). Nevertheless, whether it is raw footage or a finished VNR, a growing number of environmental organisations now invest quite considerable sums in the technology required to offer television news a new kind of 'information subsidy', to use Gandy's term (1982). Greenpeace spent £350,000 in establishing a satellite broadcasting link from the Spar to its 24 hour a day media centre in Holland to ensure that pictures were available to broadcasting organisations at any time (MacGregor, 1997: 40). Similarly, with Western news organisations either unable or unwilling to secure access to North Korea to cover the growing problems of famine, aid agencies supplied VNRs to television news organisations in Europe and the USA. WWFN now also regularly supplies VNR material to television outlets in Europe and the USA.

While budget constraints may sometimes encourage news organisations to accept VNRs, there is considerable anxiety among some journalists because they regard VNR material as 'second-hand news' (Rose, 1998: 162), produced by political actors with agendas of their own. The reaction against Greenpeace was partly a particular manifestation of a more widespread frustration arising from the conflict between the professional commitment to 'objectivity' and 'balance', on the one hand, and the economic determinants of news production, on the other.

If a growing number of environmental organisations invest in VNR technology, will this supplant or transform the exchange relationships which support the environmental beat? The answer is likely to be that while such exchange relationships may be modified, enduring and successful news media strategies will still depend upon exchanges between press officers and journalists. The case of the fax machine may help explain why. Before the arrival of the fax machine in press and media offices of politically marginal groups, press officers had to depend upon systems of mechanical reproduction and distribution for the delivery of press releases to journalists and newsrooms, unless they hired an expensive agency such as the Universal News System to disseminate releases. In the temptation to use the new electronic technology to maximum effect, many press officers forgot the old maxim, 'keep your powder dry'. Some press officers working for environmental organisations bombarded news desks with faxed press releases, as did one or two union press officers (Anderson, 1991: 470; Manning, 1998: 111–14). Not surprisingly, journalists did not welcome such an indiscriminate approach and the more thoughtful press officers chose to combine a more judicious approach to faxed press releases with a continued investment in the development of social relationships with particular journalists. Supporting press releases with telephone or face-to-face briefings allowed a press release to be placed in context and this frequently proved more successful.

The arrival of VNR technology is unlikely, in itself, to diminish the importance of exchange relationships. What might undermine their importance is not the use of new communication technology by politically marginal groups but rather the changing political–economic environment of news production and the ever intensifying pressures upon news organisations to trim costs, leading to cuts in the numbers of specialist correspondents on certain beats. Indeed, the arrival of new communication technologies can complement rather than undermine established news strategies and associated exchange relationships. For example, a website can be used as a way of securing the interest of journalists as well as disseminating information to the public. Thus, Friends of the Earth recently published a web page containing the results of its latest 'Factory Watch' survey of the 'worst polluters in Britain', as measured in kilos of carcinogens emitted.[11] This has generated considerable press interest, with the *Daily Mirror* reproducing the page in full, together with quotes from the Friends of the Earth press office 'framing' the story.[12] Greenpeace also publishes several award-winning websites targeted at journalists as well as the public.

Conclusion: Accommodative News Strategies and the Communications Dilemma

This chapter has examined the experience of two rather different categories of politically marginal organisation. Trade unions have come late to the use of accommodative news strategies. Indeed, the labour and industrial beat in the USA, Britain and parts of Western Europe was already in decline before communicative work was really formalised and coherently organised within many trade unions. The new generation of environmental organisations emerging in the 1960s, on the other hand, has embraced a variety of accommodative strategies from the outset. While the labour and industrial beat has shrunk over the last two decades, the environmental beat has prospered, as have related science and health beats. The opportunities afforded by the intensified news interest in environmental issues have clearly encouraged environmental organisations to refine and develop their news media work. Undoubtedly, the movement of certain political élites and governments in Europe and the USA to lend political credibility to environmental agendas has been a significant factor here, just as the marginalisation of labour and industrial correspondents together with unions themselves, under particular governments, has been important in the decline of news opportunities for union press officers (Manning, 1999).

While trade unions remain associated with opposition to the interests of capital in the eyes of many senior editors, environmental organisations appear to draw upon support from a broad cross-section of news media audiences, including those of the higher-income, educated strata, so often the object of advertisers' affections. As commentators such as Beck, Giddens and Cottle have pointed out, one of the defining features of late modern capitalist societies is the awareness of 'risk' (Beck et al., 1994; Cottle, 1998). The consciousness of 'risk' brings with it a heightened sensitivity to environmental issues among the public at large, which is helpful for environmentalist organisations. With falling membership revenues, trade unions in countries such as Britain are now often choosing to make cuts in press and media work. In contrast, while the attempts made by some corporations and governments to present environmental organisations as over-resourced Goliaths (Rose, 1998: 117–78) are exaggerated, it is true that the larger campaigning groups such as Greenpeace do have the material resources to support sophisticated news media operations with global reach.

In this context the greater frequency of news stories containing elements of the agendas promoted by environmental organisations, in comparison to trade unions, should come as no surprise. However, what is notable is the degree to which both trade unions and environmental organisations face a common set of communication dilemmas as politically marginal groups. First, if trade unions have suffered because political élites have actively encouraged the decline of labour reporting (Manning, 1999), some critics also claim that from time to time governments have leant heavily upon broadcasting organisations to disadvantage environmental groups in the struggle over the terms of the environmental debate (Rose, 1998: 155–6). Further to this, some commentators suggest that news source activity is relatively unimportant in shaping media agendas compared to broader factors, such as news organisations' assumptions about audience interest (Downs, 1972) or the influence of political élites as definers of 'public issues' (Protess et al., 1991; Lacey and Longman, 1993). A bleak reading of this kind of evidence might suggest that the news work of politically marginal groups is all but futile. While we have already seen that there are good grounds for supposing that news media strategies can make a difference, it is also important to acknowledge the extent to which both unions and environmental organisations are vulnerable to the complex forces shaping news production within the political and economic environment.

Thirdly, we have seen that the capacity to exercise control over information flows travelling out to public news arenas is a significant advantage but one that is itself a function of power (Chapter 5). If many trade unions are inherently 'leaky', which places press officers at a disadvantage, there are also variations in the degree to which the organisational cultures and institutional arrangements of environmental groups permit the exertion of effective control over the flow of information emerging from within. According to one study, at least, Greenpeace has fostered an organisational culture which permits a far higher degree of centralised control over media contacts and information provision than, for example, Friends of the Earth. In turn, this has been the source of some friction with environment correspondents (Anderson, 1993: 56–9). However, for most environmental groups, including Greenpeace, there exist some internal tensions between those who retain a strong commitment to the values and egalitarian ethos of the new social movements and those who seek to 'professionalise', and therefore centralise, aspects of the organisational work. In other words, there can often be a tension between the objective of developing a 'professional', accommodative news media strategy based upon effective central control, and the 'core' values upon which many environmental organisations were founded.

A final set of problems bound up with the attempt to mobilise mainstream news values perhaps best illustrates the communication dilemmas faced by the politically marginal, whether they are unions or environmental groups. To begin with, while those who enjoy formal political power are by definition newsworthy (they are 'official sources'), the politically marginal are always likely to have to work harder to secure access to news media arenas. The politics of spectacle – stunts, occupations and direct action – is a strategy that was frequently used by environmental groups to generate publicity in the past, before an established environmental beat emerged. With the labour and industrial beat already established in the post-war era, and political cultures rooted in the traditions of class and occupational politics rather than the new social movements, trade unions have often relied less heavily upon the stunts and publicity activities associated with Greenpeace and Friends of the Earth. Nevertheless, the dilemma posed by such strategies is one they cannot escape either. Direct action, whether it be the dumping of rubbish outside government buildings or engaging in nautical duels with oil companies, often generates relatively intense publicity in the short term, but may have less value in the longer term if it fails to support the communication of a coherent political argument, or worse, encourages the de-legitimation of the politically marginal group by casting its action as 'extreme' (Lowe and Morrison, 1984: 88). Bennie argues that this is precisely what happened in the controversy over Brent Spar and the later Greenpeace Rockall landing (1998: 400).

Beyond this, however, there is a further dilemma. The use of accommodative news media strategies has to involve the adoption of mainstream news values and this brings with it particular limitations in terms of the kinds of arguments that can be mobilised and the way in which they are presented. Deacon and Golding's distinction between the evaluative and the interpretative is useful here (1994). Just as the ambulance unions scored some notable successes in terms of coverage along the evaluative dimension in the early days of the 1989 dispute but struggled to encode the essential ingredients of their preferred interpretative framework, so the danger for environmental groups is that to encourage a concentration upon the features of their campaigns which immediately relate to mainstream news values – cuddly or vulnerable animals, dramatic stunts, visual elements, human interest angles, and so on – is to pander to the news media inclination to personalise or individualise issues which demand at another level, more complex, perhaps structural explanations. It is always difficult to use the mainstream news media to communicate detailed analyses of the political, economic or cultural processes which underlie 'news events'. By constructing potential news items around conventional news values and news pegs, some environmental groups, like many trade unions, fail to communicate their analytical or interpretative frameworks in their entirety. This makes them vulnerable if particular elements in their position are undermined. The revelation that Greenpeace had overestimated the volume of toxic waste inside Brent Spar was only damaging because the broader and more complex Greenpeace case against the *principle* of dumping at sea rather than recycling on land had not been communicated so effectively. Whether to remain outside the mainstream news media in order to articulate the complex, or to compromise the integrity (and, perhaps rationality) of the analysis in order to accommodate the mainstream news media remains a fundamental dilemma.

Notes

1. Nell Myers, Personal Assistant to the President of the National Union of Mineworkers, in *The Guardian*, 3 June 1985.

2. See, for example, 'How to Handle the Media', TUC, 1979, and 'TUC Strategy: Union Communications', Trade Union Congress Standing Conference of Principle Trade Union Officers, 24 January, 1985, unpublished.

3. The Labour and Industrial Correspondents Group would at its AGM award the 'Golden Bollock' to the labour correspondent who published the news report based upon the most wildly inaccurate interpretation or prediction of likely events. This was enjoyed as a good humoured ritual but also underlined the importance these journalists attached to 'intelligence gathering' and interpretative powers as measures of professional standing.

4. The 1979 'Winter of Discontent' which included a series of protracted public sector disputes and allowed a hostile press to dwell upon the inconvenience caused to the public, including the dead being left unburied, provided a potential template which could have proved highly damaging to the union cause. Trade union complaints regarding this kind of coverage were documented in the TUC pamphlet, 'A Cause for Concern' (1979).

5. See, for example, 'No-one Profits From a BA Strike' by Harry Elliott, *The Times*, Features, 5 June 1997, p. 43.

6. Author's interview with Andrew Murray, former TGWU Press Officer, 25 January 1999.

7. Author's interview with Andrew Murray, former TGWU Press Officer, 25 January 1999.

8. Author's interview with Andrew Murray, former TGWU Press officer, 25 January 1999.

9. Unfortunately, the implications of these developments for union industrial and media strategies are beyond this remit of this book. However, it is quite possible that the Internet came to replace the news media in fulfilling certain key communication functions for unions. In the past, for example, unions often depended upon the news media for the rapid dissemination of information to members involved in disputes or strikes. The case of the Liverpool dockworkers shows that the Internet can be used to develop global channels of rapid communication, independently of not only the national news media but the official union apparatus as well. See Davies (1998). Also, http://www.cf.ac.uk/ccin/union/eng.html

10. MORI Biennial Survey of Editors, October/November 1996, cited in Rose (1998: 151).

11. www.foe.co.uk/factorywatch

12. 'Revealed: 20 Worst Polluters in Britain', *Daily Mirror*, 8 February 1999, p. 19.

8 News Audiences and News Sources

The opening chapter discussed Habermas's concept of the public sphere. The point was made that for Habermas, the public sphere represents the place where 'private individuals come together as a public'. In the contemporary world it could be understood as the point at which, to use Habermas's phrase, the *lifeworld* of the individual intersects with the public beliefs and ideas circulated through mass communication systems. Exactly how the ideas and categories of meaning circulated by mass communication systems, such as news media, intersect with the beliefs of individuals and exactly how individuals or small social groups use their 'decoding skills' to make sense of media messages, are questions which continue to preoccupy media researchers. Drawing upon Bourdieu (1985) and Corner (1991), Verstraeten (1996) distinguishes separate dimensions along which news media may communicate with or 'influence' news audiences. At an obvious level, news messages register with audiences at the denotative level because they describe particular persons, events, issues or things. Such messages also communicate along a connotative dimension because persons, events, issues or things almost always suggest, or connote, deeper associations of one kind or another, in the minds of the audience, which are then processed or thought about (the cognitive level). A photograph of the Queen is likely to suggest more to readers or viewers than simply 'the woman who is monarch'; it will probably trigger thoughts of sovereignty, power, tradition or, perhaps, privilege. However, for Verstraeten there is also a dimension of categorisation, 'through which a certain world view is defined and legitimized', and which is 'established by the "primary definers" and . . . translated into a public idiom and spread by the media. . . . It is precisely here that the symbolic exercise of power within the public sphere takes place' (1996: 363). In other words, while individuals may be more or less autonomous in the way they make sense of, or decode, news messages at one level, there is also a social dimension to 'understanding the news', through which news audiences draw upon and share social categories for thinking through the news, and these categories are produced within the public sphere. The struggles between news sources to control the information flows supplying news organisations connect to news audiences through the categories of understanding which emerge in the public sphere. What kind of impact these categories have upon news audiences (i.e. the public) is the central question for this chapter. After all, if the categories which emerge through news media discourse have little influence upon the way in which we understand news or political issues (broadly defined), there would be little point in attempting to theorise or empirically describe news source activity.

Now, in order to understand the significance of the careful choice of words employed by Verstraeten, we need to briefly review how the controversies surrounding the question of the relationship between news media and news audiences have ebbed and flowed in the period since 1945. In doing this, we need to recognise the importance of clarifying what kinds of effects we are considering. Some of the earliest research attempted to measure attitudinal changes which could be attributed to the news media, while more recent work has shifted the focus away from attitudes and towards the process of agenda setting, and more recently still, the interpretative frameworks through which we draw upon a number of information resources, including the media, in constructing our understanding of the world. In tracing these shifts in research focus, we move on from a search for evidence of relatively short-term or 'immediate' media effects, to an approach that tries to explore longer term or even lifelong cumulative effects. Models of linear effects – 'transmission models' which assume that 'effects' travel in one direction only, from media source to audience – are dumped in favour of multi-linear models in which audience and media interact. Quantitative measures are displaced by qualitative methods, such as surveys by focus groups or 'script writing' exercises.

In other words, the recent history of audience research in media sociology and communication studies is a history of debates not merely over 'evidence' but methodology and epistemology too. Relatively few studies have attempted to track the impact of particular news source campaigns, through the process of news encoding, to reception within news audiences. There is a relative paucity of material dealing with the question of whether or not public relations techniques or the strategies for controlling information flows employed by interest groups and campaigning organisations actually work by registering with news audiences. For those social scientists with a preference for quantitative research and the 'control' of variables, the complexity of the task facing those hoping to 'isolate' the effect of news media strategies from other possible influences upon news audience understandings and behaviour is more than somewhat daunting. Quite apart from all the possible permutations in terms of news content form and genre, all the external and internal processes shaping newsroom practice would have to be taken into account, not to mention the variety of influences patterning the responses and decoding practices of news audiences. However, this does not mean that there is nothing to be said on the subject of the relationship between news audiences and those news sources struggling to be heard. The first step is to briefly review how news audience research has arrived at its current position.

From Masses to Consumers: Two-Step Flows, Uses and Gratifications

In the period up to 1945 there was considerable speculation about the effects of the still relatively new mass communication systems but much less empirical research. The view that mass communication systems were 'obviously' powerful in their capacity to mould public opinion was shared widely not only among commentators and politicians but also, as we saw in Chapter 2, by many social theorists. Liberal apprehensions regarding the vulnerability of 'the masses' to powerful persuasions, including both drink and political oratory, have a long history but they were given a new urgency by the apparent capacity of the new communication technologies of the twentieth century – cinema, radio and mass circulation newspapers – to sway large segments of public opinion. The skilful use made by totalitarian political movements of mass media for propaganda purposes appeared to 'work'. What else would explain the rise of 'the great dictators' in the two decades between 1918 and 1939? The scenes of panic in California following the notorious broadcast of Orson Welles' radio version of *War of the Worlds*, as a series of realistic 'news broadcasts', in 1938, seemed to confirm this new communicative power. From another perspective, the critical theorists of the Frankfurt School could only explain the triumph of capitalist advertising and marketing functions in forging new 'mass markets' for consumer goods in terms of the capacity of the 'culture industries' not only to sway opinion but to manipulate behaviour (Adorno and Horkheimer, 1977).

However, during the 1940s and 1950s, the picture of news audiences as 'masses' vulnerable to powerful mass communication systems was transformed by a series of empirical audience surveys conducted in the USA by, among others, Paul F. Lazarsfeld. Ironically, Lazarsfeld was given his first senior post in audience research by Hadley Cantril, who had been awarded a grant by the Rockefeller Foundation to establish an Office of Radio Research at Princeton University in 1937. It was Cantril who undertook the systematic study of the aftermath of the Orson Welles radio broadcast. This was at a time when the large US communications corporations, such as the Columbia Broadcasting Corporation (CBS), were beginning to consider the possibility of employing social science methodologies to enquire into the characteristics and tastes of their audiences with greater precision. Lazarsfeld developed a close working relationship with CBS and a number of other media corporations. Although an empirical tradition of audience research had already emerged in the USA in the 1930s (Macleod et al., 1991), Lazarsfeld's work is important because it represents one of the first attempts to quantify in a systematic way, the influence of political communication upon news audiences and it became the template for a tradition in political science and mass communication research that was to endure for at least a further three decades on both sides of the Atlantic. However, as we shall see, Lazarsfeld's approach has a number of weaknesses which are related both to the theoretical and methodological assumptions underpinning it and the context in which it was developed.

Two large empirical studies form the basis for what came to be called the 'two-step flow' model of mass communication (Lazarsfeld et al., 1948; Katz and Lazarsfeld, 1955). In each, a large panel of voters was selected and their political attitudes, including the way in which they received political communication, was monitored using quantitative survey techniques for the six-month duration of the presidential election campaigns (1940 and 1945); the argument being that if news media messages were to exert any influence upon publics, it would certainly be during such periods in which radio and newspaper coverage of politics grew in intensity. The findings from these studies turned the idea of powerful political media moulding mass opinion upside down. In each study, more than half of those sampled held firm views about their voting preferences at the beginning of the research period and these views were not altered by the growing intensity of the news media coverage during the course of the six-month campaigns. Only approximately one-quarter of voters – those who we might now call 'floating voters' – indicated that they made up their minds which way to vote during the course of the campaign and rather than attributing their decisions to the effect of the mass media, they were more likely to cite the influence of particular individuals – 'significant others', or what Lazarsfeld called 'molecular leaders'. A picture, then, emerges of fairly stable bodies of political opinion, either 'Democrat' or 'Republican', made up of individuals who have formed political preferences through processes of political socialisation within the home, community and workplace, rather than the mass media. For a minority of less committed individuals, political support and voting preferences were not so stable but political choices were shaped primarily by small group interaction and the influence of particular individuals. As the subtitle of the second study, *Personal Influence*, suggests, the focus was upon 'the part played by people in the flow of mass communications' (Katz and Lazarsfeld, 1955). Political media 'effects' were found to be limited and for a majority played only a small part in attitude formation, relative to the influence of family, peer group and workplace. For a minority, however, Lazarsfeld believed, salient political messages were communicated in a two-stage sequence. Some individuals would have a strong interest in political issues and would therefore pay more attention to radio or news coverage. Such individuals might also happen to be important members of particular social groups – families, friends, work colleagues and so on – and if they discussed what they made of such news coverage within small groups such as family, peer group or workplace, their ideas about the content of news coverage might register more strongly with less committed sections of the population. The two-step flow model, then, placed the emphasis upon exploring the ways in which political communications were mediated through small group interaction. Political ideas and attitudes, 'flow from radio and print to opinion leaders and from them to the less active sections of the population' (Katz and Lazarsfeld, 1955: 32).

Where as earlier ways of understanding the mass media had pictured powerful media moulding the vulnerable masses, the two-step flow model approached the question of influence by asking questions about how active individuals responded to political messages and how these messages were filtered through group interaction and discussion to be received by individual audience members. For many years, this kind of approach, in terms of both theory and methodology, largely dominated political science and communication research. Through the work of a younger generation of audience researchers – some of whom, such as Bernard Berelson and Joseph Klapper, were trained by Lazarsfeld – the two-step flow model evolved into what came to be termed the *uses and gratifications* tradition. Lazarsfeld's influence can clearly be detected in the underlying principles of uses and gratifications research. First, media influence was equated with attitudinal change. Research designs frequently involved taking measures of opinion 'before' and 'after' exposure to mass media influences. Secondly, the relationship between media and audience was modelled in terms of variables and potential correlations. Thus, for example, distinct potential independent variables, such as level of media exposure ('high', 'medium', or 'low'), were related to dependent variables such as 'degree of attitude change'. Thirdly, the search was primarily for quantifiable evidence and the thrust of the research process was towards the empirical testing of possible hypotheses (McLeod et al., 1991: 236). As with any research design, the underlying assumptions, theoretical and methodological, steered the research towards particular kinds of question and away from others. Trying to model and quantify social behaviour in terms of independent and dependent variables made it difficult to explore in much depth how audiences went about *interpreting* or trying to make sense of what they saw or read. Evidence of bald attitude changes can be quantified using questionnaires or structured interviews but they are less effective in capturing extended discussions or verbal analyses offered by respondents. Nevertheless, there was a suspicion of qualitative data, based upon the dangers of researcher bias and the difficulties in trying to 'control' the group dynamics within focus groups, which prompted a strong drive towards quantification (McQuail et al., 1972: 144; Blumler and Gurevitch, 1982: 265).

The apparent lack of strong evidence indicating changes in attitudes 'before' and 'after' exposure to mass media, encouraged Lazarsfeld's former students, such as Klapper (1960) and Berelson (1959), to concentrate increasingly upon the tastes, background and characteristics of the audience as independent variables. In other words, rather than conceptualising media content as the active determinant of audience responses, the uses and gratifications approach suggested that a more fruitful line of enquiry would be to explore the ways in which particular tastes or characteristics in media audiences determined the *selection* of particular media. The assumption underpinning this approach was that audiences selected or 'used' particular media to gratify interests which had developed according to the complex interplay of upbringing and experience that Lazarsfeld had earlier identified as playing such an important part in the two-step flow of communication. If the mass media did exert an influence it was primarily through the mechanism of reinforcement, rather than persuasion or manipulation. Thus, those with strong political commitments would seek out the political media which reinforced their perspectives and produced the minimum friction between content and preconceived understandings. As Klapper argued, 'those dispositions, are at work before, and during exposure to mass communication, and . . . largely determine the content to which the individual is exposed' (1963: 67). For Klapper, audiences actively selected and consumed media content; if the political media did exert an influence for change it was only in very particular circumstances in which a predisposition for change already existed and political media merely reinforced such an orientation. Growing political disillusionment with a particular government might be consolidated, for example, by hostile political media coverage. However, for the most part, the social effects of the media depended upon how 'society as a whole – the family, schools, churches – fashions the audience' (1963: 75).

In Britain, the 1959 General Election was the first to be extensively covered on television and this, of course, prompted academic interest. Trenaman and McQuail (1961) studied a large sample of the electorate and while detecting a sharp swing during the campaign towards the Conservative Party, they could find no evidence that this correlated with exposure to particular media. Dozens of similarly constructed studies produced similar conclusions. The political media appeared to play a relatively minor role in producing changes in political attitude. The primary function of the political media appeared to be to enable more interested voters to survey the political environment and gather information. An important study of the following 1964 British General Election undertaken at Leeds University suggested that: 'Watching political TV was a way of finding out what might be in store for oneself, one's family, or one's social group, should one or another party win the election and obtain power' (Blumler, 1970: 78). According to the Leeds researchers, television audiences would use the medium to gather political information, once their interest had been activated by the prospect of a coming election, although the Leeds team believed that only around a quarter of their sample actively sought out media that reinforced preconceived opinions. Following the uses and gratifications tradition of quantitative audience research, the Leeds team based their conclusions on the results of a quantitative survey that asked individuals to select, for example, which reasons for watching party broadcasts from a list of eight, applied to them. A key issue to consider below is the extent to which this kind of methodology can adequately capture the complexities of the relationship between political audiences and political media.

From Attitudes to Cognitions

The uses and gratifications tradition in communication research continues to thrive, particularly in the USA (Rubin, 1994). However, by the late 1970s its position of academic hegemony had been toppled and for three reasons.

First, the 'received wisdom' that audiences were the active agents in their relations with political media, that political media might supply information and perhaps in some instances reinforce political opinion but not exert influence beyond this, appeared not to square with certain kinds of 'first-hand evidence'. For example, academics in Britain could not help but notice the skilful way in which Enoch Powell used the news media to promote his racist agenda in the late 1960s and early 1970s (Seymour-Ure, 1974: 99–136). Powell certainly struck a chord with the concerns of certain sections of the white working class but it was also plain to see that the interaction between Powell as a news source and the political media had also played an important part in the framing of the politics of immigration during this period. The spiral of moral panics concerning categories of young people through the 1960s and 1970s, generated by interaction between news media, political élites and social control agencies, provided further examples where sudden eruptions in news media coverage appeared to make an immediate impact upon public opinion (Cohen, 1972).

A second set of reasons for a more sustained questioning of the uses and gratifications approach concerned the relationship between method and theoretical understanding. The commitment to quantitatively measuring possible changes in political attitude precluded the exploration of alternative ways of understanding mass media influence. Indeed, several researchers working within the two-step flow/uses and gratifications tradition recognised this. Lazarsfeld himself certainly acknowledged that the methodology he employed could not capture evidence of 'deeper' or longer-term effects through which ideological frameworks or ways of thinking might be shaped – processes which involved something more profound than relatively short-term shifts in attitude between competing parties. The two major studies of the presidential election process included several caveats and footnoted comments indicating the possible existence of other kinds of 'influence' beyond attitude change, and in a separate article Lazarsfeld discussed the possibility that the media might be in certain respects 'dysfunctional', if they provided the public with a set of vicarious experiences or pleasures which diverted attention from the task of addressing real social and political problems (Merton and Lazarsfeld, 1948). In subsequent research projects evidence suggesting the possibility of more significant and sustained media influence began to accumulate. The Leeds University 1964 study, for example, found that 'persuasibility depended upon low political motivation'. In the case of party political broadcasts, those who took little interest in politics were more vulnerable to influence because of their 'relative inability to mount counter arguments against the onslaught of unfamiliar propaganda' (Blumler, 1970: 85). Resistance to persuasion was weakened by the lack of enthusiasm for political debate which characterised this particular segment of the political audience. As Blumler argued, television might be a potentially more powerful medium precisely because of the passivity which characterised television viewing. People actively selected their newspapers and magazines but television viewing was often less discriminating, particularly, Blumler implied, among the politically uncommitted (1970: 86). The implication here was that more attention needed to be given to the social and political characteristics of social groups within the political audience and the kind of knowledge or experience which they could deploy in decoding political media texts. This was difficult to do, however, given the overriding commitment to large sample research and quantitative analysis.

Thirdly, a more far-reaching critique which challenged the fundamental theoretical and methodological assumptions underpinning the two step-flow/uses and gratifications tradition emerged (see, for example, Golding, 1974; Gitlin, 1978; Hall, 1982). For these researchers, drawing upon Marxist and critical perspectives, the fundamental flaw in the uses and gratifications tradition was that it failed to place the process of political communication in the context of the power structures that dominated contemporary society and the processes of ideological reproduction upon which these power structures depended. Questions needed to be asked about the interests shaping the production of media messages, how those interests were reflected in the ideological frameworks organising media content, and, in turn, how the extent to which audiences could resist or decode critically depended also upon position in the social structure and access to information. Gitlin (1978) produced a critique that systematically unpicked the relationship between theory, method and the context of Lazarsfeld's research in the early post-war period but the main thrust of his criticisms was regarded as having a wider applicability. Gitlin argued that Lazarsfeld's work was limited by its 'marketing orientation' (1978: 233). In other words, Lazarsfeld was concerned with generating data that would be of academic interest but, crucially, would also be of value to publishers and broadcasting organisations, upon whose support he depended not just for finance but for credibility. At each level, from the theoretical assumptions about the nature of the relationship between media and audience, to the design of the questionnaires, the research fitted closely with the objectives of market as much as social research. This inevitably limited the range and scope of the enquiry.

The behaviourist and empiricist assumptions underpinning the research design were, of course, highly compatible with a 'marketing orientation'. Thus, for example, media influence was equated with change in the choices made by individual social actors or 'consumers'. Political communication was understood in behavourist terms as the possible response produced in individuals by particular variables or 'stimuli'. Individuals engaged in politics just as they might engage in shopping, making choices between one 'product' or another. An empiricist epistemology leads to the assumption that any significant effects of media communication will register at the surface level of observable, quantifiable phenomena and can be captured via questionnaires administered to individuals and designed to record conscious preferences (Gitlin, 1978: 210–17). Although, as we have seen, Lazarsfeld was very much aware of what might be overlooked by such an approach, none the less it remains the case that such an approach encourages a 'behaviouralisation of power' (Gitlin, 1978: 213). As we saw in Chapters 6 and 7, theories which try to relate the media to the political need to take account of the dimensions beyond the level of conscious decision-making and yet in the research template left by Lazarsfeld for subsequent 'uses and grats' researchers, media influence or power is understood merely as a series of discrete 'choices' made by individuals. Politics is equated with party competition as it occurs at an exceptional moment during an election campaign and media power is assessed only within this narrow understanding of the political. One of the central thrusts of the radical critique developed by Gitlin, Hall and others, was that an adequate understanding of media power must embrace a wider definition of the political. The problem was that, 'Larger historical shifts, questions of political process and formation before and beyond the ballot box, issues of social and political power, of social structure and economic relations, were simply absent, not by chance but because they were theoretically outside the frame of reference' (Hall, 1982: 59).

Thus, for example, the very invariance detected by Lazarsfeld should have become a problem to be investigated. Why was it that American society was characterised by such stable bodies of opinion, with large unyielding bodies of political support for the main political parties simply existing 'out there'? Was this feature of the data itself a product of longer-term processes through which dominant ideological frameworks were constructed? After all, as Gitlin argues, in an era of advanced consumer capitalism, shifts in preference from one product to another are the norm. Placed in this kind of context, one which acknowledges the importance of a historical perspective and an awareness of wider social and power structures, invariance in public opinion and the extent to which the political status quo remained taken for granted might have become the starting point for an analysis which related audience understandings to media power and the interests at play in the production of media messages. This provides the starting point, for example, for the *cultivation effects* approach, associated with George Gerbner and his colleagues. We are immersed in media communication from a very early age and all the content of media is 'political' in a broad sense. All television, in particular, including drama, entertainment and advertising, as well as news and current affairs programming, projects moral and political messages about the ways in which we should 'understand' the world. Gerbner has devoted more than two decades to researching evidence of a fit between the moral maps projected through television content in the USA and the understandings developed by television audiences (Gerbner, 1969; Gerbner et al., 1994).

Three important points emerge from the critical re-evaluation of the early political audience research. First, a richer, deeper understanding of the nature of political communication can only be achieved if audience research is placed in the context of an analysis of the power structures and processes which shape news media production. This might include the politics of news sources, both powerful and marginal. Secondly, and following from the first point, the nature of the political and economic environment in which media news production and reception takes place must be taken into account, even if the primary focus of research remains with the audience. Both critical theorists such as Gitlin and Hall, and researchers associated with the uses and gratifications tradition (for example, Blumler and Gurevitch, 1982), agreed that the world had moved on in significant ways. When Lazarsfeld and his team undertook their fieldwork in the 1940s, television had yet to transform and dominate the party political process. As both critical theorists and researchers associated with the uses and gratifications tradition all acknowledged, by the 1970s television had become the primary arena of party political competition in liberal democracies, with radio and print media playing an important but subordinate role; voting behaviour was beginning to change in significant ways with the gradual dissolution of the large traditional blocks of Democrat/Republican, or Labour/Tory voters, while patterns of globalisation had begun to impact upon both media and political structures. In these circumstances, the whole question of 'media effects' required a fresh analysis.

Thirdly, attempts to devise quantitative measures of changes in public attitude which can be correlated with measures of media exposure are in danger of missing the point. It is possible that there are few circumstances in which substantial changes in public opinion can be attributed directly to the influence of the mass media. However, a more fruitful line of enquiry is to consider the cognitive rather than the attitudinal dimension. In other words, rather than searching for evidence of attitude changes, it is more useful to explore the ways in which intellectual frameworks for thinking issues through are constructed and the contribution which the news media might play in the development of such 'mental maps' among audiences. Significantly, both critical and Marxist theorists and researchers associated with pluralism and uses and gratifications research began to think of ways in which their respective theoretical frameworks could be directed towards these questions (Hall, 1980; Morley, 1980; Blumler and Gurevitch, 1982). Critical and Marxist theorists, drawing upon Gramscian and Althusserian ideas, insisted that audience research should not be undertaken in a vacuum but rather should place the question of how audiences made sense of, or decoded, media messages, in the context of the wider analysis of power structures and the political interests at play in the production of media messages. But liberal–pluralist researchers and those associated with the uses and gratifications tradition also began to recognise that a wider understanding of power, including a politics of news sources, had to inform their approach to audience research (Blumler, 1980; McLeod et al., 1991).

Embracing the Agenda

An approach that placed more emphasis upon tracing the relationship between the content of political media and the ways, or frameworks, people used to think about political issues, rather than a search for correlations between media exposure and simple attitude change, was nothing new in the 1970s. The Langs had pointed the way towards this kind of approach in the 1950s (Lang and Lang, 1955), while a few years later Bernard Cohen had captured the nub of the argument in a formulation which has been reworked again and again, when he suggested that, 'The press may not be successful much of the time in telling people what to think but, it is stunningly successful in telling its readers what to think *about*' (1963: 13). In other words, the significant influence of the news media, and perhaps other media genre too, may not lie in an ability to directly change public attitudes but in a more subtle process, set the agenda for public discussion and alert audiences to particular aspects of an issue.

This formulation offered the potential to make advances on three fronts. First, it suggested that much more attention should be given to the nature of the media text and the question of how issues were represented, alongside the analysis of audience responses. Both phases of the political communication process had to be considered alongside one another (Mcleod et al., 1994: 139). In the early uses and gratifications research the specifics of media content had been largely bracketed off as a secondary concern. However, the concept of agenda setting suggested that the ordering of ideas within the text and the inflection given to particular themes might be important to the processes through which audiences constructed their 'mental maps' or 'interpretative frameworks'. Secondly, the idea of agenda setting also immediately prompted questions about the interests at play in developing news agendas prior to their communication. This offered the potential to explore questions about power and the production of media content, relations between journalists and political élites, and the politics of news sources and news journalism, in the same context as questions about audience reception (McCombs, 1994: 9). Given the growing sophistication of the public relations industry and the media strategies employed by both governments and non-official sources, the task of linking audience research to an understanding of news production and the activity of news sources was urgent (McLeod et al., 1994: 132–3). Thirdly, the agenda setting model appeared to offer a way of reconciling the picture of a relatively active, selective and critical audience, with the theoretical and political judgement that in some circumstances, at least, the mass media *did* exert influence, even if such influence was not frequently expressed in terms of bald attitude change.

Nevertheless, despite the potential offered by this new way of conceptualising the influence of the mass media, the early agenda setting research was still very much (and arguably still is) constrained by the quantitative tradition. McCombs and Shaw (1972) are usually given the credit for the first explicit agenda setting investigation, although earlier researchers had certainly had the idea of searching for correlations between public opinion and media content. The research design for this study actually retained a number of features associated with the uses and gratifications tradition. Once again, the political was equated with the electoral process, the focus directed towards a sample of undecided voters, and the research design rested upon the possibility of correlating two quantitative measures of the political communication process: a measure of how voters ranked a list of key issues in order of priority, and a measure of the volume of coverage devoted to each of these issues in the print and broadcasting media used by the sample of voters. McCombs and Shaw found an almost perfect correlation between the two variables. Of course, to establish a correlation is not necessarily to demonstrate a causal relation. One immediate problem with this kind of research design is to establish that the media agenda is shaping public opinion, rather than the other way around. McCombs and Shaw tried to overcome this problem by isolating a subsample of floating voters who were beginning to lean towards either the Democrats or the Republicans. They were able to show that the ordering of issue priorities within these subgroups still more closely fitted the general news media agenda, rather than the particular agendas to be found in either pro-Republican or pro-Democrat newspapers. This, McCombs and Shaw argued, ruled out the possibility that 'leaning' voters were selecting media which reinforced their preconceived ideas and confirmed, instead, that the general news media were indeed effective in setting public agendas.

At almost the same time but quite independently, Funkhouser (1973) published data from his doctoral thesis which had involved a longitudinal analysis of American national opinion poll data, correlated with a longitudinal content analysis of leading US news media (including, for example, *Time* and *Newsweek*). Funkhouser was also able to demonstrate a strong correlation between media agendas and public concerns as measured by the ranking of issues in opinion polls. However, Funkhouser also matched these two variables against a set of statistical measures of 'reality', or what was 'really' going on in the real world. For example, he used the number of troops sent to the Vietnam war, the number of campus demonstrations organised in US universities, and riot damage measured in dollars, to demonstrate that media coverage and public concerns were not simply determined by 'real events'. He showed that public concerns about these issues reached their highest levels *before* the statistical indicators suggested that each issue had reached its crisis point in 'reality'. This, Funkhouser argued, pointed to the active role of the news media in constructing public agendas for concern, as distinct from the impact of 'real' problems in the 'real' world. This was not to suggest that the media had the power to override public experience but that in the ordering of issues of public concern, the news media played an active, rather than a reflective role. Again, this conclusion seemed to fit well with early work on the extent to which US policy-making appeared to be driven more by cycles of media coverage, than by developments in the 'real' world (Downs, 1972).

The great attraction of agenda setting models for orthodox political science and communications scholars, particularly in the USA, appeared to be the promise they offered to detect real, if limited, media effects but within a research design and methodological framework that retained all the 'security features' demanded by the quantitative social science tradition. Variables could be identified and measured, correlations established, and designs replicated. Indeed, some researchers have tried testing an agenda setting hypothesis in laboratory conditions (Iyengar and Kinder, 1987). An enormous agenda setting industry rapidly developed and certainly moved beyond the limited terrain of election studies. Thus, the emergence of drug addiction as a major public issue in the USA (for example, Shoemaker et al., 1989), the emergence of the AIDS crisis on the US public agenda (for example, Rogers et al., 1991), a variety of aspects of environmentalism (for example, Protess et al., 1987; Lacey and Longman, 1993; Gooch, 1996), and even the potential impeachment of an American president (Weaver et al., 1975), have all been investigated using the agenda setting model.

From food scares and environmental risks, to sudden panics about crime, or scandals involving politicians, there is no doubt that the news media can rapidly push particular themes or issues up the hierarchy of public concerns. In an age when most households in Europe and the USA have access to near-instantaneous communication through television, it is quite probable that the cycle of public issue elevation is accelerating. Quantitative agenda setting studies are very good for describing and charting in broad terms, the associations between intensities of media coverage and broad measures of public opinion. However, there are some inherent problems. First, as noted above, correlations are not causal relationships, yet it is easy to lose sight of this distinction in trying to use data from agenda setting studies to 'prove' a unilinear (one-way influence) model of political communication. This is a temptation that has to be resisted because evidence of an association between measures of media coverage and measures of public opinion does not 'prove' that media coverage shapes public opinion. It is possible, in some circumstances, to interpret such an association in a way which suggests that the direction of effect is reversed, or indeed, that a complex multi-directional relationship exists in which media agendas shape public understanding to a degree but, at the same time, public interest also influences the editorial decisions determining media content.

Brosius and Kepplinger's (1990) huge study of agenda setting processes in West Germany illustrates this very well. The authors' starting point is with the characteristic weaknesses of earlier agenda setting studies. First, newspaper influence had received a great deal more attention than television and yet it was television that provided more political information for most audiences in Western industrial societies. Secondly, following McCombs and Shaw, a large number of agenda setting studies were cross-sectional rather than longitudinal. They took a 'snapshot' of associations between media content and public opinions or agendas, at a particular moment in time, rather than tracking possible associations between the two variables. However, Brosius and Kepplinger argue that the agenda setting process is dynamic and the nature of the associations between media content and public agendas may change over time. A longitudinal perspective is required to take account of change over time and allow for the possibility that directions of causality may vary depending upon the issue and the moment. In other words, public concerns may shape media editorial policy, rather than the reverse, for certain issues at certain times, and longitudinal studies offer the prospect of exploring the time lag between media content and opinion poll changes. They allow researchers to note which comes first, media coverage or a shift in public understanding, and draw inferences about the direction of causality accordingly (Brosius and Kepplinger, 1990: 184–5).

What were their findings? Brosius and Kepplinger undertook a continuous content analysis of the four major television news programmes on West German television during 1986, and each week sampled the 'problem awareness' of the public, producing 53 separate weekly polls. As the research design tracked both television content and public awareness of problems over the course of a year, it was possible to explore time lags and to assess the direction of causality. For five issues (energy supply, environmental protection, European politics, defence, and East–West relations) evidence suggested while people's own previous knowledge was important, television coverage, particularly in the preceding week, did indeed raise public awareness. Equally, a decline in television coverage led to a decline in public awareness. Here, then, is evidence that while television may not tell the public what to think, it does have the capacity to influence what the public think about. However, this was not the complete story because for three issues, the authors found that rather than media coverage shaping public understanding, 'problem awareness exercised a significant causal influence on television coverage' (Brosius and Kepplinger, 1990: 193). These three issues were pensions, public security and public debt; in the case of a fourth, East–West relations, there appeared to be evidence that influence worked in both directions. On the basis of this evidence, the relationship between news media agendas and public understanding is highly complex, with lines of causality travelling in either direction or in both simultaneously, depending upon the context and nature of the issue in question. In providing quantitative evidence of the associations which clearly exist between audience understanding and news content, such studies are invaluable but they still leave a set of intriguing questions to be explored. Why do news audiences accept elements of the news hierarchies offered by news media but, presumably, draw upon alternative sources of information and experience to complete their lists of issue priorities? How do news audiences combine and analyse information drawn from the news media with existing knowledge and interpretative frameworks, to construct their agendas? What social conditions and contexts modify these cognitive processes? Of particular importance with regard to the politics of news sources is the question of the perceived legitimacy of the sources or institutions involved in particular issues. Do news audiences employ hierarchies of credibility in rather the same way as journalists, and if so, how do these influence the cognitive processes through which audience agendas are constructed?

The Limits of Agenda Setting Research

Dearing and Rogers (1996: 90–2), in a review of 112 agenda setting studies, provide a useful summary of what can be said with confidence about agenda setting. We know that at a given point in time or over a period, 'different media place a similar salience on a set of issues'. In other words, news organisations tend to hunt in packs, continually monitoring each other's output, and following very similar editorial strategies, so that news media agendas tend to be shared across papers and broadcasting channels. Secondly, 'real world indicators are relatively unimportant in setting the media agenda'. What happens out there in 'the real world', as measured by data such as crime statistics, economic indicators, risk probabilities and so on, does not necessarily determine levels or intensity of coverage; neither do scientific research findings. As Dearing and Rogers argue, for example, a series of scientific breakthroughs in our understanding of AIDS during the 1980s did little to shift the moral frameworks within which AIDS was reported by the news media or understood by the public

Thirdly, news audiences do combine information from media sources with other kinds of knowledge or experience, 'as clues . . . to determine the salience of an issue', and key trigger events are more important than 'real world' indicators in putting issues on the public agenda. By trigger events, Dearing and Rogers are referring to examples such as the first of Michael Buerk's BBC news reports from a refugee camp during the 1984 Ethiopian famine, or to take an example from an earlier section of this book, the early reports of dead seals being washed up on the coasts of Britain and the Netherlands. While 'real world indicators' usually take a form often regarded by journalists, and perhaps the public, as 'dry statistics', trigger events always involve a human interest angle of some kind. Images of suffering or drama, or of a potential threat, certainly attract more news interest and may play a part in the cognitive processes through which audience agendas are constructed.

Fourthly, and importantly for this book, it is possible to say something about the role of news sources from the conclusions in the general agenda setting literature. Trigger events frequently involve the powerful or the prominent. Members of political élites, governments, powerful corporations, and prominent personalities or 'showbiz' celebrities are frequently associated with trigger events. This means that the powerful frequently loom large in the thoughts of news audiences as they process information and construct their interpretative frameworks, although this does not necessarily mean that such thoughts are uncritical. Finally, and most importantly, 60 per cent of the studies reviewed by Dearing and Rogers reported a 'media agenda–public agenda relationship', or, in other words, a correlation between the two.

As several critics have pointed out (Atwater et al., 1985; Dearing and Rogers, 1996: 92–4), quantitative studies generally use large aggregated categories, such as 'defence', 'environment' and so on, but in order to explore the cognitive processes through which news audiences make sense of and analyse the news world around them, we need a finer, more nuanced set of categories. When we think politically or when we make moral judgements or draw inferences about the implications of a media-defined problem for our own lives, we very rarely sit in our living rooms trying to decide whether 'defence' should be ranked higher or lower than 'environmental degradation'. In other words, the categories employed by most quantitative agenda setting studies, and most of the processes through which respondents are required to go in order to participate in such studies (i.e. ranking issues specified in a polling questionnaire), are not sufficiently sympathetic to the ways in which most audiences actually think about news.

What is really required is an analysis that moves from the breadth of typical quantitative agenda setting studies, based as they usually are upon large samples of public opinion and mounds of content analysis, to a finer, more sensitive and detailed, analysis that explores the ways in which audiences actually construct their interpretative frameworks. Dearing and Rogers call for a 'disaggregation' of data so that the differences in the social position of sections of the audience, the different kinds of news media, and different types of issue can be separated out. One attempt to do this still within a quantitative framework was provided in the USA by Atwater et al. (1985), who broke one issue, 'environmentalism', down into a number of more concrete sub-issues such as disposal of wastes, quality of water, wildlife conservation and so on. Further to this, the researchers recognised that news media audiences might themselves distinguish between the media agenda and their own priorities. By correlating a content analysis of three regional newspapers with a survey of 304 respondents, they were able to show that a significant relationship existed between newspaper content and audience readings of the media agenda, and a slightly weaker relationship between newspaper content and respondents' own judgements as to what the most important environmental issues might be (Atwater, et al., 1985: 395–7).

Important in the Atwater design was the recognition that part of the cognitive process through which audiences constructed their own interpretative frameworks included a reflexive analysis of media content. However, the design still included measures of audience cognition based upon the ranking of priorities, which failed to do justice to the complexity of the way in which we all think about politics, social and moral issues. The crucial question remained, what was it that encouraged particular sections of the news audience to rely more heavily upon the news media agenda in the construction of interpretative frameworks for some issues but not others? The extent to which audiences have first-hand experience of an issue, or the degree to which an issue obtrudes into their daily lives seems to make a difference (Zucker, 1978; Gooch, 1996). News audiences are more actively critical where they can draw upon their own experience or knowledge as a benchmark against which to assess media coverage, and are more likely to embrace the news agenda to the degree that they depend upon the mass media as their main source of information. This may explain why Brosius and Kepplinger (discussed above) found that German television tended to shape the public agenda with regard to issues such as the environment, energy supply and defence. These were issues quite far removed from day-to-day public experience, whereas matters, such as pensions and public security touched much more directly upon first-hand experience among news audiences. On these issues, the public mood appeared to influence the television agenda. The extent to which media coverage encourages a 'snowball effect', or 'spiral of silence', through which interpretations favoured by the news media accumulate public credibility and deter people from voicing alternative, dissident ideas may also be important (Noelle-Neuman, 1984). If the news media do, in some instances, define what come to be regarded as significant problems in society, we also need to know whether news content influences how audiences analyse and explain such problems. Some studies, for example, suggest that news reports often encourage an individualisation of social problems, such as poverty or racism, so that news audiences offer explanations which focus upon the failings of individual politicians or officials, rather than inherent structural features of society (Iyengar, 1991). The jury is still out concerning the question of whether television or newspapers exert a more powerful agenda setting influence. Although television has always been regarded by governments and authorities as the more 'powerful' medium, research evidence suggests that newspapers may be more influential (McCombs, 1977; Miller, 1991; Blood and Philips, 1995), though studies such as that of Brosius and Kepplinger (1990) indicate that television is certainly influential too. The question is whether the conditions under which television or newspapers exert most influence can be specified, or whether it is more appropriate to consider the interaction of the two sources of news together, like most members of news audiences!

To pursue these lines of enquiry it is probable that a rather different methodology is required – one that allows a richer and more complex description of how news audiences draw upon the variety of information sources and experiences available to construct their inferential frameworks or ways of understanding. This suggests a qualitative dimension to audience research, not necessarily as an alternative but certainly as a way of extending news audience research. Before considering this tradition, one last important point needs to be made. Much of the agenda setting research has adopted an agnostic position with regard to the question of the relationship between the news media and the powerful. In other words, although agenda setting research tends to support the view that the mass media exert influence through the way in which issues are prioritised and events framed, this proposition can be embraced by a number of quite distinct macro theoretical approaches, from pluralism to Marxism and perspectives which stress the existence of dominant groups with a capacity to mobilise the media to their advantage. McCombs (1994: 11), for example, insists that agenda setting evidence should be interpreted within a pluralist framework. This, he argues, is because it is journalists guided by professional news values, rather than government spin doctors or economically powerful corporations, that control news production, which explains why in certain circumstances the direction of influence travels from audience to media, as journalists react to public opinion.

We have already examined in previous chapters the power relationships governing the production of news and noted the ways in which the powerful in society do exert a significant degree of control over the flow of information to news organisations, the capacity of those organisations mobilising capital to make that wealth count in terms of media power, and the efforts of subordinate and politically marginal groups to challenge and resist such power, in the news arena. The final question is whether or not an understanding of the power structures, the contests and patterns of resistance around news encoding should inform news audience research? Supporters of qualitative approaches suggest that these methodologies allow more attention to be paid to the discourses and modes of explanation employed by news audiences and to evaluate these in terms of the contested nature of the news encoding process.

Media Power and Audience Power

Early agenda setting research can be understood as an attempt to explore a dimension of media influence ignored by the earlier uses and gratifications approach but still mainly from within an American quantitative and positivistic tradition. However, the continuing influence of European Marxist writers, including Althusser and Gramsci, during the 1970s encouraged some researchers to think about ways in which the relationship between power structures, the ideological frameworks organising media texts and media audiences, could be explored. While Althusser's writing directed attention to the relationship between the structures of capitalist societies and the ideological beliefs through which understanding was 'organised', Gramsci's influence encouraged researchers to approach news media production in the context of the struggle for hegemony in society in between dominant and subordinate social groupings and classes (Althusser, 1971; Gramsci, 1971). The implication for those interested in audience research was that the ways in which audiences interpreted media messages could not be uncoupled from an analysis of the power relations involved in their production. From this emerged first Stuart Hall's well-known *encoding–decoding model* and secondly, a new tradition in audience ethnography.

Hall (1980) proposes a circular model of communication involving the distinct 'moments' of message encoding or production, circulation, distribution and audience reception or decoding. The model is circular because Hall notes that while the mass media may contribute to the ideological frameworks that organise audience understanding, such ideologies also influence the process of encoding, as journalists frequently share widely held public beliefs themselves and also have to make sure that their copy acknowledges public sentiments. Gramsci's influence is clear in the way Hall describes each 'moment' in this process. The production or encoding of messages is not straightforward but is characterised by possible tensions and conflicts, as powerful interests contest the 'meaning' of events or issues through the encoding process:

> . . . though the production structures of television originate the television discourse, they do not constitute a closed system. They draw topics, treatments, agendas, events, personnel, images of the audience, 'definitions of the situation', from other sources and other discursive formations within the wider socio-cultural and political structure of which they are a differentiated part. (Hall, 1980: 129)

Equally, the 'moment' of decoding or audience reception is not straightforward but always potentially contested because of the polysemic nature of all media texts. Media texts are always encoded within power structures which may imprint a 'preferred reading' (or 'spin' to use the contemporary term) but audiences may develop an alternative reading, or interpretation. Hall, following Parkin (1972), argues that broadly three audience positions in relation to media texts can be identified: the 'dominant hegemonic' when sections of the audience more or less embrace the 'preferred readings' produced through the expression of power relations within the process of encoding; a negotiated position where the legitimacy of a dominant, 'preferred reading' is accepted but certain criticisms are developed in the light of personal experience or local conditions; and finally, the oppositional position where an alternative political and ideological framework is deployed to question all the assumptions underpinning the 'preferred reading'. One great virtue of Hall's model was that it refused to uncouple the analysis of audience reception from an understanding of the power relations and contests involved in media message production. Equally important was the recognition in Hall's model that 'meaning' did not lie solely in the text – a point which quantitative agenda setting approaches found hard to grapple with. A preferred reading might be encoded through the political struggles and media strategies of contesting groups, together with the professional and organisational practices of media personnel, but texts were, for all that, polysemic or open to multiple interpretation.

The obvious question that follows from the presentation of this model was what was it that determined the response of particular audience groups? Why might some groups embrace, some negotiate but others oppose the dominant or 'preferred reading' in a news text? The task of first operationalising the encoding–decoding model and gathering empirical data to answer these kinds of questions fell to Dave Morley, who worked under Hall at the Birmingham University Centre for Contemporary Cultural Studies during the early 1970s. Morley employed qualitative techniques – what was later to be described as audience ethnograpy – to explore the ways in which 29 different small groups 'read' two editions of a 1970s BBC television news and current affairs programme called *Nationwide*. Morley (1980) taped the small group discussions that followed the showing of each video and tried to relate the extent to which different groups embraced, negotiated or opposed the dominant encoded 'meaning' of particular items (several, for example, concerned trade unions and industrial disputes) to the social position of each audience group in terms of class, age, ethnicity and gender. Morley certainly demonstrated that there were important differences between groups, rather than within groups. In other words, in contrast to the uses and gratifications perspective which focused primarily upon the individual and the psychology of audience reception, Morley reveals the importance of the social dimension to reception. This reception of messages is achieved through the group mobilisation of particular discourses which, in turn, reflect knowledge, experience and ideological understandings. However, given the complexity of the ways in which social class, gender, ethnicity, age and locality are likely to interact, it is hardly surprising that his attempts to make particular connections between the social position of different groups and particular readings of texts are not always convincing. What emerges from this early audience ethnography is that the meanings constructed by audience groups cannot be simply 'read off' or predicted by their social class, gender or ethnic identity. On the other hand, there is plenty of evidence that social groups do work at constructing a meaning or making sense of media texts, and that access to knowledge, experience or skills can encourage more critical negotiated or oppositional readings to be developed.

Morley's work here illustrates some of the problems with qualitative and ethnographic approaches to audience research. Critics point to the inconsistent way in which the interview material is used in his account and to the unrepresentative nature of the groups selected (Turner, 1990: 135). Nevertheless, Morley was successful in demonstrating the value of listening *at length* to the way in which social groups digested or analysed news media texts. What clearly emerges from this study is the importance of the decoding skills which individuals or groups can deploy and the extent to which access to alternative sources of information, knowledge or experience are vital in allowing audiences to decode critically. For example, those with little or no experience of industrial relations or trade unions were much more likely to embrace the dominant understanding of industrial relations 'problems' as represented by *Nationwide* during the 1970s; those with some first-hand experience of trade unions or with access to relevant theoretical knowledge through higher education were more likely to produce critical negotiated or oppositional readings. As we saw above, more recent agenda setting research has suggested that the greater the degree to which an issue obtrudes into people's lives, the more likely it is that they will think more critically about media agendas which do not relate to their own experience. Morley's qualitative work allows us to follow this process in more depth.

More Recent Qualitative Audience Research

The encoding–decoding model prompted a surge in qualitative audience research in the following two decades but this involved several distinct approaches. Morley focused next upon the conditions of media consumption and how the gendered nature of family life shaped patterns of television viewing (Morley, 1986). This, in turn, encouraged the 'domestic technology' approach which explores the way in which power relationships condition the consumption of media and communication technologies.[1] A similar but distinct trajectory developed through the study of audiences as fans, with the objective being to demonstrate that fans of soaps, pop stars, magazines or romantic fiction were not dupes but critical, even subversive, in the way they took meaning from cultural commodities.[2] These approaches engaged primarily with texts other than news media and space prohibits a more detailed consideration, but they do illustrate one of the enduring difficulties in qualitative approaches to the relationship between media text and audience. In some but by no means all cases, a recognition of the polysemic nature of the text was interpreted as a licence to present audience decoding as entirely unconstrained by either the text or the power relations involved in its production. The 1990s saw a series of critical interventions against this 'new revisionism'.[3] Some suggested that too great an emphasis upon the diversity of audience decodings without an understanding of the power relations involved in the production of media texts amounted to little more than a re-statement of faith in consumer sovereignty. In particular, critics argued that because texts might offer the possibility of more than one interpretation, this did not mean that an infinite number of interpretations were possible, or that audience decoding was not shaped by 'structural location and values, political beliefs and knowledge, and the political norms and discourse of social groups' (McLeod et al., 1994: 141).

Members of the Glasgow University Media Group have expressed similar critical reservations about much of the recent audience ethnography, and in their own use of qualitative methods to research audience reception, have tried to retain an understanding of the power relations at play in media production (Philo and Miller, 1997). Through the late 1980s and 1990s, the Glasgow team explored the ways in which news audiences approached news coverage of a number of quite different issues. These included the 1984–85 Coal dispute (Philo, 1990), the war in Northern Ireland (Miller, 1994), mental illness (Philo, 1996), AIDS (Kitzinger, 1998), and food scares (Reilly, 1999). In most of these studies, audience focus group and individual interviews were combined with a 'script-writing exercise' to explore the ways in which media definitions were mediated by news audiences. When used to explore the nature of news media influence, the script-writing exercise has involved inviting small groups to reconstruct news bulletin texts, including headlines or picture captions, after providing the groups with certain materials to aid recall, such as still photographs taken from actual news coverage (either newspaper or television). In combination, the various Glasgow projects have involved over 250 focus groups and 1500 individuals (Kitzinger, 1999: 4). The first point to emerge is that news audiences are fluent in the use of news conventions (formats, headlines, etc.) and can often reproduce close approximations to dialogue and text, even weeks or several months after an issue has lost its news media salience. The ability of audiences to recall news forms does not, of course, in itself prove that the news media influence audience ideas or ways of thinking about particular issues. Audiences might be able to reproduce news media forms and conventions while also being critical of them. Indeed, the Glasgow group have found that this frequently is the case and, accordingly, the script-writing exercises have been used as 'springboards for further discussion' (Kitzinger, 1999: 5). Research participants are encouraged to talk around the scripts they produce; to evaluate media coverage and identify the various sources of information upon which they draw (personal experience, information relayed through family and friends, alternative media, etc.) to do this. Interview and focus group discussion transcripts can then be used by the

Glasgow team to trace the ways in which audiences recall news issues, how they try to understand news coverage, and ultimately how they formulate beliefs about issues in the news.

What emerges clearly from the Glasgow team's research is that audiences are aware of the socially constructed nature of news; they recognise that news coverage employs a number of consistent textual devices, and are 'fluent in the generic conventions of news' (Kitzinger, 1999: 5). The skill and accuracy with which groups were able to recall and reproduce examples of news coverage, even if some factual details were inaccurate, is evidence of this. Secondly, the Glasgow work does not support a unilinear model of media power – a model in which power is understood to travel in one direction only, from powerful media to vulnerable audience. The Glasgow work reveals that 'people were able to resist dominant messages', particularly where they could deploy personal experience in a critical way, or knowledge acquired from alternative sources, or where people were positioned within 'interpretative communities' which encouraged the adoption of more critical discursive positions (Eldridge et al., 1997: 162). Thus, for example, miners and those close to the pit communities of the 1980s were likely to be more sceptical of news accounts of the coal strike which took picket line violence as the main organising news theme (Philo, 1990); those with direct experience of life in Northern Ireland were more likely to question the dominant news definitions of the war (Miller, 1994). As Eldridge and his colleagues acknowledge, this conclusion is very close to Hall's account of the process of decoding, although Eldridge emphasises that interpretative communities are never neatly defined or sealed but, on the contrary, are characterised by 'multiple and overlapping experiences' (1997: 162).

However, thirdly, the Glasgow team found that there were limits to the extent to which audiences could deploy personal experience in a critical way. They found that sometimes people did not trust their own personal experience, or only deployed it critically when actually prompted by a researcher, or attempted to reconcile personal experience with dominant media definitions despite contradictions between each, even where that personal experience was both powerful and painful, as in the case of child abuse (Kitzinger, 1999: 15–16). Most importantly, the Glasgow team stress the point that personal experience cannot be artificially isolated from 'broader media and cultural factors' (Kitzinger, 1999: 8). Thus, for example, people reacted to media coverage of AIDS by relating it to their own experience *and* to other media shaped images which, in turn, drew upon broad sets of cultural or ideological symbols and themes, such as the image of Africa as a 'disaster zone', characterised by 'sexual excess'. People's experience cannot be regarded as a separate resource uncontaminated by previous media exposure. Processes of reception and consumption certainly mediate but do not necessarily undermine media power (Kitzinger, 1999: 4). The Glasgow team believe that where audiences lack access to alternative sources of information or critical interpretative communities, or sometimes even where their own social location encourages a more critical response, the media can and do exert influence. In the work conducted on media coverage of AIDS (Kitzinger, 1993; Miller et al., 1998); for example, it is clear that the news media supplied the 'facts and figures' which people used to draw conclusions about the extent of the problem; the media developed a vocabulary ('safe sex', 'body fluids', etc.); which entered common public discourse; television and newspaper coverage generated images which had a powerful impact upon public understanding (the emaciated victim, etc.), and news coverage intersected with wider cultural references to create a widely shared moral calculus which distinguished 'guilty' from 'innocent' victims. The Glasgow position is neatly summarised by Philo (1999: 287):

> In conclusion it would be quite wrong to see audiences as simply absorbing all media messages. . . . But it is also wrong to see viewers and readers as effortlessly active, creating their own meanings in each encounter with the text. Our work suggests that the media can be a powerful influence on what audiences believe and what is thought to be legitimate or desirable.

Of course, the Glasgow team's work is unlikely to be received as the definitive statement about the relationship between news media and news audiences. It is based mainly upon qualitative methodologies and is unlikely to satisfy those who favour the quantitative or positivistic in audience research.[4] Nevertheless, in insisting that we return to the task of exploring media 'influence' and in reconnecting audience research to an understanding of power and control in media production, the Glasgow team have performed an invaluable service.

News Audiences and News Sources

Public relations consultants and political spin doctors are fond of pointing to the faintest of shifts in public attitudes measured by opinion polls as evidence that their techniques 'work'. However, by now it should be clear that there are huge difficulties in attempting to isolate the effectivity of news source activity upon news audiences as one independent variable to be precisely measured in a quantitative design. As we have seen, even before the point of reception there are numerous factors, from the strategies employed by other news sources, through to the different ways in which newsrooms are organised and journalists mobilised, which simply cannot be 'controlled' in a precise way. And, at the point of reception, as we have seen in this chapter, there are again a number of factors that mediate the reception of messages which simply cannot be untangled in any very precise fashion. To attempt to 'measure' the impact of particular news sources upon audiences is to revert to what Hansen has called a 'transmission model' and, consequently, to hugely oversimplify (Hansen, 1991: 446). We know, for example, that public opinion polling after the Greenpeace Brent Spar campaign suggested the public in Britain believed that Greenpeace had 'won' (Bennie, 1998: 398). Can this be attributed solely to the effectiveness of the Greenpeace news strategy, rather than a complex set of factors which might certainly include Greenpeace's media agility but also, perhaps, a growing, generalised public antipathy towards corporate power, the political and media ineptitude of the government and Shell, and the understandings shared through the various 'interpretative communities', more or less engaged in environmental politics?

This does not mean that news sources do not have an effect upon audiences, but simply that we cannot measure this in any very precise way. Given the complexity of the task, it is hardly surprising that few studies have attempted to explore each element in the political communication process as an integrated package, from the news sources strategies employed, the practice of journalists and newsrooms, through analysis of content and text, to audience reception. Studies of environmental battles have suggested that audience reception both at local and national levels is mediated by local knowledge and experience, however slick the media strategy of campaigning groups, or dominance of the news agenda (Corner et al., 1990; Burgess and Harrison, 1993). Burgess and Harrison, for example, found that despite the ability of a large leisure corporation to seize the local news agenda, local audiences grew highly sceptical of the messages generated by all the contesting groups, while Gooch (1996) concluded that the local campaigning activity of environmental organisations (as distinct from their media strategies) and the 'obtrusiveness' of particular environmental issues in the lives of local people, rather than the agendas of regional news media, were most significant in shaping public understanding in Sweden.

Yet Gooch's study, based as it is upon measures of the public agenda as expressed by quantified rank orderings of 'issues', is subject to many of the weaknesses of the quantitative agenda setting tradition discussed above. There is a tension in the study: Gooch actually wants to go much further than the quantitative measures employed will allow. He refers to the 'schemata', 'cognitive and affective frameworks' and 'territories of environmental consciousness' which need to be explored (1996: 113) but quantitative measures of 'opinion' hardly do justice to these concepts. The mismatch that Gooch finds between the media coverage and public opinion issue hierarchies cannot prove that the news media strategies of particular organisations have not played some part, together with personal experience, local environmental factors and so on, in the shaping of these 'schema' or 'cognitive frameworks'. One of the few projects to attempt to follow the complete 'circuit of communication', including the activity of news sources, news production, text and audience reception, is the Glasgow Media Group's study of the representation of AIDS (Miller et al., 1998). Given the difficulties discussed above, it is not surprising that no single source emerges with a capacity to set the news agenda or directly shape public opinion around AIDS. The picture which emerges from this Glasgow team study is that the activity of the different sources engaged in the struggle over the 'meaning' of AIDS contributed to the symbolic and political environment within which people developed their thinking about the disease but that direct links were impossible to establish, partly because news organisations sometimes had their own distinct interpretations, and partly because audiences drew upon the images and symbolic vocabularies circulating within particular 'interpretative communities', as well as the media.

Absences are sometimes as important as obvious contributions. The failure of particular news sources in struggles around the news agenda may also have important consequences in terms of audience reception. For example, the inability of the British Conservative government to primarily define the public debate over the Community Charge or 'poll tax', and the growing evidence of opposition, not only from the left, but also from sections of the political right, opened up a space which helped to encourage the widespread growth of critical opposition to the tax among news audiences during the late 1980s (Deacon and Golding, 1994). Despite their success in momentarily pricking the public's conscience in the 1960s, the inability of the campaigning groups within the 'poverty lobby' to make a significant impact upon the news agenda in England has meant that significant sections of the news media, national and local, have continued to appeal to and reinforce the long-standing concept of the 'undeserving poor' and a discourse of 'scroungerphobia', both of which are deeply embedded in public thinking and the interpretative frameworks employed by news audiences (Golding and Middleton, 1982).

Conclusion

News sources do have an influence upon news audiences but not in the direct and immediate way sometimes claimed by public relations professionals and politicians. Undoubtedly, simple models of audience manipulation seriously underestimate the extent to which people will critically engage with news texts providing they can draw upon personal experience or deploy ideas circulating within particular interpretative communities. On the other hand, we are all more vulnerable and less able to critically engage if we lack 'alternative benchmarks' against which to measure news coverage. In the case of war, famine and 'events abroad', or, for example, with many controversies concerning technical or 'expert' opinion, we are all less able to step outside the interpretative frameworks offered by the news media. For other issues, certain sections of the news audience will have access to alternative benchmarks but certain sections will be more dependent upon the frameworks for understanding offered by the news media. For certain issues (GM food being a good example), the issue touches upon most people's daily lives in such a direct way that large sections of the news audience make an unusual effort to obtain alternative information and engage critically in the news debates.

The struggles in which news sources engage do register with news audiences. Such 'effects' cannot be neatly measured in the way traditional positivistic social science might wish but nevertheless the interpretations and meanings offered by the news sources that successfully intervene in the news production process, do contribute to the symbolic environment in which news audiences are positioned. Indirectly, and occasionally directly, the strategies deployed by successful news sources, register in terms of the images and discourses deployed by news audiences. What does this imply for an analysis of the relationship between the news media and power? As earlier chapters have shown, the capacity to maintain control of the information flows which sustain news journalism is largely dependent upon the possession of material and symbolic resources. These are not evenly distributed in contemporary capitalist societies; the economically and politically dominant enjoy significant advantages, the politically marginal significant disadvantages, in the struggle to restrict or promote information and shape meaning in news encoding. Contrary to some cruder models of media domination, this does not mean that the economically powerful *always* control the circulation of ideas and images: access to the main public spheres in contemporary society is obviously not hermetically sealed and is characterised by continuing struggles and contests. Clearly, there are important moments when politically marginal or subordinate groups are successful in seizing the initiative or deploying information in ways which promote oppositional, or critical frameworks. And equally clearly, these do register with news audiences. Despite these caveats, however, the conclusion here remains a rather pessimistic one. The openings and opportunities for a diverse range of perspectives to be promoted through traditional news coverage are unlikely to significantly grow and, with the future of public service broadcasting systems uncertain in many countries, may significantly diminish, although the Internet will certainly offer some alternatives. The grip which corporate power and its political allies exert over information flows is likely to strengthen, and as argued in Chapter 4, at a structural level, the market in which news is commodified works against diversity in coverage and perspective. News audiences are active and sceptical but the political economy of news reminds us that audiences can only begin their critical decoding with the available tools, or information, to hand. The obstacles faced by subordinate news sources in the struggle to supply a wider range of sharper tools are rather more perplexing than is good for the health of democracy.

Notes

1. See, for example, Morley and Silverstone (1990) or Gillespie (1995).
2. From the huge literature see, for example, Ang (1985), Radway (1987), Livingstone (1988) or Jenkins (1992).
3. See, for example, Curran (1990), Corner et al. (1991), McGuigan (1992) and Ferguson and Golding (1997).
4. Criticisms of qualitative audience ethnography usually focus upon sampling and the dangers inherent in focus group and semi-structured interview work (see, for example, Moores, 1993: 60–9). Although the total number of participants and focus groups involved in the Glasgow work is impressive, the numbers involved in particular projects are often quite small. The Glasgow team is very much aware that the script-writing exercises measure audience media literacy rather than the 'effect' of particular messages but the dangers inherent in any research situation involving respondent group dynamics and researcher–respondent interaction are always difficult to minimise. For the Glasgow thinking about these issues, see Kitzinger (1994).

References

Adam Smith Institute (1984) *Omega Report: Communications Policy*. London: ASI.

Abercrombie, N., Hill, S. and Turner, B. (1980) *The Dominant Ideology Thesis*. London: George Allen and Unwin.

Adeney, M. (1983) 'Why can't managers be more like trade union leaders?' *The Listener*, 16 June 1983.

Adorno, T. and Horkheimer, M. (1977) 'The culture industry: Enlightenment as mass deception', in J. Curran, M. Gurevitch and J. Woolacott (eds), *Mass Communication and Society*. London: Arnold.

Ainley, B. (1998) *Black Journalists, White Media*. Stoke on Trent: Trentham.

Alexander, J. (1981) 'The mass media in systematic, historical and comparative perspective', in E. Katz and T. Szecsko (eds), *The Mass Media and Social Change*. London: Sage.

Allan, S. (1995) 'News, truth and postmodernity: unravelling the will to facticity', in B. Adams and S. Allan (eds), *Theorising Culture*. London: UCL Press.

Altheide, D.L. and Johnson, J.M. (1980) *Bureaucratic Propaganda*. Massachusetts: Allyn and Bacon.

Althusser, L. (1971) 'Ideology and ideological state apparatuses', in *Lenin and Philosophy and Other Essays*. London: New Left Books.

Anderson, A. (1991) 'Source strategies and environmental affairs', *Media Culture Society*, 13(4): 459–76.

Anderson, A. (1993) 'Source–media relations: the production of the environmental agenda', in A. Hansen (ed.), *The Mass Media and Environmental Issues*. Leicester: Leicester University Press.

Anderson, A. (1997) *Media, Culture and the Environment*. London: University College London Press.

Ang, I. (1985) *Watching Dallas*. London: Methuen.

Armstrong, S. (1998) 'You say tomato, we say genetically modified food product that's good for the planet', *The Guardian*, G2 section, 6 July 1998.

Atwater, T., Salwen, M.B. and Anderson, R.B. (1985) 'Media agenda setting with environmental issues', *Journalism Quarterly*, 62: 393–7.

Axford, B., Madgwick, P. and Turner, J. (1992) 'Image management, stunts and dirty tricks: the marketing of political brands in television campaigns', *Media Culture Society*, 14: .637–51.

Bachrach, P. and Baratz, M.S. (1962) 'The two faces of power', *American Political Science Review*, 56: 947–52.

Baistow, T. (1985) *Fourth Rate Estate*. London: Comedia.

Ball, A.R. and Millard, F. (1986) *Pressure Politics in Industrial Societies*. Basingstoke: Macmillan

Bardoel, J. (1996) 'Beyond journalism: a profession between information society and civil society', *European Journal of Communication*, 11(3): 283–302.

Barnett, S. (1997) 'New media, old problems. New technology and the political process', *European Journal of Communication*, 12(2): 193–218.

Barthes, R. (1973) *Mythologies*. London: Paladin.

Basnett, D. and Goodman, G. (1977) *The Press: Minority Report of the Royal Commission on the Press*. London: The Labour Party.

Baudrillard, J. (1975) *The Mirror of Production*. Translated by Mark Poster, St Louis: Telos Press.
Baudrillard, J. (1981) *For a Critique of the Political Economy of the Sign*. Translated by Charles Levin, St Louis: Telos Press.
Baudrillard, J. (1983) 'The precession of the simulacra', in T. Doherty (ed.), *The Postmodern Reader*. Hemel Hempstead: Harvester Press.
Bauman, Z. (1992) *Intimations of Modernity*. London: Routledge.
BBC (1995) *Report and Annual Accounts 1994/95*. London: BBC Publications.
BBC (1998) *Report and Accounts 1998*. London: BBC Publications.
Beaverbrook, Lord (undated) *Politicians and the Press*. London: Hutchinson.
Beck, V., Giddens, A. and Lash, S. (1994) *Reflexive Modernization: Politics, Tradition and Aesthetics in the Modern Social Order*. Cambridge: Polity Press.
Becker, H. (1967) 'Whose side are we on?' *Social Problems*, 14: 239–47.
Becker, H. (1972) 'Whose side are we on?' in J.D. Douglas (ed.), *The Relevance of Sociology*. New York: Appleton–Century–Crofts.
Bell, E. (1998) 'A licence to print money in White City', *The Observer*, Business Section, Media, 12 April 1998, p. 5.
Bell, E. (1999) 'No Greg, no comment . . .', *The Observer*, Media Section, 27 June 1999.
Bell, M. (1994) *In Harm's Way: Reflection of a War Zone*. London: Hamish Hamilton.
Bellos, A. (1997) 'Swampy fever', *The Guardian*, G2 Media Section, pp. 4–5.
Benjamin, I. (1995) *The Black Press in Britain*. Stoke on Trent: Trentham.
Bennett, T. (1982) 'Theories of the media, theories of society', in M. Gurevitich, T. Bennett, J. Curran and J. Woolacott (eds), *Culture Society and the Media*. London: Methuen.
Bennie, L. (1998) 'Brent Spar, Atlantic oil and Greenpeace', *Parliamentary Affairs*, 51(3): 397–410.
Berelson, B. (1959) 'The state of communication research', *Public Opinion Quarterly*, 23: 1–6.
Bielby, W.T. and Bielby, D.D. (1992) 'Cumulative versus continuous disadvantage in an unstructured labour market', *Work and Occupations*, 19(4): 366–86.
Blood, D.J. and Philips, P.C.B. (1995) 'Recession headline news, consumer sentiment, the state of the economy and presidential popularity: a time series analysis', *International Journal of Public Opinion Research*, 7: 2–22.
Blumenthal, S. (1982) *The Permanent Campaign*. New York: Simon and Schuster.
Blumler, J.G. (1970) 'The political effects of television', in J. Halloran (ed.), *The Effects of Television*. London: Panther.
Blumler, J.G. (1980) 'Mass communication research in Europe: some origins and prospects', *Media Culture Society*, 2: 367–76.
Blumler, J.G. (1992) 'Vulnerable values at stake', in J.G. Blumler (ed.), *Television and the Public Interest*. London: Sage.
Blumler, J. and Gurevitch, M. (1977) 'Linkages between the mass media and politics: a model for the analysis of political communication systems', in J. Curran, M. Gurevitch and J. Woollacott (eds.), *Mass Communication and Society*. London: Arnold.
Blumler, J. and Gurevitch, M. (1979) 'The reform of election broadcasting: a reply to Nicholas Garnham', *Media Culture Society*, 1(2): 211–19.
Blumler, J. and Gurevitch, M. (1982) 'The political effects of mass communication', in M. Gurevitch, J. Curran, T. Bennett and J. Woolacott (eds), *Culture, Society and the Media*. London: Methuen.
Bourdieu, P. (1985) 'The social space and the genesis of groups', *Theory and Society*, 14: 728–9.
Boyd-Barrett, O. (1997) 'Global news wholesalers as agents of globalization', in A. Sreberny-Mohammadi, D. Winseck, J. McKenna and O. Boyd-Barrett (eds) *Media in Global Context*. London: Edward Arnold.
Boyd-Barrett, O. (1998) '"Global" news agencies', in O. Boyd-Barrett and T. Rantenan (eds), *The Globalization of News*. London: Sage.

Boyd-Barrett, O. and Rantanen, T. (eds) (1998) *The Globalization of News*. London: Sage.

Brosius, H.B. and Kepplinger, H.M. (1990) 'The agenda setting function of television news', *Communication Research*, 17(2), April, 183–211.

Brown, M. (1997) 'Round the clock, round the bend?', *The Guardian*, Media Section, 3 November 1997, pp. 2–3.

Brown, M. (1998) 'Global Warning', *The Guardian*, Media Section, 17 August 1988, p. 4.

Burgess, J. and Harrison, C.M. (1993) 'The circulation of claims in the cultural politics of environmental change', in A. Hansen (ed.), *The Mass Media and Environmental Issues*. Leicester: Leicester University Press.

Cameron, D. (1996) 'Style policy and style politics: A neglected aspect of the language of news', *Media Culture Society*, 18(2), April

Campaign for Quality Television (1998) *Serious Documentaries on ITV*. London: Campaign for Quality Television.

Campbell, D. (1998) 'Police tighten the net', *The Guardian*, Online Section, 17 September 1998, pp. 2–3.

Camrose, Viscount (1947) *British Newspapers and Their Controllers*. London: Cassell.

Cayford, J. (1985) *Speak Up: Trade Union Responses to New Management Communications*. London: Comedia.

Chapman, S. and Lupton, D. (1994) *The Fight for Public Health*. London: BMJ Publishing Group.

Chibnall, S. (1977) *Law and Order News*. London: Tavistock.

Chippindale, P. and Franks, S. (1991) *Dished! The Rise and Fall of British Satellite Broadcasting*. London: Simon and Schuster.

Chomsky, N. (1989) *Necessary Illusions, Thought Control in Democratic Societies*. London: Pluto Press.

Cockerall, M. et al. (1984) *Sources Close to the Prime Minister*. London: Macmillan.

Cohen, A., Levy, M.R., Roch, I. and Gurevitch, M. (1996) *Global Newsrooms. Local Audiences. A Study of the Eurovision News Exchange*. London: John Libbey.

Cohen, B. (1963) *The Press and Foreign Policy*. Princeton, NJ: Princeton University Press.

Cohen, S. (1972) *Folk Devils and Moral Panics: The Creation of the Mods and Rockers*. London: MacGibbon and Kee.

Cohen, S. and Young, J. (eds) (1978) *The Manufacture of News*. London: Constable.

Coles, J. (1997) 'Boyzone story', *The Guardian*, Media Section, 28 April 1997, pp. 4–5.

Collins, R. (1993) 'Public service versus the market ten years on: reflections on critical theory and the debate on broadcasting policy in the UK', *Screen*, 34(3): 249–65.

Connell, I. (1991) 'Tales from Tellyland: the popular press and television in the UK', in P. Dahlgren and C. Sparks (eds), *Communication and Citizenship: Journalism and the Public Sphere in the New Media Age*. London: Routledge.

Conway, G. (1997) *Islamaphobia*: *Its Features and Dangers*. Runnymede Trust Consultation Paper, London: Runnymede Trust.

Corner, J. (1991) 'Meaning, genre and context: The problematics of "Public Knowledge" in the New Audience Studies', in J. Curran, M. Gurevitch and J. Woolacott (eds), *Mass Communication and Society*. London: Arnold.

Corner, J., Richardson, K. and Fenton, N. (1990) *Nuclear Reactions: Form and Response in 'Public Issue' Television*. London: John Libbey.

Costigan, R. (1996) 'Fleet Street blues: police seisure of journalists' material', *Criminal Law Review*, April: 231–9.

Cottle, S. (1993) *TV News, Urban Conflict and the Inner City*. Leicester: University of Leicester Press.

Cottle, S. (1995) 'The production of news formats: determinants of mediated public contestation', *Media Culture Society*, 17(2): 275–91.

Cottle, S. (1998) 'Ulrich Beck, "Risk Society", and the media. a catastrophic View?', *European Journal of Communication*, 13(1): 5–32.
Cox, G., Lowe, P. and Winter, M. (1986) 'Agriculture and conservation in Britain: a policy community under seige', in G. Cox, P. Lowe and M. Winter (eds), *Agriculture: People and Policies*. London: Allen and Unwin.
Crenson, M. (1971) *The Un-politics of Air Pollution: A Study of Non-Decision Making in the Cities*. London: John Hopkins Press.
Cronkite, W. (1997) 'More bad news', *The Guardian*, Media Section, 27 January 1997, p. 2.
Cudlipp, H. (1953) *Publish and Be Damned*. London: Andrew Dakers.
Cumberbatch, G., McGregor, R. and Brown, J. (1986) *Television and the Miners' Strike*. Mimeo, London: Broadcasting Research Unit.
Cunnison, S. and Stageman, J. (1993) *Feminising the Unions*. Aldershot: Avebury.
Curran, J. (1978) 'Advertising and the press', in J. Curran (ed.), *The British Press: A Manifesto*. London: Macmillan.
Curran, J. (1990) 'The new revisionism in mass communication research: A reappraisal', *European Journal of Communication*, 5.
Curran, J. (1991) 'Rethinking the media as a public sphere', in P. Dahlgren and C. Sparks (eds), *Communication and Citizenship: Journalism and the Public Sphere in the New Media Age*. London: Routledge.
Curran, J. (1996) 'Rethinking mass communications', in J. Curran, D. Morley and V. Walkerdine (eds), *Cultural Studies and Communications*. London: Arnold.
Curran, J. (1997) 'The liberal theory of press freedom', in J. Curran and J. Seaton (eds), *Power Without Responsibility*, 5th edition. London: Routledge.
Curran, J. and Seaton, J. (1997) *Power Without Responsibility*, 5th edition. London: Routledge.
Dahl, R.A. (1961) *Who Governs?* New Haven: Yale University Press.
Dahl, R.A. (1982) *Dilemmas of Pluralist Democracy: Autonomy versus Control*. New Haven: Yale University Press.
Dahlgren, P. (1991) 'Introduction', in P. Dahlgren and C. Sparks (eds), *Communication and Citizenship: Journalism and the Public Sphere in the New Media Age*. London: Routledge.
Davies, S. (1998) 'Workers of the world – online', *People Management*, September.
Davis, A. (2000) 'Public relations campaigning and news production: the case of the new unionism in Britain', in J. Curran (ed.), *Media Organisations in Society*. London: Arnold.
Deacon, D. (1996) 'Voluntary activity in a changing communication environment', *European Journal of Communication*, 11(2): 173–98.
Deacon, D. and Golding, P. (1994) *Taxation and Representation: The Media, Political Communication and the Poll Tax*. London: John Libbey.
Deacon, D., Fenton, N. and Bryman, A. (1999) 'From inception to reception: the natural history of a news item', *Media Culture Society*, 21(1): 5–31.
Dearing, J.W. and Rogers, E.M. (1996) *Agenda Setting*. London: Sage.
De Bens, E. and Østbye, H. (1998) 'The European newspaper market', in D. McQuail and K. Siune (eds), *Media Policy. Convergence, Concentration and Commerce*. London: Sage.
Denny, C. (1999) 'Cyber Utopia? Only the usual candidates need apply', *The Guardian*, 12 July 1999, p. 23.
Douglas, S. (1986) *Labor's New Voice*. New Jersey: Ablex Publishing.
Doward, J. (1999) 'Gotcha Yahoo! Tabloids on line', *The Observer*, Business Section, 4 April 1999.
Dowmunt, T. (ed.) (1993) *Channels of Resistance*. London: BFI and Channel Four.
Downs, A. (1972) 'Up and down with ecology – the issue attention cycle', *Public Interest*, 28: 38–50.
Driberg, T. (1956) *Beaverbrook: A Study in Power and Frustration*. London: Weidenfeld and Nicolson.

Drier, P. (1988) 'The corporate complaint against the media', in R.E. Hiebert and C. Reuss (eds), *The Impact of the Mass Media*. New York: Longman.
Dugdale, J. (1999) 'Sticks and stones', *The Guardian*, Media Section, 21 June 1999, p.2.
Dunleavy, P. (1990) 'Government at the centre', in P. Dunleavy, A. Gamble and G. Peele (eds), *Developments in British Politics 3*. Basingstoke: Macmillan.
Easthope, A. (1990) 'Trade unions in British television news', *The Year Book of English Studies*, 20 (Literature in the Modern Media).
Eckstein, H. (1960) *Pressure Group Politics*. London: George Allen.
Edwards, R., Garrona, P. and Todtling, F. (eds) (1986) *Unions in Crisis and Beyond*. Aldershot: Auburn House.
Edwards, P. Hall, M. Hyman, R. Marginson, P., Sissons K., Waddington, J. and Winchester, S. (1992) 'Great Britain: still muddling through', in A. Ferner and R. Hyman (eds), *Industrial Relations in the New Europe*. Oxford: Blackwell.
Eide, M. (1997) 'A new kind of newspaper? Understanding a popularization process', *Media Culture Society*, 19(2): 173–82.
Ekecrantz, J. (1997) 'Journalism's "discursive events" and sociopolitical change in Sweden 1925–87', *Media Culture Society*, 19(3): 393–412.
Eldridge, J., Kitzinger, J. and Williams, K. (1997) *The Mass Media and Power in Britain*. Oxford: Oxford University Press.
Eley, G. (1992) 'Nations, publics and political cultures: placing Habermas in the nineteenth century', in C. Calhoun (ed.), *Habermas and the Public Sphere*. Cambridge, MA: MIT Press.
Elliott, P. (1981) 'Review of more bad news', *Sociological Review*, 29(1): 169–71.
Emmison, M. (1983) '"The Economy": its emergence in media discourse', in P. Walton (ed.), *Language, Image Text*. Oxford: Basil Blackwell.
Epstein, E. (1973) *News from Nowhere*. New York: Random House.
Ericson, R.V., Baranek, P.M. and Chan, J.B. (1989) *Negotiating Control: A Study of News Sources*. Milton Keynes: Open University Press.
Esaiason, P. and Moring, T. (1994) 'Codes of professionalism: journalists versus politicians in Finland and Sweden', *European Journal of Communication*, 9(3): 271–89.
Euromedia Research Group (1992) *The Media in Western Europe*. London: Sage.
European Institute for the Media (1998) *More Colour in the Media*. Dusseldorf: European Institute for the Media.
Evans, H. (1983) *Good Times, Bad Times*. London: Weidenfield and Nicolson.
Eyerman, R. and Jamison, A. (1989) 'Environmental knowledge as an organisational weapon', *Social Science Information*, 1989.
Fawcett Society (1997) *Watching Women*. London: Fawcett Society.
Fenton, N., Bryman, A., Deacon, D. and Birmingham, P. (1997) 'Sod off and find us a boffin': journalists and the social science conference', *The Sociological Review*, 45(1): 1–23.
Ferguson, M. and Golding, P. (eds) (1997) *Cultural Studies in Question*. London: Sage.
Ferner, A. and Hyman, R. (eds) (1992) *Industrial Relations in the New Europe*. Oxford: Blackwell.
Ferrell-Lowe, G. and Alm, A. (1997) 'Public service broadcasting as cultural industry value transformation in the Finnish market place', *European Journal of Communication*, 12 (2), June.
Finer, S.E. (1966) *Anonymous Empire*. London: Pall Mall Press.
Fishman, M. (1980) *Manufacturing the News*. Austin, TX: University of Texas Press.
Foucault, M. (1979a) *Discipline and Punish. The Birth of the Prison*. Harmondsworth: Penguin Books.
Foucault, M. (1979b) 'Governmentality', *Ideology and Consciousness*, 6: 5–21.
Foucault, M. (1984) 'Nietzsche, genealogy, history', in P. Rabinow (ed.), *The Foucault Reader*. New York: Pantheon Books.
Franklin, B. (1994) *Packaging Politics: Political Communication in Britain's Media Democracy*. London: Edward Arnold.

Franklin, B. (1998) 'Tough on soundbites, tough on the causes of soundbites', *Free Press*, Campaign for Press and Broadcasting Freedom, 102, January–February.
Franklin, B. and Murphy, D. (1991) *What News? The Market, Politics and the Local Press*. London: Routledge.
Fraser, N. (1990) 'Rethinking the public sphere: a contribution to the critique of actually existing democracy', *Social Text*, 25/26: 56–80.
Friedland, J. (1998) 'Barracking the Beeb', *The Guardian*, Media Section, 9 February 1998, p. 8.
Funkhouser, G.R.(1973) 'The issues of the sixties: an exploratory study in the dynamics of public opinion', *Public Opinion Quarterly,* 37: 62–75.
Gall, G. (1993) 'The employers' offensive in the provincial newspaper industry', *British Journal of Industrial Relations*, 31(4): 615–24.
Gall, G. (1997) 'Looking in the mirror: a case study of industrial relations in a national newspaper', in M. Bromley and T. O'Malley (eds), *A Journalism Reader*. London: Routledge.
Galtung, J. and Ruge, M. (1973) 'Structuring and selecting the news', in S. Cohen and J. Young (eds), *The Manufacture of News*. London: Constable.
Gamson, W. and Modigliani, A. (1989) 'Media discourse and public opinion on nuclear power: a constructionist approach', *American Journal of Sociology*, 95(1): 1–37.
Gamson, W. and Wolfsfeld, G. (1993) 'Movements and medias interacting systems', in R. Dalton (ed.), *Citizens Protest and Democracy*, Annals of the American Academy of Political and Social Science, 528 (July): 114–25.
Gandy, O. (1982) *Beyond Agenda Setting: Information Subsidies and Public Policy*, Norwood, NJ: Ablex Publishing.
Gandy, O. (1998) *Communication and Race*. London: Arnold.
Garnham, N. (1979) 'Contribution to a political economy of mass communication', *Media Culture Society*, 1(1).
Garnham, N. (1986) 'The media and the public sphere', in P. Golding, G. Murdock and P. Schlesinger (eds), *Communicating Politics*. Leicester: University of Leicester Press.
Garrett, A. (1998) 'Is your advertising really necessary?', *The Observer*, Media Section, 22 February 1998, p. 7.
Geiber, W. (1956) 'Across the desk: a study of 16 television editors', *Journalism Quarterly*, 33 (Fall): 423–32.
Gerbner, G. (1969) 'Toward "cultural indicators": the analysis of mass mediated message systems', *AV Communication Review*, 17(2): 137–48.
Gerbner, G., Gross, L., Morgan, M. and Signorielli, N. (1994) 'Growing up with television: the cultivation perspective', in J. Bryant and D. Zillman (eds), *Media Effects Advances in Theory and Research*. Hove: Lawrence Erlbaum Associates.
Gillespie, M. (1995) *Television, Ethnicity and Social Change*. London: Routledge.
Gitlin, T. (1978) 'Media sociology: the dominant paradigm', *Theory and Society*, 6(2), September: 205–53.
Gitlin, T. (1980) *The Whole World is Watching*. London: University of California Press.
Glasgow University Media Group (1976) *Bad News*. London: Routledge and Kegan Paul.
Glasgow University Media Group (1980) *More Bad News*. London: Routledge and Kegan Paul.
Glasgow University Media Group (1985) *War and Peace News*. London: Routledge.
Goldenberg, E.N. (1975) *Making the Papers*. Lexington, MA: D.C. Heath.
Goldie, G.W. (1977) *Facing the Nation: Television and Politics 1936–76*. London: The Bodley Head.
Golding, P. (1974) 'Media role in national development: critique of a theoretical orthodoxy', *Journal of Communication*, 24: 39–53.
Golding, P. (1981) 'The missing dimensions – news media and the management of

social change', in E. Katz and T. Szecsko (eds), *The Mass Media and Social Change*. London: Sage.
Golding, P. (1990) Political communication and citizenship: the media and democracy in an inegalitarian social order", in M. Ferguson (ed.), *Public Communication. The New Imperatives*. London: Sage.
Golding, P. (1992) 'Communicating capitalism: resisting and restructuring state ideology – the case of "Thatcherism"', *Media Culture Society*, 14: 503–21.
Golding, P. (1996) 'World Wide Wedge: Division and Contradiction in the Global Information Infrastructure', *Monthly Review*, 48(3): 70–85.
Golding, P. and Elliott, P. (1979) *Making the News*. London: Longmans.
Golding, P. and Middleton, S. (1982) *Images of Welfare. Press and Public Attitudes to Poverty*. Oxford: Martin Robertson.
Golding, P. and Murdock, G. (1977) 'Capitalism, communications and class relations', in J. Curran, M. Gurevitch and J. Woollacott (eds), *Mass Communication and Society*. London: Edward Arnold.
Golding, P. and Murdock, G. (1991) 'Culture, communications and political economy', in J. Curran and M. Gurevitch (eds), *Mass Media and Society*. London: Edward Arnold.
Gooch, G. (1996) 'Environmental concern and the Swedish press', *European Journal of Communication*, 11(1): 107–27.
Graber, D.A. (1993) 'Failures in news transmissions: reasons and remedies', in P. Gaunt (ed.), *Beyond Agendas: New Directions in Communication Research*. Westport, CT: Greenwood Press.
Gramsci, A. (1971) *The Prison Notebooks*. London: Lawrence and Wishart.
Grant, W. (1987) *Business and Politics in Britain*. Basingstoke: Macmillan.
Grant, W. (1990) *Pressure Groups Politics and Democracy*. Hemel Hempstead: Philip Allan.
Grant, W., Paterson, W. and Whitson, C. (1988) *Government and the Chemical Industry: A Comparative Study of Britain and West Germany*. Oxford: Clarendon Press.
Greenberg, D.W. (1985) 'Staging media events to achieve legitimacy: a case study of Britain's Friends of the Earth', *Political Communication and Persuasion*, 2 (4): 347–62.
Greenslade, R. (1998) 'Murdoch's big bucks stir up Saturday morning fever', *The Guardian*, Media Section, 12 January 1998, p. 7.
Greer, A. (1998) 'Pesticides, sheepdips and science', *Parliamentary Affairs*, 51(3): 411–23.
Gurevitch, M. and Blumler, J. (1977) 'Linkages between the mass media and politics: a model for the analysis of political communication systems', in J. Curran, M. Gurevitch and J. Woolacott (eds), *Mass Communication and Society*, London: Edward Arnold.
Gurevitch, M. and Blumler, J. (1990) 'Political communication systems and democratic values', in J. Lichtenberg (ed.), *Democracy and the Mass Media*. Cambridge: Cambridge University Press.
Gurevitch, M., Levy, M. and Roeh, I. (1991) 'The global newsroom: convergences, and diversities in the globalization of television news', in P. Dahlgren and C. Sparks (eds), *Communication and Citizenship: Journalism and the Public Sphere in the New Media Age*. London: Routledge.
Habermas, J. (1983) 'Modernity – an incomplete project', in H. Foster (ed.), *Postmodern Culture*. London: Pluto Press.
Habermas, J. (1987) *The Theory of Communicative Action: Volume Two. Lifeworld and System. A Critique of Functionalist Reason*. Boston: Beacon Press.
Habermas, J. (1989) *The Structural Transformation of the Public Sphere*. Cambridge: Polity Press.
Habermas, J. (1992) 'Further reflections on the public sphere', in C. Calhoun (ed.), *Habermas and the Public Sphere*. London: The MIT Press.

Hall, S. (1971) 'Politics, deviancy and the media', Centre for Contemporary Cultural Studies, Occasional Paper, University of Birmingham.
Hall, S. (1973a) 'A world at one with itself', in S. Cohen and J. Young (eds), *The Manufacture of News*. London: Constable.
Hall, S. (1973b) 'The determination of news photographs', in S. Cohen and J. Young (eds), *The Manufacture of News*. London: Constable.
Hall, S. (1973c) 'The structured communication of events', Paper for the Obstacles to Communication Symposium, Unesco Division of Philosophy, Centre for Contemporary Cultural Studies Occasional Paper, University of Birmingham.
Hall, S. (1980) 'Encoding/decoding', in S. Hall, D. Hobson, A. Lowe and P. Willis (eds.) *Culture Media Language*. London: Hutchinson.
Hall, S. (1982) 'The re–discovery of "ideology": return of the repressed in media studies', in M. Gurevitch, T. Bennett, J. Curran and J. Woollacott (eds), *Culture Society and the Media*. London: Methuen.
Hall, S. (1993) 'Which public, whose service?' in W. Stevenson (ed.), *All Our Futures.* London: BFI Publications.
Hall, S. (1996) 'On postmodernism and articulation: an interview with Stuart Hall', edited by Larry Grossberg, in D. Morley and K. Chen (eds.), *Stuart Hall Critical Dialogues in Cultural Studies*. London: Routledge.
Hall, S., Chritcher, C., Jefferson, T., Clarke, J., and Roberts, B. (1978) *Policing the Crisis. Mugging, the State and Law and Order*. London: Macmillan.
Hallin, D.C. (1986) *The 'Uncensored War': The Media and Vietnam*. Oxford: Oxford University Press.
Hall-Jamieson, K. (1992) *Dirty Politics: Deception Distraction and Democracy*. Oxford: Oxford University Press.
Hansen, A. (1991) 'The media and the social construction of the environment', *Media Culture Society*, 13: 443–58.
Hansen, A. (ed.) (1993) *The Mass Media and Environmental Issues*. Leicester: Leicester University Press.
Harris, R. (1990) *Good and Faithful Servant*. London: Faber and Faber.
Harrison, M. (1985) *TV News: Whose Bias?* Berkhamsted Policy Journals.
Hattersley, R. (1998) 'Let's hear it for Tony . . . or else', *The Observer*, Review Section, 22 February 1998, p. 3.
Hennesey, P. and Bevins, A. (1990) 'The crippling of the scribes', *British Journalism Review*, 1(2), Winter.
Hennesey, P. (1999) 'For he was a jolly good fellow', *New Statesman*, 8 January 1999, p. 11.
Henningham, J. (1995) 'Political journalists' professional and political values', *Australian Journal of Political Science*, 30(2): 321–34.
Herman, E.S. and Chomsky, N. (1988) *Manufacturing Consent: The Political Economy of the Mass Media*. New York: Pantheon Books.
Herman, E.S. and McChesney, R.W. (1997) *The Global Media – The New Missionaries of Global Capitalism*. London: Cassell.
Hetherington, A. (1981) *Guardian Years*. London: Chatto and Windus.
Hickey, N. (1998) 'Sell the Front Page', *Columbia Journalism Review*, July/August.
Hirsch, F. and Gordon, D. (1975) *Newspaper Money*. London: Hutchinson.
Hirsch, M. and Petersen, V.G. (1998) 'European policy initiatives', in D. McQuail and K. Siune (eds), *Media Policy. Convergence, Concentration and Commerce*. London: Sage.
Hirst, P. and Thompson, G. (1996) *Globalization In Question: The International Economy and the Possibilities of Governance*. Cambridge: Polity Press.
Hobsbawm, E. (1994) *The Age of Extremes, The Short Twentieth Century 1914–1991*, London: Abacus.
Hobsbawm, E. (1997) 'To see the future, look at the past', *The Guardian*, Comment and Essay Section, 7 June 1997.

Hoge, J. (1988) 'Business and the media: stereotyping each other', in R.E. Hiebert and C. Reuss (eds), *The Impact of the Mass Media*. New York: Longman.
Holland, P. (1998) 'The politics of the smile: "soft news" and the sexualisation of the popular press', in C. Carter, G. Branston and S. Allan (eds), *News Gender and Power*. London: Routledge.
Hollingsworth, M. (1986) *The Press and Political Dissent*. London: Pluto Press.
Hoyt, M. (1984) 'Downtime for labor', *Columbian Journalism Review*, 22: 34–8.
Humphreys, P. (1994) *Media and Media Policy in Germany*, Rev. Ed., Oxford: Berg.
Humphreys, P. (1996) *Mass Media and Media Policy in Western Europe*. Manchester: Manchester University Press.
Hutton, W. (1996) *The State We're In*. London: Vintage.
Hyman, R. (1985) 'Class struggle and the trade union movement', in D. Coates, G. Johnston and R. Bush (eds), *A Socialist Anatomy of Britain*. Cambridge: Polity Press.
ITC (1996) *Annual Report and Accounts*. London: ITC.
Iyengar, S. (1991) *Is Anyone Responsible? How Television Frames Political Issues*. Chicago: University of Chicago Press.
Iyengar, S. and Kinder, D.R. (1987) *News That Matters: Agenda Setting and Priming in a Television Age.* Chicago: Chicago University Press.
Jack, I. (1998) 'Now for the bad news', *The Guardian*, Saturday Review, 8 August, p. 3.
Jacobs, R.N. (1996) 'Producing the news, producing the crisis: narrativity, television and news work', *Media Culture Society*, 18(3): 373–97.
Jameson, F. (1984) 'Postmodernism, or the cultural logic of late capitalism', *New Left Review*, 146 (July/August,): 53–92.
Jamieson, K.H. (1992) *Dirty Politics: Deception, Distraction and Democracy*. Oxford: Oxford University Press.
Jenkins, H. (1992) *Textual Poachers*. London: Routledge.
Jessop, B. (1990) *State Theory: Putting Capitalist States in their Place*. Cambridge: Polity Press.
Jones, B. (1993) 'The pitiless probing eye: politicians and the broadcast political Interview', *Parliamentary Affairs*, 46(1): 66–90.
Jones, N. (1986) *Strikes and the Media*. Oxford: Basil Blackwell.
Jones, N. (1995) *Soundbites and Spindoctors*. London: Cassell.
Jordan, G. (1981) 'Iron triangles, wooly corporatism and elastic nets: images of the policy process', *Journal of Public Policy*, 1: 95–123.
Katz, E. (1992) 'The end of journalism: notes on watching the war', *Journal of Communication*, 42(3): 5–13.
Katz, E. and Lazarsfeld, P.F. (1955) *Personal Influence: The Part Played by People in the Flow of Mass Communication*. New York: Free Press.
Keane, J. (1991) *The Media and Democracy*. Cambridge: Polity Press.
Kelly, J. (1990) 'British trade unionism 1979–1989: changes, continuity and contradictions', *Work Employment Society*, Special Issue: 29–65.
King, A. (1998) 'Thatcherism and the emergence of Sky', *Media Culture Society*, 20: 277–93.
Kingdon, J. (1984) *Agendas, Alternatives and Public Policies*. Boston: Little Brown and Co.
Kitzinger, J. (1993) 'Understanding AIDS: media messages and what people know about AIDS', in J. Eldridge (ed.), *Getting the Message, News Truth and Power*. London: Routledge.
Kitzinger, J. (1994) 'Focus groups: method or madness?', in M. Boulton (ed.), *Challenge and Innovation: Methodological Advances in Social Research on HIV/AIDS*. London: Taylor Francis.
Kitzinger, J. (1998) 'Media impact on public beliefs about AIDS', in D. Miller, J. Kitzinger, K. Williams and P. Beharrell (eds), *The Circuit of Mass Communication*. London: Sage.
Kitzinger, J. (1999) 'A sociology of media power: key issues in audience reception research', in G. Philo (ed.), *Message Received.* Harlow: Longman.

Klapper, J. (1960) *The Effects of Mass Communication*. New York: Free Press.
Klapper, J. (1963) 'The social effects of communication', in W. Schramm (ed.), *The Science of Communication*. New York: Basic Books.
Kleinsteuber, H.J. (1997) 'Germany', in Euromedia Research Group (eds), *The Media in Western Europe*, 2nd edition. London: Sage.
Kleinsteuber, H.J. and Peters, B. (1991) 'Media Moguls in Germany', in J. Tunstall and M. Palmer (eds), *Media Moguls*. London: Routledge.
Knightley, P. (1989) *The First Casualty*. London: Pan Books.
Koch, T. (1991) *Journalism for the 21st Century, On-line Information, Databases and the News*. Westport, CT: Greenwood Press.
Koss, S. (1973) *Fleet Street. A.G. Gardiner and the Daily News*. London: Allen Lane.
Kuhn, R. (1995) *The Media in France*. London: Routledge.
Lacey, C. and Longman, D. (1993) 'The press and public access to the environment and development debate', *Sociological Review*, 41(2): 207–43.
Lamb, L. (1989) *Sunrise*. London: Macmillan.
Lang, K. and Lang, G. (1953) 'The unique perspective of television and its effect: a pilot study', *American Sociological Review*, 18(1): 3–12.
Lang, K. and Lang, G. (1955) 'The inferential structure of political communication', *Public Opinion Quarterly*. pp. 168–83.
Lash, S. and Urry, J. (1987) *The End of Organised Capitalism*. Oxford: Blackwell.
Lasswell, H. (1960) 'The structure and function of communication in society', in W. Schramm (ed.), *Mass Communications*. Urbana: University of Illinois Press.
Lazarsfeld, P.F., Berelson, B. and Gaudet, H. (1948) *The People's Choice*. 2nd edition. New York: Columbia University Press.
Lee, E. (1996) *The New Internationalism*. London: Pluto Press.
Lennon, T. (1996) 'Digital doubts', *Free Press*, Journal of the Campaign for Press and Broadcasting Freedom, 91 (March–April): 7.
Lichtenberg, J. (1991) 'In defence of objectivity', in J. Curran and M. Gurevitich (eds.), *Mass Media and Society*. London: Edward Arnold.
Lichter, R. and Rothman, S. (1988) 'Media and business elites', in R.E. Hiebert and C. Reuss (eds), *The Impact of the Mass Media*. New York: Longman.
Linne, O. (1993) 'Professional practice and organisation: environmental broadcasters and their sources', in A. Hansen (ed.), *The Mass Media and Environmental Issues*. Leicester: Leicester University Press.
Livingstone, S. (1988) 'Why people watch soap operas: an analysis of the explanations of British viewers', *European Journal of Communication*, 3: 55–80.
Livingstone, S. and Lunt, P. (1994) *Talk on Television*. London: Routledge.
Love, A. (1990) 'The production of environmental meanings in the media: a new era', *Media Education Journal*, 10 (Winter): 18–20.
Lowe, P. and Morrison, D. (1984) 'Bad news or good news: environmental politics and the mass media, *Sociological Review*, 32 (1): 75–90.
Lowe, P., Cox, G., MacEwan, M., O'Riordan, T. and Winter, M. (1986) *Countryside Conflicts*. Aldershot: Gower.
Lukes, S. (1974) *Power*. London: Macmillan.
MacAskill, E. (1997):'Spin doctoring: it takes one to know one', *The Guardian*, 30 October 1997.
MacGregor, B. (1997) *Live, Direct and Biased? Making Television News in the Satellite Age*. London: Arnold.
Machill, M. (1998) 'Euronews: the European channel as a case study for media industry development in Europe and for spectra transnational journalism in Europe,' *Media Culture and Society*, 20: 427–50.
McCarthy, M. (1986) *Campaigning for the Poor*. Beckenham: Croom Helm.
McChesney, R.W. (1997) *Corporate Media and the Threat to Democracy*. New York: Seven Stories Press.
McCombs, M.E. (1977) 'Newspaper versus television: mass communication effects

across time', in D.L. Shaw and M.E. McCombs (eds), *The Emergence of American Political Issues: The Agenda Setting Function of the Press*. St Paul: West Publishing Company.

McCombs, M.E. (1994) 'New influences on our pictures of the world', in J. Bryant and D. Zillmann (eds) *Media Effects: Advances in Theory and Research*. Hove: Lawrence Erlbaum Associates.

McCombs, M.E. and Shaw, D.L. (1972) 'The agenda setting function of the mass media', *Public Opinion Quarterly*, 36: 176–87.

McCormick, J. (1991) *British Politics and the Environment*. London: Earthscan.

McDonald, S. (1998) 'Tell us how it really is', *The Guardian*, Media Section, 20 April 1998, p. 9.

McGuigan, J. (1992) *Cultural Populism*. London: Routledge.

McGuire, S. (1999) 'Set free – in spite of the red tape', *The Guardian*, Media Section, 11 October 1999, p. 10.

McIntyre, S., Miller, D. and Reilly, J. (1998) 'Food choice, food scares, and health: the role of the media', in A. Murcott (ed.), *The Nation's Diet: The Social Science of Food Choice*. London: Longman

McLaughlin, L. (1993) 'Feminism, the public sphere, media and democracy', *Media Culture Society*, 15: 599–620.

McLeod, J.M., Kosicki, G. and Zhongdang, P. (1991) 'On understanding and misunderstanding media effects', in J. Curran and M. Gurevitch (eds.), *Mass Media and Society*, 1st edition. London: Edward Arnold.

McLeod, J.M., Kosicki, G. and McLeod, D. (1994) 'The expanding boundaries of political communication effects', in J. Bryant and D. Zillmann (eds), *Media Effects. Advances in Theory and Research*. Hove: Lawrence and Erlbaum Associates.

McQuail, D., Blumber, J.G. and Brown, J.R. (1972) 'The television audience: A revised perspective', in D. McQuail (ed.) *Sociology of Mass Communications*. Harmondsworth: Penguin Books.

Mancini, P. (1993) 'Between trust and Suspicion: how political journalists solve the dilemma', *European Journal of Communication*, 8(1): 33–51.

Manning, P. (1991) 'The media and pressure politics', *Social Studies Review*, 6(4) 159–63.

Manning, P. (1998) *Spinning for Labour: Trade Unions and the New Media Environment*. Aldershot: Ashgate.

Manning, P. (1999) 'Categories of knowledge and information flows: reasons for the decline of the British labour and industrial correspondents' group', *Media Culture Society*, 21(3): 313–36.

Marquez, G.G. (1997) 'Hacks in the time of tape recorders', *The Observer*, 25 May 1997.

Marx, K. (1968) 'The eighteenth brumaire of Louis Bonaparte', in K. Marx and F. Engels (eds), *Selected Works*. London: Lawrence and Wishart.

Marx, K. and Engels, F. (1968) *Selected Works*. London: Lawrence and Wishart.

Marx, K. and Engels, F. (1970) *The German Ideology*, edited by C.J. Arthur. London: Lawrence and Wishart.

Mazzoleni, G. (1991) 'Media moguls in Italy', in J. Tunstall and J. Palmer (eds), *Media Moguls*. London: Routledge.

Mazzoleni, G. (1997) 'Italy', in The Euromedia Research Group, B.S. Ostergaard (ed.), *The Media in Western Europe*, 2nd edition. London: Sage.

Merton, R.K. and Lazarsfeld, P.F. (1948) 'Mass communication, popular taste, and organised social action', in L. Bryson (ed.), *The Communication of Ideas*. New York: Institute for Religious and Social Studies.

Michie, D. (1998) *The Invisible Persuaders. How Britain's Spin Doctors Manipulate the Media*. London: Bantam Press.

Miliband, R. (1972) 'The problem of the capitalist state', in R. Blackburn (ed.), *Ideology in Social Science*. London: Fontana/Collins.

Miliband, R. (1973) *The State in Capitalist Society*. London: Quartet Books.

Miliband, R. (1991) *Divided Societies*. Oxford: Oxford University Press.

Miliband, R. (1994) *Socialism for a Sceptical Age*. Cambridge: Polity Press.

Miller, D. (1993) 'The Northern Ireland Information Service: aims, strategy and tactics', in J. Eldridge (ed.), *Getting the Message: News Truth and Power*. London: Routledge.

Miller, D. (1994) *Don't Mention the War*. London: Pluto Press.

Miller, D. and Dinan, W. (2000) 'The rise of the PR industry in Britain, 1979–98', *European Journal of Communication*, 15(1): 5–35.

Miller, D. and Reilly, J. (1994) 'Food and the media: the reporting of food "risks"', in S. Henson and S. Gregory (eds), *The Politics of Food*. Reading: University of Reading.

Miller, D. and Williams, K. (1998) 'Sourcing AIDS News', in D. Miller , J. Kitzinger, K. Williams and P. Beharrell (eds), *The Circuit of Mass Communication*. London: Sage.

Miller, D. and Williams, K. (1993) 'Negotiating HIV/AIDS information: agendas, media strategies and the news', in J. Eldridge (ed.), *Getting the Message: News Truth and Power*. London: Routledge.

Miller, D., Kitzinger, J., Williams, K. and Beharrell, P. (1998) *The Circuit of Communication*. London: Sage.

Miller, P. and Rose, N. (1993) 'Governing economic life', in M. Gane and T. Johnson (eds), *Foucault's New Domains*. London: Routledge.

Miller, W. (1991) *Media and Voters: the Audience, Content and Influence of Press and Television at the 1987 General Election*. Oxford: Clarendon Press.

Mills, C.W. (1956) *The Power Elite*. London: Oxford University Press.

Milne, S. (1994) *The Enemy Within. The Secret War Against the Miners* London: Verso.

Milne, S. (1997) 'The battle of British Airways', *The Guardian*, G2 Media Section, 14 July 1997, p.1 0.

Milne, S. (1998) 'After the brothers', *The Guardian*, Jobs and Money Section, 14 March 1998, pp. 2–3.

Molotoch, H. and Lester, H. (1974) 'News as purposive behaviour', *American Sociological Review*, 39 (February): 101–12.

Moores, S. (1993) *Interpreting Audiences: The Ethnography of Media Consumption*. London: Sage.

Moran, M. (1983) *Politics and Society in Britain*. Basingstoke: Macmillan.

Moran, M. (1984) *The Politics of Banking*. Basingstoke: Macmillan.

MORI (1993) *Survey of Britain's Industrial and Labour Reporters*. London: MORI, unpublished.

Morley, D. (1976) 'Industrial conflict and the mass media', *Sociological Review*, 24(2): 245–68.

Morley, D. (1980) *The Nationwide Audience*. London: BFI.

Morley, D. (1986) *Family Television*. London: Comedia/Routledge.

Morley, D. and Chen, K. (1996) *Stuart Hall Critical Dialogues in Cultural Studies*. London: Routledge.

Morley, D. and Robins, K. (1995) *Spaces of Identity. Global Media, Electronic Landscapes and Cultural Boundaries*. London: Routledge.

Morley, D. and Silverstone, R. (1990) 'Domestic communication – technologies and meanings', *Media Culture Society*, 12 (1): 31–55.

Mosco, V. (1996) *The Political Economy of Communication*. London: Sage.

Mountfield Report (1997) 'Report of the Working Group on the Government Information Service'. Cabinet Office, London: HMSO.

Mulgan, G. (1993) 'Why the constitution of the air waves has to change' in W. Stevenson (ed.), *All Our Futures*. London: BFI Publishing.

Mulgan, G. (1996) 'Union future is mutual satisfaction', *The Guardian*, Comment, 3 September 1996.

Murdock, G. (1992) 'Large corporations and the control of the communications industries', in M. Gurevitch, T. Bennett, J. Curran and J. Woolacott (eds), *Culture, Society and the Media*. London: Methuen.
Negrine, R. (1993) 'The organisation of British journalism and specialist correspondents: a study of newspaper reporting', Centre for Mass Communication Research Occasional Paper No MC9311, University of Leicester.
Negrine, R. (1994) *Politics and the Mass Media*. London: Routledge.
Negroponte, N. (1995) *Being Digital*. New York: Hodder and Stoughton.
Neil, A. (1996) *Full Disclosure*. London: Macmillan.
Neil, A. (1998) 'You can cuddle up to Rupert, but its not worth it – he doesn't love you, Tony, he only loves his wallet', *The Observer*, 29 March 1998.
Newman, K. (1984) *Financial Marketing and Communication*. London: Holt Reinhardt and Winston.
Noelle-Neuman, E. (1984) *The Spiral of Silence: Public Opinion our Social Skin*. Chicago: Chicago University Press.
Nugent, N. (1979) 'The National Association of Freedom', in R. King and N. Nugent (eds), *Respectable Rebels*. London: Hodder and Stoughton.
Offe, C. (1985) *Disorganised Capitalism*. Cambridge: Polity Press.
Ogilvy-Webb, M. (1965) *The Government Explains: A Study of the Information Services*. London: George Allen and Unwin.
O'Shaugnessey, N.J. (1990) *The Phenomenon of Political Marketing*. Basingstoke: Macmillan.
Paletz, D.L. and Entman, R.M. (1981) *Media Power and Politics*. New York: Free Press.
Parkin, F. (1972) *Class Inequality and Political Order*. St Albans: Paladin.
Parsons, D.W. (1989) *The Power of the Financial Press*. Aldershot: Edward Elgar.
Patterson, C. (1998) 'Global Battlefields', in O. Boyd-Barrett and T. Rantanen, (eds.), *The Globalization of News*. London: Sage.
Pearson, G. (1983) *Hooligan. A History of Respectable Fears*. Basingstoke: Macmillan.
Peters, B.G. (1986) *American Public Policy*. London: Macmillan.
Peters, J.D. (1993) 'Distrust of representation: Habermas on the public sphere', *Media Culture Society*, 15: 541–71.
Pfetsch, B. (1996) 'Convergence through privatisation: changing media environments and televised politics in Germany', *European Journal of Communication*, 11(4), December.
Phillips, E.B. (1977) 'Approaches to objectivity: journalists versus social science perspectives', in P.M. Hirsch et al. (eds), *Strategies for Communication Research*. Beverley Hills: Sage.
Philo, G. (1990) *Seeing and Believing*. London: Routledge.
Philo, G. (1995) 'Political advertising and popular belief', in G. Philo (ed.), *Glasgow University Media Group Reader, Vol. 2: Industry Economy War and Politics*. London: Routledge.
Philo, G. (ed.) (1996) *The Media and Mental Distress*. London: Longman.
Philo, G. (ed.) (1999) *Message Received*. Harlow: Longman.
Philo, G. and Lamb, R. (1986) *Television and the Eithiopian Famine. From Buerk to Band Aid*. Report prepared by Glasgow University Media Group and Television Trust for the Environment, for UNESCO.
Philo, G. and Miller, D. (1997) 'Cultural compliance: dead ends of media/cultural studies and social science', Glasgow Media Group, University of Glasgow, occasional paper.
Pilger, J. (1997) 'Gutted!', *The Guardian*, Weekend Section, 15 February 1997, pp. 32–38.
Pomper, G. (1959) 'The public relations of labor', *Public Opinion Quarterly*, 23: 483–94.
Poster, M. (1990) *The Mode of Information: Poststructuralism and Social Context*. Cambridge: Polity Press.

Potter, A. (1961) *Organised Groups in Britain*. London: Faber.
Poulantzas, N. (1969) 'The problem of the capitalist state', *New Left Review*, 58.
Preston, P. (1998) 'Time for some home truths from abroad', *The Observer*, Media Section, 7 June 1998.
Protess, D.L., Cook, F.L., Curtin, T.R., Gordon, M.T., Leff, D.R., McCombs, M.E. and Miller, P. (1987) 'The impact of investigative reporting on public opinion and policy making: targeting toxic waste', *Public Opinion Quarterly*, 51(2): 166–85.
Protess, D.L. et al. (1991) *The Journalism of Outrage. Investigative Reporting and Agenda Building in America*. London: The Guildford Press.
Puette, W. (1992) *Through Jaundiced Eyes*. Ithaca, NY: ILR Press.
Radway, J. (1987) *Reading the Romance: Women Patriarchy and Popular Literature*. London: Verso.
Reilly, J. (1999) 'Just another food scare', in G.Philo (ed.), *Message Received*. Harlow: Addison Wesley Longman.
Rhodes, R.A.W. (1988) *Beyond Westminster and Whitehall*. London: Unwin Hyman.
Rhodes, R.A.W. and Marsh, D. (1992) 'Policy networks in British politics. A critique of existing approaches', in D. Marsh and R.A.W. Rhodes (eds), *Policy Networks in British Government*. Oxford: Clarendon Press.
Richardson, J.J. and Jordan, A.G. (1985) *Governing Under Pressure*. Oxford: Basil Blackwell.
Robinson, B. (1995) 'Market share as a measure of media concentration', in T. Congdon, A. Graham, D. Green and B. Robinson (eds), *The Cross Media Revolution, Ownership and Control*. London: John Libbey.
Rogers, E.M., Dearing, J.W. and Chang, S. (1991) 'AIDS in the 1980s: the agenda setting process for a public issue', *Journalism Monographs*, 126.
Rose, C. (1998) *The Turning of the Spar*. London: Greenpeace.
Rose, R. (1974) *Politics in England Today*. London: Faber and Faber.
Royal Commission on the Press (1962) *Royal Commission on the Press 1961–62 Report*, Cmd 1811.
Royal Commission on the Press (1977) *Royal Commission on the Press 1974–77 Final Report*, Cmnd 6810.
Rubin, A.M. (1994) 'Media uses and effects: a uses and gratifications perspective', in J. Bryant and D. Zillman (eds), *Media Effects Advances in Theory and Research*. Hove: Lawrence Erlbaum Associates.
Rucht, D. (1995) 'Greenpeace and earth first! in comparative perspective', in W. Rudig (ed.), *Green Politics Three*. Edinburgh: Edinburgh University Press.
Rusbridger, A. (1997) 'Burdened with proof', *The Guardian*, 26 June 1997.
Ryan, M. (1992) 'Gender and public access: women's politics in nineteenth century America', in C. Calhoun (ed.), *Habermas and the Public Sphere*. Cambridge, MA: MIT Press.
Sabato, L. (1981) *The Rise of Political Consultants*. New York: Basic Books.
Scammell, M. (1995) *Designer Politics. How Elections Are Won*. Basingstoke: Macmillan.
Scannell, P. (1992) 'Public service broadcasting and modern life', in P. Scannell, P. Schlesinger and C. Sparks (eds), *Culture and Power*. London: Sage.
Schlesinger, P. (1978) *Putting Reality Together*. London: Constable.
Schlesinger, P. (1980) 'Between sociology and journalism', in H. Christian (ed.) *The Sociology of Journalism, Sociological Review Monograph 29*. Staffordshire: University of Keele.
Schlesinger, P. (1989) 'From production to propaganda?', *Media Culture Society*, 11: 283–306.
Schlesinger, P. (1990) 'Rethinking the Sociology of Journalism: source strategies and the limits of media centrism', in M. Ferguson (ed.), *Public Communication: The New Imperatives*. London: Sage.

Schlesinger, P. and Tumber, H. (1994) *Reporting Crime. The Media Politics of Criminal Justice*. Oxford: Clarendon Press.

Schattschneider, E.E. (1960) *The Semi-Sovereign People: A Realist's View of Democracy in America*. New York: Holt, Rinehart and Winston.

Schudson, M. (1991) 'The sociology of news production revisited', in J. Curran and M. Gurevitich (eds), *Mass Media and Society*. London: Edward Arnold.

Schumpeter, J.A. (1976) *Capitalism, Socialism and Democracy*. London: Allen and Unwin.

Scott, J. (1997) 'Communication campaigns and the neo-liberal policy agenda', *Media Culture Society*, 19: 183–99.

Seibert, F., Peterson, T. and Schramm, W. (1956) *Four Theories of the Press*. Urbana, IL: University of Illinois Press.

Seiden, M. (1974) *Who Controls the Mass Media? Popular Myths and Economic Realities*. New York: Basic Books.

Self, P. and Storing, H. (1974) 'The farmers and the state', in R. Kimber and J.J. Richardson (eds), *Pressure Groups in Britain*. London: J.M. Dent.

Seyd, P. (1975) 'Shelter: The National Campaign for the Homeless', *Political Quarterly*, 46: 418–31.

Seyd, P. (1976) 'The Child Poverty Action Group', *Political Quarterly*, 47: 189–202.

Seymour-Ure, C. (1974) *The Political Impact of Mass Media*. London: Constable.

Seymour-Ure, C. (1991) *The British Press and Broadcasting Since 1945*. Oxford: Blackwell.

Shoemaker, P. (1989) 'Public relations versus journalism?', *American Behavioural Scientist*, 33(2): 213–15.

Shoemaker, P.J., Wanta, W. and Leggett, D. (1989) 'Drug coverage and public opinion, 1972–1986', in P.J. Shoemaker (ed.), *Communication Campaigns About Drugs: Government, Media and the Public*. Hillsdale, NJ: Lawrence Erlbaum Associates.

Siebert, F., Peterson, T. and Schramm, W. (1956) *Four Theories of the Press*. Urbana, IL: University of Illinois Press.

Sigal, L.V. (1973) *Reporters and Officials*. Lexington, MA: D.C. Heath.

Simons, J. (1995) *Foucault and the Political*. London: Routledge.

Simpson, J. (1998) 'Global warning', *The Guardian*, Media Section, 17 August 1998, pp. 4–5.

Siune, K., McQuail, D. and Truetzschler, W. (1992) 'From structures to dynamics', in K. Siuene and W. Truetzschler (eds), *Dynamics of Media Politics*. London: Sage.

Skirrow, G. (1980) 'More bad news – a review of the reviews', *Screen*, 21(2): .95–9.

Smith, M.J. (1990) *The Politics of Agricultural Support in Britain: The Development of the Agricultural Policy Community*. Aldershot: Dartmouth.

Smith, M.J. (1991) 'From policy community to issue network: salmonella in eggs and the new politics of food', *Public Administration*, 69: 235–55.

Smith, M.J. (1993) *Pressure Power and Policy*. Hemel Hempstead: Harvester Wheatsheaf.

Snow, J. (1997) 'More bad news', *The Guardian*, Media Section, 27 January 1997, pp. 2–3.

Soloski, J. (1989) 'News reporting and professionalism: some constraints on the reporting of news', *Media Culture Society*, 11: 207–28.

Sparks, C. (1992) 'Popular journalism: theories and practice', in P. Dahlgren and C. Sparks (eds), *Journalism and Popular Culture*. London: Sage.

Sreberny-Mohammadi, A. and Mohammadi, A. (1994) *Small Media and Revolutionary Change: Communication, Culture and the Iranian Revolution*. Minneapolis, MN: University of Minnesota Press.

Sreberny-Mohammadi, A., Winseck, D., McKenna, J. and Boyd-Barrett, O. (eds) (1997) *Media in Global Context*. London: Edward Arnold.

Statham, P. (1996) 'Television news and the public sphere in Italy', *The European Journal of Communication*, 11(4): 511–56.

Stothard, P. (1997) 'The Times they aren't changing', *The Guardian*, Media Section, 16 June 1997, pp. 4–5.
Sweeney, J. (1998) 'How the New Labour mafia took revenge on Martin Bell', *The Observer*, 25 January 1998, p. 22.
Thompson, E.P. (1970) 'Sir, writing by candlelight . . .', *New Society*, 24 December 1970, pp. 1135–6.
Thompson, K. (1997) 'Regulation, de-regulation and re-regulation', in K. Thompson (ed.), *Media and Cultural Regulation*. London: Sage.
Tiffen, R. (1989) *News and Power*. Sydney: Allen and Unwin.
Tracey, M. (1978) *The Production of Political Television*. London: Routledge.
Trenamen, J. and McQuail, D. (1961) *Television and the Political Image*. London: Methuen.
Triandafyllidou, A. (1996) '"Green" Corruption in the Italian press. Does a political culture matter?', *European Journal of Communication*, 11(3): 371–91.
Truman, D. (1951) *The Governmental Process*. New York: Alfred A. Knopf.
TUC (1985) *Guidelines on Advertising*. London: Trade Union Congress.
TUC (1979) *A Cause for Concern*. London: Trade Union Congress.
Tuchman, G. (1972) 'Objectivity as a strategic ritual', *American Journal of Sociology*, 77(4): 660–79.
Tulloch, J. (1993) 'Policing the public sphere – the British machinery of news management', *Media Culture Society*, 15: 363–84.
Tumber, H. (1993) ' "Selling Scandal": business and the media', *Media Culture Society*, 15: 345–61.
Tunstall, J. (1971) *Journalists at Work*. London: Constable.
Tunstall, J. (1993) *Television Producers*. London: Routledge.
Tunstall, J. and Palmer, M. (1991) *Media Moguls*. London: Routledge.
Turk, J.V. (1986) 'Information subsidies and media content: a study of public relations influence on the news', *Journalism Monograph 100*, Association for Education in Journalism and Mass Communication, Columbia, SC, December.
Turner, G. (1990) *British Cultural Studies: An Introduction*. London: Unwin Hyman.
Van Zoonen, L. (1998) 'One of the girls? The changing gender of journalism', in C. Carter, G. Branston and S. Allan (eds), *News, Gender and Power*. London: Routledge.
Veljanovski, C. (ed.) (1989) *Freedom in Broadcasting*. London: Institute of Economic Affairs.
Verstraeten, H. (1996) 'The media and the transformation of the public sphere. A contribution for a critical political economy of the public sphere', *European Journal of Communication*, 11(3): 347–70.
Vidal, J. (1999) 'Get the net – the Internet environment: global conflict@ the net', *The Guardian*, Society Section, 13 January 1999, p. 4.
Wallack, L.-et al. (1993) *Media Advocacy and Public Health: Power for Prevention*. London: Sage.
Warner, K. and Molotoch, H. (1993) 'Information in the marketplace: media explanations of the '87 Crash', *Social Problems*, 40 (2): 167–88.
Waterhouse, K. (1995) *Streets Ahead*. London: Hodder and Stoughton.
Waterman, P. (1990) 'Communicating labour internationalism: a review of relevant literature and resources', *European Journal of Communication*, 15(1/2): 85–103.
Weaver, D.H., McCombs, M.E. and Spellman, C. (1975) 'Watergate and the media: a case study of agenda setting', *American Politics Quarterly*, 3: 458–72.
Weymouth, A. and Lamizet, B. (eds) (1996) *Markets and Myths: Forces for Change in the Media of Western Europe*. London: Longman.
Whale, J. (1977) *The Politics of the Media*. London: Fontana.
White, D.M. (1950) 'The gatekeeper: a case study in the selection of news', *Journalism Quarterly*, 27 (Fall): 383–90.
Whitely, P. and Winyard, S. (1983) 'Influencing social policy: the effectiveness of the poverty lobby in Britain', *Journal of Social Policy*, 12: 1–26.

Wickens, P. (1987) *The Road to Nissan*. Basingstoke: Macmillan.
Williams, F. (1946) *Parliament, Press and the Public*. London: Heinemann.
Williams, G. (1998) 'How Monsanto is massaging its message', *Free Press*, 107 (Nov.–Dec.): 4–5.
Williams, K. and Miller, D. (1998) 'Producing AIDS news', in D. Miller , J. Kitzinger, K. Williams and P. Beharrell (eds), *The Circuit of Mass Communication*. London: Sage.
Williams, R. (1961) *The Long Revolution*. London: Chatto and Windus.
Williams, R. (1974) *Television: Technology and Cultural Form*. London: Fontana.
Wilson, C. and Gutierrez, F. (1995) *Race Multiculturalism and the Media*. London: Sage.
Wilson, D. (1984) *Pressure: The A–Z of Campaigning in Britain*. London: Heinemann.
Winterton, J. and Winterton, R. (1989) *Coal Crisis and Conflict*. Manchester: Manchester University Press.
Wintour, P. and Mills, H. (1997) 'Labour's health scare was an accident waiting to happen', *The Observer*, 16 June 1997.
Wirth, L. (1948) 'Consensus and mass communication', *American Sociological Review*, 13(1): 1–15.
Women in Journalism (1998) *The Cheaper Sex: How Women Lose Out in Journalism*. London: Women in Journalism.
Woolas, P. (1990) 'Television's first aid', *New Socialist*, April/May.
Wooton, G. (1978) *Pressure Politics in Contemporary Britain*. Lexington, MA: D.C. Heath.
Worcester, R. (1996) 'Not so green as cabbage looking: comparing environmental activism of the public and of journalists', *MORI Research Paper*, 19 May. London: MORI.
Wright-Mills, C. (1970) *The Sociological Imagination*. Harmondsworth: Penguin.
Wylie, L. (1974) *Village in Vaucluse*. Cambridge, MA: Harvard University Press.
Young, H. (1998) 'Murdoch's victim is not football, What is lost is honest news', *The Guardian*, 8th September 1998.
Younge, G. (1999) 'In our own backyard', *The Guardian*, Media Section, 1st March, p. 2.
Zucker, H.G. (1978) 'The variable nature of news media influence', in B.D. Ruben (ed.), *Communication Yearbook*, Volume 2. New Jersey: Transaction Books.

Index